CANADIAN MILITARY INTELLIGENCE

Georgetown Studies in Intelligence History

Series Editors: Christopher Moran, Mark Phythian, and Mark Stout

CANADIAN MILITARY INTELLIGENCE

OPERATIONS AND EVOLUTION FROM THE OCTOBER CRISIS TO THE WAR IN AFGHANISTAN

DAVID A. CHARTERS

GEORGETOWN UNIVERSITY PRESS / WASHINGTON, DC

Published in cooperation with the Canadian Military Intelligence Association

© 2022 Canadian Military Intelligence Association. All rights reserved. No part of this book may be reproduced or utilized in any form or by any means, electronic or mechanical, including photocopying and recording, or by any information storage and retrieval system, without permission in writing from the publisher.

The publisher is not responsible for third-party websites or their content. URL links were active at time of publication.

Library of Congress Cataloging-in-Publication Data

Names: Charters, David A. (David Anderson), 1949– author.
Title: Canadian military intelligence: operations and evolution from the October crisis to the War in Afghanistan / David A. Charters.
Description: Washington, DC: Georgetown University Press, [2022] | Series: Georgetown studies in intelligence history | "Published in cooperation with the Canadian Military Intelligence Association." | Includes bibliographical references and index.
Identifiers: LCCN 2022005193 (print) | LCCN 2022005194 (ebook) | ISBN 9781647122935 (hardcover) | ISBN 9781647122942 (paperback) | ISBN 9781647122959 (ebook)
Subjects: LCSH: Military intelligence—Canada—History.
Classification: LCC UB251.C2 C48 2022 (print) | LCC UB251.C2 (ebook) | DDC 355.3/4320971—dc23/eng/20220215
LC record available at https://lccn.loc.gov/2022005193
LC ebook record available at https://lccn.loc.gov/2022005194

23 22   9 8 7 6 5 4 3 2 First printing

Printed in the United States of America

Cover design by Erin Kirk
Interior design by BookComp, Inc.

CONTENTS

List of Photographs — vii
Acknowledgments — ix
List of Acronyms and Abbreviations — xi

Introduction — 1

PART I. THE EVOLUTION OF CANADIAN DEFENCE AND MILITARY INTELLIGENCE, 1945–2005

1 Policies, Budgets, Resources, and Commitments: Canadian Defence in Context — 13

2 Uncertain Foundations: Canadian Defence and Military Intelligence, 1945–1970 — 30

3 When in Debt, Reorganize: Canadian Defence Intelligence, 1975–2005 — 41

4 From Adaptation to Transformation: Canadian Military Intelligence, 1975–2005 — 67

PART II. INTELLIGENCE SUPPORT TO CANADIAN MILITARY OPERATIONS, 1970–2010

5 The October Crisis: Countering Terrorism in Québec, 1970 — 103

6 Operation SALON: Internal Security Operations in the Oka Crisis, 1990 — 123

7 Operation FRICTION: Naval and Air Operations in the Persian Gulf War, 1990–1991 — 148

8 Peacekeeping in the Balkans: The UN Years, 1992–1995 — 171

9 Peace Enforcement in Bosnia: The NATO Years, 1996–2004 — 198

10 Peace Enforcement in Kosovo: Air and Ground Operations, 1999–2000   215

11 Kandahar and Kabul: Stabilizing Afghanistan, 2001–2005   244

12 Return to Kandahar: Counterinsurgency in Afghanistan, 2005–2010   259

    Conclusion   303

Select Bibliography   313
Index   321
About the Author   335

PHOTOGRAPHS

3.1	Lt.-Gen. Michel Gauthier, the first chief of defence intelligence	53
4.1	An intelligence section briefing for Lt.-Gen. Stanley Waters	71
8.1	The tactical compartment on a CP-140 Aurora maritime patrol aircraft	191
9.1	The Canadian National Intelligence Centre, Bosnia, 1997	202
10.1	A Coyote LAV, Kosovo, 1999	234
11.1	Combat Operations room on a Canadian patrol frigate	246
11.2	The All-Source Intelligence Centre, Camp Julien, Kabul, Afghanistan, 2004	251
11.3	A Sperwer Tactical UAV	253

ACKNOWLEDGMENTS

While I am the author of record, this book is the result of a collective effort by many people. First, I wish to thank the Canadian Military Intelligence Association (CMIA) for proposing this project and for providing the support and the funding to bring the book to fruition. In particular, I owe a great debt of gratitude to the CMIA's "editorial board": Lt.-Col. Greg Jensen and Capt. (N) Andrea Siew. They facilitated contacts for interviews, ferreted out source material, read and reread draft chapters, shared insights and wise counsel, and corrected my occasional missteps. This book would not have been possible without their assistance. Second, I am grateful for the help provided by many serving and retired members of the military intelligence community who consented to be interviewed, corresponded with me, and offered comments on drafts of the book. They are too numerous to be listed here; all have been cited in the chapter notes. I greatly appreciated their generosity and patience. Their vital contributions filled in many of the gaps in the incomplete document record. Third, I wish to thank the staffs of Library and Archives Canada and the Directorate of History and Heritage of the Department of National Defence, who provided access to valuable original sources. Larus Technologies was generous in sponsoring my security clearance, which made my research that much easier.

Many colleagues and friends offered encouragement and advice during the project. In particular, I would like to thank Cindy Brown, Isabel Campbell, Howard Coombs, Phil Davies, Sean Kennedy, Glenn Leonard, Sean Maloney, Marc Milner, Hal Skaarup, Reg Whitaker, and Lee Windsor. Two individuals deserve special mention: Alan Barnes, who created and maintains the Canadian Foreign Intelligence History Project's vast digital archive of declassified documents, and Professor Timothy Winegard of Colorado Mesa University, who generously donated his collection of declassified sources on the Oka Crisis to the Gregg Centre at the University of New Brunswick.

It was a pleasure and a privilege to work with the thoroughly professional staff at Georgetown University Press. I would like to thank especially Senior Acquisitions Editor Donald Jacobs, who patiently accommodated the joint approach of the CMIA and the author; Mark Stout, the series editor; and my copy editor, M. Yvonne Ramsey, who turned a challenging manuscript into the fine book that it is. I also benefited from the comments and suggestions offered by the two external reviewers. Martin Ainsley deserves a hearty thanks for formatting the manuscript to meet the press's standards.

My wife and family were supportive throughout and undoubtedly were grateful that I had something to occupy my time while we hunkered down during the pandemic. Finally, this collective effort not withstanding, I alone am responsible for any shortcomings in the recounting of this history.

ACRONYMS AND ABBREVIATIONS

1 CAD	1 Canadian Air Division
A2	Air Command Intelligence Section (first designation)
AAA	antiaircraft artillery
ABCCC	Airborne Battlefield Command and Control Centre
ACP	Aid to the Civil Power
ADP	automated data processing
ANA	Afghan National Army
AOR	area of responsibility
ASIC	All-Source Intelligence Centre
ASW	antisubmarine warfare
ATN	attack the network
BG	battle group
BIOC	Basic Officers Intelligence Course
C2	command and control
C4ISR	command, control, communications, computers, intelligence, surveillance, and reconnaissance
CAF	Canadian Armed Forces
CANBAT	Canadian battalion
CANFORME	Canadian Forces Middle East
CANIC	Canadian National Intelligence Centre
CANTASS	Canadian Towed Array Sonar System
CAOC	Combined Air Operations Center
CATGME	Canadian Air Task Group Middle East
CBNRC	Communications Branch of the National Research Council
CDI	chief of defence intelligence
CDS	Chief of Defence Staff
CENTAF	US Central Command Air Forces
CENTCOM	US Central Command
CFB	Canadian Forces Base
CFHQ	Canadian Forces Headquarters
CFIHP	Canadian Foreign Intelligence History Project

CFINTCOM	Canadian Forces Intelligence Command
CFIOG	Canadian Forces Information Operations Group
CFSMI	Canadian Forces School of Military Intelligence
C-IED	counter-IED
CIMIC	civil-military cooperation
CIS	chief of intelligence and security
CJIC	Canadian Joint Intelligence Committee
CMIA	Canadian Military Intelligence Association
CSE	Communications Security Establishment
CSIS	Canadian Security Intelligence Service
CW	chemical warfare
DA	direct action
DCDS	deputy chief of the Defence Staff
DDI	Directorate of Defence Intelligence
DEA	Department of External Affairs
DGI	director general of intelligence
DHH	Directorate of History and Heritage
DI	Defence Intelligence
DIE	Directorate of Imagery Exploitation
DIR	*Defence Intelligence Review*
DM	deputy minister
DND	Department of National Defence
DSTI	Directorate of Scientific and Technical Intelligence
ECM	electronic countermeasures
ELINT	Electronic Intelligence
EW	electronic warfare
FHT	field human intelligence team
FLQ	Front de Libération du Québec
FMC	Force Mobile Command
G2	Air Command Intelligence Section (second designation)
HUMINT	human source intelligence
HVT	high-value target
ICAC	Intelligence Collection and Analysis Centre
IED	improvised explosive device
IFOR	Implementation Force
ILO	intelligence-led operation
ISAF	International Security Assistance Force
ISR	intelligence, surveillance, and reconnaissance
ISTAR	intelligence, surveillance, target acquisition, and reconnaissance
ISTARCC	ISTAR Coordination Centre

ISX	Intelligence and Security Complex
IT	information technology
JCC	Joint Coordination Center
JC2IS	Joint Command and Control Information System
JIC	Joint Intelligence Centre
JNA	Yugoslav People's Army
JTF-A	Joint Task Force–Afghanistan
JTF2	Joint Task Force 2
JTFSWA	Joint Task Force South West Asia
KAF	Kandahar Airfield
KFOR	Kosovo Force
KLA	Kosovo Liberation Army
KMNB	Kabul Multi-National Brigade
LAV	light armoured vehicle
MARCOM	Maritime Command
MI	military intelligence
MIF	Maritime Interdiction Force
MNB	multinational brigade
MND-SW	Multi-National Division South West
MRG	Management Review Group
NATO	North Atlantic Treaty Organization
NAVCENT	Naval Forces Central Command
NCO	noncommissioned officer
NDHQ	National Defence Headquarters
NDIC	National Defence Intelligence Centre
NDOC	National Defence Operations Centre
NORAD	North American Aerospace Defense Command
OGDs	other government departments
OP	observation post
PPC	Production Planning Coordinator
PPCLI	Princess Patricia's Canadian Light Infantry
PRT	Provincial Reconstruction Team
RCAF	Royal Canadian Air Force
RCMP	Royal Canadian Mounted Police
RCN	Royal Canadian Navy
RCR	Royal Canadian Regiment
RC-S	Regional Command–South
RMA	revolution in military affairs
ROE	rules of engagement
R22eR	Royal 22nd Regiment
SA	situational awareness

SAM	surface-to-air missile
SCIF	secure compartmented intelligence facility
SFOR	Stabilization Force
SHAPE	Supreme Headquarters Allied Powers Europe
SIGINT	Signals intelligence
SIU	Special Investigation Unit
SOC	Strategic Operations Centre
SOF	Special Operations Forces
SOIC	Special Operations Intelligence Centre
SQ	Sûreté du Québec (Québec Provincial Police)
TOW	tube-launched, optically tracked, wire-guided
TUA	TOW missile under armour
UAV	unmanned aerial vehicle
UN	United Nations
UNHCR	United Nations High Commission for Refugees
UNMIK	United Nations Mission in Kosovo
UNPA	United Nations Protected Area
UNPROFOR	United Nations Protection Force
USAF	United States Air Force
USN	US Navy
VCDS	vice-chief of the Defence Staff
YCC	Yugoslav Crisis Cell

INTRODUCTION

On 1 December 2011, the Canadian flag was lowered for the last time at Kandahar airfield, a decade after the first Canadian troops arrived there. This brought to an end not only Canada's longest—and perhaps most controversial—war but also the largest overseas deployment of Canadian intelligence personnel since World War II. It would be gratifying to be able to say that this deployment was the result of years of careful planning and preparation. However, it was in fact the result of a sudden, dramatic change in the strategic environment; a series of hasty commitments of Canadian troops to an unlikely theatre of conflict; and an improvised adaptation of Canadian defence and military intelligence (MI) personnel, structures, and systems to meet an unprecedented need for intelligence support to combat forces.

That said, the ability of the Canadian Armed Forces (CAF) intelligence branch to adapt to that task did not spring fully formed out of nothing. It was able to draw upon accepted doctrines,[1] modified as needed, as well as trained personnel and decades of operational experience. The latter is the focus of this book, which was commissioned by the Canadian Military Intelligence Association (CMIA), an independent nonprofit professional association of the Canadian MI community. The aim of the book is to provide a history of intelligence support to a selection of CAF operations from 1970 to 2010. The chapters that follow will show how that support developed and changed over time; what trends, technologies, policies, and decisions shaped it; and what effect it had on CAF operations at home and abroad. What emerges from this is a story of transformation of Canadian MI from a marginal to a central military and defence activity.

Why is this book needed? Simply put, to fill a significant gap in post-1945 Canadian military history and in the history of Canadian intelligence activity. The Department of National Defence (DND) Directorate of History and Heritage (DHH) has produced official histories of Canadian operations in the Korean

War and is due to publish one on the CAF in peacekeeping. An authorized history of the Canadian Army in Afghanistan is also in the offing.[2] Scholars and journalists have published studies of the CAF in Somalia, Bosnia, the Oka Crisis, Kosovo, and the Persian Gulf War, and many, including this author, have written about the CAF in Afghanistan.[3] High-profile retired generals Lewis MacKenzie and Rick Hillier have published their memoirs.[4] The report of the Somalia Commission of Inquiry[5] is one of the few studies that makes more than a passing reference to intelligence.[6]

This should not be surprising. Because of the secrecy surrounding intelligence—a legacy of both World War II and the Cold War—the study of intelligence is relatively new. Few academic studies existed before the late 1970s.[7] It was "the missing dimension" of military and diplomatic history.[8] There were, however, a few memoirs[9] and policy-oriented studies.[10] It was the near-simultaneous unmasking of the secret British Ultra signals intelligence (SIGINT) and the congressional inquiries into the actions of the US intelligence community in the mid-1970s that opened the floodgates and ushered in the new field of intelligence studies. The number of books in the field now runs into the hundreds, and there are also scholarly journals, academic and professional associations, conferences, and research projects devoted to intelligence topics.

Yet even so, this body of work falls well short of being comprehensive. First, the vast majority of the literature focuses on the United States, Britain, and Soviet Russia. This reflects their prominent roles in the world, especially during the Cold War and in the use of intelligence. In the case of Britain and the United States, it also reflects the availability of original source material.[11] The literature on intelligence in other countries, including Canada, is fragmentary and of uneven quality. Second, the literature devotes disproportionate attention to the operations of secret foreign intelligence services—particularly the US Central Intelligence Agency, Britain's Secret Intelligence Service, and the Soviet KGB—while giving short shrift to other services and their activities, defence intelligence (DI) and MI among them. There are popular histories of MI organizations and a few scholarly studies of intelligence in specific campaigns and battles, with emphasis on intelligence failures and surprise attacks.[12] But compared to studies of secret intelligence services, these are a distinct minority.

Reflecting both a more modest role in intelligence and limited access to classified material, Canadian intelligence studies have lagged behind their British and American counterparts. Much of the writing on Canadian intelligence is policy-oriented and, since Canada lacks a foreign human intelligence service, is focused on domestic security intelligence, which has had a troubled history chronicled in part in the McDonald Commission of Inquiry reports.[13] There is one full-length scholarly study of the security service[14] and another of Canadian SIGINT in World War II.[15] Recently, several highly informative internal histories of parts of the Canadian intelligence community have been declassified.[16] There are numerous scholarly articles and several major studies dealing with issues of efficacy and propriety of domestic security intelligence activities,[17] and there are also a handful of memoirs[18] which are not very enlightening. Neither are the reports of the Security Intelligence Review Committee or those of the several inspectors-general. The conferences of the Canadian Association for Security and Intelligence Studies, founded in 1985, have focused largely on domestic security intelligence issues.

With few exceptions, outside of the official professional publications, Canadian MI has received little study.[19] For example, Douglas Bland's studies of defence administration and of the Chiefs of Defence Staff barely mention intelligence. A recent volume on the Canadian intelligence and security community includes one chapter each on Canadian Armed Forces/DND intelligence and the Communications Security Establishment (CSE). Both are relatively short and focused on current activities and offer little historical perspective.[20]

The first exception is *Scarlet to Green*, S. R. Elliot's history of the Canadian Army Intelligence Corps from its nineteenth-century origins to the early post-war era. Published in 1979 and reissued in 2018, this pioneering work based on original sources focuses mostly on Canadian Army tactical and operational intelligence in World War II. The second is Maj. (ret.) Harold Skaarup's *Out of Darkness—Light*, which in four volumes provides an anthology of useful documents, memoirs, anecdotes, and articles about the history of the intelligence branch focusing in large measure on training courses, personnel, operations, and other significant events.[21] But it falls short of being a comprehensive, analytical history. Finally, Brig.-Gen. (ret.) James Cox's 2004 Royal Military College of Canada war studies master's thesis usefully examines changes in the organization and functioning of DI at the highest levels of civil-military command and decision making from 1990 to 2004.[22]

The main obstacle is access to information. Most of the relevant documents in this field are classified as secret or higher and thus are inaccessible to historians. Using the Access to Information Act process is unsatisfactory due to the lengthy time frame needed to review documents for release. Since Canadian intelligence activity is often integrated with that of our alliance or coalition partners, they need to be consulted regarding release of sensitive material. Thus, only three chapters in this volume rely on extensive use of original documents. In addition to these, the author used unclassified or declassified official sources, such as doctrine and planning documents. Some of these are aspirational—looking toward the future—rather than historical. However, the 1970 Isbister Report on Canadian intelligence and the 2003 *Defence Intelligence Review* were helpful in tracking the processes of change in Canadian MI. Many of the chapters exploit interviews to fill in gaps in the document record, but most rely heavily on published sources such as articles in scholarly and military professional journals.

Although the leading scholarly journal *Intelligence and National Security* has published many articles on Canadian subjects, intelligence support to military operations is all but absent. The *International Journal of Intelligence and Counterintelligence* published only two that specifically addressed Canadian MI/DI. None of the articles searched in *Canadian Military History* addressed intelligence as a subject in its own right, but some discussed it within other topics.

Not surprisingly, the CAF's professional education journals devote more attention to MI. In its first decade (2000–10), the *Canadian Military Journal* published thirty articles that dealt with MI, DI, or both in whole or in part. The majority focused on current activities and anticipated requirements and capabilities. One-third discussed intelligence in the context of operations from the October Crisis to Afghanistan. However, they mentioned intelligence only as part of the main topic and not necessarily the most significant part. Between 1998 and 2014 the *Army Doctrine and Training Bulletin* and its successor, the *Canadian Army Journal*, published eleven articles each on intelligence. Most were devoted to practical issues of support to operations, as was appropriate for publications devoted to professional development of an army at war. Between 2005 and 2013, the *Canadian Naval Review* published a dozen articles on various aspects of naval intelligence and surveillance. The *Air Force Journal*, by contrast, devoted little attention to intelligence for reasons that will be made clear in chapter 4.

Thus, until now the post-1960s history of intelligence support to CAF operations has existed only in fragments, scattered across a wide range of sources none of which in themselves could provide a comprehensive overview of the whole. This book is intended to do just that: take the reader beyond the door that has kept post-1970 Canadian MI/DI locked away in secrecy and consequently overlooked by historians.

In addition to the introduction and the conclusion, this book tells the story in two parts. Part One provides the wider framework for understanding how Canadian MI and DI supported CAF operations from 1970 forward. The first chapter sets the essential context, outlining the frequent changes in defence policies and decisions about force structures, priorities, budgets, and commitments that shaped the ability of the CAF to perform its missions, from the unification/reorganization process of the mid-1960s to the transformation of the armed forces during the Afghanistan War. Chapter 2 explains how the changes brought about by unification/reorganization laid the foundation for the post-1970 intelligence structures. But to make sense of those changes chapter 2 also explains briefly the MI structures that existed from 1945 to 1964. The chapter draws particular attention to the creation of Canada's post-1945 SIGINT service and its place in the Five Eyes intelligence alliance. Both the service and the alliance would come to play important roles in supporting CAF operations from 1990 on.

Chapter 3 discusses the constant reorganization of DI from 1975 to 2005 and how this affected its ability to support CAF operations and strategic-level decision making. Chapter 4 examines the development and integration of CAF intelligence technologies and operational concepts and the changes in training that professionalized the intelligence cadre.

Over the course of eight chapters, Part Two examines intelligence support to a selection of CAF operations from 1970 to 2010. All of the chapters explain the operational setting, Canadian (or coalition) mission(s) and tasks, the CAF formations deployed, intelligence requirements and resources, the conduct of operations, intelligence support (collection, production, dissemination, and exploitation) to them, and an assessment of the impact of intelligence on operations.

Part Two opens with two domestic internal security operations: the October Crisis of 1970 and the Oka Crisis of 1990. These two events, twenty years apart, illustrate dramatic changes in the CAF's ability to provide intelligence support to operations in the fields of intelligence collection, exploitation, and cooperation with police and security services.

The six subsequent chapters examine intelligence support to overseas operations: the 1990–91 Persian Gulf War; United Nations (UN) peacekeeping in the Balkans, 1992–95; the peace enforcement in Bosnia led by the North Atlantic Treaty Organization (NATO), 1996–2004; the air and ground peace enforcement operations in Kosovo, 1999–2000; and two phases of Canadian operations in Afghanistan, counterterrorism and stability actions (2001–5) and the counterinsurgency campaign (2005–10). These operations forced the Canadian DI/MI enterprise to adapt to new complex missions within multinational coalitions and to adopt new practices and technologies, in particular the fusion of intelligence from a wide range of sources and methods.

The conclusion will, first, attempt to assess the quality and utility of the intelligence support provided to the CAF in those operations. Did it make a difference, allowing them to achieve their goals, and if so or not, why? What practices and systems changed over time to make this possible? Second, the conclusion will provide a brief survey of developments since the end of the Canadian involvement in Afghanistan and, in particular, will discuss the creation of the Canadian Forces Intelligence Command and its significance for the role of intelligence in military decision making. Third, the conclusion will identify current trends, from hybrid warfare to cyber warfare, and try to assess their implications for future intelligence support to the CAF.

Having laid out that agenda, the author is obligated to provide several cautionary notes. First, as the foregoing makes clear, the book does not cover all

CAF operations for that forty-year period; such a study would require several volumes and would take many more years to complete. Those included were significant operations in their own right or can be seen as having been typical or representative of similar operations conducted throughout the period. But the book does not include any of the domestic or international disaster assistance operations.

Second, owing to limitations of space and access to source material, this cannot be considered a definitive history. It is comprehensive in scope but less so in detail. Indeed, of necessity it simplifies the complex, multifaceted nature of the MI process.[23] These limitations notwithstanding, until new sources become available this book should have lasting utility for the MI profession and historians of Canadian intelligence.

Third, setting the temporal boundaries of any historical work is always a somewhat arbitrary process. Every event, decision, action, organization, and development has roots that predate the start line of any historical study. But, choosing 1970 makes sense for several reasons. First, the processes of unification and reorganization of the Canadian forces that had begun with the 1964 *White Paper on Defence* were largely complete by this date. This included significant changes to the CAF intelligence enterprise. Second, in 1970 the CAF conducted a major internal security operation that tested the capabilities and limits of the newly restructured armed forces. Finally, that same year the government received the Isbister Report, a detailed external review of Canada's intelligence community. Recommendations arising from it set in motion a number of initiatives that would modernize that community, including MI and DI.

Likewise, setting the end date is a challenge. It is tempting to try to bring the end date as close to the present as possible—history as it was the day before the book went to press. But realistically, that is more likely to date the book quickly than an earlier closing point. Access to original sources also limits how close one can come to the present, and this book is no exception. Although the CAF did not formally end its Afghan mission until December 2011, active operations had drawn down about six months earlier. I had no access to sources covering 2011. So, the book ends forty years after the starting date in the final full year of the active campaign in Afghanistan at the point when the Canadian intelligence contingent, its capabilities, and its human and technical resources in theatre and in Canada had reached a degree of maturity. This puts a distance of more than a decade between that point in time and the author's attempt to reflect on and draw some useful conclusions about those years of operational experience.

Intelligence studies does not sit comfortably within a single discipline. It is multidisciplinary, this book being a case in point. *Canadian Military Intelligence: Operations and Evolution from the October Crisis to the War in Afghani-*

stan is a work of intelligence history, nested within the field of military history, that also draws upon political studies, defence studies, international relations, organization theory, anthropology, and cultural studies. As such, the book is a hybrid.

This final product is therefore very similar to an intelligence assessment: an informed best guess based on the collection, analysis, interpretation, and exploitation of a range of sources. This book captures the big picture but does not provide definitive answers to all of the detailed questions one might wish to ask. As such, it is unlikely to satisfy every reader, especially those who were there and experienced the events described herein. But given the challenges of access to original sources, intelligence history, like intelligence itself, is always inherently untidy and incomplete, a work in progress not to be completed by a single author or book. It will be up to future historians to revise and reimagine the past presented here, but they will benefit greatly from the CMIA's efforts to preserve the institutional and individual memories of the Canadian MI community.

NOTES

1. For example, the CAF used NATO Standardization Office, *AINTP-1(A) Intelligence Doctrine* (NATO, January 1995).
2. Written by Royal Military College professor Sean Maloney, it is due for release in 2022.
3. See, for example, Grant Dawson, *"Here Is Hell": Canada's Engagement in Somalia* (Vancouver: University of British Columbia Press, 2006); Carol Off, *The Ghosts of Medak Pocket: The Story of Canada's Secret War* (Toronto: Vintage, 2005); Timothy C. Winegard, *Oka: A Convergence of Cultures and the Canadian Forces* (Kingston, Ontario: Canadian Defence Academy Press, 2008); Bob Bergen, *Scattering Chaff: Canadian Air Power and Censorship during the Kosovo War* (Calgary: University of Calgary Press, 2019); Marc Milner, *Canada's Navy: The First Century* (Toronto: University of Toronto Press, 1999), 295–300; Janice Gross Stein and J. Eugene Lang, *The Unexpected War: Canada in Kandahar* (Toronto: Viking, 2007); Lee Windsor, David A. Charters, and Brent Wilson, *Kandahar Tour: The Turning Point in Canada's Afghan Mission* (Mississauga, Ontario: Wiley, 2008); and Murray Brewster, *The Savage War: The Untold Battles of Afghanistan* (Mississauga, Ontario: Wiley, 2011).
4. See Lewis MacKenzie, *Peacekeeper: The Road to Sarajevo* (Vancouver: Douglas & McIntyre, 1993); and Rick Hillier, *A Soldier First: Bullets, Bureaucrats and the Politics of War* (Toronto: HarperCollins, 2009).
5. Commission of Inquiry into the Deployment of Canadian Forces to Somalia, *Dishonoured Legacy: The Lessons of the Somalia Affair; Report*, 5 vols. (Ottawa: Minister of Public Works and Government Services, 1997).
6. Others include David Fraser and Brian Hanington, *Operation Medusa: The Furious Battle That Saved Afghanistan from the Taliban* (Toronto: McClelland & Stewart, 2018); and David A. Charters, "Canadian Military Intelligence in Afghanistan," *International Journal of Intelligence and Counter Intelligence* 25, no. 3 (2012):

470–507. See also Sean Maloney's three unofficial histories of the CAF in Afghanistan: *Enduring the Freedom: A Rogue Historian in Afghanistan* (Lincoln, NE: Potomac Books, 2007); *Confronting the Chaos: A Rogue Military Historian Returns to Afghanistan* (Annapolis, MD: Naval Institute Press, 2009); and *Fighting for Afghanistan: A Rogue Historian at War* (Annapolis, MD: Naval Institute Press, 2011).
7. Among the exceptions were Harry Howe Ransom, *Central Intelligence and National Security* (Cambridge, MA: Harvard University Press, 1959); and David Kahn, *The Codebreakers: The Story of Secret Writing* (1967; repr., London: Macmillan, 1969).
8. Christopher M. Andrew and David Dilks, *The Missing Dimension: Governments and Intelligence Communities in the Twentieth Century* (London: Macmillan, 1984).
9. Maj.-Gen. Sir Kenneth Strong, *Intelligence at the Top: The Recollections of an Intelligence Officer* (London: Cassell, 1968).
10. Sherman Kent, *Strategic Intelligence for American World Policy* (Princeton, NJ: Princeton University Press, 1949).
11. In this respect Britain has remained in the forefront, having produced an official history, F. H. Hinsley et al., *British Intelligence in the Second World War*, 6 vols. (London: HMSO, 1979), and permitted the publication of authorized histories of MI5, MI6, and the Government Communications Headquarters.
12. Richard K. Betts, *Surprise Attack: Lessons for Defense Planning* (Washington, DC: Brookings Institution, 1982); and James J. Wirtz, *The Tet Offensive: Intelligence Failure in War* (Ithaca, NY: Cornell University Press, 1991).
13. Commission of Inquiry Concerning Certain Activities of the Royal Canadian Mounted Police, D. C. McDonald, *Report*, 4 vols. (Ottawa: Minister of Supply and Services, 1980).
14. Reginald Whitaker, Gregory S. Kealey, and Andrew Parnaby, *Secret Service: Political Policing in Canada: From the Fenians to Fortress America* (Toronto: University of Toronto Press, 2012).
15. John Bryden, *Best-Kept Secret: Canadian Secret Intelligence in the Second World War* (Toronto: Key Porter, 1993).
16. Wesley K. Wark, *A History of the Creation of Canada's Post–World War II Intelligence Community, 1945–1970* (Ottawa: [Privy Council Office], 2000–2002); and N. K. O'Neill and K. J. Hughes, *History of the Communications Branch of the National Research Council* (Ottawa: CSE, 1987). Both of these sources are declassified unpublished reports held by the digital archive of the Canadian Foreign Intelligence History Project, https://carleton.ca/csids/canadian-foreign-intelligence-history-project/.
17. See Craig Forcese and Kent Roach, *False Security: The Radicalization of Canadian Anti-Terrorism* (Toronto: Irwin Law, 2015).
18. John Starnes, *Closely Guarded: A Life in Canadian Security and Intelligence* (Toronto: University of Toronto Press, 1998); and Mike Frost and Michel Gratton, *Spyworld: Inside the Canadian and American Intelligence Establishments* (Toronto: Doubleday, 1994).
19. MI is mentioned in Tim Cook, *Shock Troops: Canadians Fighting the Great War, 1917–1918* (Toronto: Viking, 2008); and in Milner, *Canada's Navy*.
20. See Stephanie Carvin, Thomas Juneau, and Craig Forcese, eds., *Top Secret Canada: Understanding the Canadian Intelligence and National Security Community* (Toronto: University of Toronto Press, 2020).

21. Harold A. Skaarup, *Out of Darkness—Light: A History of Canadian Military Intelligence*, 3 [4] vols. (New York: iUniverse, 2005). A fourth volume is not yet published (manuscript in author's possession, received 2018).
22. James Cox, "The Transformation of Canadian Defence Intelligence since the End of the Cold War" (MA thesis, Royal Military College of Canada, 2004), Canadian Foreign Intelligence History Project.
23. See, for example, Department of National Defence, *Canadian Forces Joint Publication 2-1 Intelligence Operations*, 2nd ed., promulgation draft (Ottawa: DND, 2021).

PART I

THE EVOLUTION OF CANADIAN DEFENCE AND MILITARY INTELLIGENCE, 1945–2005

1

POLICIES, BUDGETS, RESOURCES, AND COMMITMENTS

Canadian Defence in Context

The operational history of Canadian MI and DI between 1970 and 2010 did not occur in a strategic or political vacuum. At the strategic level it began during the Cold War. That tense standoff between the Soviet bloc and the NATO alliance was the touchstone that anchored all Western foreign and defence policies. The standoff shaped their armed forces and defined how they prepared for conventional and nuclear war. But that all changed between 1989 and 1991 when the Soviet bloc—and the Soviet Union itself—disintegrated. The period since has been marked by a proliferation of conflicts that spanned the spectrum from high-intensity conventional wars, the 1990–91 Persian Gulf War being the major case in point, to low-intensity unconventional wars, such as those in the Balkans, Africa, and Afghanistan. It was these latter conflicts that most profoundly shaped the operational experience of the CAF and of its intelligence component from 1990 through 2010.

Trying to understand and develop effective responses to these changes in the strategic environment taxed the minds of defence staffs of many countries, and Canada was no exception. But those were not the only factors at work. The four decades from 1970 to 2010 also were marked by constant but inconsistent and frequently ineffective efforts to "square a circle": limiting military commitments and defence spending, while at the same time trying to support allies, respond to crises, and manage domestic policies, budgets, and public expectations.

In 2018 Dr. Ross Fetterly, a retired Royal Canadian Air Force (RCAF) colonel, offered a succinct summary of the defence policy challenges that have faced all Canadian governments since the mid-1960s. "The history of defence reform in Canada has been one of a constant struggle to renew both core military capabilities and personnel strengths, while searching for increased efficiency within a limited budget."[1] Declaratory policies were frequently overtaken by unforeseen events that required rapid and unplanned adaptation. As a result, CAF formations and units—and their intelligence support—that deployed to conduct operations were shaped as much by domestic constraints as by the requirements of their missions and the environments in which they occurred. With rare exceptions, that support came up short. But before exploring the post-1970 period, it is essential to set the policy, fiscal and structural context that laid the foundation for that era.

CANADIAN DEFENCE POLICY AND ARMED FORCES ORGANIZATION, 1964–69

Emerging from World War II and drawn quickly into the precarious Cold War, Canadian governments began to define Canada's defence needs and commitments in terms of collective security through bilateral arrangements with the United States and multilateral institutions such as the newly created UN and currently NATO. This meant that if and when Canadian forces fought again, they would do so only within some kind of military coalition or alliance.

Consequently, by the mid-1960s the Canadian military (over one hundred thousand strong) were assigned to commitments and missions that were not mutually supporting. The RCAF, for example, operated two air forces: one in Canada, committed to air defence of North America (from 1958 on under the joint Canadian-American North American Aerospace Defense Command [NORAD]), and a second one in Europe, assigned to fight an air/ground war within the NATO command structure. Likewise, under the auspices of NATO the Royal Canadian Navy (RCN) was prepared for antisubmarine warfare (ASW) to secure sea lines of communication to Europe. The Canadian Army raised a mechanized brigade for the Korean War, while a similar one—the forward element of what was meant to be a mechanized division—was deployed in Germany for NATO.[2] From 1957 on, units and personnel also participated in numerous peacekeeping operations. So, the forces and their missions were fragmented and mutually nonsupporting, and as shown later they would largely conceive of their intelligence needs and practices within this context.

In 1947, Defence Minister Brooke Claxton had created the single Department of National Defence (DND) under a deputy minister (DM). His intention was to foster "the maximum degree of coordination and to eliminate duplication of functions."[3] But his focus was on the policy domain, not on operational matters; military command was a separate function to be exercised only by the uniformed chain of command. The result was not "two solitudes" working in silos, but neither was there complete unity of effort.

Liberal government member Paul Hellyer became minister of national defence in 1963 and set out to rectify what he had identified as serious problems in the Canadian military: the absence of a single command authority and service voice on military matters, the fact that the DND administered but did not control the armed forces, duplication of functions among three service chains of command and support structures, and the fact that the three services did not work together. Hellyer was determined to rectify this problem, and make the DND and the armed forces more effective and efficient.

His solution, outlined initially in the 1964 *White Paper on Defence*, was threefold: first, to create a single chain of command and an integrated military headquarters and staff, headed by a Chief of Defence Staff (CDS) who would be the sole military adviser to the minister of national defence. But as defence analyst and former Canadian Army officer Douglas Bland points out, the role and responsibilities of the CDS position were never clarified before it was created and remained elusive thereafter.[4] Second, the DND would come under the sole direction of a DM who reported directly to the minister of national defence. Finally, in 1967 the three services were unified into a single service, organized into six triservice commands. The intention was to make CAF formations more efficient and more mobile and better organized to support each other in combined operations.[5]

But all defence white papers must be understood as "aspirational" documents. They reveal how the government of the day *wants* to see the strategic environment, how it *wants* its defence efforts to reflect that vision, and *what* it is (or is not) prepared to do and to spend on it. Under the 1964 and later white papers these three things were not necessarily synchronized. The result often was a disconnect between what the government aspired to do and what it actually did. There were inherent contradictions between the government's "vision" of the strategic environment and intentions and how it prepared the CAF to translate them into relevant capabilities and missions that advanced the government's objectives. The latter goal was defeated by the fact that the government found that it could not easily shed alliance commitments that imposed the different roles and equipment on the forces. The "unified" services remained equipped and trained for major war in Europe but not in concert with each other. They were no more capable of joint and combined operations than they had been before.

DEFENCE IN THE '70S AND THE MANAGEMENT REVIEW GROUP, 1971–72

In 1971 the government published a new white paper that was meant to solve the dilemmas the previous one had created. At the outset *Defence in the '70s*, which was developed outside the DND and without advice from the CAF,[6] asserted logically that defence policy could not be developed in isolation from national interests and foreign policy. The paper acknowledged the changing international environment, but legacy defence priorities—defence of North

America, collective security for Europe within NATO, and UN peacekeeping—remained unchanged.

The paper then shifted its focus to domestic concerns, including "the threat to society posed by violent revolutionaries and the implications of the recent crisis."[7] The October Crisis internal security operation (examined in chapter 5) had ended only a few months before the paper was published. So, it made sense that the preamble drew attention to the "internal aspects of national defence," including Aid to the Civil Power (ACP) and assistance to civil authorities.[8]

That apart, the paper outlined national aims and policies that were defined mostly in ways that made it difficult to discern what the CAF could contribute to them. This introduced some incoherence to defence policy and to force posture. For example, although the Soviet navy had greatly increased its missile-firing submarine capability, the CAF's new Maritime Command (MARCOM), which brought together naval vessels and rotary- and fixed-wing patrol aircraft, would reduce its ASW role against such threats and develop more versatile general-purpose naval capabilities. Similarly, in spite of Canadians' proud embrace of UN peacekeeping, the paper was not optimistic about its future.[9]

As Bland astutely observed, "The real dilemma for the [Pierre Trudeau] government was that they had established defence objectives from which they could not escape but which they did not wish to honour."[10] Fiscal concerns provided a useful cover for this conundrum. The foundation for defence planning in the white paper was financial. It noted that there was "substantial pressure" to reduce defence spending to meet social and economic priorities. Indeed, it made the curious assertion that there was "no obvious level for defence expenditures in Canada."[11] This made no sense, since the government had to assign funds to meet actual NORAD and NATO commitments. But instead of a threat- and capability-based defence budget, once spending had been decided for other departments and programs, the DND would get the "leftovers."[12]

Further changes were to come. A Management Review Group (MRG) had been appointed to review the direction and organization of the DND. However, the new minister of national defence, Edgar Benson, started to make changes even before the MRG issued its final report. The most important was his March 1972 decision to integrate civilian and military elements of the DND and the integrated military headquarters into a single National Defence Headquarters (NDHQ). This new structure placed the DM and the CDS directly under the minister, with assistant deputy ministers assigned to a range of functional responsibilities. The military chain of command went from the CDS to the vice-chief of the Defence Staff (VCDS), then to two deputy chiefs of the Defense Staff (DCDSs): for operations, and support. Although the CDS was meant to be the sole source for military advice to the minister, the new structure gave senior civil servants a voice on military issues.[13]

But these changes also gave them a role in defence policymaking that strayed into areas that previously had been solely the domain of the uniformed chiefs. In 1972 the new CDS, Gen. J. A. Dextraze, met with the MRG and told them he did not object to the proposed structure so long as it gave the CDS "without any restraint . . . the total ability to effectively *control and administer* the Forces."[14] He separated policymaking from policy execution; the DM was responsible for the former and the CDS the latter. Still, the CDS necessarily played a policy-making role. But the reorganization driven by the MRG report also took the VCDS out of the policy planning process (which went to the assistant deputy minister's Policy branch) and separated policy from operational planning, when the two should have been closely linked. Similarly, the DCDS lost control of future operational policy. By February 1973, the operational branch headed by the VCDS disappeared, replaced by a single DCDS, and "the VCDS was relieved of direct operational responsibilities."[15]

Instead, the VCDS became the chief "manager" of NDHQ, and the DCDS became the chief "operator" of the armed forces. Assisted by a joint staff, that office had inherited most of the traditional responsibilities previously exercised by the vice-chiefs of the three services: operational planning, training, and overseeing the ongoing operations of the CAF. But intelligence, plans, and operational requirements had been delegated to the assistant chief of the Defence Staff, so the DCDS's authority was fragmented. In Bland's view, this change represented "the complete loss of the continuity of policy and command and control once enjoyed by the CDS/VCDS."[16]

THE DEFENCE STRUCTURE REVIEW, 1974

These changes were barely under way when the government initiated another review. Having failed twice to reconcile defence policies, commitments, force structures, and the budget, it launched the *Defence Structure Review* in 1974 in an attempt to do just that. And there was much to be reconciled. First, in 1969 Canada had reduced its NATO commitments at the very time when the alliance had adopted the flexible response doctrine, which was based on maintaining larger conventional forces in Europe. Second, by the mid-1970s CAF personnel strength had fallen to seventy-eight thousand, forty-six thousand below its strength in 1963–64. This was at a time when it was the world's largest source of peacekeeping troops, and the brigade in Germany was 60 percent below its peacetime strength. Third, defence spending had not kept pace with inflation.[17]

The *Defence Structure Review* reaffirmed for the CAF the tasks set out in the 1971 white paper, but the government finally put money and muscle where its mouth was. Defence spending was indexed to inflation, and then the DND went on a spending spree: Leopard tanks for the brigade in Germany, ASW frigates and CP-140 (Aurora) long-range patrol aircraft for MARCOM, and CF-18 fighter aircraft for NATO and NORAD. The tanks recommitted Canada to a heavy armoured mechanized force in NATO, not the light airmobile one envisioned in *Defence in the '70s*, bringing its posture into synch with the flexible response doctrine. Defence spending increased fivefold and reached the 20 percent capital spending target in 1977–78 but still struggled to keep pace with inflation. And while the new equipment was much better, there was less of it: 128 Leopard tanks replaced 334 Centurions, and 18 Aurora long-range patrol aircraft replaced 33 Argus ASW aircraft. Personnel increased to over eighty-three thousand by the end of 1984. Still, academic defence analyst Dr. Rod Byers wrote in 1986 that the *Defence Structure Review* was realistic but "too little too late."[18]

Consequently, when the new Conservative government came into office in 1984, the "commitment-capability" gap still had not been closed.[19] From the mid-1970s, "a general consensus has emerged that Canadian commitments to NATO and western security are mismatched, given the current size and capabilities of the Canadian Forces."[20] And not just mismatched but also inadequate. In 1983–84 the minister of national defence had told the cabinet that "if a major national crisis were to occur, the Canadian Forces could not make a credible contribution to deterrence; and in the event of hostilities . . . would not be sufficiently manned and equipped to carry out the tasks expected of them in support of the allied effort and consequently would be overly vulnerable to enemy attack."[21]

CHALLENGE AND COMMITMENT: THE 1987 WHITE PAPER AND THE AFTERMATH

The Conservative government of Prime Minister Brian Mulroney conducted a foreign policy review that blended global engagement with the importance of NATO and NORAD and the sovereignty protection theme of the early Trudeau years. The NATO brigade in Germany was strengthened by 1,200 troops, bringing it closer to wartime strength. The CAF also tested the Canadian air-sea transportable brigade commitment to Norway (established in 1969) for the first time in 1986 and found that it could not be deployed in time or be sustained once it got there.[22]

These initiatives presaged the next white paper, released in June 1987. Titled *Challenge and Commitment: A Defence Policy for Canada*, it tried to distance itself from the policy of previous government. In reality, it did not represent a fundamental break with prevailing Cold War policy themes. But it did offer a radically different prescription to deal with the legacy of the Trudeau-era defence policies and what the government perceived as a more hostile international environment. Unlike its 1971 counterpart, the 1987 white paper actually addressed the Soviet military threat. The 1987 paper identified new threats to

Canadian territory and airspace: Soviet bombers equipped with cruise missiles. Providing Canadian capabilities to deal with these was couched in terms of protecting sovereignty, since failure to do so would result in the United States doing it on Canada's behalf.[23]

The government dropped the Canadian air-sea transportable brigade, and reassigned it and other elements to form a division for service in Germany. Likewise, the two air squadrons originally designated to support that brigade were reallocated to bring air contingent in Germany up to air division strength in a crisis. The government ambitiously envisioned a "three-ocean navy," so MARCOM was to be the beneficiary of a major spending splurge. This would include six more frigates, ten to twelve nuclear-powered attack submarines, new shipborne ASW helicopters to replace the aging Sea Kings, and six new long-range patrol aircraft. The government planned to increase defence spending by 2 percent per year over a five-year period, with major purchases being funded above this level.[24]

But the ink was barely dry on the white paper when the Soviet bloc collapsed in 1989 and then the Soviet Union dissolved in 1991. These events largely undermined the rationale for much of the 1987 white paper and its programs. In the 1990 budget, responding to the dramatic changes in Europe, the government announced the closure of Canada's bases in Germany and that the forces there would return to Canada. There was much talk of a budgetary "peace dividend."

That optimism was quickly shattered by a series of unexpected military developments starting with the Oka Crisis in Canada, a small but politically charged First Nations insurrection in the summer of 1990. It was quickly followed by the 1990–91 Persian Gulf War, the outbreak of the civil war in Yugoslavia, and a humanitarian crisis in Somalia. Most of these involved Canadian military operations discussed later. So, it was no surprise that once the Liberals came back to power in 1993, they would initiate yet another defence policy review. This launched an era of multiple reviews of Canadian military affairs and of continued and declining defence spending, giving the 1990s the stigma of being the "Decade of Darkness."[25]

THE 1994 WHITE PAPER

Prime Minister Jean Chretien set the tone when, immediately upon taking office, he cancelled the controversial contract for new shipborne helicopters. In the *1994 Defence White Paper* Minister of National Defence David Collenette stated bluntly that the CAF and the DND were going to experience serious reductions. This was due in part to the changes in the international environment but equally if not more to the government's commitment to maintain social programs while trying to get spending under control. The white paper predicted that by fiscal year 2000, the defence budget would be only about 60 percent of the level anticipated in the 1987 white paper. The 1994 white paper acknowledged that the DND and the CAF had "already made a large contribution to the national effort to reduce the deficit, [but] the Government believes that additional cuts are both necessary and possible." The paper added that "as a consequence of the further decline in defence expenditure that forms the fiscal context of this paper, cuts will be deeper, and there will be more reductions, cancellations, and delay."[26]

The 1994 white paper reaffirmed Canada's traditional defence commitments. But just as for previous governments, how to fulfil those obligations proved to be a challenge. On the one hand, the government wanted to have combat capable forces able to fight "alongside the best, against the best."[27] On the other, the CAF would have to do so within a reduced funding envelope, with fewer personnel, and would not be able to cover the entire spectrum of conflict. Yet, there was no real reduction in tasks across that spectrum. The CAF had to do sovereignty protection and defence of Canada, ACP, search and rescue, fisheries and counternarcotics patrols, and disaster relief. Forces were designated for the defence of North America and for the NATO Immediate Reaction Force. One additional ship would occasionally sail with the NATO standing naval force in the Mediterranean. Up to four thousand personnel would be set aside to support UN peacekeeping.[28] This was what the government aspired to provide even though the CAF lacked the resources to fulfil these aspirations.

Nevertheless, defence analyst Dr. Joel Sokolsky praised the white paper for having "gotten it right."[29] He argued that it "more closely matches commitments with capabilities" not because the CAF were to be given previously denied capabilities "but rather because the current policy adopts a leaner view of what Canada's commitments should be."[30] In his view, Canada was "cutting its sail to fit its cloth."

But just as with previous white papers, the contradictions of this approach were obvious. The Army was to gain three thousand additional troops, but the CAF overall would lose fifteen thousand regular force personnel. The paper did not attempt to reconcile that disconnect. Headquarters staffs would be reduced by one-third. Funding for major procurement projects would be scaled back by $15 billion, with projects cancelled, reduced, or delayed. Canada's role in NORAD surveillance, warning, and air defence would be "significantly reduced." The number of operational CF-18s would be reduced, with flying hours also scaled back. The North Warning System radars would be maintained at a reduced level of readiness.[31] That, at least, was consistent with what the United States was doing in continental aerospace defence. Ironically, Canada was committing forces to counternarcotics operations just as the United States was considering a reduction in that task, having concluded that it was having little impact.[32] Ideally, the CAF was supposed to be able to field at any time what it called "main contingency forces" composed of a naval task force, a brigade group plus an infantry battalion, a fighter wing, a tactical air transport squadron, and a joint task force headquarters totalling some ten thousand personnel. While oriented to war fighting, main contingency force units could be deployed for low-intensity missions such as peacekeeping.[33]

The CAF could not meet all of these commitments without double-tasking units and formations. For example, the UN standby battalion was also designated the NATO Immediate Reaction Force.[34] In any case, the forces were already plagued by personnel and equipment shortages that rendered many units and formations "hollow," unable to meet the commitments assigned to them. To conduct the many ongoing operations and those mounted in the wake of the white paper, the CAF had to cobble units together.[35]

Having praised the "realism" of the white paper, Sokolsky warned that if the economy performed worse than expected, the proposed spending cuts might not be the last. He believed that in the view of the government, "there is always room for less defence spending."[36] In short, realism was mutable.

THE DEFENCE "REENGINEERING" EXPERIMENT, 1995–99

Defence spending continued to decline for the next two years before being increased in 1999.[37] Even after 9/11, defence spending increased only gradually until the middle of the decade.[38] The changes imposed by the white paper and the 1994 and 1995 budgets forced the DND and the CAF to seek ways to preserve operational capability. One of initiatives to achieve this was "reengineering," described as, "the radical redesign of an organization's processes, intended to result in dramatic improvements to delivered products and/or services. The specific CF [Canadian Forces] embodiment of this . . . was the Management Command and Control Re-engineering Team."[39]

The Management Command and Control Re-engineering Team was launched in January 1995. Guided by concepts proposed in the white paper, its mandate was to redesign the DND/CAF structures for command and control (C2) and for resource management. It focused primarily on restructuring and reducing the sizes of various headquarters, although NDHQ continued to serve as an integrated civilian/military headquarters. The key features of this process included: reducing resources for headquarters functions by one-third (later extended to 50%); moving the chiefs of environmental staffs (air, land, and sea) to NDHQ, where they would continue to act as service commanders, but also act as the strategic staff of the CDS and the DM; and eliminating separate command headquarters.[40] This new structure looked remarkably like Canadian

Forces Headquarters (CFHQ) before Hellyer's reorganization. In thirty years, it had come full circle.

Driven as much by business management practices and fads as by government priorities, the bottom line of reengineering was about limiting spending and maximizing fewer resources. In short: "doing more with less."[41] But in this case, reduced spending and fewer personnel were not the results of reengineering, but predetermined parameters within which changes had to work. Not surprisingly, the Management Command and Control Re-engineering Team exercise had its skeptics, and not without good reason. It proved impossible to apply these processes exactly to the DND for reasons related to its unique responsibilities. Nor were the processes applied across the department as a whole. They also encountered resistance and inertia, so some parts of the DND never were reengineered. The result was that instead of creating a whole new management structure, the old one was largely retained with only some internal tinkering and fewer personnel. By 1999, the DND could not provide an agreed "view of the impact or effectiveness of its reorganization." And as late as 2004 there was "little evidence that any component of the MCCRT [Management Command and Control Re-engineering Team] was even measured."[42]

THE CANADIAN ARMED FORCES AND THE REVOLUTION IN MILITARY AFFAIRS

While this was happening, new strategic thinking was starting to push the DND and the CAF to imagine a more ambitious vision of their future. The rapid coalition victory in the Persian Gulf War, shaped by the integration of air, land, and sea power as well as surveillance systems, computers, and communications, was being hailed as marking a "revolution in military affairs" (RMA).[43] By the late 1990s, RMA-derived concepts were infiltrating Canadian defence thinking. In 1998 the Defence Management Committee directed the DND to develop a Canadian perspective on the RMA.[44] In a 1999 paper Dr. Andrew Richter states, "To say that... the Department of National Defence—has approached the RMA in a slow and deliberate fashion would be an understatement."[45] The topic had been all but absent in the 1994 white paper.[46]

But according to Dr. Elinor Sloan, the RCN already had highlighted the technical implications of the RMA in its 1997 strategy paper *Adjusting Course: A Naval Strategy for Canada*, which stated that the RCN should expect radical changes in the areas of data management, communications, situational awareness, and stealth technology. This would have implications for training, C2 (blurring the lines between strategic, operational, and tactical), and coalition operations.[47] Shortly thereafter the Canadian Army published a similar "vision" paper, *Canada's Army: We Stand on Guard for Thee*. Like the RCN, the paper acknowledged the blurring of command boundaries; drew attention to the expansive information/awareness domain and "smart" weapons, demonstrated by the Persian Gulf War; and noted that these would shape how future armies would be organized, led, trained, and equipped.[48] It is clear, then, that the services had been studying the implications of the RMA for some time. Dr. Sloan also pointed to two other documents that identified themes that resonated with the RMA: *Shaping the Future of the Canadian Forces: A Strategy for 2020* (June 1999) and the *Defence Planning Guidance 2000* (August 1999).[49] She pointed to acquisitions that showed some commitment to adapt to the RMA: precision-guided bombs for the CF-18s, which were used in the 1999 Kosovo air campaign; a Canadian military satellite communications package that piggybacked on American satellites; and upgraded communications systems for the Canadian Army and RCN. But she also drew attention to the absence of any unmanned aerial vehicle (UAV) capability.[50]

Canada's capacity to adapt to the RMA was seriously constrained at that time by limits on spending, a point the official papers acknowledged. As the CDS stated in the *Defence Planning Guidance*, "We continue to experience short term and longer term affordability issues which limit flexibility."[51] Unconstrained by the need to adhere to an official line, Richter was even more blunt: "Canada's participation in the RMA will be limited both by its modest military establishment and niche-oriented civilian technology sector, which appears poorly suited to supplying DND with technology platforms for advanced weapons systems. Thus, it is not entirely clear whether and how Canada can participate in the RMA, and these concerns raise doubts about our military's ability to function effectively in an information/technology environment."[52]

Even as the reengineering process was ongoing and the CAF and the DND were trying to grapple with the implications of the RMA, the forces carried out a wide range of missions. In addition to the NATO-led peace-enforcement operations in Bosnia and Kosovo discussed later, CAF units deployed to three UN missions in Haiti (750 troops each) and to twenty-one other operations. Additionally, in 1997 some 8,500 troops conducted flood relief operations in Manitoba, and 16,000 deployed across Ontario and Québec after the 1998 ice storm.[53]

If the foregoing was not enough, during this period the CAF and the DND also were subjected to intense and scathing public scrutiny during the formal inquiry into two murders committed during the Somalia mission. Launched in 1994 and ended in 1997, the inquiry examined every aspect of the operation.[54] The hearings stripped away many illusions about the nature of the "new" peacekeeping.[55] But they also exposed lapses of leadership and discipline that tarnished the reputation of the CAF and cost the careers of several CDSs and other high-ranking officers. Evidence of continuing and pervasive ill discipline and racism in the deployed unit—the Canadian Airborne Regiment—led to its unfortunate disbandment in 1995. The commission's final report offered an extensive list of recommendations to improve C2 and leadership, reinforce discipline and legal norms, change institutional culture, and improve predeployment training.[56] It was a dark end to a dark decade.

DEFENCE AFTER 9/11

Then came 9/11, and everything changed again. During the next ten years, the CAF conducted stability and combat operations in Afghanistan and related activities in the region. As shown in chapters 11 and 12, the CAF mission grew from a handful of special operations forces in late 2001 to a brigade-size task force from 2008 to 2011. Starting from a readiness, personnel, equipment, and funding deficit, the CAF and the DND adapted and improvised to meet the changing operational requirements. An independent study published in 2003 concluded that "years of over-commitment and under-investment in national defence had taken the Canadian Forces to a perilous point of no return, where many essential capabilities would fail before they could be rescued."[57] Ironically, the Afghanistan War (2001–11) may have saved the CAF from complete rust-out and personnel burnout. Defence spending almost doubled over the decade following 9/11 until the troops were withdrawn from combat in 2011.[58] And the operations in Afghanistan took place while the Canadian Army was undergoing a process of institutional reform, reorganization, and reinvestment, often referred to as "Transformation."

While the fundamentals of defence policy remained unchanged after 9/11, continuing efforts to find economies and efficiencies in organization were taking place "at a time when global security demands our constant attention, and when the CAF operates outside Canada in a less permissive and uncertain environment, . . . increasingly one of unilateralism and multi-dimensional conflict, with unconventional means used to disrupt both national institutions and long-standing multi-national arrangements."[59] Barely a year before 9/11, the divisional headquarters established in 1989 was disbanded and reorganized into the Canadian Forces Joint Operations Group, which came under control of the DCDS. It comprised a joint headquarters, a signals regiment, and a support group, all to be deployable into a theatre of operations.[60] The divisional headquarters was an army-only formation, while the Canadian Forces Joint Operations Group was "joint." But even if that change could produce a more effective C2 structure for deployed forces, broad structural problems remained.

Bland pointed out in 2005 that while the CAF establishment was set at only sixty thousand regular force personnel, myriad administrative tasks unrelated to the primary focus of the CAF—"to have an instrument to apply coercive and, if necessary, deadly force on others in pursuit of the government's objectives"[61]—were draining many uniformed personnel at NDHQ away from that focus. The defence procurement process was a case in point. It did not seem to be directed at getting "a bigger bang for the buck" for the CAF to fulfil its raison d'être. Rather, it seemed to be aimed at satisfying political, regional, and national industrial policies.[62]

Indeed, in spite of the reengineering exercise, which did eliminate some headquarters, the number of CAF personnel assigned to administration continued to grow at the expense of personnel at the "sharp end." At the same time, the DND/CAF was spending large amounts of money to maintain aging vehicles and aircraft rather than investing in new ones, which would be less costly over the long term.[63] This was unsustainable if the CAF was to retain any credible operational capability,[64] but the Liberal government did not address the problem publicly until 2005, when it issued its *International Policy Statement*.

THE *INTERNATIONAL POLICY STATEMENT* AND "TRANSFORMATION," 2005–8

The defence portion of the *International Policy Statement* acknowledged the volatility of the strategic environment and the consequent need for armed forces to exert influence therein. The policy statement announced a "new vision" for the CAF that proposed to "fundamentally and permanently transform the military from its lingering Cold War paradigms into a very new, strategically relevant, operationally responsive and tactically decisive joint force."[65] The driving force behind this was the new CDS, Gen. Rick Hillier, who took command of the CAF in February 2005.

One of the main features of this initiative was the reorganization of major portions of the DND and the CAF into several new operational commands led by a strategic-level joint staff. Announced in January 2006 but under development internally for some time prior, they included four new structures: the Canada Command, the Expeditionary Forces Command, the Special Operations Forces Command, and the Operational Support Command. This shifted command authority from the environmental chiefs and staffs within NDHQ and devolved it onto forces and commanders more directly involved in operations. To give force to these changes, in the February 2005 budget the government committed to providing $13 billion in new defence spending over five years and adding five thousand new regular force members and three thousand reservists. Among the beneficiaries of this largesse was the Special Operations Forces Command. Its Joint Task Force 2 counterterrorism force was expanded, and a command headquarters, a special operations regiment, an aviation squadron, and a special incident response unit were created. As shown in chapters 11 and 12, the Special Operations Forces Command forces were both drivers of and beneficiaries of the changes in Canadian approaches to military intelligence that the Afghanistan War demanded.[66]

These changes were not without challenges and critics. According to Lt.-Gen. (ret.) Mike Jeffery, Hillier's initial vision lacked the details needed to turn ideas into realities. Hillier bypassed the environmental chiefs, who then were not wholly committed to the process. Not enough time was devoted to planning before implementing the vision, and the personnel targets proved hard to meet. So, in 2006 an external review recommended "mid-course corrections." To his credit, the CDS responded positively to the review, and by 2007 the new command structure was firmly in place.[67]

The government was defeated in an election not long after issuing the *International Policy Statement*. But the new Conservative government did not materially change the approach to defence. If anything, its June 2008 defence policy statement, *The Canada First Defence Strategy*, enhanced and accelerated what the *International Policy Statement* already had put in place.[68] The new command structure remained unchanged until the creation of Canadian Joint Operations Command in 2012.

IMPLICATIONS FOR INTELLIGENCE

Canadian defence policies, budgets, and command and force structures were in constant flux from 1970 to 2010. The single dominant trend, especially after 1990, was that the CAF always had to do more with less: people, equipment, and money. As subsequent chapters will show, this policy, budgetary, and organizational turmoil impacted defence and military intelligence no less, sometimes enhancing but mostly inhibiting their ability to provide optimal support to the deployed forces. The fact that most of the relevant public policy and other documents are all but silent about intelligence speaks volumes. There were people inside the DND and the CAF who did the work and recognized its value and its limits. But, few in number and labouring in secrecy, their voices were rarely heard outside the "Green Door." It took the onslaught of operations in the post–Cold War period to generate an intelligence-savvy culture within the CAF and the DND, force open that door, and bring intelligence support to operations in from the cold.

NOTES

1. Ross Fetterly, "Defence Business Planning in Canada," *Canadian Global Affairs Institute*, Policy Perspectives, October 2018, https://www.cgai.ca/defence_business_planning_in_canada.

2. Douglas L. Bland, *The Administration of Defence Policy in Canada, 1947 to 1985* (Kingston, Ontario: Ronald P. Frye, 1987), 14–15, 21.
3. Bland, 3.
4. Douglas L. Bland, *Chiefs of Defence: Government and the Unified Command of the Canadian Armed Forces* (Toronto: Canadian Institute of Strategic Studies, 1995), 71–76.
5. DND, *White Paper on Defence* (Ottawa: Queen's Printer and Controller of Stationery, 1964), 17, 21–22.
6. Bland, *Administration of Defence Policy*, 59.
7. DND, *Defence in the '70s: White Paper on Defence* (Ottawa: Information Canada, 1971), 1.
8. DND, *Defence in the '70s*, 3.
9. DND, *Defence in the '70s*, 1, 27–30, 34–36, 39–40.
10. Bland, *Administration of Defence Policy*, 61.
11. DND, *Defence in the '70s*, 41, and opening remarks by the minister of defence.
12. DND, *Defence in the '70s*, 41; Bland, *Administration of Defence Policy*, 60–61.
13. DND, *Defence in the '70s*, 42; Bland, *Administration of Defence Policy*, 81–82, fig. 5, 96–107.
14. Quoted in Bland, *Chiefs of Defence*, 3, and in Bland, *Administration of Defence Policy*, 104.
15. Bland, *Chiefs of Defence*, 27; Bland, *Administration of Defence Policy*, 103, 111.
16. Bland, *Administration of Defence Policy*, 112–15; James Cox, "The Transformation of Canadian Defence Intelligence since the End of the Cold War" (master's thesis, Royal Military College of Canada, 2004), 23, Canadian Foreign Intelligence History Project.
17. D. W. Middlemiss and J. J. Sokolsky, *Canadian Defence: Decisions and Determinants* (Toronto: Harcourt Brace Jovanovich, 1989), 32, 35–42; R. B. Byers, *Canadian Security and Defence: The Legacy and the Challenges* (London: International Institute for Strategic Studies, 1986), 10.
18. Middlemiss and Sokolsky, *Canadian Defence*, 39–40, 43–44; Byers, *Canadian Security and Defence*, 11.
19. Middlemiss and Sokolsky, *Canadian Defence*, 45.
20. Byers, *Canadian Security and Defence*, 10.
21. Byers, 11.
22. Middlemiss and Sokolsky, *Canadian Defence*, 46–47, 52, 191–92.
23. Middlemiss and Sokolsky, 49, 54; Byers, *Canadian Security and Defence*, 16; DND, *Challenge and Commitment: A Defence Policy for Canada.* (Ottawa: DND, 1987), 1–3, 5–15, 17, 55, 59.
24. DND, *Challenge and Commitment*, 49–64; Middlemiss and Sokolsky, *Canadian Defence*, 51–53; Maj.-Gen. J. K. Dangerfield, "The 1st Canadian Division: Enigma, Contradiction or Requirement?," *Canadian Defence Quarterly* 19, no. 5 (Spring 1990): 8.
25. Gloria Galloway, "Hillier Decries Military's 'Decade of Darkness,'" Globe and Mail, 16 February 2007, https://www.theglobeandmail.com/news/national/hillier-decries-militarys-decade-of-darkness/article20393158/.
26. DND, *1994 White Paper on Defence* (Ottawa: DND, 1994), 3–7, 9–10.
27. DND, *1994 White Paper on Defence*, 12, 14, 15, 20, 27.

28. DND, *1994 White Paper on Defence*, 13, 15–39, 46.
29. Joel J. Sokolsky, *Canada, Getting It Right This Time: The 1994 Defence White Paper* (Carlisle Barracks, PA: Strategic Studies Institute, US Army War College, 1995), 1.
30. Sokolsky, 2.
31. DND, *1994 White Paper on Defence*, 23, 40–42, 46, 48.
32. Sokolsky, *Canada, Getting It Right*, 15.
33. Joseph T. Jockel, *The Canadian Forces: Hard Choices, Soft Power* (Toronto: Canadian Institute of Strategic Studies, 1999), 3–4.
34. DND, *1994 Defence White Paper*, 39; Sokolsky, *Canada, Getting It Right*, 15.
35. Jockel, *Canadian Forces*, 37–40, 44–49, 52–56.
36. Sokolsky, *Canada, Getting It Right*, 14.
37. Bill Robinson and Peter Ibbott, *Canadian Military Spending: How Does the Current Level Compare to Historical Levels? . . . To Allied Spending? . . . To Potential Threats?* (Waterloo, Ontario: Project Ploughshares, 2003), 6, chart 1, http://ploughshares.ca/wp-content/uploads/2012/08/WP3.1.pdf.
38. David Macdonald, *The Cost of 9/11: Tracking the Creation of a National Security Establishment in Canada* (Ottawa: Rideau Institute, 2011), 4, table 2.
39. Lt.-Col. Michael Rostek, "A Framework for Fundamental Change? The Management Command and Control Re-Engineering Initiative," *Canadian Military Journal* 4, no. 5 (Winter 2004–5): 66, http://www.journal.forces.gc.ca/vo5/no4/manageme-gestion-eng.asp.
40. Rostek, 71n5; DND, *1994 Defence White Paper*, 41; DND, *Organization and Accountability: Guidance for Members of the Canadian Forces and Employees of the Department of National Defence*, 2nd ed. (Ottawa: DND, 1999), 7, 14.
41. Rostek, "Framework for Fundamental Change," 67–68.
42. Cox, "Transformation of Canadian Defence," 112; Rostek, "Framework for Fundamental Change," 67–68, 71.
43. Lawrence Freedman, *The Transformation of Strategic Affairs* (London: Routledge, The International Institute for Strategic Studies, 2006), 12–13.
44. Elinor Sloan, "Canada and the Revolution in Military Affairs: Current Response and Future Opportunities," *Canadian Military Journal* 1, no. 3 (Autumn 2000): 8.
45. Andrew Richter, *The Revolution in Military Affairs and Its Impact on Canada: The Challenge and the Consequences* (Vancouver: Institute of International Relations, University of British Columbia Press, 1999), 17.
46. Richter, 18.
47. Sloan, "Canada and the Revolution," 8; DND, *Adjusting Course: A Naval Strategy for Canada* (Ottawa: Canada Communications Group, 1997), 21–24.
48. DND, *Canada's Army: We Stand on Guard for Thee* (Ottawa: DND, 1998), 78–79, 113–14.
49. DND, *Shaping the Future of Canadian Defence: A Strategy for 2020* (Ottawa: DND, 1999), 1, 4, 7; DND, Vice Chief of the Defence Staff, *Defence Planning Guidance, 2000* (Ottawa: DND, 1999), chap. 1, 1.
50. Sloan, "Canada and the Revolution," 9.
51. DM/CDS message in Vice Chief of the Defence Staff, *Defence Planning Guidance*.
52. Richter, *Revolution in Military Affairs*, 17–18.
53. Jockel, *Canadian Forces*, 20–22, 25–26.
54. Commission of Inquiry into the Deployment of Canadian Forces to Somalia, *Dishonoured Legacy: The Lessons of the Somalia Affair; Report of the Commission of*

Inquiry into the Deployment of Canadian Forces to Somalia, Executive Summary (Ottawa: Minister of Public Works and Government Services, 1997), 12–14.
55. Allen Gregory Sens and Commission of Inquiry into the Deployment of Canadian Forces to Somalia, *Somalia and the Changing Nature of Peacekeeping: The Implications for Canada* (Ottawa: Minister of Public Works and Government Services, 1997), 45–46, 50–59, 99, 102–3, 113–14; Jockel, *Canadian Forces*, 30–31.
56. Commission of Inquiry, *Dishonoured Legacy*, Executive Summary: 52–81.
57. Douglas L. Bland, *Canada without Armed Forces?* (2003), quoted in Douglas L. Bland, *Transforming National Defence Administration* (Kingston, Ontario: School of Policy Studies, Queen's University, 2005), viii.
58. Macdonald, *The Cost of 9/11*, 4, table 2.
59. Fetterly, "Defence Business Planning."
60. "Canadian Forces Joint Operations Group," DND Backgrounder, 19 May 2004 (web page accessed 8 December 2018, no longer active, http://www.forces.gc.ca/en/news/article.page?doc=canadian-forces-joint-operations-group/hnocfniy&wbdisable=true).
61. Bland, *Transforming National Defence Administration*, 2, 4.
62. Bland, 2–5.
63. Bland, 8, 27–29.
64. Scot Robertson, "The Defence Review: Attacking the Strategy–Resources Mismatch," *Canadian Military Journal* 3, no. 3 (Autumn 2002): 21.
65. Quoted in Andrew B. Godefroy, *Canada's International Policy Statement Five Years Later* (Calgary, Alberta: Canadian Defence & Foreign Affairs Institute, 2010), 5.
66. See Harold A. Skaarup, "Out of Darkness—Light: A History of Canadian Military Intelligence," [vol. 4] (unpublished manuscript, 2018, author's copy), 148–53.
67. Lt.-Gen. (ret.) Michael K. Jeffery, "Inside Canadian Forces Transformation," *Canadian Military Journal* 10, no. 2 (2010): 10, 12, 14–17, https://epe.lac-bac.gc.ca/100/201/301/cdn_military_journal/2009/v10no2/www.journal.forces.gc.ca/vol10/no2/04-jeffery-eng.html. See also Allan English, "Outside CF Transformation Looking In," *Canadian Military Journal* 11, no. 2 (Spring 2011): 12–20, https://epe.lac-bac.gc.ca/100/201/301/cdn_military_journal/2010/v11no2/www.journal.forces.gc.ca/vol11/no2/04-english-eng.html. Surprisingly, General Hillier doesn't devote much space to the subject in his memoir.
68. Godefroy, *Canada's International Policy Statement*, 6.

2

UNCERTAIN FOUNDATIONS

Canadian Defence and Military Intelligence,
1945–1970

The post-1970 DI and MI enterprise did not emerge from nothing. But neither was it a natural extension of what had gone before. It rested on an uncertain foundation built between 1945 and 1970.

CANADIAN WARTIME INTELLIGENCE, 1939–45

Canada had entered World War II as a relative intelligence neophyte.[1] However, Canada emerged from the war as an experienced intelligence producer and consumer at the tactical, operational, and strategic levels. In 1942 the three services created the Canadian Joint Intelligence Committee (CJIC) to conduct studies to inform higher authorities.[2] Canada also had created a cryptographic Examination Unit and an analysis branch in External Affairs, known as the Special Intelligence Section.[3] The RCN had stood up an Operational Intelligence Centre, supported by a SIGINT network, that played a major role in ASW, protecting convoys and hunting U-boats.[4] But the greatest growth had occurred in the Canadian Army, which created an Intelligence Corps in 1942 and trained and deployed more than seventy-five intelligence and field security units and many more individual soldiers who supported Army operations in Canada and overseas.[5] Working in collaboration with its allies, the Canadian military had gained valuable intelligence experience.

Although many in government and the military understood the value of that experience, as the war ended there was a fractious debate over the need for and shape of a peacetime intelligence community.[6] However, as Canada confronted the emerging Cold War, several crucial steps were taken that would define its postwar intelligence structures and functions.

CANADIAN POSTWAR DECISION MAKING ON INTELLIGENCE

Canada's allies reduced some of their wartime intelligence organizations after 1945 but did not eliminate them altogether. Britain needed them to support its efforts to retain control of its empire.[7] In 1947, spurred by the emerging Cold War, the United States established a new foreign intelligence service, the Central Intelligence Agency. The United States also continued its SIGINT alliance with Britain that had been established during the war.[8]

By contrast, Canada opted not to create a secret foreign intelligence service.[9] In some respects this seems surprising. Canada had played a role in training secret agents—Canadians among them—during the war.[10] Moreover, the 1945–46 Gouzenko affair had exposed extensive Soviet espionage in Canada just as Canadian officials were considering Canada's postwar intelligence needs and options.[11] Gen. Charles Foulkes, chief of the General Staff from 1945 to 1951, made a case in 1946 for a full-service intelligence capability, but the government was unpersuaded of the need for it. Nor did it establish a central national-level intelligence coordinating body, only an Intelligence Policy Committee.[12]

However, after fierce debate Canada decided in 1945 to retain a SIGINT/communications security service. Known as the Communications Branch of the National Research Council (CBNRC), it was a stand-alone agency from 1946 to 1975.[13] The government also recognized the benefits of wartime intelligence sharing, particularly in the SIGINT field, and after much debate and lengthy negotiations agreed to join a postwar intelligence alliance with the United States and Britain. That network later expanded to include Australia and New Zealand and has since become known as the "Five Eyes."[14] This unique alliance allowed the United States and the United Kingdom to devolve some of the collection burden onto their partners while giving the latter access to SIGINT products they would not have seen otherwise.

Because the Soviet Union was America's top intelligence priority, the close proximity of Canada's Arctic archipelago to the Soviet Union gave it a unique place in the Five Eyes collection efforts. From the late 1950s, the Canadian SIGINT station at Alert, at the northern tip of Ellesmere Island, directed its intercept capacity "over the pole" into the Soviet Union.[15]

But Five Eyes activity was not limited to collection burden sharing. Since many personnel stayed on after the war or returned as the Cold War heated up, the network was built initially on a foundation of trusted relationships, both formal and informal. Cross-posting of personnel was common although never in large numbers. This facilitated the establishment of common procedures for intelligence sharing, liaison, security standards, terminology, and training. Joint committees and conferences examined a wide range of topics. Most important, raw intelligence and processed reports and assessments flowed between the partners.[16]

The decisions taken in the early postwar period meant that the Canadian government and its military would be dependent on their allies for much of their raw and processed defence-related intelligence. In a July 1947 statement to the House of Commons on Canada's defence needs and organization, Defence Minister Brooke Claxton identified as his second long-term goal: "Joint intelligence and planning groups to review defence appreciations and plans."[17] Decades would pass before intelligence was accorded such a high priority in a public statement on defence policy. Canada retained a limited capacity for independent analysis and assessment in the form of the CJIC and its Joint Intelligence Staff on which all three services and key civilian departments were represented. This eventually ensured that Canadian assessments contained some "Canadian" perspective. But its products were directed to the military chiefs of staff and allied agencies, not to senior government decision makers. Moreover, given its limited collection resources, Canada struggled to develop well-informed, sound assessments.[18]

DEFENCE AND MILITARY INTELLIGENCE, 1947–64

Within the Canadian military the three services maintained separate intelligence branches at national headquarters and between their units and formations. At Army headquarters up to 1964, the intelligence branch was called the Director or Directorate of Military Intelligence, the terms being applied interchangeably. Likewise, naval intelligence was housed within the office of the Director or Directorate of Naval Intelligence, which was reestablished in 1948. The RCAF had a Director or Directorate of Intelligence–Air until 1952, when the term "air intelligence" came into use. Each service had regional subsections and sections for operations, training, foreign liaison, technical intelligence, security, and counterintelligence or some portion thereof. But the Director/Directorate of Military Intelligence had limited analysis capability and lacked access to original intelligence sources. Defence-related scientific intelligence was housed within the Defence Research Board until 1965, when it was placed under the new Director General of Intelligence (DGI).[19]

The separation manifested at national headquarters was matched at formation and unit levels, since the services were independent entities and were structured and deployed on distinct and separate missions. The intelligence components of these units and formations tended to be small. Typically, an infantry battalion would have a single intelligence officer, assisted by a noncommissioned officer (NCO) and perhaps a clerk private. They were responsible for preparing enemy order of battle data and maps for exercises and operations, maintaining the unit war diary, and briefing the command team. This staff might include intelligence-trained personnel. But, Lt.-Col. Kent Dowell notes that military "intelligence" was not a high priority for battalion commanders in the postwar army. Thinking in 1945 suggested that commanders were better placed to do their own estimate of enemy intentions, a perspective that has lingered to the present.[20]

During the early postwar years, there were few military intelligence units. The Korean War and the deployment of forces to Germany brought about new regular force Field Security Sections. Militia intelligence training companies were established in 1948 in several cities. They were to provide personnel to augment the regular force, and many were taken on strength of the new Field Security Sections. The RCAF had only intelligence clerks (NCOs) but formed four auxiliary (reserve) intelligence units in 1951–52 to provide trained air intelligence personnel for wartime units. However, they were disbanded in 1958 as a result of budget cuts. To train both regular and reserve army intelligence personnel, the chief of the General Staff created in October 1949 the Canadian School of Military Intelligence.[21]

From 1957 on, units and troops (including MI personnel) participated in a number of peacekeeping operations in Egypt, the Congo, and Cyprus. By their intent and nature they involved monitoring, observing, patrolling, and reporting, normal MI activities. For reasons of political sensitivity, the products of their efforts were referred to as military "information," not "intelligence."[22]

By design that incorporates radars, sonars, and other sensors, modern naval surface combatants and submarines are simultaneously intelligence collectors and consumers, tasks they can conduct independently relying on their shipborne systems or through intelligence sharing with other vessels in naval task forces. As noted above, from 1950 on the RCN operated extensively in coalitions with allied naval forces. For example, in the 1962 Cuban Missile Crisis, RCN ships and RCAF aircraft tracked Soviet submarines in the Atlantic using their own sensors, but most of their intelligence came from the US Navy (USN). However, they also would have received data from the joint Canadian-US Sound Surveillance System, a network of seabed-based hydrophones and onshore tracking stations (located at Argentia, Newfoundland, and Shelburne, Nova Scotia) that had been created in the 1950s.[23] What is important to note here is that on naval vessels, intelligence was closely integrated within the operations staff, who were not trained intelligence personnel themselves but performed those tasks as part of their operations duties.[24] In this regard, the RCN pioneered intelligence "fusion" within the CAF, although the kind of near-instant "sensor-to-shooter" fusion the navy developed was unique to its operational requirements.

The RCN also played a major role in land-based SIGINT. Until all of the CBNRC's intercept stations were consolidated into the Supplementary Radio System within the DND after unification, the RCN was responsible for operating seven of them: six in Canada and one in Bermuda. The Canadian Army's Royal Corps of Signals ran three more, including Alert.[25]

In 1959 the DND created the Joint Photo Interpretation Centre for the analysis of aerial surveillance imagery. This gave Canadian DI a niche of expertise that was useful not just to the DND and the forces but also to Canada's allies. Like the CBNRC and Canadian-US Sound Surveillance System, this helped to justify Canada's "seat" at the Five Eyes table.

This brief summary makes clear that, SIGINT apart, intelligence was not a distinct high-priority function in any of the three services before 1964. And since they had separate and discrete missions, tasks, and environments, their intelligence capabilities were not interoperable.

THE IMPACT OF UNIFICATION AND INTEGRATION ON DEFENCE INTELLIGENCE, 1964–69

Unification and integration of the armed forces had a profound impact on DI. First, in 1964 it was unified and centralized under a single DGI, that post being held until 1968 by Brig.-Gen. Lloyd Kenyon, who had served previously in the Directorate of Military Intelligence.[26] Second, in 1967 following two studies, the intelligence function was merged with counterintelligence (Security) and military police to form the Security Branch under a deputy chief of intelligence and security.[27] This was an awkward marriage of two related but different tasks. However, the third change, placing the deputy chief of intelligence and security under the VCDS,[28] raised the profile of DI. This reflected changes in the defence management structure, such that within NDHQ, DI was now serving two masters: military and civilian.

Creating a new centralized and integrated DI enterprise was no small task. To guide Kenyon in this mission, in August 1964 assistant chief of the Defence Staff Air Vice-Marshal Wilfred Bean laid out the DGI's terms of reference in specific language. The DGI (and latterly the deputy chief of intelligence and security) was to be responsible for

1. "Advice on all aspects of intelligence policy" required by the DND;
2. "Development of policies and plans for the management, operation, future development, and wartime employment of the intelligence resources" of the DND;
3. "The efficient management and optimum security of the intelligence resources";

4. "The production of intelligence on the capabilities, activities, and likely courses of action of foreign armed forces" as required by the CAF and the DND;
5. "The production of economic and geographic intelligence" for the DND and interdepartmental purposes;
6. "The collection of intelligence from such Canadian sources . . . subject to the concurrence of other departments for activities involving their personnel, interests or responsibilities";
7. "Participation in inter-departmental intelligence committees, such as the Joint Intelligence Committee";
8. "Liaison for intelligence purposes and exchange of intelligence" on the DND's behalf with other Canadian government departments;
9. "Cooperation for intelligence purposes and exchange of intelligence" on the DND's behalf "with such foreign countries as may be designated";
10. "DND policy in regard to foreign attache [sic] activities in Canada";
11. "Management of the Canadian attaché program"; and
12. "Security policy in conjunction with Directorate of Security."[29]

This detailed guidance notwithstanding, Bean gave Kenyon a free hand to develop and run the division. His later reflections on this period shed some useful light on how he did so.

Upon arrival, Kenyon was dismayed to find that senior NDHQ officers were apathetic with regard to intelligence matters. Fortunately, the second CDS (Gen. Jean V. Allard) was "intensely interested" in intelligence, as he had been an attaché in Moscow. Likewise, Defence Minister Hellyer was very supportive; he received regular intelligence briefings. He did, however, order substantial reductions in military personnel strength that impacted DI.[30] In December 1964 Bean presented his terms of reference and setup to the Defence Council, which was examining the proposed command structure. Bean said that his staff could not be reduced by 30 percent and still do the work. He received support from Arthur Menzies (External Affairs) "to shore up his contention that the intelligence group would suffer if cut substantially." But Hellyer wasn't convinced. He wrote in his diary that "we are spending far too much money in this area."[31] Kenyon was to lose 14 of his 140 staff but made the savings among the support staff so that the DGI did not lose analytic capability. He shifted that function from service-based to topic-based, with triservice teams covering most functional topics. By November 1965 the DGI had five directorates, including Operations (attachés), and Production.[32]

In November 1965 the DGI absorbed the Directorate of Scientific Intelligence (DSI) from the Defence Research Board. The DSI's director, L. G. Eon, had initially told Kenyon that the scientists wanted to be directed by other scientists and did not want to come under military command. However, according to Kenyon, after he included some DSI analysts in a briefing to the minister, Eon told him that "I've never seen intelligence get to the top before.... [A]ll these big papers we write, nobody ever reads those. You're getting the intelligence right in there."[33] With the understanding that the DGI would not micromanage scientific work, which would be directed by a scientist, the DSI moved to DGI, and became the Directorate of Scientific and Technical Intelligence (DSTI). It also absorbed the technical analysts from the service intelligence directorates.[34]

The DGI downgraded the status of the CJIC. The CJIC produced a limited number of studies, and while Kenyon thought their quality was very good, he did not believe the Cabinet ever read the papers or used them to support decision making. So, he stopped the current intelligence briefings to the CJIC, reassigned the briefing team to the intelligence production directorate, and worked to improve the quality of briefings to senior officials—all in an effort to "sell" the value of intelligence to decision makers. In 1966, the DGI had given an on-camera briefing to the House of Commons Standing Committee on External Affairs and National Defence "of the type that is routine for congressmen in Washington, but was unheard of in Canada except in wartime."[35] As a result, political leaders began to show greater appreciation for it. Prime Minister Lester Pearson in particular had a good grasp of international issues and valued Kenyon's efforts. By contrast, Pierre Trudeau showed little interest in intelligence matters when he first became prime minister.[36] As will be shown in chapter 5, that attitude came back to haunt him in 1970 when he ignored intelligence warnings about emerging terrorism threats in Québec.

The DGI was acutely aware of the risk of being too dependent on the United States for intelligence. The US intelligence community shared a lot of material (imagery and SIGINT reports) with their Canadian counterparts, with the clear intention of persuading them to accept the US view on issues that mattered to them. The CBNRC's strategic SIGINT program also contributed intelligence to the United States and the United Kingdom. In return, CBNRC received much more "finished" intelligence than it could consume, but having access to it when needed was important. During Kenyon's tenure the intercept stations were transferred temporarily to DGI control, becoming the Supplementary Radio System and adding some 1,500 personnel to his organization.[37]

DGI's photo interpretation unit (originally the Joint Photo Interpretation Centre) received satellite photos from the Central Intelligence Agency and the US Defense Intelligence Agency, which did not have enough capacity to process all of the photos they collected. Neither did the DGI, but Kenyon worked hard to get the extra staff and new computers needed to do so. This also entailed building a secure compartmented intelligence facility (SCIF) known as the National Special Centre, accessible only to a tightly controlled list of people cleared to see the photos. The high security was intended to limit knowledge of the degree of resolution the American satellite cameras could achieve. By agreement with the United States and the United Kingdom, Canadian analysis focused on Soviet and Chinese aerospace and naval forces (missiles in particular) and Soviet and Warsaw Pact theatre forces.[38] When analysed alongside other sources, this imagery material was, in Kenyon's words, "most useful as confirmatory evidence in process of analysis of Soviet strengths and capabilities and future developments. It hardens the process of estimation into 'near certainty' and thus is an invaluable tool of analysis. It is becoming the primary tool of strategic intelligence collection and analysis in respect to foreign armed forces."[39] It was, he later said, "one of our most valuable sources."[40] This makes sense, since in the 1960s Canadian intelligence priorities and collection efforts were focused primarily on the Soviet Union's military intentions and capabilities. But the Cold War also was largely stable and predictable, so DI did not expect a major war between the Soviet Union and NATO.[41]

When Kenyon relinquished his position as director general of intelligence and security in 1968, he left behind a more integrated and more comprehensive DI organization than he had inherited four years earlier. He oversaw the work and staffs of seven sections—Production, Services (which provided support functions), Operations, Scientific and Technical Intelligence, Foreign Liaison, Security, and the Joint Intelligence Bureau (which focused on economic intelligence)—until it was transferred to External Affairs.[42] The absence of service-specific sections is striking; DGI was one of the first unified directorates within the DND. The merger of intelligence with security would remain troubled until their separation in 1982. Nevertheless, the creation of the DGI had laid the foundation for unified DI, the starting point from which it supported the DND and government decision making and CAF operations in the period 1970 to 2010. However, as chapter 3 will show, over those thirty years frequent budget cuts and attempts to restructure DI gradually eroded its ability to fulfil its mission.

NOTES

1. S. R. Elliot, *Scarlet to Green: A History of Intelligence in the Canadian Army, 1903–1963*, 2nd ed. (Ottawa: Canadian Military Intelligence Association, 2018), 55–62, 63–69, 74–75, 81–82, 84, 85–88; Lt.-Col. J. A. E. K. Dowell, *Intelligence for the Canadian Army in the 21st Century: "Enabling Land Operations"* (Kingston, Ontario: DLCD, 2012), 8. See also Wesley K. Wark, "Cryptographic Innocence: The Origins of Signals Intelligence in Canada in the Second World War," *Journal of Contemporary History* 22, no. 4 (1987): 639.
2. Wesley K. Wark and Canada, Privy Council Office, "Creating a Post-War Intelligence Community," chap. 1 in *A History of the Creation of Canada's Post–World*

War II Intelligence Community, 1945–1970 (Ottawa: [Privy Council Office], 2000–2002), 3, accessed through the Canadian Foreign Intelligence History Project.

3. N. K. O'Neill and K. J. Hughes, *History of the Communications Branch of the National Research Council*, Vol. 1 (Ottawa: CSE, 1987), chap. 1:5–7, accessed through the Canadian Foreign Intelligence History Project; Wark, "Creating a Post-War," 2.
4. O'Neill and Hughes, *History of the Communications Branch*, Vol. 1, chap. 1:8; Marc Milner, *Canada's Navy: The First Century* (Toronto: University of Toronto Press, 1999), 92, 102, 122; Roger Sarty, *War in the St. Lawrence: The Forgotten U-Boat Battles on Canada's Shores* (Toronto: Allen Lane, 2012), 238–39.
5. Elliot, *Scarlet to Green*, 434–35, 755–56; Dowell, *Intelligence*, 8.
6. Wark, "Creating a Post-War," 4–21.
7. Christopher M. Andrew, *The Defence of the Realm: The Authorized History of MI5* (Toronto: Viking, 2009), 447, 461, 462. See also David French, *The British Way in Counter-Insurgency, 1945–1967* (Oxford: Oxford University Press, 2011), 32.
8. John Robert Ferris, *Behind the Enigma: The Authorised History of GCHQ, Britain's Secret Cyber-Intelligence Agency* (London: Bloomsbury, 2021), 326–35. See also Richard J. Aldrich, *GCHQ: The Uncensored Story of Britain's Most Secret Intelligence Agency* (London: HarperCollins, 2011), 38–43, 96.
9. Wesley K. Wark, "Harvest at Nightfall: To Spy or Not to Spy," chap. 4 in *History of the Creation*, 1.
10. David Stafford, *Camp X* (New York: Dodd, Mead, 1987).
11. Reginald Whitaker, Gregory S. Kealey, and Andrew Parnaby, *Secret Service: Political Policing in Canada; From the Fenians to Fortress America* (Toronto: University of Toronto Press, 2012), 156, 179–81.
12. Wark, "Creating a Post-War," 12–14. The Intelligence Policy Committee coordinated intelligence "policy direction" but not the functions of the intelligence services. See Intelligence Advisory Committee, *The Canadian Intelligence Community*, n.d., appendix A, para. 2, Library and Archives Canada (LAC), RG25, BAN 2017-00437-5, box 2, file 3-5-5, part 1.
13. O'Neill and Hughes, *History of the Communications Branch*, Vol. 1, chap. 1:1–2, chap. 2:2, and Vol. 7 [Chronological Summary]; Wesley K. Wark, "Do Gentlemen Read Each Other's Mail? The Debate over a Post-War Canadian SIGINT Agency," chap. 2 in *History of the Creation*.
14. N. K. O'Neill and K. J. Hughes, *History of the Communications Branch*, Vol. 2, chap. 2:5, 12, and annex G, Vol. 1, chap. 4:2, 6–8, 17, 20, Vol. 3, chap. 11:9–12, 29–36 [pages 13–28 redacted]; Wesley K. Wark, "The Road to CANUSA: How Canadian Signals Intelligence Won Its Independence and Helped Create the Five Eyes," *Intelligence and National Security* 35, no. 1 (2020): 20–34. See also Matthew M. Aid, *The Secret Sentry: The Untold History of the National Security Agency* (New York: Bloomsbury, 2010), 11–13; James Bamford, *Body of Secrets: Anatomy of the Ultra-Secret National Security Agency; From the Cold War through the Dawn of a New Century* (New York: Doubleday, 2001), 394–97; Ferris, *Behind the Enigma*, 338, 340–45; Aldrich, *GCHQ*, 89–90, 92–95, 97–98.
15. Wesley K. Wark, "Favourable Geography: Canada's Arctic Signals Intelligence Mission," *Intelligence and National Security* 35, no. 3 (2020): 319–30, stresses that the Canadian Arctic SIGINT role was not a foregone conclusion but rather was the subject of much internal bureaucratic posturing and fiscal debates.

16. See Ferris, *Behind the Enigma*, 358–59; James Cox, *Canada and the Five Eyes Intelligence Community* (Calgary, Alberta: Canadian Defence & Foreign Affairs Institute, 2012), 7; Aid, *Secret Sentry*, 398; Communications Security Establishment, *Briefing Book for Minister*, 2015, part 1, tab A, part 3, tab K, Canadian Foreign Intelligence History Project; C. M. Isbister, *Intelligence Operations in the Canadian Government*, Privy Council Office Report 70-11-09 (9 November 1970), 6, appendix A, Canadian Foreign Intelligence History Project (hereafter cited as Isbister Report).
17. Douglas L. Bland, *The Administration of Defence Policy in Canada, 1947 to 1985* (Kingston, Ontario: Ronald P. Frye, 1987), 15.
18. Wesley K. Wark, "The Canadian Joint Intelligence Committee," chap. 6 in *History of the Creation*.
19. Alan Barnes, "Defence Intelligence Assessment Groups," 31 October 2018, Canadian Foreign Intelligence History Project; Brig.-Gen. Lloyd Everett Kenyon, interviews by Chris Bell, 1983–1984, University of Victoria Oral History Program. Notes compiled from interview tapes by Alan Barnes. See also Harold A. Skaarup, *Out of Darkness—Light: A History of Canadian Military Intelligence*, Vol. 1 (New York: iUniverse, 2005), 159. Messages and memoranda regarding creation of the DSTI are from Defence Research Board files in LAC, RG24, vol. 7440, file DRBS-255-35/7.
20. Dowell, *Intelligence*, 10–11.
21. Skaarup, *Out of Darkness—Light*, 1:161, 162, 164–65, 167–68, 495; Elliot, *Scarlet to Green*, 534–35, 539, 541–45.
22. Elliot, *Scarlet to Green*, 557; Skaarup, *Out of Darkness—Light*, 1:288; Maj.-Gen. A. J. Tedlie (deputy chief of intelligence and security) to Claude Isbister, 18 September 1970, in Isbister Report, appendix C, makes a strong, clear case for the importance of intelligence in peacekeeping operations.
23. Milner, *Canada's Navy*, 233–35; Skaarup, *Out of Darkness—Light*, 3:403.
24. "1976, Position Paper of the CISA, Brief to the CDA," in Skaarup, *Out of Darkness—Light*, 1:495.
25. See "History of Canadian CESM," RCSigs.ca, 2020, http://www.rcsigs.ca/index.php/History_of_Canadian_CESM.
26. "BGen Kenyon's Comments on Intelligence," in Skaarup, *Out of Darkness—Light*, 1:307; Kenyon interviews.
27. Barnes, "Defence Intelligence," has the director general of intelligence and security in place by October 1967; see brief summaries of the Turcot and Piquet reports in Skaarup, *Out of Darkness—Light*, 1:383–84. The deputy chief of intelligence and security position came into effect in 1969.
28. Bland, *Administration of Defence Policy*, 109, fig. 10, 114, fig. 11.
29. Assistant Chief of Defence Staff, Memorandum: "ACDS Staff Organization," 1 August 1964, Director General Intelligence, DG INT TORs, DND, DHH, 73/1223, file 567.
30. Kenyon interviews.
31. Paul Hellyer, *Damn the Torpedoes: My Fight to Unify Canada's Armed Forces* (Toronto: McClelland & Stewart, 1990), 118–19, citing his diary entry for 30 December 1964.
32. Kenyon interviews; Barnes, "Defence Intelligence."
33. Kenyon; Barnes.

34. Kenyon; letters, Chairman, Defence Research Board, to CDS, re: "Integration of Scientific Intelligence," 2 September 1965; L. G. Eon to DC/DRB, re: "Integration of DSI with DGI," 24 September 1965; L. G. Eon, Memorandum, 19 October 1965, LAC, RG24, vol. 7440, file DRBS-255-35/7; Air Chief Marshal Miller CDS to Chairman, Defence Research Board, re: "Integration of Scientific Intelligence" and annex A, 4 August 1965; "Excerpt from Minutes of 220th Meeting of the Defence Research Management Committee," 9 September 1965, LAC, RG24, vol. 7440, file DRBS-255-35/7.
35. Hellyer, *Damn the Torpedoes*, 155–56.
36. Kenyon interviews.
37. Kenyon; DND, "SIGINT Box—Factual Statement on the Decision-Making Points and Processes within the Canadian Intelligence Community," input to Isbister Report, n.d., LAC, RG25, BAN 2017-00434-0, box 21, file 1-1-1-1, part 1; Barnes, "Defence Intelligence," doesn't show the Supplementary Radio System under the deputy chief of intelligence and security until 1972.
38. Kenyon interviews; DND, "Special Centre Box—Factual Statement," input to Isbister Report, n.d., LAC, RG25, BAN 2017-00434-0, box 21, file 1-1-1-1, part 1.
39. DND, "Special Centre Box."
40. Kenyon interviews.
41. "The Canadian Intelligence Programme," annex to CJIC 8-96(69) Final, 13 November 1969, para. 6–7, 13–14, 35, 37–38, 46–50, 57, *DEA Documents: Canadian Intelligence Programme*, LAC, RG25, BAN 2017-00434-0, box 21, file 1-1-1-1, part 6.
42. Barnes, "Defence Intelligence," entry for October 1967.

3

WHEN IN DEBT, REORGANIZE

Canadian Defence Intelligence, 1975–2005

The DI structure that Brig.-Gen. Lloyd Kenyon had created underwent frequent reorganizations from 1975 on. The rationale in many cases was financial, since fiscal restraint was a major driving force behind most DND "reforms" in this period. That in turn was shaped largely by domestic policy rather than by the international environment. But a "penny wise, pound foolish" approach to funding DI and constantly "reinventing the wheel" constrained its ability to adapt to the shifting operational environment and to adopt new technologies. As subsequent chapters will show, this turmoil yielded mostly negative but eventually some positive impacts on DI support to CAF operations.

DEFENCE INTELLIGENCE STRUCTURE AND DIRECTION, 1975–84

In the wake of the *Defence Structure Review* and the reshaping of the command and authority structure within the DND, DI underwent several reorganizations between 1975 and 1984. Brig.-Gen. Reginald Weeks, the director general of intelligence and security, first ordered a review of the Directorate of Intelligence Production to establish a new structure. But the key document does not explain why he felt changes were needed.[1]

By 1976 the new structure had four directorates: the Directorate of Defence Intelligence (DDI), previously the Directorate of Intelligence Production; the program support directorate (DISPS); the DSTI; and security. The DDI had three estimates cells (strategic, general purpose, and stability) and also included a new 24/7 "watch" unit, the National Defence Intelligence Centre (NDIC). Its role consisted of collating, preparing, and delivering current intelligence briefings. The DISPS' services included foreign liaison (attachés).[2]

But in 1979 the program support directorate vanished. The director general of intelligence and security took control of operations, plans and training, administration, production, and attaché administration. The following year the DSTI was reduced from five topic sections to three. Technical Intelligence looked at the major conventional weapons. Scientific Intelligence studied advanced and strategic weapons (missiles), while Systems Analysis focused on space systems, activities, and telemetry. The DSTI was also responsible for the National Special Centre (the SCIF for handling US-generated imagery). By 1982 the DDI had added an imagery exploitation section (formerly the Joint Photo Interpretation Centre). Finally, a chief of intelligence and security (CIS) replaced the director general of intelligence and security in the reporting chain to the VCDS.[3]

As the DND's adviser on intelligence and security, the CIS's role included developing policies and plans for and managing the DND's intelligence and security resources, planning and directing DI production and dissemination for the DND and other government departments (OGDs), deciding and implementing security policies and procedures for the department, and controlling the activities of CAF attachés and advisers and of foreign attachés accredited to Canada. The CIS served on the two subcommittees of the Privy Council's Interdepartmental Committee on Security and Intelligence: the Security Advisory Committee and the Intelligence Advisory Committee.[4]

The CIS also exercised authority over the NDIC, the newly separate Directorate of Imagery Exploitation (DIE), and the National Special Centre. The CIS directed planning and DI collection activities; represented the branch on interdepartmental and international programs for production and exchange of DI; controlled development of branch objectives, priorities, and standards for intelligence production and dissemination; exercised "technical control" of the Supplementary Radio System (the SIGINT intercept stations); carried out a range of tasks related to security; advised on training at the intelligence school; and was expected to serve as "the focal point for professional defence intelligence and security knowledge within the department."[5] In addition to reporting to the VCDS, the CIS would provide support to the minister of national defence, the DND's senior civilian leadership, the DCDS, the heads of the unified commands, OGDs, and foreign and international staffs and agencies. As of 1983 the CIS was assisted by three directors: intelligence, security, and intelligence and security support.[6]

By 1984 many of these duties had been delegated to the DGI. This included developing intelligence production priorities and allocating resources to meet them; tasking attachés and defence advisers with collection requirements; training, briefing, and debriefing them; maintaining the flow of intelligence and liaison among the Five Eyes; maintaining and updating the DDI's foreign forces databases; monitoring indications and warning and providing crisis intelligence support via the NDIC; and reviewing current intelligence to select items to brief the CIS, CDS, and the National Defence Operations Centre. The DGI was to provide studies and in-depth analysis of threats to Canada, North America, and global stability and would also participate in international conferences intended to produce agreed estimates for NATO and NORAD. Finally, the DGI would serve as the intelligence adviser to the CIS and attend the Intelligence Advisory Committee as an ex-officio member and as a permanent member of its priorities, requirements, and resources subcommittee.[7]

The sources explain what was changed in these relationships but don't explain why. Furthermore, they do not indicate whether the new structures made DI more efficient and effective. The fact that further changes followed suggests that they did not.

COORDINATING INTELLIGENCE PRODUCTION, 1984–88

In 1984 the DGI added a production planning coordinator (PPC) and a director of current intelligence to run the NDIC and had assigned the director of the DIE to run the Canadian Forces Joint Imagery Centre.[8] A 1986 review of the PPC position offered a clear rationale for it: "Within DDI there was no cohesive and coherent intelligence production plan beyond section head level. Consequently, deadlines were being missed and some essential intelligence never was disseminated because there was no cell specifically designated to oversee production, planning and coordination."[9] Likewise, the resources of the CAF attaché program were being squandered due to an absence of collection, tasking, and control. Overall, there was no quality control of intelligence products.[10]

The PPC was allocated eight staff positions but started with only one: a major. As a result, it was largely unable to fulfil its mandate, which was then limited to deciding intelligence requirements and production and editing selected intelligence products. But the review claimed that the PPC was functioning "more as a coordination/odd jobs cell than as a collection and production management organization."[11] This criticism was supported by the many extra tasks assigned to it, such as developing the briefing program and preserving the briefings, coordinating visits to the DGI, assisting in preparing the intelligence analyst course and maintaining the course handbook, and preparing the *Weekly Intelligence Review* for the DND's senior leadership. Maj. Patrick Crandell, head of the PPC, noted that as a result "the fulfilment of PPC primary responsibilities has suffered accordingly."[12]

Major Crandell elaborated on the PPC's problems: separation of collection and production management from operations and plans, duplication of effort, and lack of control over attaché collection, *Weekly Intelligence Review* production, and quality and dissemination of reports. The latter were in "disarray" due to the absence of any central distribution control authority. On the separation issue, Crandell noted that Operations, Plans and Training "has developed the intelligence planning input to national-level plans/operations without reference to or cognizance of specified national or allied collection requirements or production programmes which may have impacted on the plan and planning process. Conversely, PPC has developed force-wide requirements without linkage to national plans.... The only guaranteed way of eliminating this problem is to integrate ... PPC's collection and production management functions with OP&T's [Operations, Plans and Training] operations and plans responsibilities."[13] In addition, he recommended that the PPC be divested of responsibility for attaché control and for the *Weekly Intelligence Review*, which he felt should be retained by the CIS's attaché administration branch and by the DDI, respectively. In fact, he felt that most of the tasks assigned to the PPC should be handed back to the units originally tasked to do them, leaving it with collection and production management, dissemination control, production of selected publications, and liaison with OGDs and agencies and the CAF to support those activities.[14]

The CIS heeded this advice, at least in the short term. Under the new structure announced in December 1986 the PPC was moved directly under the DGI, and the new Directorate of Intelligence Plans and Doctrine absorbed Operations, Plans and Training.[15] But by August 1988, the PPC had become Directorate of Intelligence Plans and Doctrine's Section 5, and many of the tasks that the PPC had shed were reassigned to Section 5. Its head, Maj. Ken F. Binda, complained that intelligence requirements had been formulated but not circulated to producers and were not coordinated with production or dissemination; the DGI had no coherent or cohesive collection plan; there was no production or quality control; attaché collection, tasking, and control were neglected; and intelligence products were being circulated without reference to requirements. He urged that Section 5 "be allowed to function in the manner for which it was formed ... 'Production and Dissemination control.'"[16]

Major Binda's list of tasks that the section should retain or shed was similar to Crandell's. The fact that Binda had to make this plea two years after the review shows that the reorganization had not been implemented properly. The need for coordination had been clear. What was lacking was a plan to integrate the position effectively into the existing DI structure. The result was dysfunction and failure to fulfil the intent of reorganization.

THE TAIL WAGS THE DOG:
AUTOMATION VERSUS STAFFING, 1984–96

Following the lead of the US intelligence community, the director general of intelligence and security had begun planning for the introduction of automated (computerized) data processing (ADP) in 1973. By the end of the 1970s the director general of intelligence and security had acquired an interactive graphics display for missile telemetry analysis. The NDIC was to have an automated message-handling system, identical to that used by the US Defense Intelligence Agency, by March 1980. Imagery analysis was a third area identified for ADP. But further advances toward automation were not expected to take place until 1990.[17]

In 1983 the DSTI added an intelligence and security automation section, which got its own director of defence intelligence and security automation in 1984. By 1988 that director had been moved directly under the CIS.[18] The creation of this position made sense in light of the decision in 1984 to acquire an ADP system, the Intelligence and Security Complex (ISX), "to produce strategic military intelligence and handle security information in an automated environment."[19] Two factors drove this change: the increasing volume of intelligence that had to be processed manually and the expectation that by the 1990s most US material would be in digital format, which the DND would not be able to access if it did not move to ADP as well.[20]

However, the Mulroney government's decision to rein in its initial ambitious plans and spending presented the CIS and the DGI with serious cost and personnel challenges, as it moved into the computer age. In a March 1988 memo to the VCDS (Lt.-Gen. Jack Vance), the CIS (Maj.-Gen. William Hewson) had expressed "very serious misgivings about the impact on my Branch of the current force development process."[21]

The proposed force levels made no allowance for promised additional positions, such as those needed to set up and run the ISX project. The CIS would have to forgo new positions and function within current staffing levels. These decisions, made without consultation, cast aside the progress made for approval of the new ADP systems, which were deemed essential if the CAF and the government "are to benefit from the vastly improved intelligence capabilities and security procedures which are now possible."[22] Hewson complained bluntly that "my staff is being directed to accept an unrealistic personnel ceiling . . . and then to produce a plan which will lead to an organization less capable than the one which now exists. They are loyally doing so despite the futility of their exercise."[23]

Hewson laid out in detail the negative implications of the proposed personnel ceilings and reductions. The problem, as he saw it, was that the Total Force Development Plan required a reduction in CIS staff positions that already had been allocated to meet the needs of well-advanced plans such as the ISX. He requested that the supplement to the CIS branch development plan be consulted along with the plan itself.[24]

The supplement asserted that the primary deficiencies in the DND strategic intelligence production and security capabilities were in personnel and computer support. Although the CIS branch was "the primary DND producer of strategic foreign intelligence," the supplement stated, the CIS lacked sufficient people to do the job. Five years earlier the VCDS had approved a manpower review that identified a personnel shortfall of over one hundred positions. The CIS had received twenty-nine new people, with a further seventeen promised for fiscal year 1988–89, but would lose all of these under the Total Force Development Plan's proposed ceiling. This would reduce strategic intelligence production to "a barely acceptable level" and would undermine the ability to meet its intelligence-sharing obligations. The lack of adequate computer support would exacerbate these effects. In ADP the CIS was already ten to fifteen years behind the US military intelligence services. While the CIS had some computer support there was no integrated architecture, so "the bulk of all-source collation, analysis and production is performed without the benefit of automation."[25] The ISX project was designed to solve this problem and was vital to ensure interoperability with Canada's allies. But implementing it required seventy-three positions to operate and manage the project effectively. Hewson insisted that "these positions must be accepted as a legitimate requirement in excess of the CDS allocation."[26]

Hewson received no sympathy from the VCDS, who asked him to allow the force development process to move forward. Vance stated that "all branches will be expected to manage within a personnel establishment that will give DND the minimum viable structure to implement the White Paper initiatives." He added that the process was meant "to ensure that a balanced solution is found that will enable DND to operate effectively and efficiently in peace-time and, if necessary, during war."[27] At this point the document record on this debate goes silent for over a year. In the meantime, Hewson was posted to NATO, succeeded as CIS for one year by Maj.-Gen R. Percival Pattee and then by Rear Adm. John Slade, who served from 1989 through 1991.[28]

The exchange between Hewson and Vance reveals two competing visions of the need for DI and of how the capability should be maintained. Hewson's view was that strategic DI was a "foundational" capability within the DND that served the department's needs and those of the wider government and Canada's allies. That could be sustained only by an investment in people. The Total Force Development Plan undermined the DND's ability to perform its essential functions and risked Canadian DI falling even further behind, unable to interact with its allies.

Bureaucracies resist change, especially reductions, but Hewson's case does not appear to have been special pleading. He was able to demonstrate the costs arising from the personnel ceilings and reductions. The VCDS, by contrast, faced the pressures of implementing an ambitious defence policy in a time of fiscal constraint and a consequent effort to restructure the forces in a way that would serve policy, meet budget goals, and still yield effective military power. The total force concept may have been unrealistic, but the VCDS had no choice but to try to make it work. To ensure that the larger project reached its goal, all of the parts that made up the whole would have to adjust. For Vance, the needs of the many trumped the needs of the few, however essential those few might be.

But the issue remained unresolved. In June 1989 CIS Major-General Pattee wrote to Vance's successor, Lt.-Gen. John de Chastelain, noting that Vance had asked the CIS to be patient and let the force development process evolve to a solution. "We have been patient," Pattee wrote, "but the problems of a year ago have not disappeared, but have been exacerbated."[29] The ISX project needed more people, but the CIS could not get them because of the "arbitrary" ceilings; new positions would have to be found within the existing establishments. Looking at the future implications, Pattee wrote that the "essential question" was "whether DND can stay in the intelligence business if we are unable to accept automated information from our allies."[30] His attached appendix laid out the personnel shortfalls: nearly five hundred positions, most of them associated with the ISX.

While Pattee's plea did not fall on entirely deaf ears, neither did he get any relief. A marginal note by the VCDS stuck to the same policy line that Vance had stated: "This problem must be considered in the overall context of NDHQ ceilings/reduction."[31]

Shortly after Pattee's memo Lt.-Col. Ray J. Taylor submitted a report, at the DGI's request, on how the CIS could implement the ISX project using existing personnel. The study focused on meeting the needs for only the first of three ISX phases: the Foundation Group of Systems, which would be introduced in two stages by August 1990 and January 1996. The Treasury Board had approved only the first stage, but the report reviewed the needs of the Foundation Group of Systems through the completion of stage two. Taylor analysed the duties and staffing of all DGI directorates, carefully trying to identify absolutely vital functions and those where some reductions could be made. There really were no superfluous tasks or people. Every reduction entailed some loss of capability. Within the CIS as a whole, the DGI would sustain 60 percent of the cuts, the remainder coming from the security and support sections: forty-six positions in all. It would be a huge loss but would allow the ISX project to proceed.[32]

Moreover, personnel issues and costs were only part of the problem. Mike Bowen, who served as a special assistant to the CIS at the time, explained that creating a secure ADP facility imposed physical security requirements: a floor-to-ceiling shielded room with vacuum-sealed doors. Every piece of equipment had to meet Tempest (emission-limiting) specifications. He observed that "it was hard to manage the tempo of changing technology in a government environment."[33] The pace at which each moved was out of synch with the other.

That aside, Taylor's report was not well received within the DGI. Lt.-Col. Gordon Graham, the head of DIE, remarked that "it seems counter-productive to continue to increase DISA [defence intelligence and security automation] at the expense of the production directorates. If we continue to do this ... we will end up with more computer support staff than analysts to work the available terminals ... the classic situation of the tail wagging the dog."[34] Graham went on to assert that every iteration of the proposed changes had already been tried and had failed. Dissecting some of the reductions and changes in Taylor's memo, Graham pointed out that the DIE exploited only 3 percent of the imagery it received. So, any reduction threatened an already weak function and could prompt the United States to send less, a net loss for Canada.[35]

Taylor had acknowledged that owing to the most recent budget cuts, the goals of the Total Force Development Plan and of the 1987 white paper itself could no longer be achieved.[36] So, it might appear that trying to enforce artificial personnel ceilings and cuts for a plan that was no longer workable did not make sense. But fiscal constraints and the need to create computing capacity overrode outdated personnel planning logic. The ISX Foundation Group of Systems had to go ahead to ensure that the CIS branch could do its job even if only on a reduced scale. In any case, within a few months the Berlin Wall came down, and the strategic calculus that had driven Canadian DI for four decades all but vanished overnight.

Two points are worth making here. First, it is clear that at the start of this period DI did not see support to deployed forces as its primary function. Todd Fitzgerald and Michael Hennessy assert that as NDHQ transitioned from an administrative focus to an operational one in 1990, intelligence coordination "posed a challenge for NDHQ."[37] The DGI adapted to the demands for support to operations by creating temporary crisis intelligence response cells.[38] Second, adapting to this role was challenging in part because the DGI's leaders still had to wrestle with more reviews, budget cuts, staffing issues, and incorporating ADP.

The "Functional Review" of 1990, like those that preceded it, was focused on finding economies of scale and cost to improve efficiency. And as usual, this meant finding ways to do more with fewer people. On 5 November the CIS (Rear Admiral Slade) issued a briefing paper for the review. It first identified the staffing shortfall: the CIS branch was sixteen positions below its establishment. The paper then pointed out that the manning levels were not sufficient to maintain the 24/7 watch brief required by the Oka and Gulf operations while also carrying out the normal branch activities. Moreover, the ISX project had priority in new staffing, leaving other divisions within the CIS short-staffed. Any further reductions would leave the CIS unable to fulfil some important tasks.[39]

The 1991 Persian Gulf War did not stop the review, but the proposed reductions in the CIS branch were postponed until after the CAF deployment ended.⁴⁰ That said, even as the war continued the CIS asked his branch to plan for postwar implementation of the review. He told them to identify the major activities they could accomplish with the (reduced) staffing assigned to them and to create a short list of important activities they felt should be included but that they could not fulfil due to staffing constraints. The CIS had his own priorities he regarded as mandatory, including procuring and staffing ISX Foundation Group of Systems phase one and the creation of an operational intelligence tasking cell.⁴¹ Slade reiterated the capability losses that the "Functional Review" necessitated. And while he made some personnel reductions in the CIS branch overall, he resisted pressure to cut staff in the DGI largely to ensure that the first phase of the ISX project could be implemented.⁴²

The ink was barely dry on the "Functional Review" when the CDS and DM ordered a review specifically focused on DI. At the direction of the VCDS, Lt.-Gen. (ret.) D. M. McNaughton did the study, whose final report was due on 31 January 1992.⁴³ The McNaughton report made eighteen recommendations, including more reorganization of the DGI. Crucially, the report recommended that the ISX project be ended upon completion of the first phase. Instead of creating a bespoke system, a team would examine the option of purchasing "off-the-shelf" systems even though this would constrain future hardware and software solutions and would require a new procurement strategy.⁴⁴

This seemed to be reasonable plan, but a year later very little progress had been made. The amalgamation of the VCDS/DCDS branches during the summer of 1992 had delayed progress, as did the need to consult the heads of all affected groups. So, almost everything was still under consideration.⁴⁵ A 1994 auditor general's report noted that the DND had been unable to resolve its IT problems (which became apparent during the Persian Gulf War) that included networking, interoperability, stovepiping, and security classification obstacles. The auditor general recommended an "evolutionary" approach to ADP/IT acquisition "rather than attempting to provide complete systems, which could take years to deliver a product."⁴⁶

The DCDS tasked the director of intelligence security and operations automation, Kevin O'Keefe, to review and rationalise the C2 IT requirements. Later in 1994 the director and his counterpart in Information Systems Engineering launched a "proof of concept" project for a prototype Joint Command and Control Information System modeled on the American Global Command and Control System. After testing, the project yielded a "capable and expandable" system that went into prototype service, was funded at $72 million in February 1995, and by July was recognized as the "keystone" NDHQ command control and intelligence project.⁴⁷

This was a major step forward. Capt. (N) Andrea Siew, who served in the Directorate of Intelligence Security and Operations Automation at the time, notes that the DND had two IT big projects on the books then: "ISX, and RAS (Rapid Access System—for imagery). They had hundreds of millions of dollars tied up in those projects, and they were going nowhere fast.... ISX was a massive program, but would never be able to deliver the needed intelligence capability."[48] Walking away from those costly investments midstream and introducing a cheaper substitute took courage. But it proved to be the right decision. It provided NDHQ with an encrypted secret-level Defence Wide Area Network and a top secret–level link to the Australia, Canada, United Kingdom, and United States network. It became the foundation for the Canadian Forces Communication System, which would serve all three services and the joint staff. The Chief Review Services 2001 report on the Joint Command and Control Information System stated that it had "enjoyed considerable success."[49] In Siew's view, "it was much cheaper than ISX, delivered what was needed in a defined period of time.... They could buy off-the-shelf computers and software, everybody used common systems."[50] But the project was still a "work in progress." It was delayed in part by the diversion of resources to address the anticipated year 2000 rollover problem and by the lack of an agreed DND C2 doctrine. Nevertheless, the Chief Review Services concluded that "a 75 per cent to 80 per cent solution is considered acceptable."[51] Brig.-Gen. Ken Hague acknowledged in a DGI draft business plan that "the implementation of Information Technology within the Division since 1990 has been modest and evolutionary."[52] But the latter, at least, was what the auditor general had recommended.

REENGINEERING DEFENCE INTELLIGENCE, 1995–99

The DND reengineering project discussed in chapter 1 exerted a negative impact on DI, although planning for reductions preceded it. In March 1994 the DGI was advised that it would lose ten positions. The DDI was pared down to three sections: current intelligence and two global/regional sections. The DIE would lose fifteen military positions, even though it was taking on new imagery-production responsibilities under an agreement with the United States. Consequently, some capabilities, such as imagery support to NATO, would be lost or reduced. But in spite of the cuts, the DGI had to fulfil real-world intelligence requirements. For example, to support CAF operations in the Balkans, the DDI created the Yugoslavia Crisis Cell (YCC) within the current intelligence section, with a team of seven watch officers and noncommissioned members.[53]

Since 1990 the DCDS group had taken responsibility for J2 (intelligence) and J3 (operations). The DCDS represented both, although the DGI actually performed the J2 function.[54] By mid-1995, reengineering imposed further changes on J2/DGI to bring its structure more in line with that of J3. This first iteration of the plan divided it into three branches: Operations, Plans/Policy, and

Geomatics. Operations was responsible for intelligence production and would comprise the DDI, the DSTI, the NDIC, and the DIE. Plans/Policy was a catch-all. Its tasks would include plans, doctrine, policy, requirements, international liaison, automation, coordination, dissemination, exercises, and publications. A full colonel would head each branch to provide experience as well as to represent the DGI at the appropriate levels in intergovernmental and international forums. The DCDS strongly endorsed the structural changes and the position ranks.[55] And while all of this was being debated, CAF troops were under fire or being taken hostage in the Balkans.

J2/DGI commodore Ted Heath and his successor, Brigadier-General Hague, believed that they had strong cases for retaining existing DI capabilities if not for strengthening them. However, according to Brig.-Gen. (ret.) James Cox, the reengineering team felt that J2/DGI had failed to demonstrate "operational value added" and just did not "get it."[56] By that the team meant that DI did not grasp that the exercise was not about getting more resources or protecting what they had; it was all about doing more with less. In fact, one goal was to reduce the number of colonels in the DGI.[57] So, it was to be cut yet again.

By the end of July 1995 a new, even leaner J2/DGI structure had been approved with few changes (J2 Plans lost policy). J2 Geomatics absorbed the Mapping and Charting Establishment.[58] The NDIC also was revising the YCC to better meet DND/CAF needs.[59] But this was just an interim reorganization. Under the next phase J2 Plans would regain a policy function. J2 Ops would include current intelligence (the NDIC), strategic and regional assessments, scientific and technical intelligence, and imagery. Not long after, the National Special Centre was transferred from scientific and technical intelligence to J2 Coordination.[60]

By late 1996, the effects of reengineering were readily apparent. Like the rest of the DND, J2/DGI had to produce plans that included mission statements and detailed accounting procedures covering everything from salaries to expenditures on pens and paper. But reengineering had achieved little within J2/DGI except some internal restructuring in pursuit of minor efficiencies that resulted largely in retaining the status quo.[61]

Indeed, an internal reengineering team document indicates that the process had fallen short. The team observed that the DGI branch had "already undergone reorganization as a result of earlier initiatives, resulting in an increased focus on support to operations."[62] But the team identified unresolved issues, including staffing levels (further reductions were expected), the creation of a strategic intelligence unit, the amalgamation of the DIE and the Canadian Forces Photographic Unit, and how to integrate twenty-two personnel offered by Land Force Command to staff crisis cells (which would complicate efforts to reach lower staffing levels).[63] In March 1997 Hague identified thirteen positions to be eliminated through 1997–98 while explaining the implications of the losses. He also pointed out that if the DND approved creating the strategic intelligence unit, there would be no personnel or cost savings at all.[64]

By May 1997 scientific and technical intelligence was claiming that it was in crisis. Three years earlier it had established an S&T human source intelligence (HUMINT) program, using CAF sources and access to allied HUMINT to generate Canadian analysis. That in turn leveraged access to UK HUMINT, so much in fact that scientific and technical intelligence had a backlog. But budget constraints were limiting its ability to access that and material from the Defense Intelligence Agency.[65] In a January 1998 briefing to the DCDS, the J2 made a strong case that the J2/DGI division had been pared down to the bare minimum such that certain functions (e.g., the 24/7 watch) were understaffed and had no depth or redundancy.[66] Yet, further cuts were forthcoming. J2 Ops was to lose five military and one civilian positions for fiscal year 1999–2000.[67] In a notable change, however, DI's focus had shifted significantly. The 1999 draft *Defence Intelligence Priorities* document ranked "current/warning intelligence and support to deployed forces" first among its three priorities, with support to strategic-level decision making and to allies shown as second and third, respectively.[68]

What is striking about reengineering is that the documents were replete with the jargon and processes of the business world. This was symptomatic of the extent to which civilian bureaucratic thinking and practices had come to permeate defence planning. It had occurred over several decades but became much more noticeable after 1993. The tone was set from the top. Determined to get the debt and deficit spending under control, the civilian leadership—from the prime minister and minister of finance through the DND bureaucracy—had adopted a business model to run the DND and the CAF. Whether that was appropriate remains very much open to question. Certainly, the uneven and unmeasured impact of the reengineering program on the CAF and the DND cast that experiment into considerable doubt.

With regard to DI/MI, the most notable effect was less capability. When 9/11 happened, the regular force Intelligence Branch totalled only 420 personnel, comprising less than 1 percent of the entire CAF. They were augmented by 160 reservists and several hundred nonbranch uniform personnel and civilians. Some 500 CAF personnel and civilians worked in DGI staffing the NDIC, filling the analyst positions, and running the national counterintelligence unit. The remainder served outside NDHQ, at units and joint headquarters, international headquarters, liaison positions in London and Washington, militia intelligence companies, and the School of Military Intelligence. The CAF's DI personnel had earned an enviable reputation for their "quality, training, adaptability, and experience."[69] However, there was concern about the fact that junior MI officers received no formal training beyond the Basic Intelligence Officer's Course (BIOC), which was conducted at the unclassified level and offered a very limited introduction to the subject.[70] Yet, the CAF's operating environment demanded more than its understaffed and overtasked DI structure could provide.

THE CHIEF REVIEW SERVICES REPORT, 2001–2

The senior leaders in the CAF and the DND were sufficiently concerned about the quality of the intelligence effort[71] that they commissioned the Chief Review Services to conduct another review of DI. The resulting report made twenty recommendations grouped into four categories: governance, integration, interoperability, and human resources. Some of the concerns these raised found their way into the media. The *Ottawa Citizen* reported in June 2001 that the CAF's collection capabilities had been seriously degraded in recent years. Staffing had declined "to the point where the associated risk is barely acceptable," yielding "unreliable and uncorroborated intelligence products" that could leave commanders and their political masters poorly informed.[72] DI's "voice" was not being heard, and this wasn't satisfying its customers. Lt.-Gen. Michel Gauthier (figure 3.1), who served as J2/DGI and then as chief of defence intelligence (CDI) from 2002 to 2005, later put it bluntly: "Post–Cold War defence intelligence had lost its way."[73] Constant reorganization and cuts in funding and people clearly had taken their toll. The result was that in spite of all the relevant operational experience of the previous decade, on the eve of the war in Afghanistan DI was not ready to support the CAF at war. It would take that war and a wide-ranging *Defence Intelligence Review* (*DIR*) to transform intelligence support to operations. In fact, Gauthier says, the review and the war acted in synergy, each

FIGURE 3.1. Lt.-Gen. Michel Gauthier, the first chief of defence intelligence, 2004–5, shown in Afghanistan. *Michel Gauthier*

forcing the pace of the other. "What we learned from our DIR deliberations informed how we did business strategically and tactically, ... [and] how we did business strategically and tactically informed how we did the DIR."[74]

THE *DEFENCE INTELLIGENCE REVIEW*, 2002–4

The *DIR* was the most comprehensive examination of DI since unification. The DCDS, Vice-Adm. Greg Maddison, and the associate deputy minister, Margaret Purdy, managed the review jointly, with a large team doing the research and drafting. The J2/DGI (Gauthier) was not formally part of the team but played a central role in informally overseeing the process to ensure that it met DI's needs. He helped "to steer consultations, define what the important questions were, and more so as the time came to draw the main conclusions."[75]

Taking the Chief Review Services report as its starting point, the *DIR* was to develop recommendations to ensure that its functions would support "client and partner requirements," resources were "effectively allocated" to meet them, "appropriate links and cooperation with the Canadian intelligence community" were defined, DI had effective international cooperation, and requirements for policy and legal changes were identified. The team was tasked to address DI's clients in the DND and the CAF, direction of the DI function, intelligence architecture, oversight/review/accountability mechanisms, ongoing intelligence/information projects, and human resources.[76]

The draft was completed in June 2003, with the final version delivered in May 2004. The implementation plan called for a two-year, three-stage process: first, setting the conditions, with minimal staff augmentation; second, transitioning to the new structure, with management and oversight processes and procedures fully implemented; and third, enacting the plans developed in the second stage to "enhance analysis and collection capabilities."[77]

Before briefing the CDS, the team sought input from the VCDS, the environmental chiefs, and the six key associate deputy ministers. All broadly supported creating a DI authority and strengthening the management framework and intelligence capabilities. They raised concerns over the extent of functional responsibilities and how to provide the resources. After the CDS was briefed in May 2004, the Defence Management Committee discussed the report.[78] Finally, in October, the CDS (Gen. Ray Hennault) and the DM (Ward Elcock) gave approval in principle to begin implementation, although with some caveats since the DND was "operating in a period of constrained resources with a wide variety of competing demands."[79]

The final report ran to 171 pages and recommended more than seventy changes, encompassing the entire span of Canadian DI.[80] This allowed the report's authors to assert that it had met the goals of the review and provided "a definitive plan to transform defence intelligence into a fully integrated DND/ CF [Canadian Forces] capability" in line with the "Defence Intelligence Vision." The key ideas were transformation and the integration of capabilities. In the vision statement, DI was a "DND/CF wide capability" that "will be purposefully joined together by a protected and fully interoperable secure information infrastructure seamlessly integrating tactical, operational, and strategic capabilities with service, joint, national and international data and products."[81] The intent was that all DI components would function within a "cohesive process framework" that gathered and prioritized requirements and tasked the collection and production assets of the CAF and its partners, ultimately delivering "the right product to the right decision maker at the right time and in the right format." The report also called for "all strategic collection and production capabilities" to be "fully harmonized" and "21st century capabilities" to be developed under the direction of the new DI authority.[82]

Examining all of the *DIR* recommendations and how they were or were not implemented lies beyond the scope of this chapter. What follows is a digest of the key elements that—once approved (or not)—impacted DI's ability to support CAF operations in Afghanistan and the strategic-level decision making that influenced them. But this selective analysis has been shaped in part by the perspectives of those who were involved in implementation and relies on only a handful of original documents. So, this is not a complete or wholly disinterested account.

The most important changes arising from the *DIR* were in governance. The report concluded that DI needed to be governed and managed as a DND/CAF-wide capability and that the DND needed to appoint a "senior level national defence intelligence authority,"[83] guided by a clear DI policy and supported by a governance structure. The *DIR* recommended that in the short-term the J2/DGI be designated as that authority, reporting to the CDS and the DM for strategic intelligence and to the DCDS for support to operations.[84] This change was essential because the J2/DGI had authority over only about 20 percent of DI's resources and could not direct outputs from them.[85] The new authority would exercise direction over the entire DI enterprise. It would become a command rather than a staff position. The J2/DGI position also was to be renamed chief of defence intelligence.[86] According to Gauthier, a significant change that followed from this was to make the CDI a two-star position, "because there's an important difference in how two stars are perceived versus one stars by civilians in DND [and] in PCO."[87] It would give DI a higher profile and stronger voice within government.

The *DIR* also spelled out in detail the authorities and responsibilities of the new position. The CDI would serve as the "principal Defence Intelligence advisor to DND/CF strategic decision-makers" and as the senior DND/CAF authority on all matters relating to DI relations with allies; provide "oversight and policy direction" for all DI activities; provide "functional direction" to all elements of DI, including deployed forces, "consistent with departmental and CF priorities"; ensure that the function meets the DI needs of decision makers and commanders at the strategic, operational, and tactical levels; plan and oversee the DI force generation process in support of deployed CAF operations; coordinate the annual development of the DND's DI priorities; "co-ordinate advice concerning the allocation of resources" within the DI community; ensure that all DI personnel are "effectively trained, sufficient in numbers and efficiently distributed" across the DI community; act as the DND lead for the development of future DI capabilities; provide advice "concerning the intelligence component of all C4ISR [command, control, communications, computers, intelligence, surveillance, and reconnaissance] projects and programs"; coordinate DI information management requirements and priorities; and exercise authority over designated secure information management systems.[88]

The report first recommended that the CDI be supported by two new staffs: legal and policy. In addition, DI needed a new staff structure to address human resources development, a new education and training program for military and civilian personnel, the information management requirements for supporting DI architecture, national and international partnerships, and current and future strategic capabilities. New staff procedures and tools were needed to "systematically manage the collection, production, and dissemination of intelligence" across the DND/CAF and develop dynamic interaction with DI's strategic-level clients. The report recommended ten new analyst positions to meet short-term operational requirements, directed the CDI to "formalize the accountability relationship" between the CDI and the Canadian Forces Information Operations Group (CFIOG) in concert with the associate deputy minister of information management and initiate studies to "fully define needs and propose options to deliver sustainable HUMINT and counter-intelligence (CI) capabilities."[89] Both would also require legal guidance to ensure that their activities complied with Canadian legislation and laws.[90] Transforming the DI staff in this way was essential, given the CDI's wide responsibilities.

The second area in which major changes were recommended and implemented was intelligence production. An analysis of DND/CAF capability needs and shortfalls circulated in July 2002 had yielded a mixed record. The information/intelligence category showed a "very serious shortfall" at "military strategic" level even though it was ranked as being of "High" importance.[91] DI's collection and analysis assets were distributed across various Level 1 (executive) domains and several levels of the operational chain of command but with only limited horizontal coordination. The report noted that the DND and the CAF had "no formal documentation that sets out areas of responsibility for the conduct of intelligence activities or for the provision of intelligence products."[92] Consequently, "at the strategic/national level there is no single agency that knows the disposition of all available information sources and has the responsibility to task the best sources in anticipation of the decision-maker's needs.... There is neither a centralized fusion process nor an organization that has the responsibility to bring together all available information from a multitude of sources to create an integrated assessment of information that can be provided to the appropriate commander."[93] Being able to coordinate and integrate collection assets was important because new collection capabilities were increasingly blurring the lines between the levels of intelligence. The *DIR* noted that "tactical sensors will collect information that has value to strategic-level decision-makers; conversely, strategic intelligence capabilities[,] such as space-based assets, will increasingly be capable of supporting tactical level objectives, particularly targeting."[94]

But strategic analysis and intelligence production had been degraded by the constant cuts, reviews, and structural reorganizations. One former DND official told the author that while there were some very good analysts in the organization, conditions there did not allow them to flourish. "Intelligence Production was a mess. People didn't know who they were reporting to or why."[95] Moreover, it was hard to acquire and create good analysts. Solving this problem would not be easy. For the civilian members of DI in particular, there was not just insufficient analytical training but also the lack of a career path.[96] The CDI was directed to "determine the staff and funding requirements and procedural framework necessary to manage" development—in concert with the two associate deputy ministers for human resources—of an "HR strategy and a training and education plan" to address "the future needs of both civilian and military components" of DI.[97]

The *DIR* proposed the creation of a new Intelligence Production division under a senior executive-level civilian. The division would have four sections: production management, client management, global/regional analysis, and scientific/technical analysis, all linked to the National Defence Command Centre.[98] So, one of Gauthier's first initiatives was to bring in an experienced senior intelligence official from outside the DND to help DI get back on its feet. The new director general of intelligence production, Dr. Linda Goldthorp, spent six months planning to create a "road ahead," then "stole" or "borrowed" civilian analysts from OGDs to meet her division's demands. On-the-job training and mentoring improved the quality of analysis. The best of these analysts became the CDI's voice in government circles and among Canada's allies. Gauthier was impressed by CSE's focused approach using customer relations officers and thought that DI should seek some ways to emulate it.[99]

Writing for the CDI's internal newsletter in 2008, Dr. Goldthorp explained the role of the Intelligence Production division and its organization and products and was able to show how it had been revitalized. Her essay clarified tasks of the Intelligence Production division: "leading and co-ordinating the defence intelligence function and ... producing all source intelligence analysis to support the DND/CF, other government departments and allies."[100] The Directorate of Intelligence Operations was responsible for coordinating the development of DI priorities by drawing upon input from across the DND and the CAF and also oversaw the "Collection Co-ordination and Intelligence Requirements Management (CCIRM) process" and the distribution of DI products by the Intelligence Dissemination Centre.[101]

Three intelligence directorates carried out the analytic work: regional, transnational, and the DSTI. The regional directorate focused on leadership intentions of specific countries. The transnational directorate examined occurring or anticipated events, such as missile launches. The DSTI continued its focus on understanding conventional and unconventional weapons system capabilities. The analytic teams contained a mix of CAF personnel with operational experience, scientists and engineers, and civilians with academic credentials or work experience in OGDs. This talent pool allowed the Intelligence Production division to generate daily one-page executive and operations intelligence summaries; a DI digest and a "Global Scan," each twice per week; intelligence assessments as requested; and a daily report on Afghanistan during the Canadian deployment there.[102]

This unit apart, only one of the *DIR*'s many human resources recommendations—a personnel resourcing plan—was fully implemented. Most of the force-generation recommendations were put in place. However, although the CDI received some new analytic staff, it also lost some to provide support to the new commands or to serve in Afghanistan. Some of these had to be clawed back to ensure that DI retained the analytical capabilities it required. The creation of military and civilian career fields in intelligence was partially implemented, but other human resources recommendations were not completed before being overtaken by new requirements.[103]

Third, the information revolution had generated an "exponential growth" of data, requiring increased productivity, coordination, and interoperability of all DI assets. The diverse character of intelligence requirements "and *the need for information fusion* across an increasing spectrum of data types" highlighted "the need for integration and interoperability of information systems and architecture across operational, analytical and leadership domains."[104] This required the CDI to review and revise DI's approaches to managing C4ISR programs generally and SIGINT relationships in particular.

At this time some Level 1 DND officials were championing more than one hundred C4ISR-related projects. But neither DI generally nor the DGI specifically played any formal role in the governance framework for "intelligence-related capability development" or provided input to it. And although the DGI would be the major users of C4ISR and related capabilities, there were no dedicated staff within the DGI assigned to deal with their development. Shortfalls in IT support staff impeded the ability of intelligence staffs at all levels to provide all-source intelligence to their commanders. Moreover, there was an inconsistent approach to connectivity: no overarching, coherent process within DI to rationalize and prioritize the various IT and information management requirements from the intelligence staffs. The DND and the CAF needed a single point of authority to aggregate requirements and develop standard software tools and database requirements.[105] However, although the CAF was using its own and allied intelligence, surveillance, and reconnaissance (ISR) capabilities daily in Afghanistan, due to governance issues and divergent views DI was unable to establish "an overarching ISR management framework and collection policy that aims to ensure CF ISR assets, including tactical assets with organic collection capabilities of potential 'strategic' significance, are maximized to fulfill standing requirements and fully leveraged to contribute to allied burden-sharing arrangements."[106]

A related initiative—driven as much by the war as by the *DIR*—was to forge a new relationship between the CSE (the national SIGINT agency) and the CFIOG, the CAF's tactical SIGINT organization. On operations, the CFIOG was tasked by the CAF but operated under the CSE's policies, which dictated what it could and could not do. But the Chief Review Services report had concluded that the CFIOG was "dislocated" from the broader DI enterprise. The *DIR* recommended that the CDI exercise authority over its SIGINT and related functions. The CDI was to work with the associate deputy minister of information management to develop recommendations on its "organizational and command relationships" to clarify "the accountability relationship between the CDI and the CFIOG."[107] This was expected to establish "centralized intelligence strategic capability planning, priorities and resource control" and would strengthen "the integration, accountability and coordination of SIGINT to support operations and strategic requirements."[108]

To facilitate this, in a joint initiative with CSE head John Adams, CDI head Gauthier created a new position: director general of military SIGINT, held initially by Brig.-Gen. Glenn Nordick as a part-time position while he was CDI (2004–5), then by Capt. (N) Andrea Siew full-time from 2005 to 2008. In tandem with the director general, a J2 SIGINT staff was created within the new Intelligence Capabilities Division. These changes served several purposes. For the CAF, it would inform field force commanders and their staffs (especially their intelligence staff) about the national capabilities available to support them and how to access them. From the CSE's perspective, it would minimize duplication of effort and costs. This was important because Canada could not afford to have the CAF and the CSE competing with each other to fund expensive SIGINT systems. Bringing strategic and tactical SIGINT together was, in Siew's words, "a whole new way of doing business."[109] Its impact on operations in Afghanistan is discussed in chapter 12.

Although not a direct result of the *DIR*, its vision was clearly realized in the collaborative efforts of the Mapping and Charting Establishment and the Canadian Forces Joint Imagery Centre. In line with Canada's allies, they had begun to combine their products into geospatial intelligence. The RMA drove technological advances especially in long-range communications, allowing them to generate deployable Geomatics and Imagery Support Teams to support major operations. This use of strategic assets to support operational/tactical-level activities was a visible manifestation of the compression of intelligence collection capabilities and its utility at the sharp end. Subject only to bandwidth limits, improved connectivity would allow information to be shared across different command levels in near real time.[110]

Finally, the *DIR* recommended the creation of new counterintelligence and HUMINT capabilities. The CDI formed a new counterintelligence/HUMINT section (J2X) within the Intelligence Capabilities Division, along with a deployable HUMINT unit (Joint Task Force X). The review had also recommended creation of the Defence Debriefing Team, modeled on the British practice, that would debrief "key military personnel" who had served in or visited overseas deployments. This was partially implemented through the Policy Intelligence Group, J2X, and occasional taskings of Joint Task Force X.[111] More will be said about this in chapters 11 and 12. However, the proposal to create a deployable counterintelligence unit was considered too controversial and was not enacted.

The list of responsibilities and authorities the *DIR* proposed for the new DI authority and its staff was remarkably similar to the terms of reference given to Brigadier-General Kenyon forty years earlier. That the *DIR* team felt it was necessary to make these recommendations confirms that DI had indeed lost its way in the intervening years. It may be fair to suggest that over successive decades Kenyon's bold vision had died the death of a thousand budget cuts. The *DIR* represented a rare opportunity to rectify that if possible.

In October 2004 the senior DND/CAF leadership approved almost everything the *DIR* had recommended. If implemented fully this would have amounted to a wholesale transformation of DI. But these were not ordinary times. The CAF was about to go through its own transformation, with three new operational commands being stood up over the next eighteen months. It also had been engaged in operations in Afghanistan for over three years, and the government was considering an expanded mission. Overshadowing all of this was the ever-present imperative to limit defence spending. The net effect of these factors was that they limited the scope of DI transformation. A former senior DND official observed that "there was push and pull between the desire to implement the 'pure' version of the *DIR* versus one that matched reality," supporting the Afghan mission and meeting other operational needs. Some of the recommendations looked sensible on paper but were impossible to implement in the context of the CAF's then high-tempo operational environment and in light of changes to the command structure. So, reality won out, but "implementation did follow the 'spirit' of the *DIR*."[112] And as Gauthier explained, "implementing was all about resources. You get into resources allocation bureaucracy... and organizational capacity to absorb those resources. It was a little bit now, with a lot more later. The immediate focus was 'what do I need for the next year', then 'what will I need for subsequent years'?"[113]

CONCLUSION

Between 1975 and 2005 DI experienced at least eight distinct reviews and multiple organizational changes. The reasons for those changes were clear in some cases, such as the move to ADP, but less so in others. However, with the exception of the *DIR*, the effects they had were consistent over time: budget and resource constraints. But the documents cited here represent only a tiny fraction of the paperwork generated in each case. So, all conclusions drawn here are tentative.

What stands out among four of these reorganizations is systemic failures: poor definition of the problem, the absence of clearly defined goals, poor planning, and often prolonged and ineffective execution of the tasks. This is remarkable, given that it occurred in two organizations (the DND and the CAF) whose very raison d'être was planning for life-and-death decision making. This can be attributed in part to fiscal constraints, but that does not tell the whole story. It is also tempting to fault individuals. But the evidence—as incomplete as it is—shows that DI leaders at all levels struggled to preserve essential capabilities even as they tried to make flawed reforms work. Rather, as Douglas Bland suggests, the problem lay within the DND and the CAF. They were subjected to frequent reviews and reorganizations, guided by business management concepts,[114] in pursuit of an elusive ideal functionality that would meld effective civilian administration, accountability, and political control with effective military command and operational capabilities, all at an acceptable (minimal) cost. Prior to the *DIR*, these efforts yielded less than optimal results. With the evidence at hand, we can only infer a cause-and-effect link between them and the flawed attempts to reorganize DI to fulfil its mission: to provide high-quality intelligence support to military and civilian leaders and to deployed forces.

James Cox faults the reform process for falling short of a full transformation of DI.[115] But the *DIR* stands in stark contrast to all previous efforts. It was comprehensive, guided by a clear intent and plan, focused on essential capabilities, and yielded specific recommendations for change that would make a measurable, positive difference. DI did not get everything it needed, at least initially, and implementing the approved recommendations was gradual and uneven. But most of the very important initiatives were put into effect. These were most apparent in DI governance, intelligence production, SIGINT coordination, geospatial intelligence, and HUMINT collection. Underpinning all of this was a major shift in the institutional culture of the CAF/DND toward intelligence-driven operations. Lieutenant-General Gauthier stressed that "all of a sudden the organizational focus on intelligence was real, and really important, whereas in the previous decade it had not been at all."[116]

That change of mindset was the real transformation. The implementation of the *DIR* did not so much create this shift as reflect what had been happening gradually and piecemeal since 1990. As the case study chapters will show, it was driven by operational necessity. This, as much as the changes arising from the *DIR*, laid the foundation for the creation of the Canadian Forces Intelligence Command (CFINTCOM) in 2013.

NOTES

1. "Proposed DINTP Reorganization," 2 June 1975, LAC, RG24, BAN 2005-00285-2, box 11, file 1901-1, part 1 (1966–77).
2. "DDI Organization Chart," 19 May 1976, LAC, RG24, BAN 2005-00285-2, box 11, file 1901-1, part 1; Alan Barnes, "Defence Intelligence Assessment Groups," entry for summer/autumn 1976, Canadian Foreign Intelligence History Project.
3. "Directorate of Scientific and Technical Intelligence [organization chart]," annex A to "IAC [Intelligence Advisory Committee] 1302 DSTI Reorganization," 30 December 1980 [sic; 1979], LAC, RG73, BAN 2016-00616 box 7, file 7/10, part 29; Barnes, entry for spring 1982.
4. "Chief Intelligence and Security TORs," 3 February 1983, 1, LAC, RG24, BAN 2005-00285-2, box 14, file 1920-1, part 2.
5. "Chief Intelligence and Security TORs," 2–5. "Technical control" of the Supplementary Radio System stations was limited mostly to procedures and machinery.
6. "Chief Intelligence and Security TORs," 6–7.
7. Memorandum, "Chief Intelligence and Security Branch, Director General Intelligence [draft TOR]," 31 October 1984, 1–2, LAC, RG24, BAN 2005-00285-2, box 11, file 1901-1, part 3.
8. Barnes, "Defence Intelligence Assessment Groups," entry for spring 1987; Memorandum, "NDHQ Organization Chief Intelligence and Security Branch. Creation of Three New Directorates in Director General Intelligence Division," 26 November 1986, LAC, RG24, BAN 2005-00285-2, box 11, file 1901-1, part 3.
9. "PPC Structure Review," January 1986, 1, LAC, RG24, BAN 2005-00285-2, box 14, file 1920-1, part 3.
10. "PPC Structure Review," 1.
11. "PPC Structure Review," 2.
12. "PPC Structure Review," 5.
13. "PPC Structure Review," 5–6.

14. "PPC Structure Review," 11–13.
15. Commodore J. C. Slade, Memorandum, "DDI Organization," 3 December 1986, LAC, RG24, BAN 2005-00285-2, box 11, file 1901-1, part 3, and "CIS Organization Chart," n.d., box 14, file 1920-1, part 4.
16. Maj. K. F. Binda (Directorate of Intelligence Plans and Doctrine Section 5), "Memo—DIPD5 Mandate," 24 August 1988, LAC, RG24, BAN 2005-00285-2, box 14, file 1920-1, part 4.
17. Commodore J. Rodocanachi (director general of intelligence and security), Memorandum, "Automatic Data Processing in DGIS," 13 March 1980, IAC, Privy Council Office, LAC, RG73, BAN 2016-00616, box 7, file 7/10, part 27.
18. *DND Telephone Directory*, autumn 1983, E-43; Barnes, "Defence Intelligence Assessment Groups," entry for autumn 1984.
19. Gaétan Lavertu, DGI Foreign Intelligence Bureau, Department of External Affairs, "Note on DND ISX Project for ICSI [Interdepartmental Committee on Security and Intelligence] Meeting," 19 February 1987, LAC, RG25, BAN 2017-00434-0, box 14, file 29-4-ICSI, part 4.
20. Lavertu.
21. Maj.-Gen. C. W. Hewson (CIS) to VCDS, Memorandum, "Defence Planning and Force Development Process—CIS Branch," 25 March 1988, LAC, RG24, BAN 2008-00172-5, box 10, file 1901-CIS, part 10.
22. Hewson.
23. Hewson.
24. Hewson, Memorandum, "Canadian Forces Total Force Development Plan," 28 March 1988, LAC, RG24, BAN 2008-00172-5, box 9, file 1901-CIS-2.
25. Addendum to Hewson, "Canadian Forces," 6–7.
26. Hewson, "Canadian Forces," 7.
27. Lt.-Gen. J. E. Vance (VCDS) to Hewson (CIS), 8 April 1988, LAC, RG24, BAN 2008-00172-5, box 9, file 1901-CIS-2.
28. Harold A. Skaarup, *Out of Darkness—Light: A History of Canadian Military Intelligence*, Vol. 2 (New York: iUniverse, 2005), 463–64.
29. Maj.-Gen. R. P. Pattee (CIS), Memorandum, "Defence Planning and Force Development Process—CIS Branch," 7 June 1989, LAC, RG24, BAN 2008-00172-5, box 9, file 1901-CIS-2.
30. Pattee.
31. Pattee, with VCDS marginal comment (undated).
32. Lt.-Col. R. J. Taylor, Memorandum Draft, "FGS Personnel Requirements," and "Service Paper," 21 June 1989, LAC, RG24 BAN 2005-00285-2, box 14, file 1920-1, part 5.
33. Mike Bowen, interview with the author, 13 June 2019.
34. Lt.-Col. G. S. Graham (DIE), Memorandum, "Manpower Reductions," 26 June 1989, LAC, RG24 BAN 2005-00285-2, box 14, file 1920-1, part 5.
35. Graham.
36. Taylor, "FGS Personnel Requirements."
37. Michael A. Hennessy and Todd Fitzgerald, "An Expedient Reorganization: The NDHQ J-Staff System in the Gulf War," *Canadian Military Journal* 4, no. 1 (2003): 23, 25, 27.
38. Rear-Adm. J. C. Slade (J2), Memorandum, "NDHQ Joint Intelligence and Security Intelligence Organization—J2—Persian Gulf Crisis," 11 January 1991, LAC, RG24, BAN 2008-00172-5, box 10, file 1901-CIS, part 11.

39. Slade to NDHQ Functional Review Coordinator, Memorandum, "NDHQ Functional Review—CIS Briefing Document, 2nd Submission," 5 November 1990, LAC, RG24, BAN 2005-00285-2, box 14, file 1920-1, part 1 (1990–92).
40. Col. P. S. Hargreaves, Memorandum, "CIS Functional Review Reduction Implementation Plan—Op FRICTION Implications," 25 January 1991, LAC, RG24, BAN 2005-00285-2, box 14, file 1920-1, part 7.
41. M. P. Bowen (SA/CIS), Memorandum, "Post-War Post-Functional Review Implementation—CIS Branch Structure," 4 February 1991, LAC, RG24, BAN 2005-00285-2, box 14, file 1920-1, part 1 (1990–92).
42. VCDS, Memorandum, "CIS Branch Structure Post-Functional Review" (including memorandum and annexes by CIS), 24 April 1991, LAC, RG24, BAN 2005-00285-2, box 12, file 1901-1, part 5.
43. *NDHQ Action Directive C4/91 Review of DND/CF Intelligence Requirements*, 15 October 1991, LAC, RG24, box 9, file 1243-J2/DGI, part 1.
44. M. P. Bowen SA/CIS Memorandum to VCDS, "Review of DND/CF Intelligence Requirements McNaughton Report—Implementation Plan," 13 July 1992, LAC, RG24, BAN 2005-00285-2, box 11, file 1901-1, part 1 (1975–93).
45. *NDHQ Action Directive D_/93 Implementation of the Final Report: Review of DND/CF Intelligence Requirements*, issued by CDS and DM, 6 July 1993, and Brig.-Gen. B. N. Cameron (DGI), Memorandum, "Review of DND/CF Intelligence Requirements—Implementation of Final Report," 30 August 1993, LAC, RG24, box 9, file 1243-J2/DGI, part 2.
46. Chief—Review Services, *Joint Command Control Intelligence System (JC2IS)*, April 2001, 1, author's copy; Capt. (N) (ret.) Andrea Siew, interview with author, 7 November 2019.
47. *Joint Command Control Intelligence System (JC2IS)*, 1.
48. Siew interview.
49. *Joint Command Control Intelligence System (JC2IS)*, i–iii.
50. Siew interview.
51. *Joint Command Control Intelligence System (JC2IS)*, i.
52. Brig.-Gen. K. C. Hague, *DCDS Group Intelligence Division Level 2 Business Plan 1996/97–1997/98* [Draft], annex to minute sheet, DGI Coordinator to J2/DGI, 14 April 1996, LAC, RG24, BAN 2005-00285-2, box 13, file 1901-1, part 11.
53. Brig.-Gen. B. N. Cameron (DGI) to SA (DCDS), Memorandum, "Budget Reductions—Personnel Plan," 18 March 1994, and Col. Victor Ashdown, Memorandum, "DDI Reorganization," 6 July 1994, LAC, RG24, BAN 2005-00285-2, box 15, file 1920-1, part 12.
54. Maj. J. W. Nixon to A/DGI, Memorandum, "J2 Reorganization," 12 July 1994, LAC, RG24, BAN 2005-00285-2, box 12, file 1901-1, part 9.
55. DCDS (Vice-Admiral Mason), Memorandum to ADM (Per), "DCDS Group ECP 188/94," 19 June 1995, LAC, RG24, BAN 2005-00285-2, box 15, file 1920-1, part 12.
56. James Cox, "The Transformation of Canadian Defence Intelligence since the End of the Cold War" (master's thesis, Royal Military College of Canada, 2004), 112–14, Canadian Foreign Intelligence History Project.
57. Mason to ADM (Per), 19 June 1995.
58. Commodore T. C. Heath (J2/DGI), Memorandum, "DG INT Organization Change," 27 July 1995, LAC, RG24, BAN 2005-00285-2, box 12, file 1901-1, part 10A.

59. Col. V. V. Ashdown (J2 Ops), Memorandum, "J2 Current/YCC Re-Engineering," 17 August 1995, LAC, RG24, BAN 2005-00285-2, box 12, file 1901-1, part 10A.
60. K. D. Brigden (DGI Coord), *J2 DG INT Phase 2 Reorganization*, 16 November 1995, LAC, RG24, BAN 2005-00285-2, box 12, file 1901-1, part 10B, and K. D. Brigden, *New Titles*, 31 July 1996, box 13, file 1901-1, part 12.
61. G. J. Kolisnek (Directorate of Defence Intelligence 3), *J2 OPS Business Plan FY 97/98*, 6 August 1996; and *DCDS Update C-6 Re-engineering Progress Steps 7 & 8*, 8 October 1996, LAC, RG24, BAN 2005-00285-2, box 13, file 1901-1, part 12.
62. *MCCRT Assessment—Overview DCDS Organization*, 15 October 1996, LAC, RG24, BAN 2005-00285-2, box 13, file 1901-1, part 12.
63. *MCCRT Assessment*.
64. Brig.-Gen. K. C. Hague (J2 DGI) to Chief of Staff DCDS, "Draft DG INT Reductions," 17 March 1997, LAC, RG24, BAN 2005-00285-2, box 13, file 1901-1, part 13.
65. Dr. B. H. Harrison (J2 scientific and technical intelligence) to J2 Ops, Message, "J2 STI in Crisis Again," 13 May 1997, LAC, RG24, BAN 2005-00285-2, box 11, file 1901-1, part 3 (1996–2000).
66. DGI, *Business Plan Brief to DCDS*, 23 January 1998, LAC, RG24, BAN 2005-00285-2, box 13, file 1901-1, part 15.
67. K. D. Brigden (J2 Coordinator), *J2 Division Authorized Strength*, 15 September 1998, box 13, file 1901-1, part 16.
68. *1999 Defence Intelligence Priorities* [Draft], n.d. [file dated 27 November 1998], LAC, RG24, BAN 2005-00285-2, box 13, file 1901-1, part 16.
69. David A. Charters, "The Future of Military Intelligence within the Canadian Forces," *Canadian Military Journal* 2, no. 4 (2002): 48.
70. Siew interview. See also chapter 4.
71. Cox, "Transformation of Canadian Defence," 136.
72. David Pugliese, "Budget Cuts Damaged Military's Intelligence-Gathering Ability," *Ottawa Citizen*, 16 June 2001.
73. Lt.-Gen. Michel Gauthier, interview with author, Ottawa, 5 November 2019.
74. Gauthier interview.
75. Gauthier interview and his comments on the draft chapter.
76. J2/DGI, *Defence Intelligence Review* [*DIR*], i. This was stated in the DM/CDS memorandum to all Level 1 staff in a memo, 18 November 2002. See also "Executive Summary," i; and slide, "DIR Directed Study Areas," J2/Director General Intelligence, *Defence Intelligence Review Briefing to CDS and A/DM*, slide deck, 20 May 2004, copy in possession of author (cited hereafter as *DIRB*). The wording of the *DIR* and the slide differ slightly. Author's copy is from Lt.-Gen. Gauthier, who did the briefing.
77. *DIRB*.
78. *DIRB*.
79. CDS (Gen. Ray Hennault) and DM (Ward Elcock), letter, "Departmental Approval Defence Intelligence Review," October 2004, author's copy.
80. J2/DGI, *DIR*; and "CRS Conclusions" in *DIRB*. See also *Defence Intelligence and Enterprise Renewal (DI&ER), Initial Assessment of the Defence Intelligence Review, 2019* (hereafter cited as *DI&ER*).
81. *DIR*, i–ii.
82. *DIR*, ii.
83. *DIR*, i; and "CRS Conclusions" in *DIRB*.

84. *DIR*, v; and *DIRB*.
85. Gauthier interview.
86. *DIRB*; and Glenn Nordick, interview with author, 11 June 2019.
87. Gauthier interview. His immediate successor, Glenn Nordick, remained at the brigadier-general rank but exercised full authority as CDI.
88. *DIRB*.
89. *DIRB*.
90. Gauthier interview.
91. *DIR*, 11, fig. 1.
92. *DIR*, iv, 4, 18; and Cox, "Transformation of Canadian Defence," 112–15, 178.
93. *DIR*, 65–66.
94. *DIR*, 77.
95. Former DND official, who requested anonymity, interview with author, 4 November 2019.
96. *DIR*, 52, 54; and Siew interview.
97. CDS/DM, "Departmental Approval."
98. *DIRB* and *DI&ER*, 2019, serial 49.
99. Gauthier interview; interview with a former DND official who requested anonymity, 4 November 2019.
100. "Director General Intelligence Production Dr. Linda Goldthorp," *CDI Internal Newsletter* 1 no. 1 (Spring 2008), quoted in Harold A. Skaarup, "Out of Darkness—Light: A History of Canadian Military Intelligence," [vol. 4] (unpublished manuscript, 2018, author's copy), 156.
101. "Director General," in Skaarup, [4]:156
102. "Director General," in Skaarup, [4]:156–57.
103. *DI&ER*, 2019; anonymous former DND official, interview.
104. *DIR*, 18 (my emphasis).
105. *DIR*, 59–60, 63–65.
106. *DI&ER*, 2019, serial 24.
107. *DIRB*.
108. *DI&ER*, 2019, serial 60. See also Siew interview.
109. John Adams, interview with author, 6 November 2019; Nordick interview; Siew interview; and *DI&ER*, 2019, serial 60.
110. *DIR*, 77, 96–97.
111. *DI&ER*, 2019, serials 61, 63.
112. Anonymous former DND official, interview, and written comments, January 2022.
113. Gauthier interview.
114. Douglas L. Bland, *The Administration of Defence Policy in Canada, 1947 to 1985* (Kingston, Ontario: Ronald P. Frye, 1987), 11.
115. Cox, "Transformation of Canadian Defence," 196, 206.
116. Cox, 199; quote from Gauthier interview; and Siew interview. See also Lewis MacKenzie, *Peacekeeper: The Road to Sarajevo* (Vancouver: Douglas & McIntyre, 1993), 284–85, 330.

4

FROM ADAPTATION TO TRANSFORMATION

Canadian Military Intelligence, 1975–2005

The organizational turmoil that plagued DI was not matched to the same degree in the deployable forces. But neither were they completely immune to the factors shaping national level DI. Driven in part by operational requirements—especially the need for interoperability with coalition partners—and in part by new thinking about and new technologies for combat intelligence, MI underwent three adjustments in approaches to providing support to commanders. These included new structures, new technologies, and new concepts. All three interacted with each other, leaving the observer with a chicken-and-egg conundrum: which came first? Combined with a cultural shift in the forces toward recognition of the utility of intelligence, they led to what is now referred to as "intelligence fusion." Arguably, this amounted to a transformation of Canadian MI.

INTELLIGENCE FUSION

The term "intelligence fusion" refers to the integration of intelligence processes and products to create a more complete picture of the intelligence target(s).[1] The emerging ISR systems allowed armed forces to see more of the conventional battlefield, at longer range and with greater clarity, and to accumulate and process more data about the enemy. The technologies associated with the RMA, especially computers and communications,[2] have made possible more effective fusion of all this data. Operations in complex operating environments against elusive, unstructured adversaries, which impose diverse information sources and high-volume intelligence inputs, have made intelligence fusion essential.

Intelligence fusion may entail some or all of the following. The first is *functional*: the integrated analysis of information and data from across the collection/source spectrum. This includes SIGINT, imagery intelligence, HUMINT, and technical, open-source, and direct observation of or contact with the adversary (e.g., reconnaissance, patrolling, observation posts [OPs]). The second is *organizational*, bringing together the collection and analysis functions of national intelligence agencies, deployed forces, OGDs, and intelligence services of allies and coalition partners. The third is the *cultural* shift mentioned above: a paradigm shift in how force commanders and civilian leaders come to recognize the value of intelligence and integrate it into planning, decision making, and directing operations. Likewise, intelligence producers have had to adapt their practices and products to meet their consumers' needs. Fourth, fusion is *holistic*, inclusive of all aspects of the conflict environment and recognizing the complexity of the adversary. Finally, fusion now entails *compression* of the strategic, operational, and tactical levels of intelligence into an integrated, synergistic relationship. The operational chapters (5–12) will illustrate these changes.

PROCESSES OF CHANGE IN CANADIAN MILITARY INTELLIGENCE

The following sections trace the changes in approaches to intelligence undertaken by the three services. Each approach was shaped by the structures, functions, practices, and responsibilities unique to those services; by the environments in which they were expected to operate and to a greater or lesser degree by the intelligence requirements they would have to fulfil.

The DND Inherits Strategic SIGINT, 1975–77

The most significant change in Canadian strategic intelligence during the 1970s occurred in April 1975, when Canada's SIGINT/communications security agency, the CBNRC, was transferred to the DND. There it became the CSE. The question of authority and responsibility for SIGINT had been raised during the 1970 review of the Canadian intelligence program, commissioned by the Intelligence Policy Committee, and carried out by Claude Isbister.

Since 1960 the Intelligence Policy Committee had been responsible for SIGINT policy, at least in theory. The director of communications security, who was head of intelligence and security within the Department of External Affairs and also chaired the CJIC, was in turn responsible for executing those policies, planning and controlling the CBNRC's budget, and maintaining relations with its Five Eyes partners. But by 1970 the Intelligence Policy Committee had all but ceased to function. So, operational responsibility was divided between the CBNRC's director, who managed the SIGINT processing and reporting programs, and the DND, which looked after administration, staffing, and (from the late 1960s) operations and maintenance of the intercept stations, the Supplementary Radio System. Isbister stressed that the existing system was unwieldy, since the director of communications security had no authority over military SIGINT activities, and the position was overtasked and untenable. He recommended that the position be terminated, with the director of the CBNRC assuming all managerial duties.[3]

The idea of moving the service seems to have been raised first in 1971 by Sir Leonard Hooper, director of the Government Communications Headquarters, Britain's SIGINT service. Maj.-Gen. Roland Reid, deputy chief of intelligence and security, had told him that the National Research Council was eager to rid itself of responsibility for SIGINT.[4] Then in 1974, a Canadian Broadcasting Corporation documentary did an exposé on the CBNRC's SIGINT role.[5] This prompted the government to act. Meeting in January 1975, the Cabinet Committee on Security and Intelligence confirmed the National Research Council's discomfort with the SIGINT task and that the publicity about it had been an "important factor" in bringing about a review of its status. A memorandum to the Cabinet Committee on Security and Intelligence recommended the transfer of the CBNRC to the DND, where it would be renamed the CSE. This made sense financially and administratively, since DI operated the (then) five intercept stations, and the DND provided $24 million of the $32 million SIGINT budget.[6]

Since the CSE was regarded as a national as opposed to a departmental asset, it was not integrated into the DI structure. Instead, the CSE became a stand-alone organization within the DND, reporting to the minister of national defence. The Interdepartmental Committee on Security and Intelligence assumed responsibility for SIGINT policy, although there was some uncertainty about what "policy" meant in the SIGINT context. Moreover, some inside the CSE felt that its head (preferably a full-time SIGINT professional) should be responsible for policy.[7]

But in 1977 the Interdepartmental Committee on Security and Intelligence's Intelligence Advisory Committee vested control of SIGINT in bifurcated form: the Intelligence Advisory Committee had control for "national" (i.e. nonmilitary) SIGINT, while the DCDS controlled "tactical COMINT [communications intelligence] and ELINT [electronic intelligence] for operational purposes."[8] The latter collection task later devolved onto the CFIOG (previously the Supplementary Radio System), and DI has remained the primary consumer of SIGINT products generated by the CSE[9] or shared by its Five Eyes partners. As encrypted data became more complex to break, the supercomputer became vital to cryptanalysis, so in 1985 the CSE acquired a Cray X-MP/11.[10] The CSE's position within the DND remained unchanged during the period, although after 9/11 it gained a statutory mandate, new powers, and more resources.[11]

Army Intelligence: The Intelligence Collection and Analysis Centre and the Divisional Intelligence Company, 1985–90

The Cold War had defined the focus of Canadian MI since the 1950s. It was organized and trained to support high-intensity combat against the Warsaw Pact.[12] In the 1980s, the Canadian Army was starting to grapple with the challenge of managing all-source tactical and operational intelligence. As mentioned in chapter 2, up to this time MI had been a marginal activity within the Army. Since infantry battalions were not expected to engage in combat on their own, Canadian combat intelligence doctrine said little about the subject below brigade level. According to Lt.-Col. J.A.E.K. Dowell, battalion commanders in the 1960s were not thought to need intelligence per se, only "accurate and timely information."[13] So, battalions usually had only a tiny intelligence section.[14]

The exception to this was the Canadian Airborne Regiment, the "high-readiness" unit within the Land Force.[15] As such, the regiment needed indications and warning intelligence and background and terrain information on potential deployment areas. So, it normally had eight professional intelligence and security staff, augmented as needed by soldiers trained in combat intelligence. Brigade intelligence staffs also were small (although 4 Canadian Mechanized Brigade Group in Germany had a "modestly robust" staff) but were composed of professional intelligence officers and noncommissioned members (figure 4.1). One notable weakness was in augmentation and sustainment. The reserve intelligence companies were disbanded in 1969–70, converted to "sections" (later platoons), and attached to various headquarters and units. By the late 1980s, fewer than fifty reserve personnel remained on strength. The companies were reactivated in 1994–95 and rapidly grew in strength,[16] and a significant number of intelligence reservists later deployed on operations.

Army units relied on their patrols and "recce" (reconnaissance) platoons for information. Intelligence staffs maintained the maps on exercises in which combat intelligence flowed from notional higher or allied sources. Brigades or combat groups depended on armoured reconnaissance squadrons and a limited tactical SIGINT capability. One exception was 2 Electronic Warfare (EW) Squadron, which contained a high concentration of field intelligence and EW analysis expertise. In the event of a war in Europe, the CAF expected to receive some intelligence from NATO headquarters and allied forces, but as Brig.-Gen (ret.) Glenn Nordick explained, the Army expected that it would have to use its reconnaissance assets to "fight for intelligence."[17]

The Army's experimentation with intelligence fusion at the operational/tactical level can be traced to the 1985 *Combat Development Combat Intelligence Study*. The study laid out the concept for the Intelligence Collection and Analysis Centre (ICAC) based on the "Required War Structure" of a task force

FIGURE 4.1. An intelligence section briefing for Lt.-Gen. Stanley Waters (center), commander of Mobile Command, during 1 Canadian Brigade Group Exercise WAINCON, ca. 1974. Note the talc map overlays and grease pencils. *Canadian Forces Intelligence Command*

intelligence company. Neither organization existed at the time. According to MI historian Maj. (ret.) Harold Skaarup, building on the conceptual and experimental work of the Land Force intelligence staff, the initiative to create a deployable ICAC operational "test bed" came from Capt. Greg Jensen with the support and guidance of the senior staff intelligence officer of the Force Mobile Command (FMC, the Land Force headquarters), Lt.-Col. Paul O'Leary, and the FMC intelligence section. O'Leary called it "the most important initiative in Canadian Army Combat Intelligence operations in many years."[18] In tune with the Army's role, it was oriented toward high-intensity conventional war against Soviet and Warsaw Pact forces in Europe.

The first experimental field trial of the ICAC concept took place at Canadian Forces Base (CFB) Valcartier in late October 1985 during brigade- and division-level command post exercises. The exercise report states that "for the first time, the ICAC allowed the G2 to present to the commander a detailed estimate of the enemy's intentions based on a coordinated all source assessment."[19] During the trial the team worked out procedures to coordinate the work of artillery, engineer intelligence, and EW staffs. They also created an effective tactical-level collection and tasking management system. Not surprisingly, given the pioneering nature of this test, it also highlighted the need for more training of all involved.[20]

The report stated that the Army had long recognized that higher formation (division, task force) commanders required all-source intelligence and needed an intelligence company to provide it. The report explained in detail the role of the G2 as the intelligence adviser to the division commander and the staff's role in support of the G2. The divisional intelligence company would be responsible for directing and conducting intelligence collection and analysis to support the work of the G2 and the staff. The company would have sections to conduct imagery exploitation, HUMINT collection via prisoner-of-war and refugee interrogation, counterintelligence, and UAV collection (and imagery analysis from it). The ICAC's role would be to take the G2's requirements and turn them into taskings for the intelligence company, the EW coordination centre, UAVs, and so on. As that data flowed in from all sources, the ICAC would collate, analyse, and cross-check it before producing a finished intelligence report for the G2 staff.[21] That was the very essence of tactical intelligence fusion.

The trial also was notable for the CAF's first use of computers for field intelligence ADP. This consisted of three Apple IIe computers using a mix of Canadian and US Army software. The exercise showed that owing to ADP and communications limitations, the ICAC should be located close to the divisional command post. Likewise, colocating the Electronic Warfare Coordination Centre with the ICAC was seen as being very effective. The report said that having all of the external agencies (EW, artillery, engineer, meteorological) represented in the ICAC on a 24/7 basis (with dedicated communications to their parent headquarters) was "vital for a coordinated all-source picture to be developed."[22]

The concept was tested again during the Army exercise RV 87 at CFB Wainright in April 1987. Dowell later explained that in the field training exercise that followed, the ICAC tested sensor management using aerial reconnaissance. Since the CAF had no UAVs, it simulated one by mounting a sensor package on a Cessna aircraft. The imagery quality was poor, but the data links allowed the ICAC to pass the reports in near real time, saving both manual effort and time. The major success was establishing "greater understanding of the concept and operation of the all-source collection and analysis centre."[23] Indeed, the lessons learned from the trials and exercises and from the evolving doctrines of Canada's allies led to the production of a detailed combat intelligence operations doctrine by the summer of 1988. *Canadian Forces Joint Publication 315-2* provided a conceptual and doctrinal guide to the conduct of deployed intelligence operations, with the ICAC at the very center, providing situational awareness (SA), target development, and indications and warning for force protection, for at least the next decade.[24]

These efforts had yielded a proof of concept for the ICAC and the divisional intelligence company. And when the headquarters of the 1st Canadian Division opened in Kingston on 28 February 1989, the proposed structure included an intelligence company along the lines of what had been tested. But two successive budget cuts (1989 and 1990) scaled back the size of the division. Major capital projects, such as new tanks, were scrapped or put on hold. Some units were dropped from the order of battle or would be formed only from individual postings during a crisis.²⁵ The intelligence company was not spared; it was staffed only to cadre strength (about 25% of its war establishment). When it deployed during the 1990 Oka Crisis, discussed in chapter 6, it had only fourteen members.²⁶ Still, its performance in that operation was the proof of practice for the ICAC and for the all-source fusion concept.

But innovation did not end there. The ICAC laid the foundation for four new units that were created during subsequent deployments: the Canadian National Intelligence Centre (CANIC) in the Balkans under NATO, and the All-Source Intelligence Centre (ASIC), the ISTAR (intelligence, surveillance, target acquisition, and reconnaissance) Company, and the Special Operations Intelligence Centre (SOIC) that were established during the Afghanistan War.

(Re)Imagining Intelligence

The thinking about Army intelligence also changed in two ways during this period. The first of these was conceptual: about what intelligence is and where it fits in the conduct of war. This, in turn, was shaped by RMA-driven technological changes, the US Army's "rediscovery" of the operational level of war, and assumptions about how a war in Europe might be fought.

The result was several attempts to redefine the essential combat functions in a holistic way and distill them down to a minimal list. As might be expected, the American services could not agree on the same list, and neither could NATO. So, the number of items varied but usually included command, information operations, maneuver, firepower, protection, and sustainment. In the process, MI was variously dropped from the list (reduced to a support function), subsumed under information operations, and redefined as the "sense" rubric before being reinstated as an essential function in its own right. Canadian thinking mirrored that of the United States and NATO.²⁷ This did not really change how MI and DI staffs performed their tasks. They still had to collect data, collate and analyse it, and produce reports, briefings, and assessments to yield what is called "information superiority."²⁸ But this said a great deal about how force commanders regarded intelligence. Treating it as a support function—as opposed to a coequal enabler—explicitly diminished its perceived value and relevance to those commanders in relation to hard combat power, such as fire and maneuver. Clearly it was seen not as a function essential to guiding hard power, but instead as just one more tool in the toolbox.

As Philip Davies points out, one complicating issue was whether to adopt the American concept of collection as consisting solely of ISR or the British approach, which added target acquisition to the mix to yield the ISTAR rubric. Advocates for ISTAR asserted that it enhanced the link between intelligence and operations, while critics claimed that it introduced some uncertainty about who is responsible for target acquisition: the intelligence staff or the operations staff.[29] As indicated above, the Canadian Army adopted the ISTAR approach and created structures to perform that function.[30]

Likewise, grouping intelligence under information operations alongside operations security, military deception, psychological operations (psyops), and EW muddied the waters. This conflated an activity (called "relevant information") that informs commanders with active measures directed against the enemy or others.[31] If all were assigned to the same staff, they would divert or dilute resources that would be needed to ensure that the commander was well informed before conducting operations. Nor did this conflation clarify the difference between relevant information (which sounded like 1960s terminology) and intelligence. Finally, redefining intelligence simply as a "sense" function simplifies what is a multifaceted activity. To sense is merely to detect or at best identify. Intelligence work entails more than simply detecting the enemy; it tries to understand what the enemy—and other elements in the battle space—is doing, how, and, in irregular conflicts, why, to what end.

That said, this new thinking about information operations drew attention to a dramatic change in the MI knowledge base. Reflecting the impact of computer-generated and internet-linked ADP systems, it pointed to the emergence of a massive "Global Information Environment."[32] This would be both a blessing and a curse. On the one hand, intelligence collectors and analysts would have access to a lot of data that had not existed in an accessible way previously. On the other, the ability to collect it on a large scale could dwarf their ability to make sense of and convey it to commanders in a timely manner. This put a premium on information management.

What was probably more significant was the dramatic shift in the attitude of commanders in the field toward intelligence. This was driven not by arcane debates over its place in war-fighting doctrine but instead by the experience of operations. The following chapters will show that from the Oka Crisis to Afghanistan, intelligence proved its value when it was available, timely, relevant, and accurate and its negative impact when it was not. In the Canadian Army from the 1990s forward, MI moved from the margins to begin playing a central role in planning and conduct of operations. Commanders learned to appreciate it, expect it, and rely on it. As former CDI lieutenant-general Michel Gauthier told the author, "They screamed for it."[33] This represented a sea change in attitudes toward intelligence and how it was employed in the CAF.

Evolution of Canadian Naval Intelligence

Changes in naval intelligence in this era appear more incremental because the navy started from a more fully developed position. Since modern naval surface combatants and submarines incorporate closely linked sensors and weapons systems, the distinction between intelligence collection and its tactical exploitation is almost nonexistent. In this sense, the RCN pioneered nearly instant sensor-to-shooter intelligence fusion in the CAF.[34] On RCN vessels, intelligence was closely integrated with the operations staff, which until quite recently did not necessarily include professionally trained intelligence personnel. In fact, prior to unification, operations staff serving aboard in combat information centres were selected to perform intelligence tasks "as required."[35] Of course, what happened aboard ships was only part of the naval intelligence story. A number of developments also happened ashore that shaped intelligence operations afloat, and much of it was technology-driven. And initially at least, it was designed for conventional (or even nuclear) war.

As discussed in chapter 2, the *Defence in the '70s* white paper proposed that the navy (MARCOM) should shift from its NATO-defined ASW role to a more general-purpose capability. However, several factors precluded an early transition. First, so long as the Cold War was the navy's dominant paradigm, it could not forsake the ASW function. It was essential to ensure that sea lines of communication remained open and Soviet submarines were kept at bay. That did not change until the 1990s. Second, converting the navy to a general-purpose role would entail building new ships and modernizing older ones. That would require a more expensive commitment than the governments of the day were prepared to make. Instead, during the first half of the 1970s the fleet was pared down significantly.[36] After that, modernization took priority over new construction.

The Destroyer Life Extension Program, initiated in 1978, and the Tribal Update and Modernization Program of the 1980s gave the navy improved weapons, sensors, and C2 systems. But the new Canadian Patrol Frigate Program build did not begin until the late 1980s, with the ships entering service only in the 1990s. In the meantime, the four tribal-class (DDH 280) destroyers—converted to air-defence ships under the Tribal Update and Modernization Program—were the only ones that could operate effectively in a modern naval war that would see the use of high-velocity sea-skimming antiship missiles and submarine-launched cruise missiles. By the mid-1990s even once all twelve new patrol frigates had joined the fleet, the navy was smaller and still lacked a modern shipborne helicopter. Nevertheless, the patrol frigates and the tribal-class destroyers were capable enough to deploy regularly with USN carrier task forces.[37]

MARCOM was not exempt from the reductions imposed by the 1994 white paper, but its long-standing commitments remained.[38] It would have to meet these with fewer people and less money. That meant reduced ship readiness and longer response times to prepare for overseas deployments.[39] Even so, as shown in chapter 12, the navy was able to deploy a rotating naval task force to the Persian Gulf area of operations from October 2001 to December 2003.[40]

During the 1990s, MARCOM was also thinking ahead about the future of naval warfare and operations and what it would need to do to stay effective and relevant. The 1993 *Maritime Command Vision* document emphasised the integration of surveillance and command, control, communications, and intelligence.[41] MARCOM's 1997 policy paper *Adjusting Course: A Naval Strategy for Canada* and its successor *Leadmark* (2001) presented assessments of the likely future maritime operating environment. They highlighted the information revolution, weapons proliferation, changes in international politics, the Canadian national security milieu (with all of its constraints), and the emerging threats to naval forces. Before identifying missions and operational roles, the policy papers stressed several strategic signposts, two of which are closely linked and most relevant to this chapter: multinational operations and the interoperability of command, control, communications, and intelligence.[42] The ISR implications were significant and challenging. *Adjusting Course* noted that new technologies would provide navies with the means to achieve

> far better situational awareness. The growing utility of coordinated weapon and sensor systems, better communications, along with more intelligent analysis systems, will allow partially or fully assessed data, from joint and possibly combined sensors, to be transmitted to a centrally located collation and processing site that integrate[s] all inputs to produce a superior situational assessment. This data can then be summarized and redistributed to all relevant platforms. It can also be used to facilitate weapon engagement or assignment decisions. . . . Realizing this potential will require a consistent effort to intelligently exploit automated and operator-assisted systems to produce significant improvements in effectiveness and efficiency.[43]

By allowing ship commanders to do their own long-range surveillance, these technical advances blurred the lines between strategic, operational, and tactical activities. *Adjusting Course* quoted American defense analyst Anthony Cordesman to the effect that "high volume, long distance, secure and intelligence related C3I [command, control, communications, and intelligence] systems are likely to be critical operational problems in mid- to high-intensity conflicts and could prove critical in many multinational peacekeeping and low intensity operations."[44]

But *Adjusting Course* also highlighted a conundrum for Canadian naval forces. On the one hand, they needed to "have access to integral and independent surveillance information to avoid over-dependence on foreign sources."[45] Yet on the other hand, the policy paper said that "the most essential requirement will be a capability to interact with coalition partners." The level of equipment interoperability needed to survive in future naval combat operations would likely increase "to the point where sensor and weapon systems aboard different platforms will need to cooperate seamlessly when engaging targets."[46] In short, naval intelligence will inform naval force employment.[47]

Clearly, this not only imposed C4ISR capability and funding requirements but also had major national command authority implications, possibly to include creating a national ISR centre.[48] Finding and following an independent path in an interoperable coalition world was a challenge for Canadian DI as a whole and for naval intelligence no less.

Once the DND articulated its vision in what is called *Strategy 2020* in June 1999, the navy followed suit with its *MARCOM Capability Planning Guidance 2000*, issued in September 1999. While the guide stated that the goals of the *1994 Defence White Paper* remained appropriate, it called for a review of the strategy articulated in *Adjusting Course*. The *MARCOM Capability Planning Guidance 2000* drew attention to the constraints imposed on the operational readiness of the navy. Even so, it identified interoperability with the USN as a key feature of Canada's fleet and gave C4ISR the highest priority for research and development. Surveillance was ranked first among the operational capabilities of Canada's "combat capable Maritime Forces."[49] To flesh out what this meant for naval intelligence, Andrea Siew, at the time a commander, worked with a team to draft the navy's *Operational Intelligence, Surveillance and Reconnaissance Blueprint to 2010*. It set the ISR architecture within the context of the navy's maritime missions, concepts of surveillance and intelligence, existing and needed capabilities, and key technology goals. The study concluded with recommendations on force structure, modernization, human resources, deployability, jointness, and interoperability.[50]

Against this background, from the late 1970s to the 1990s MARCOM incorporated new or updated technology and systems that enhanced surveillance/intelligence collection and analysis capacity. *Adjusting Course* asserted that "surveillance systems are at the heart of all naval operations,"[51] so these improvements offset to some degree the wider erosion of the navy's capabilities. The following summary addresses only those systems that played a role in the naval operations discussed later in this book in the Persian Gulf, the Adriatic Sea, and the Arabian Sea.

Variable-depth sonar, which had entered service in the 1960s, remained the primary shipboard submarine detection system until the mid-1990s, when the Canadian Towed Array Sonar System (CANTASS) replaced it. Unlike variable-depth sonar, which was an active system that used a powerful ping and echo to find a submarine, CANTASS is passive. It consists of low-power microphones arrayed along a cable towed up to 2 kilometres behind the ship plus onboard signal processors. Quieter detection apart, CANTASS also picks up less of its own ship noise, allowing the operator a clearer subsurface acoustic picture. These systems could detect submarines at ranges in excess of 160 kilometres.[52]

Ordered after the 1975 *Defence Structure Review* committed the government to buying a new long-range patrol aircraft, the CP-140 Aurora entered CAF service in 1980. The CP-140 Aurora was essentially identical to the USN's P-3 Orion but carried the updated electronics suite of the USN's S-3A Viking aircraft. As noted earlier, only eighteen Auroras replaced the thirty-two Argus long-range patrol aircraft—better capability but less of it.[53] The requirement for a Sea King shipborne helicopter replacement was identified as early as 1983, but for the political and budgetary reasons explained in chapter 1, the successor—the Sikorsky CH-148 Cyclone—did not enter service until 2015. However, the Cyclone represents a quantum leap in surface and subsurface surveillance capability.[54]

The principal detection device deployed by maritime patrol aircraft was the sonobuoy. Directional, variable-depth, passive sonobuoys allowed the aircraft to detect submarines at an approximate range of about 8–16 kilometres. Precise indication of range was left to active sonobuoys, but their range was quite short, 1.5–3 kilometres. They also required computer support, available only on the Aurora. Their magnetic anomaly detectors had a range of only about 300 metres and so were useful only in the final approach to the submarine target. Helicopters used dunking sonars, similar to the variable-depth sonar, lowered into and dragged through the sea at slow speeds. They had a limited range of perhaps as little as 3–4 kilometres.[55]

These systems were, of course, optimized for ASW and were not always relevant to the tasks assigned to vessels deployed in the theatres examined in subsequent chapters. What was relevant, however, were two capabilities. First, based on decades of training and experience, MARCOM vessels could integrate (or fuse) data from their shipboard, aerial, and shore-based surveillance and target-acquisition sources. Second, equipped with updated communications and ADP, they were able to share with and receive data from allied and coalition vessels to produce a common recognized maritime picture: "a composite picture of activity over the maritime AORs [areas of responsibility], from subsurface to the exosphere."[56]

There were notable changes ashore as well. Within the DGI organization, for example, shifting priorities and the reorganizations and reductions explained in chapter 3 reshaped naval intelligence analysis. Once the Cold War ended and the Soviet naval threat began to decline, analytic resources that survived budget cuts increasingly were shifted to studying the rest of the world's navies, such as that of China, that were becoming bigger and more capable. Since the RCN was operating more frequently outside its Atlantic AOR, refocusing some analytic capacity to navies in the rest of the world was a logical choice. Lt.-Cmdr. (ret.) George Kolisnek, whose naval career had been devoted to studying the Soviet submarine threat, created the Canadian Submarine Analysis Group within DGI at the end of the 1980s. The Canadian Submarine Analysis Group was very active, keeping track of the Russian submarine threat, which in spite of the end of the Cold War had not dissipated, and of various submarines from the rest of the world's navies.[57]

In the 1990s, MARCOM established two specialized units—TRINITY and ATHENA—at its Halifax and Esquimalt bases, respectively, to focus more resources and a more cohesive way on surveillance and control of Canada's Atlantic and Pacific approaches. At that time, the N2s (naval intelligence officers) of Maritime Forces Atlantic and the Maritime Command Pacific were double-hatted commanders of TRINITY and ATHENA. The intelligence staff at Maritime Forces Atlantic/TRINITY consisted of three sections: N21, the Maritime Operations Centre; N22, Information Management and Collation; and N23, Plans, Policy and Doctrine. Those sections encompassed other functions, including current intelligence support, USN liaison, SIGINT/cryptologic support, C2 warfare, and a maritime air component representative responsible for surveillance. In 1997 this totalled about seventy-five personnel.[58]

According to Capt. (N) Darren Knight, who helped establish TRINITY, it became the navy's operational information and intelligence fusion centre. Two factors raised its profile in that regard. First, the advent of the internet allowed the naval intelligence staff to do web-based data searches and intelligence sharing, vastly improving the accessibility and utility of intelligence products. This aided not only developing the recognized maritime picture but also understanding the background to it. Second, the "reengineering" process within the CAF facilitated personnel and organizational changes that allowed the navy to unify a number of operational and intelligence production entities, in accordance with the emerging planning guidance for C4ISR. As a result, the complement within TRINITY grew over time to some two hundred to three hundred from numerous trades and classifications, including forty-four intelligence professionals.[59] Maritime Forces Atlantic headquarters also acquired the Maritime Command and Control Information System (based on the USN's Joint Maritime Command Information System). Although its primary focus was on Canada's maritime AOR, this command, control, communications, computers, and intelligence (C4I) system allowed it to locate, direct, inform, and support CAF naval operations and coordinate them with allied forces anywhere in the world.[60]

There was also a concerted effort to integrate—or at least coordinate— naval and other maritime operations within a consolidated headquarters. Knight says that the 1995 Canadian-Spanish fishing dispute, often referred to as the Turbot War, boosted the concept of all-source intelligence fusion and coordination across government.[61] The navy's ISR blueprint, drafted on the cusp of the new millennium, recognized that the scale of Canada's maritime surveillance task was greater than could be managed by the navy alone. If

Canada's littoral areas were a national asset and resource, then the responsibility for them could not be just "whole of government" but also "whole of nation." This vision, articulated in the ISR blueprint, took concrete form in 2004 with the creation of a Marine Security Operations Centre on each coast. Their littoral security mandate lay outside of the scope of this book, but what they represented is relevant. Belying their slightly misleading name, the Marine Security Operations Centres were multiagency "maritime intelligence analytical fusion centres."[62] The ISR blueprint had envisioned that they would support domestic or deployed international operations, using all-source information management systems and intelligence processes "including direction, collection, data fusion, analysis and dissemination," all supported by an architecture of surveillance capabilities.[63]

As originally conceived, these centres would be linked to each other and to the land, air, and naval forces intelligence systems at NDHQ via the Canadian Forces Command System. The blueprint also recommended the integration of the Canadian Maritime Network (which allowed the DND to exchange data with OGDs) with the MARCOM Operational Information Network. The MARCOM network was to be connected to allies through the US Global Command and Control System. When naval units deployed, the centres would provide them with "data marts," databases that would provide background information needed for their assigned tasks.[64]

As the navy shifted away from its Cold War role and toward low-intensity stability and sovereignty protection operations, its ISR requirements actually expanded and changed. It needed to know more, and what it needed to know was not necessarily resolved by technology or solely by the navy's own (and allied) ISR resources. Technology was an essential enabler, but the sources now included OGDs and private enterprise, the content included a significant sociopolitical element, and decision making required thorough assessment by intelligence professionals embarked aboard. A task group intelligence officer, an Intelligence Branch lieutenant (N), became a permanent member of afloat staff in 1997. Embarked intelligence teams deployed for expeditionary operations normally consisted of an Intelligence Branch officer, a cryptologic support detachment, and up to twelve intelligence operators.[65] That was perhaps the most transformational change in Canadian naval intelligence in this period.

The unclassified sources cited here are only a fraction of those extant on Canadian naval intelligence for the period since 1970. However, they probably provide a fairly representative snapshot of both CAF concepts of maritime C4ISR and the navy's efforts to develop those capabilities to operate effectively in its evolving environment. Like the other services, the navy's ability to adapt was evolutionary. Pulled in conflicting directions by the competing demands of domestic and alliance commitments, multiple simultaneous operations, declining vessel and aircraft resources, personnel limits, budgetary constraints, and shifting road maps toward an uncertain future, it could not have been otherwise.

Changes in Air Intelligence

The Canadian air force that emerged from unification had five major missions in 1970: air defence of North America under the NORAD treaty,[66] offensive nuclear strike missions in wartime under NATO, ASW, search and rescue, and strategic and tactical airlift.[67] With three exceptions—removing the nuclear weapons from the NORAD and the NATO roles in 1972 and deployments of CF-18 fighter-bombers into combat in the 1990–91 Persian Gulf War and the 1999 Kosovo air campaign—the missions of the air force did not change over the next thirty years.

What did change was, first, how the air force was organized to carry out these missions. The general trend was toward consolidation of C2 and of resources. In 1970, the air force was divided into Air Defence Command, 1 Canadian Air Group, the Maritime Air Group, the Air Transport Command, and 10 Tactical Air Group, the latter two splitting responsibility for strategic airlift and tactical aviation. Initially, 10 Tactical Air Group was part of the FMC, and also operated CF-5 fighters to support land forces. The Maritime Air Group and the Air Transport Command shared responsibility for search and rescue. The Training Command was responsible for all aircrew training. Each had its own headquarters, dispersed across the country, plus 1 Canadian Air Group's headquarters in Germany (it became 1 Canadian Air Division [1CAD] in 1988).[68]

Given the intent of unification, some of these structures made sense: the Maritime Air Group worked closely with the navy (MARCOM), and until 1970 10 Tactical Air Group gave the FMC integral air support. But 1 Canadian Air Group/1CAD in Europe did not support Canada's mechanized brigade, and the other formations functioned independently of each other. It was an unwieldy command arrangement, and standards suffered. So, five years later the DND/CAF began consolidating these functions and assets under a single authority by creating the Air Command.[69]

Under this structure, all the previously separate commands were redesignated air groups (air transport, fighter, maritime, tactical air, training, and air reserve). The next major change followed the end of the Cold War. 1CAD was disbanded in Germany in 1992–93, with its aircraft reassigned to the Fighter Group back in Canada. The division was reconstituted in 1997 and took over operational command of all Canadian air force resources. At the same time, Air Command headquarters was disbanded and moved to NDHQ, where it became the Air Staff.[70] Finally, in 2011 the air component of the CAF was renamed the Royal Canadian Air Force.

Second, due to budget reductions, the air force got smaller during the 1990s. The number of aircraft in service declined from about 725 in 1991 to 525 in 1999. The air force lost part of its CF-18 fleet, all 45 CF-5 fighters, 16 medium transport, and 63 light observation helicopters and aerial refueling aircraft. The Sea King replacement was cancelled, and several modernization projects were put on hold. The air force did acquire new CC-130 transports and the Griffon utility helicopter (the four CC-177 strategic transports did not appear until 2007). But the air force also lost vital personnel: pilots and maintainers. As chapter 11 shows, during the Kosovo air campaign the air force drew heavily on more limited resources than had been available in the 1990–91 Persian Gulf War. As such, it was a "combat capable" but not a "full spectrum" air force.[71]

Third, like the navy, the air force came late to employing professionally trained intelligence personnel. For example, having finished the BIOC in 1977, Maj. Alex Chambers became the first professional intelligence officer at CFB Shearwater, replacing a pilot major in that position. In 1986 Chambers became the first intelligence professional to serve as senior staff officer of intelligence at Air Command headquarters, a position previously filled by pilots. His successor, Maj. Susan Beharriell, was also a professional intelligence officer. In 1 Canadian Air Group/1CAD in Europe, the air intelligence staff were either intelligence officers or navigators serving in intelligence slots. Within 1CAD, each fighter squadron had an intelligence staff consisting of a captain, a sergeant, and two junior noncommissioned members. The 4 Wing (Cold Lake) had a ten-person staff headed by a major, but the 3 Wing (Bagotville) had only three personnel. The 1CAD intelligence unit in Germany consisted of only a single captain, but it was represented by a major at NATO's 4 Allied Tactical Air Force headquarters.[72]

The rationale for this was clear. Writing in 2002 from the perspective of supporting tactical fighter operations, Capt. Paul Johnston explained first that CAF fighter squadrons have no integral intelligence collection capabilities. Those were concentrated in specialized aerial reconnaissance squadrons (primarily operated by Canada's allies).[73] This had not always been the case. Both the CF-104 and the CF-5 had a limited photoreconnaissance capability, but it was lost when they retired[74] and was not restored in the CF-18. Likewise, from 1972 to 1995 the air element had operated the Kiowa light observation helicopters for reconnaissance, target marking, and observation in support of ground operations. That too was not replaced. With the important exception of the CP-140 Aurora in the ASW/maritime surveillance role, the gradual erosion of the CAF's integral aerial reconnaissance capability greatly increased the CAF's dependence on allied resources. However, as will be shown in chapters 7 and 10–12, those assets were not always available to the CAF when needed or optimized for their required tasks.

Thus, the flow of intelligence was top-down from higher headquarters or formations, such as NORAD and NATO, and by other intelligence organizations. The intelligence that CAF squadrons received already had been collated and analysed by an external intelligence staff. Furthermore, fighters are a theatre-wide asset; they usually have a larger AOR than would an army unit and may be directed to different parts of it at different times or even simultaneously. So, their target and self-defence intelligence needs are wide-ranging. The CAF air element saw intelligence as a support or enabling function.[75]

The CAF's air intelligence policy, as summarized in 1986, provided more breadth to this. It started by emphasising that successful operations depend on timely and accurate intelligence and that providing it was the responsibility of Air Command intelligence staffs. They had to be prepared to provide "basic and current Intelligence as well as Intelligence advice to commanders during training and planning for contingency tasks" and "Combat Intelligence in the field during actual operations and training exercises." The policy stated that Air Command's intelligence interests would be broader in peacetime (due to multiple taskings) than during operations. If this assertion is taken to mean that commitment to an operation would tend to focus intelligence assets mostly on that mission, then it makes sense. Nevertheless, the policy argued that this made it imperative that Air Command be supported by "professional Intelligence organizations" at all levels.[76] Here we can see the rationale for assigning professional intelligence personnel to the positions previously held by nonspecialists.

Air Intelligence priorities included, first, maintaining a "basic foreign intelligence data bank" and providing current intelligence on the commander's areas of intelligence interest. Second, the Air Command Intelligence Section (A2) would be expected to "disseminate intelligence information" to facilitate planning by the command headquarters staff and by formation and unit commanders and their staffs "in support of their assigned operational roles."[77] Third, they were required to "perform key functions" during operations and exercises and to support operational planning. They would also carry out other tasks based on the type and content of intelligence requirements stated in the annual submission to Air Command, NDHQ, and the CIS; the present tasks assigned to Air Command; and the factors already identified as basic to the command's intelligence policy. Training was given highest priority.[78]

The policy recognized that the intelligence requirements of units and formations would vary between them and according to tasking priorities and changes of commanders. Those requirements were to be reviewed annually and submitted to the A2 section. The section itself was responsible to the commander of Air Command for "initiating, interpreting and monitoring of the Command's Intelligence plans, policies and procedures."[79] Their other duties included providing the commander with intelligence regarding potential enemy capabilities against North America, NATO, and other areas where command resources might be deployed; maintaining an "orderly and timely" flow of intelligence and information to command units and formations to meet operational training needs; developing and implementing Air Command intelligence policy; and performing staff assistance visits and operational evaluations of formation and unit A2 section functions and capabilities.[80] In 1CAD (1997), the head of A2 was a lieutenant-colonel.[81]

Air Command headquarters assumed responsibility for foreign intelligence production and, with assistance from the NDHQ/CIS staff, for distributing it to units and formations as resources and security restrictions allowed. Subordinate A2 sections were discouraged from maintaining "extensive" files on any countries other than those in which they had "a direct interest due to current tasking."[82] They were expected to limit their production to intelligence received from Air Command headquarters and to briefing their commanders and staffs. This was intended to allow the A2 sections to concentrate on professional development and continuation training of nonintelligence unit personnel. Command policy was clear on one thing: A2 section personnel were not to be assigned non–intelligence-related duties that might inhibit their ability to perform their intelligence functions. And nothing was to jeopardize or interfere with their intelligence training.[83] This policy articulated a firm commitment to professionalizing air intelligence.

When 1CAD withdrew from Europe in the early 1990s, its intelligence personnel were reassigned to units and bases in Canada. At about the same time Air Command established an operational/general (G) staff, with the senior staff officer A2 becoming the command G2. The G staff (including G2) would be stood up to exercise control over specific operations. While this source (the March 1991 issue of the *Air Command Intelligencer*) explained that the G2 staff would be responsible for identifying potential threats to aircraft and aircrew, it made no mention of targeting.[84] This seems like a significant oversight, given the role of CAF CF-18s in the Persian Gulf War at that very time.[85] But it was consistent with the fighter concept of operations that targeting intelligence would come from higher headquarters and formations.

Fighter Group headquarters, which also incorporated Canada's NORAD regional headquarters, was unique in being a joint national and binational chain of command, with missions to both protect Canadian sovereignty and defend North America. These missions lie outside the scope of this book and so are not discussed further. What can be said is that the group's A2 section was organized to support the commander's efforts to fulfil both responsibilities. But the Persian Gulf War had shown that Canada might deploy its fighters overseas again, so by the summer of 1992 the A2 section was standing up an intelligence cell to cover contingency operations.[86]

Lt.-Col. Susan Beharriell, the Air Command A2/G2, laid out in 1996 the intelligence implications of the changes arising from the 1994 defence white paper. The new 1CAD headquarters intelligence centre was charged with providing "timely, accurate and relevant intelligence support to Air Force operations."[87] Since the centre would be the normal recipient of intelligence and special products from the DGI, NORAD, and other agencies, it should have been responsible for "planning, mounting and sustaining Intelligence support to Contingency Operations."[88] In fact, it was constructing a shielded facility for that very purpose. But "reengineering" reduced staffing at headquarters and freed up intelligence personnel to be reassigned to tactical-level formations. So, that role devolved onto wings. In 1998, eighty-eight air intelligence personnel were serving in 1CAD headquarters, its various wings, and the air staff at NDHQ. Furthermore, air force intelligence took on the targeting task. Air intelligence personnel had begun training to staff coalition air operations centres, and targeting was to be introduced into the BIOC curriculum. Yet, the increased demands on the air force after 9/11 made it clear that air intelligence lacked the personnel to support all of the air force missions. In response, the commander of Air Command authorized new positions.[89]

Within the new Air Staff at NDHQ, an intelligence adviser worked under the assistant chief of the Air Staff for plans and requirements in the Directorate of Force Employment, whose role was "to influence strategic level decisions" on providing and utilizing air force resources. The Directorate of Force Employment kept the Air Staff chief informed about current air operations and force employment issues. During joint or combined operations, the director of the Directorate of Force Employment served as the J3 (air operations) on the NDHQ Joint Staff Action Team, a "virtual team" composed of all the joint staffs that met weekly and controlled all CAF operations. The adviser's job was to provide intelligence advice to help define the air force posture for operations and "influencing national force employment decisions."[90] This yielded five main tasks: providing advice on intelligence issues to the Air Staff chief, the staff itself, and subordinate formations; influencing national intelligence "procedures, policies and doctrine" and producing strategic-level air intelligence doctrinal inputs (in coordination with the Directorate of Force Employment [air division intelligence section] and the 1CAD A2); coordinating strategic intelligence input into contingency planning; participating in "strategic/mission analysis and long-term planning"; and conducting liaison with the land and naval staffs, NDHQ staffs, OGDs, and foreign intelligence agencies.[91] This role in effect made the intelligence adviser the main conduit for strategic air intelligence input from the DGI and other sources to the Air Staff.

According to Cox, based on *Defence Intelligence Review* data, as of 2003 1CAD headquarters' A2 section had the largest concentration of intelligence personnel in the air force. And it remained the headquarters for Canada's NORAD region. Within the A2 a lieutenant-colonel was principal adviser and staff officer for intelligence matters in 1CAD, whose tasks included developing, monitoring, and coordinating intelligence architecture and systems and ensuring connectivity and liaison with other intelligence agencies and subordinate units. As before, there were smaller A2 sections at the five operational wings plus the Data Interpretation and Analysis Centres at the Maritime Air Component wings at CFBs Comox and Greenwood.[92] Air defence of North America under NORAD does not feature in the operations discussed in this book. However, that task—which serves primarily an indications and warning intelligence function—involves CAF personnel in high-level C4ISR activities and consumes some CAF intelligence resources.[93]

One major change in air intelligence support to operations was the CAF's adoption of UAVs. Compared to its allies, Canada came late to the UAV capability. This is more remarkable for the fact that Canada was a pioneer in UAV development. Canadair Limited developed the CL-89 drone in the 1960s for the Canadian, British, and West German armed forces, though it never entered service with the CAF. Both the CL-89 and the larger CL-289 (designed in the 1970s–80s) were jet-powered drones, launched from a ground vehicle, and carried small cameras or other sensors. They flew preprogrammed paths to intelligence targets and then on to a recovery site. Canadair (later Bombardier) developed the CL-227 "Peanut" and two successors but could not find any buyers. So, Canada's interest in UAVs languished until the end of the 1990s. In 2000 the DND announced the Joint UAV Surveillance and Target Acquisition System project, with the CAF launching test and evaluation experiments the following year.[94]

The war in Afghanistan accelerated the acquisition process. When Canada agreed to take command of the International Security Assistance Force (ISAF) in Kabul in 2003, it had to quickly fulfil its commitment to provide a UAV capability to the multinational brigade. As a result, the CAF purchased "off the shelf" four Sperwer UAVs produced by the Canadian-French consortium Oerlikon-Contraves/SAGEM. Additional units were bought later to replace operational losses. Like the CL-89/289, the Sperwer was rail-launched and recovered by parachute but was propeller-driven.[95] The Sperwer's performance and utility in support of operations is discussed in chapters 12 and 13.

When the CAF shifted its AOR from Kabul to Kandahar in 2005, it began to search for a successor to the Sperwer. The military created a new UAV/ISR project and in July 2007 solicited proposals from Canadian industry for systems that could meet the CAF's needs, which spanned the spectrum from tactical-level operations to theatre-level assessments. The 2008 report of the government's Afghanistan panel, headed by John Manley, strongly endorsed the acquisition of a "high-performance" UAV with ISR capabilities. The winning candidate was the Israeli-designed Heron, which the CAF had trialed in 2003. It was a long-range (twenty-four-hour endurance), medium-altitude UAV that carried electro-optical and infrared sensor systems, synthetic aperture radar, and an EW package and could be launched and retrieved on airport runways. The CAF leased three units from MacDonald-Dettwiler for a three-year period. In what must be a record in Canadian defence procurement, only five months passed between awarding of the contract and deployment of the aircraft.[96] Chapter 13 discusses the Heron's use on operations. In the meantime, the CAF also acquired and deployed on operations a number of smaller tactical UAVs: Scan Eagle, Maveric, and Skylark-I.[97] The Afghanistan War did not create the CAF's need for UAVs but gave it an impetus that previously had been lacking.

Writing in 2008, Lt.-Col. Bill MacLean, the 1CAD A2, highlighted several major changes in the air force intelligence function over the previous sixteen years. His first instinct was to discuss how technology "has transformed the way we collect, process and disseminate Intelligence within the Air Force—as it has in all environments."[98] But he chose instead to focus on how air intelligence has supported an increasingly "expeditionary" air force. It has deployed widely, but "the Intelligence footprint has often been small in size. As a result, those Intelligence personnel posted to Air units had few opportunities to deploy in direct support of our air assets."[99] They occasionally filled slots supporting army operations.

With its increased demand for air intelligence products, the Afghanistan War expanded opportunities for A2 operators. They have served in the ISAF Combined Air Operations Centre (CAOC), and as imagery analysts for the CAF Sperwer UAV detachment. The stand-up of the Joint Task Force–Afghanistan (JTF-A) air wing at Kandahar airfield in March 2008 brought air intelligence engagement to a new level. The wing had its own A2 staff, whose tasks were to provide intelligence support to all wing air units and contribute to the overall JTF-A intelligence architecture. This created demands for product and personnel, imagery analysts in particular, to the extent that the A2 staff expanded threefold within six months. The Heron UAV required an intelligence support team to run its sensors and to analyse the data it collected. All of this raised force generation issues, since supporting the wing, meeting the demands for the imagery analysts, and sustaining A2 operations for the whole air force all had to be met by drawing from the same pool of personnel.[100] This challenge probably prompted the 1CAD A2 to mount the Air Intelligence Working Group in November 2009. Its intent was to determine how to continue to develop the A2 function while finding sustainable solutions to improving support to deployed operations.[101]

Like the navy, the air force came late to professionalizing its intelligence staffs. Given its missions, this is understandable. Unlike the Maritime Patrol Aircraft, which were directed to ocean areas to conduct searches, tactical fighters did not have to locate targets themselves. Their missions were shaped by higher external technical sources that directed them to specific targets in the air or on the ground. But the CAF came to see the value of having trained intelligence personnel providing mission support. These did not appear out of nowhere; they were the products of a small but steady flow of officers and noncommissioned members who came out of the CAF's intelligence school, their taught skills also honed by real-life operational experience.

Intelligence Training

From 1970 to 2000, the Canadian Forces School of Intelligence and Security was located at CFB Borden, Ontario. Since then, it has been housed at CFB Kingston, renamed the Canadian Forces School of Military Intelligence (CFSMI). At Borden, intelligence training was one small section of the two-discipline school. Course data show that between 1970 and 2010 intelligence trainers conducted nearly one hundred courses: at least twenty-five serials of the BIOC and seventy-three of the Trade Qualification Intelligence Operators course. At least a dozen of these were for reserve intelligence personnel. They graduated over three hundred MI officers and over nine hundred MI operators. Ten of the BIOC courses and thirty operator courses were conducted from 2002 on, when wartime increased demand. In 2000–1 the trade qualification course content focused on "briefing presentation skills, research and writing, equipment recognition, and a strong information technology component."[102]

The move to Kingston came about after an external consultants' study recommended that intelligence training remain at Borden. Drawing upon arguments developed by the Army G2 (then Lieutenant-Colonel Jensen), Land Forces headquarters made a strong opposing case (later supported by the air force and the navy) that ultimately carried the day. Their central point was that the nature of the MI function was changing to meet the demands of the evolving operating environments and of incorporating new capabilities, and thus the training programs had to change as well. This required a new stand-alone facility.[103]

The army buttressed its argument first by quoting its capstone doctrine publication, *CFP 300*, which asserted that "intelligence and information gathering will be a major activity." This would require "a more sophisticated understanding" of how to manage collection capabilities "and most important how to process and analyze the collected data and information" by adopting a "system of systems approach."[104] Second, training efficiencies required access to schools and units that provided these capabilities. These were available at CFB Kingston, not at Borden.

So, the move went ahead in 1999–2000. But because of the high demand placed on the CFSMI—as of 2005 it was running courses for one thousand students per year with a staff of fifty-seven—it outsourced some courses (including BIOCs) for regular and reserve naval officers to the Canadian Forces Fleet School at Québec City (on-site and by distance learning) and for Land Force officers and noncommissioned members to the army reserve units.[105] In addition, there were combat intelligence courses (run at brigade headquarters), specialized courses for naval and air intelligence, and an initial HUMINT course run by British instructors. There were also efforts to introduce cultural awareness training and intelligence analysis skills. In 2008, the CFSMI graduated its first class of interrogators course students in fourteen years. Prior to 2003, all CAF imagery analysts were trained at intelligence schools in the United States and the United Kingdom. But in 2002 after several years of preparation, the Canadian Forces Joint Imagery Centre formed its own training squadron. Within a few years it had graduated eighty-four CAF members, DND civilians, and Five Eyes personnel and was mounting advanced courses, such as motion imagery analysis. Many of these graduates deployed to Afghanistan to support the JTF-A Air Wing Heron UAV surveillance operations. Professional development continued with conferences, allied personnel exchanges, and courses at foreign intelligence schools.[106]

As always, numbers tell only part of the story. The value of training depends on the course content and the quality of the instructors. Without access to curriculum documents and course evaluations, the author is unable to comment on these components. However, some published and personal accounts offer insights into the relevance of the content to the conflicts the MI personnel eventually faced and the operations they had to support.

Overall responsibility for the program lay with the training authority. In the 1990s, that was the Canadian Forces Recruiting, Education and Training System. But in 1982 when the Intelligence Branch was separated from the Security Branch, the position of Intelligence Branch adviser was created. Once or twice a year the adviser would meet with the Intelligence Branch Council (the senior MI officers and chief warrant officers from NDHQ and the CAF commands and services) to discuss the state of the branch, including training. The Intelligence Training Steering Committee was "ultimately responsible for identifying deficiencies and recommending the way forward."[107]

Maj. Jerry Mayer, commanding officer of the Intelligence Training Company, Canadian Forces School of Intelligence and Security, from 1997 to 1999, and commandant of the CFSMI from 1999 to 2000, says that the Intelligence Training Steering Committee could recommend to the Canadian Forces Recruiting, Education and Training System the creation of a new course or changes to an existing one. The next step was to create a course training standard writing board chaired by a branch senior officer and including branch representatives from the services and commands. Once the training standard was approved, a course training plan writing board would convene. Upon approval of the training plan, the school would set a date for a pilot course based on the new course training standard and plan. The commander of the Intelligence Training Company/commandant of the school then would assign instructors, who would develop lesson plans based on the course training plan and its teaching points.[108]

Capt. (N) Andrea Siew, who served as branch adviser from 2001 to 2003, said that the Intelligence Branch Council's focus on training was about "professionalization of the Intelligence Branch," ensuring that "it has the right people with the right training in the right locations to meet the demands of operational commanders."[109] Mayer goes on to add that while the school was still at Borden, the BIOC had four major phases: three service-oriented and one strategic. Course content was mostly unclassified, and "there was limited insight into sources and methods, such as IMINT [imagery intelligence] and SIGINT." Course members received an "elementary understanding" of the "principal functions and capabilities" related to those disciplines. They would not develop those more specialized skills until they received the necessary clearances and were posted to the relevant organizations. Mayer concedes that the first BIOC was very basic and that those in the early 1980s were "very much lacking."[110] Captain (N) Siew, for example, who completed the BIOC in 1986, recalls that the one skill set she took away from it was how to do different types of briefings. She acquired the essential specialized service-specific knowledge she needed— "oceanography, acoustics, ASW, tactics"—only upon being posted to 14 Wing at CFB Greenwood. There it was all learned "on the job."[111]

As a captain, Rhe Probert took the Serial 8701 BIOC. He recalls that being run while the Cold War was still on, it focused on the Soviet military threat, "with a strong emphasis on threat organizations and equipment." The Serial 8701 BIOC was organized and conducted "to introduce students attending the course on intelligence matters at tactical, operational and strategic levels . . . [and] in all three environments."[112] He felt that it was sufficient to start national-level intelligence work.

Capt. Michel Beauvais, who had rebadged from armour to intelligence, took the BIOC in 1990. At that time it was just short of six months in length and consisted of three main parts. The first covered "the basics of Military Intelligence, including definitions, int doctrine, strategic intelligence, indications and warning, sources and agencies."[113] The second part covered the three environmental services, and all course members, regardless of service, participated. The course finished with a joint phase that was underdeveloped at the time. Few classes or briefings were classified. This phase placed great emphasis on (mostly Soviet) equipment recognition, how to produce intelligence estimates and reports, and how to deliver intelligence briefings. Beauvais felt that "it gave me good grounding to start my Int career."[114]

Intelligence training changed over time. In 1996 after serving as an analyst in the DGI, then as a brigade G2 and as the intelligence staff officer at UN headquarters in Cyprus, Captain Beauvais returned to the Canadian Forces School of Intelligence and Security as the course officer for the BIOC, the reserve equivalent, and the Advanced Combat Intelligence course. He was also tasked to refresh the BIOC, which had not been updated for several years. There was concern about its relevance to the conflicts and operations the CAF had experienced in the Balkans, Somalia, and Haiti. He and the Intelligence Training Company team adjusted the course content to provide more service-specific and less cross-environmental training. This meant that, for example, an army intelligence officer spent more time on intelligence preparation of the battlefield and less on air or naval material.[115]

The basic and joint portions of the course were updated. However, it remained mostly at the unclassified level because creating classified training material was time-consuming and security clearances presented an obstacle. There was also pressure to graduate as many officers as possible. The trainers also revamped the three noncommissioned member courses. Those for warrant officers saw the most revision because of the high demand for them on operations. Battle group commanders specifically sought the warrant officers' skill and experience levels to reinforce their intelligence sections.[116]

Content changed and eventually included guest lecturers, site visits, crisis/country studies, and classified material. The revamped 1997 BIOC included not only the standard skill sets but also guest lectures and visits to relevant sites: the CSE's main SIGINT station (Canadian Forces Station Leitrim); the Canadian Forces Joint Imagery Centre; the Canadian Forces Electronic Warfare Centre; and the DGI. In addition, the navy students visited the Atlantic region Maritime Air Group bases and TRINITY, while air force students visited the air transport wing at CFB Trenton and the fighter squadron at CFB Bagotville.[117] Lt.-Cmdr. Shawn Osborne, the CFSMI commandant in 2004–6, conceded that the heavy demand placed on the school at that time due to wartime intelligence personnel requirements meant that the school did not have "enough time to conduct revision of training material or to incorporate lessons from various operations. As a result, we continue to focus on the processes necessary to support the Intelligence Function over all other aspects of training."[118]

Beauvais concurs. He says that after the 9/11 attacks and the operations in Afghanistan that followed, "there was growing pressure to change the BIOC once more." This was to ensure that CAF intelligence officers had "the right skills to be immediately employable in high-pressure jobs in Kabul and later Kandahar."[119] Even so, some had to be sent home from the Afghan mission because they could not meet the demands of the job. Beauvais says that many blamed this on the compression of training to generate greater throughput. In 2006 he chaired a review board on qualification standards, and the result was the return to a longer BIOC course that devoted more attention to asymmetric warfare and counterinsurgency. Similar, but not so drastic, changes were applied to the noncommissioned member courses. The review board also recognized the need for more than one level of intelligence training. Informally it suggested creating the Advanced Intelligence Officer Course, and the concept received rapid approval. The course was aimed at senior captains and junior majors who, on graduation, could be assigned to run units such as an All-Source Intelligence Centre or to develop intelligence architectures to support many different types of operations, which were often very complicated. The course trained the candidates in intelligence theory and planning and drew heavily upon guest lecturers, who shared their knowledge and experience.[120]

Beauvais took command of the CFSMI in November 2007 and remained in charge until 2009. During his tenure, the school was reorganized into three branches: occupational (basic), which reverted to unclassified content to eliminate lengthy candidate backlogs due to the growth of the Intelligence Branch and delays with security clearances; speciality (including HUMINT, counterintelligence, and strategic analysis); and collective training for those deploying to Afghanistan. The CFSMI also had been designated the training establishment responsible for managing the Canadian Imagery Analyst training program run by the Canadian Forces Joint Imagery Centre. Due to the classified content and the equipment requirements, the centre taught the course in-house. But to meet the demand imposed by these new courses and added responsibilities, the CFSMI staff increased from an establishment of forty-seven to about sixty. The commanding officer's rank was set at lieutenant-colonel.[121]

However, given that the school's main focus in the late 1990s was still on intelligence support to those being posted to the navy, army, and air force, Mayer felt that it was unrealistic to expect its graduates to be "fully prepared" to fill many of the DGI (analyst) slots. Before the Afghanistan War, courses made a limited effort to prepare students for the strategic- and operational-level intelligence jobs but "did not sufficiently cover analytical methodologies" largely because there was a lack of doctrine and specific reference material at that time.[122] Out of necessity, those shortfalls received more attention once the CAF engaged in the war. But until the Advanced Intelligence Officer Course started, there was little available beyond the BIOC to prepare MI personnel for the analyst role. As one former DND official put it, "Just plugging anyone into an analyst's slot doesn't make them one. Even with training, some 'get it' and some don't, or they don't get the right training. There wasn't much training available anyway: The courses at the CF [Canadian Forces] Intelligence School weren't optimal for analytical training. PCO/IAS [Privy Council Office/International Assessments Secretariat] ran a formal course for all govt analysts. DND civilians and some military took it, but it fell short too. It was mostly 'who's who in the zoo,' not strong on analytics."[123] The *DIR* had recommended the creation of a permanent "centre of excellence" for DI analyst training, but it ran into obstacles. Likewise, the CDI was unable to develop training partnerships with other government departments.[124]

The upshot of this was that the CAF's intelligence training programs left it with highly skilled tactical MI officers and intelligence operators—though never in sufficient numbers to meet demand—but short of qualified strategic intelligence analysts. That was problematic when the CAF entered the Afghanistan War because its very nature required strategic-level analytical thinking not just within NDHQ but also at the deployed operational and tactical levels. That said, Lt.-Col. Jensen argues that the operators also had to be able to "design an intelligence architecture, plan and execute ISR collection operations, provide skilled leadership" in the various intelligence centres to which they were assigned, "and be highly skilled in providing dynamic support to operational and tactical commanders."[125]

CONCLUSION

Even as he highlighted expeditionary air intelligence, Lieutenant-Colonel MacLean's initial instinct to focus on the influence of technology on it was not misplaced. The interaction of technology and intelligence processes is one of the prominent themes that emerges in this chapter. Technological changes in weapons and in the conduct of operations inevitably shaped how intelligence would be collected, analysed, distributed, and exploited. Reflecting on this, Col. Michel Foucreault asserted that "there has not been any revolution in Intelligence processes and techniques since the end of the Cold War. Rather, there has been a surge of evolutions based on the types of adversaries and leaps in technologies."[126] Indeed, arguably most of the technical revolutions in intelligence had occurred long before the end of the Cold War. The computer was central to this. The emerging battle spaces—actual and anticipated—required increasingly rapid intelligence collection and processing, hence the need for all-source fusion. The C4ISR "system of systems" made that possible. All three services moved in that direction, but except aboard naval vessels until the Afghanistan War made new equipment, personnel, and funding available, fully fused C4ISR remained more aspirational than real.

That said, there was a transformation of MI during this period that occurred in the human domain. It had two dimensions: first, the professionalization of intelligence. From an organizational perspective, this entailed integrating professionally trained intelligence personnel into headquarters staff positions and into positions supporting sharp-end units.

The second dimension was related to the first: a change in attitude toward intelligence. While the need for this always had been acknowledged, perceptions about it varied widely. It was closely integrated with operations on navy ships. Until the 1980s the army treated it as a marginal activity, and the air force had no responsibility for collecting it—it always came to them from remote organizations. But as the following chapters will show, CAF operations in the 1990s and after forced commanders to rethink their views on the utility of intelligence. Time and again, intelligence proved itself essential to the conduct of operations, especially in politically charged conflicts where local situational awareness could help tactical actions achieve strategic effects. In this respect, the CAF's Special Operations Forces (SOF) led the way. SOF operational and tactical commanders conducted "command-led and intelligence-driven" operations. Out of necessity, "they were informed, educated and voracious consumers of intelligence" who depended upon the intelligence producers to be on their game.[127] By the end of the Afghanistan War especially in the army, intelligence personnel, processes, and products had moved from the margins to center stage. If the new attitude toward intelligence could be summed up in a single slogan, it might be "Don't leave home without it."[128]

NOTES

1. Ben Connable, *Military Intelligence Fusion for Complex Operations: A New Paradigm*, Occasional Paper, OP-377-RC (Santa Monica, CA: Rand, 2012), 4.
2. *Director Intelligence Report Defence Intelligence Review—Report to the DCDS*, 20 May 2004, 14, obtained by Alan Barnes under Access to Information, available in the Canadian Foreign Intelligence History Project.
3. C. M. Isbister, *Intelligence Operations in the Canadian Government*, Privy Council Office Report 70-11-09 (9 November 1970), 31, 34–36, 52.
4. R. J. Robson, British Liaison Officer, to Acting Director, CBNRC, re: "Recent Comments by Director GCHQ," 7 June 1971, Intelligence Policy Committee documents 70-11-03 to 72-01-07—Isbister review, LAC, RG25, BAN 2017-00430-0, box 21, file 1-1-1-1, part 2.
5. "The Espionage Establishment of 1974," produced and directed by William I. Macadam, research directed by James R. Dubro, *The Fifth Estate*, aired 9 January 1974 on CBC Television, https://www.cbc.ca/player/play/2661556131 (video), https://docs.google.com/file/d/0B0wdLKxvw1xsam9FSU9XcXRPSWs/edit (transcript).
6. Cabinet Committee on Security and Intelligence, Minutes, 15 January 1975, CCSI documents 66-06 to 80-04, LAC, RG 25, BAN 2017-00440-5, box 59, file 29-4-CCSI, part 1; and N. K. O'Neill and K. J. Hughes, *History of the Communications Branch of the National Research Council*, Canadian Foreign Intelligence History Project, 7 vols. (Ottawa: CSE, 1987), 1: chap. 2, 27; 4: chap. 25, 14, chap. 26, 39–40.
7. O'Neill and Hughes, vol. 1, chap. 2: 28, 31.

8. O'Neill and Hughes, vol. 1, chap. 2, 1 and 4, annex G, Intelligence Advisory Committee, SIGINT Memorandum no. 1, "Control of Signal Intelligence (SIGINT) in Canada," 24 August 1977.
9. O'Neill and Hughes, vol. 1, chap. 3, annex L (n.p.). The CSE organizational chart for 1975 shows that three of its five SIGINT production groups were dedicated solely to MI. On the CFIOG, see Bill Robinson, "The Communications Security Establishment (CSE)," in *Top Secret Canada: Understanding the Canadian Intelligence and National Security Community*, ed. Stephanie Carvin, Thomas Juneau, and Craig Forcese (Toronto: University of Toronto Press, 2020), 87n31.
10. James Bamford, *The Shadow Factory: The Ultra-Secret NSA from 9/11 to the Eavesdropping on America* (New York: Anchor, 2009), 2, 336–39; Martin Rudner, "Canada's Communications Security Establishment from Cold War to Globalization," *Intelligence and National Security* 16, no. 1 (2001): 111; John Adams, former chief of the CSE, interview with author, 6 November 2019.
11. Robinson, "Communications Security Establishment," 73.
12. Lt.-Col. Daniel Villeneuve, "A Study of the Changing Face of Canada's Army Intelligence," *Canadian Army Journal* 9, no. 2 (Summer 2006): 18.
13. J.A.E.K. Dowell, *Intelligence for the Canadian Army in the 21st Century: "Enabling Land Operations"* (Kingston, Ontario: DLCD, 2012), 10.
14. Capt. Robert Martin [Martyn], "Trends in Tactical Intelligence: Global Conflict and the Canadian Forces," *Army Doctrine and Training Bulletin* 1, no. 2 (Fall 1998): n.p., http://publications.gc.ca/collections/Collection/D12-9-1-2E.pdf.
15. *Canadian Forces Publication CFP 310 (1): Airborne*, Vol. 1, *Canadian Airborne Regiment* (Canadian Forces Headquarters, 10 October 1968), preface. See also Maj. K. G. Roberts, "Canadian Airborne Regiment," *Sentinel: Magazine of the Canadian Forces*, June 1968, 1–3.
16. Lt.-Col. Greg Jensen, comments on draft chapter, 7 January 2021, with corrections in email, 27 January 2021. See also Harold A. Skaarup, *Out of Darkness—Light: A History of Canadian Military Intelligence*, 4 vols. (New York: iUniverse, 2005), 1:424–27, 429–30, 2:157, 257, 296–97.
17. Brig.-Gen. Glenn Nordick, interview with author, 9 June 2019.
18. Mobile Command Headquarters, *Intelligence Collection and Analysis Centre Field Trial, Post Exercise Report*, 13 February 1986, cover letter by Lt.-Col. P. O'Leary and p. 1, Lt.-Col. Greg Jensen, private papers (loaned to author); H. A. Skaarup to author, email, 6 January 2020.
19. O'Leary, cover letter to MCH, *Intelligence Collection*.
20. O'Leary, cover letter.
21. MCH, *Intelligence Collection*, 3–5. Note that UAVs were referred to as remotely piloted vehicles in the document.
22. MCH, *Intelligence Collection*, 1–2, 6; 1st Canadian Division, *JFHQ Organization and Responsibilities*, fig. 2, "Organization JFHQ & Sig Regt" (1992), Jensen Papers, states that on operations, "maximum benefit is gained by collocating the EWCC/ICAC near the JTFHQ."
23. J.A.E.K. Dowell, "RV 87 Intelligence and Analysis Collection Centre," *Intelligence Branch Journal*, no. 6 (Spring 1988): 11–13, reprinted in Skaarup, *Out of Darkness—Light*, 2:91–94. The ICAC concept was also incorporated into the Land Forces Staff College annual course CPX.

24. Comment on draft manuscript by Lt.-Col. Greg Jensen, received by author, 7 January 2021. Jensen was the chief writer, assisted by Maj. J.A.E.K. Dowell and Capt. Keith Sutton.
25. Maj.-Gen. J. K. Dangerfield, "The 1st Canadian Division: Enigma, Contradiction or Requirement?," *Canadian Defence Quarterly* 19, no. 5 (Spring 1990): 7–14.
26. Maj. Gordon Ohlke, interview with author, 13 June 2019. Ohlke commanded the Intelligence Company during the crisis.
27. Thomas Crosbie, "Getting the Joint Functions Right," *Joint Forces Quarterly*, no. 94 (2019): 99, https://ndupress.ndu.edu/Portals/68/Documents/jfq/jfq-94/jfq-94_108-112_Crosbie.pdf?ver=2019-07-25-162025-397. See also "The Army Doctrine Hierarchy [Organizational Chart]," *Army Doctrine and Training Bulletin* 1, no. 1 (1998): 1.
28. Martin Rudner, *Intelligence and Information Superiority in the Future of Canadian Defence Policy* (Ottawa: Carleton University, Norman Paterson School of International Affairs, Centre for Security and Defence Studies, 2001), 1, 3–4; NATO Standardization Office, *AINTP-1(A) Intelligence Doctrine* (January 1995), chaps. 1, 4–7, 11, Lt.-Col. Greg Jensen, private papers.
29. Philip H. J. Davies, "ISR versus ISTAR: A Conceptual Crisis in British Military Intelligence," *International Journal of Intelligence and CounterIntelligence* 35, no. 1 (2021): 73–100.
30. Col. Glenn Nordick, "Guest Editorial—Exploiting Opportunity: Thoughts on ISTAR," 1–2, and Capt. Dave Travers, "Brigade ISTAR Operations," 43–49, both in *Army Doctrine and Training Bulletin* 3/4, no. 4/1 (Winter 2000/Spring 2001), touted the benefits of the ISTAR approach.
31. Maj. George Franz, *Information—The Fifth Element of Combat Power* (Fort Leavenworth, KS: School of Advanced Military Studies, US Army Command and General Staff College, 1996), https://apps.dtic.mil/dtic/tr/fulltext/u2/a314297.pdf; Directorate of Army Doctrine, "Information Operations," *Army Doctrine and Training Bulletin* 1, no. 2 (1998): n.p., https://publications.gc.ca/collections/Collection/D12-9-1-2E.pdf; DND, B-GG-005-004/AF-010 *CF* [Canadian Forces] *Information Operations* (Ottawa: DND, 15 April 1998), Lt.-Col. Greg Jensen, private papers.
32. Electronic Warfare Associates–Canada, *DG INT Report: Information Warfare and the Canadian Forces* (Ottawa: NDHQ, 1996), 1–14.
33. Lt.-Gen. (ret.) Michel Gauthier, interview with author, 5 November 2019.
34. Lt. (N) Darren Knight, interview with author, 6 November 2019; Lt.-Cmdr. Alexandre Lebel, "The Royal Canadian Navy's Intelligence Function: In Line, Off Focus," *Canadian Forces College, JCSP*, no. 41 (2014/2015): 7–8.
35. "The CISA Brief," in Skaarup, *Out of Darkness—Light*, 1:495 and 3:195.
36. Marc Milner, *Canada's Navy: The First Century* (Toronto: University of Toronto Press, 1999), 258–76. See also Cmdr. (ret.) Peter T. Haydon, "What Naval Capabilities Does Canada Need?," *Canadian Military Journal* 2, no. 1 (Spring 2001): 25–26.
37. Milner, *Canada's Navy*, 277–310. Integration of the Canadian patrol frigates with USN carrier battle groups was possible only because the RCN and the USN used common C4I systems.
38. Canada, DND, *Shaping the Future of Canadian Defence: A Strategy for 2020* (Ottawa: DND, 1999), 2; Canada, DND, Maritime Command, *Adjusting Course: A Naval Strategy for Canada* (Ottawa: Canada Communications Group, 1997), 27–29; Canada, Directorate of Maritime Strategy, *Leadmark: The Navy's*

Strategy for 2020 (Ottawa: DND, 2001), 4, https://www.files.ethz.ch/isn/15017/ENG_LEADMARK_FULL_72DPI.pdf.
39. Canada, DND, *MARCOM Capability Planning Guidance 2000* (September 1999), chap. 1: 3–4, author's copy. See also Capt. (N) D. E. Collinson, "Maritime Operations in the 1990s," *Niobe Papers* 5 (1993): 37.
40. Richard Howard Gimblett, *Operation Apollo: The Golden Age of the Canadian Navy in the War against Terrorism* (Ottawa: Magic Light for DND, 2004), 80.
41. Canada, CAF, Maritime Command, *The Maritime Command Vision: Charting the Course to Navy 2008* (Halifax: Maritime Command, 1993), chap. 1, 5 and 12; chap. 2, 6–7.
42. Canada, DND, *Adjusting Course*; Canada, Directorate of Maritime Strategy, *Leadmark*, 87–89, 95, 108, 112, 117.
43. Canada, DND, *Adjusting Course*, 22.
44. *Adjusting Course*, 23, 26.
45. *Adjusting Course*, 35.
46. *Adjusting Course*, 36.
47. Lebel, "Navy's Intelligence Function," 5–6.
48. Lt. (N) Darren Knight, "The Intelligence Function and the Fleet of the Future," *Intelligence Branch Journal* (Fall 1988), quoted in Skaarup, *Out of Darkness—Light*, 2:129–30. See also "DCDS Planning Guidance—Intelligence, Surveillance and Reconnaissance (ISR) for the CF," draft, 7 November 2000; and "Concept of Operations National/CF ISR Centre," draft, n.d. [post-1999].
49. Canada, DND, "MARCOM Capability Planning," chap. 1: 1, 4; chap. 2: 9; chap. 3: 6, 8; and Canada. DMS, *Leadmark*, 128.
50. Canada, Maritime Command, *The Canadian Navy's Operational Intelligence Surveillance and Reconnaissance (ISR) Blueprint to 2010*, Executive Summary, n.d. [1990s], author's copy (hereafter cited as *ISR Blueprint*).
51. Canada, DND, *Adjusting Course*, 35.
52. See the entry for the SQR-501 (CANTASS) at "Canadian Navy SONAR Systems," Haze Gray & Underway: Naval History and Photography, www.hazegray.org/navhist/canada/systems/sonar/; "AN/SQR-501 CANTASS," Military Periscope, https://www.militaryperiscope.com/weapons/sensorselectronics/sonars/ansqr-501-cantass; and Brian E. Cooke, *Uses of Spatial Audio in Sonar* (Downsview, Ontario: Defence & Civil Institute of Environmental Medicine, 2002), 4–5, 15.
53. Milner, *Canada's Navy*, 272, 274.
54. Maj. Neil Scott, "A Vision for the Future of Maritime Aviation," *Canadian Air Force Journal* 3, no. 3 (Summer 2010): 22–23.
55. Canada, Senate, Sub-Committee on National Defence, and Paul C. Lafond, *Canada's Maritime Defence: Report of the Sub-Committee on National Defence of the Standing Senate Committee on Foreign Affairs* (Ottawa: Sub-Committee, 1983), 17–18. See also Maj. Graham Edwards, "The Future of the CP140 Aurora," *Canadian Air Force Journal* 3, no. 3 (Summer 2010): 30–33.
56. *ISR Blueprint*, 22.
57. Dr. George Kolisnek, interview with author, 5 November 2019.
58. Skaarup, *Out of Darkness—Light*, 2:432–33; James Cox, "The Transformation of Canadian Defence Intelligence since the End of the Cold War" (master's thesis, Royal Military College of Canada, 2004), Canadian Foreign Intelligence History Project, 27; Lebel, "Navy's Intelligence Function," 17–19.

59. Knight, interview, and his comments on the naval intelligence section draft, 22 November 2020; and Lebel, "Navy's Intelligence Function," 15n46. On the timeliness of the recognized maritime picture, see Cox, "Transformation of Canadian Defence," 88.
60. GlobalSecurity.org, https://www.globalsecurity.org/intell/systems/jmcis.htm. On the Maritime Command and Control Information System, see Cox, "Transformation of Canadian Defence," 88.
61. Knight, interview. See also Capt. (N) Peter Avis, "Surveillance and Canadian Domestic Maritime Security," *Canadian Military Journal* 4, no. 1 (Spring 2003): 11.
62. Andrea Charron, "Ode to Canada's Maritime Security Operation Centres," Broadsides Forum (blog), *Canadian Naval Review*, 10 February 2020, https://www.navalreview.ca/2020/02/ode-to-canadas-maritime-security-operation-centres/; DND, "Naval Intelligence Enterprise Review," draft, n.d. [2019], 2, para. 4, author's copy.
63. *ISR Blueprint*.
64. *ISR Blueprint*, 16, 22, and 23.
65. Skaarup, *Out of Darkness—Light*, 2:433; Lebel, "Navy's Intelligence Function," 21.
66. North American Air [later Aerospace] Defence Command.
67. Canada, DND, *Defence in the '70s: White Paper on Defence* (Ottawa: DND/Information Canada, 1971).
68. Lt.-Gen. (ret.) W. K. (Bill) Carr, "Canadian Forces Air Command: Evolution to Founding," *Royal Canadian Air Force Journal* 1, no. 1 (Winter 2012): 13–14; Allan D. English, *Command & Control of Canadian Aerospace Forces: Conceptual Foundations* (Ottawa: DND, 2008), 52.
69. Carr, "Canadian Forces Air Command," 15–23, offers a personal perspective on the creation of Air Command. See also English, *Command & Control*, 52–53, 56.
70. English, *Command & Control*, 57–59, 71–72.
71. Martin Shadwick, "The Vanishing Air Force?," *Canadian Military Journal*, Commentary, 1, no. 3 (Autumn 2000): 64; Canada, Chief of the Defence Staff, *The Aerospace Capability Framework* (Ottawa: Director General Air Force Development, 2003), 33, 43.
72. Skaarup, *Out of Darkness—Light*, 1:163, 531–32; Cox, "Transformation of Canadian Defence," 50.
73. Skaarup, *Out of Darkness—Light*, 3:161.
74. Canada, Chief of the Defence Staff, *Aerospace Capability*, 44.
75. Canada, Chief of the Defence Staff, 13–14; Skaarup, *Out of Darkness—Light*, 2:51–52, 3:160–62.
76. Skaarup, 2:51–52. The command A2 section was expanded to twelve persons at this time.
77. Skaarup, 2:51–52.
78. Skaarup, 2:51–52.
79. Skaarup, 2:53.
80. Skaarup, 2:54.
81. English, *Command & Control*, 72. The A1, A3, and A4 slots were brigadier-general rank.
82. Skaarup, *Out of Darkness—Light*, 2:54.
83. Skaarup, 2:54–55.
84. Skaarup, 2:183–84.

85. See chapter 9.
86. Skaarup, *Out of Darkness—Light*, 2:209–10; Cox, "Transformation of Canadian Defence," 47; Dixie Dysart, "'Committed to Make a Difference': Canada's Role in the Inception of NORAD Counter-Drug Operations," in *Sic Itur Ad Astra: Canadian Aerospace Power Studies*, Vol. 2, *Big Sky, Little Air Force*, ed. W. A. March, 107–16 (Ottawa: DND, 2011).
87. 1996 Air Command Report, in Skaarup, *Out of Darkness—Light*, 2:352–53.
88. 1996 Air Command Report, 2:353.
89. Skaarup, *Out of Darkness—Light*, 2:354, 375, 433.
90. Skaarup, 2:429–30.
91. Skaarup, 2:430.
92. Cox, "Transformation of Canadian Defence," 99.
93. Skaarup, *Out of Darkness—Light*, 2:72, 208–9, 406–7, and 3:37–38, 77–78, 94–95, 408–11; Cox, "Transformation of Canadian Defence," 48.
94. Andrew Carryer, *A History of Unmanned Aviation in Canada* (Brampton, Ontario: MacDonald, Dettwiler, 2008), 2–4; Skaarup, *Out of Darkness—Light*, 2:134–35, provides a 1988 status report on the CL-227 project; Danny Garrett-Rempel, "Will JUSTAS Prevail? Procuring a UAS Capability for Canada," *Royal Canadian Air Force Journal* 4, no. 1 (Winter 2015): 19–20. The Joint UAV Surveillance and Target Acquisition System project was superseded by the Remotely Piloted Airborne System project.
95. Carryer, *Unmanned Aviation in Canada*, 4, 7; Garrett-Rempel, "Will JUSTAS Prevail?," 20–21.
96. Carryer, 5–8; Garrett-Rempel, 21–22.
97. Garrett-Rempel, 21.
98. Lt.-Col. Bill MacLean, "Intelligence in the Air Force: How Far We've Come—How Far We'll Go," in Harold A. Skaarup, "Out of Darkness—Light: A History of Canadian Military Intelligence," [vol. 4] (unpublished manuscript, 2018, author's copy), 109.
99. MacLean, 109.
100. MacLean, 109–10; Capt. Kyle Welsh, "Task Force Erebus: Providing Essential Support to Canada's Mission in Afghanistan," *Canadian Air Force Journal* 3, no. 2 (Spring 2010): 20–22.
101. Maj. Bill Becker and Lt. Scott Dauk, "Air Intelligence Working Group 2009," in Skaarup, "Out of Darkness—Light," [4]:111.
102. Course data gathered from Skaarup, Vols. 1–4. Figures should be considered approximate. See also his Vol. 1, 531, and Vol. 3, 99. In 1977, Maj. (ret.) Jerry Mayer and Maj. Alex Chambers were among the students on the first professional intelligence officers course run in seventeen years. Mayer, email to author, 10 January 2021.
103. Maj.-Gen. N. B. Jeffries (assistant chief of the Land Staff) to NDHQ, 18 December 1998; Maj.-Gen. P. Gartenburg (assistant chief of the Air Staff) to distribution list, February 1999. Copies provided in email to author by Lt.-Col. Greg Jensen, 4 May 2021. The navy's concurrence was explained in a separate email.
104. Jeffries to NDHQ.
105. Skaarup, "Out of Darkness—Light," [4]:118, 208–9.
106. Skaarup's volumes, especially the unpublished volume 4, 164–65, 188–90, 193–95. Lt.-Col. Rhe Probert, interview with author, 12 June 2019, discussed the additional professional development courses.

107. Skaarup, *Out of Darkness—Light*, 1:555, 560–61, 564; and Mayer, email to author, 10 January 2021.
108. Mayer.
109. Capt. (N) Andrea Siew, interview with author, 7 November 2019.
110. Mayer, email to author, 10 January 2021.
111. Siew interview.
112. Lt.-Col. Rhe Probert, interview with author, 12 June 2019 (written answers).
113. Lt.-Col. (ret.) Michel Beauvais, email to author, 27 January 2021.
114. Beauvais.
115. Beauvais.
116. Beauvais.
117. Mayer, email to author, 10 January 2021; Skaarup, *Out of Darkness—Light*, 3:147. The Canadian Forces Fleet School in Québec City also ran BIOCs. See Skaarup, "Out of Darkness—Light," [4]:118.
118. Skaarup, [4]:209.
119. Beauvais, email to author, 27 January 2021.
120. Beauvais.
121. Beauvais; Lt. (N) Steven Morris, "CFJIC—The Evolution of Imagery Analyst Training," in Skaarup, "Out of Darkness—Light," [4]:164.
122. Mayer, email to author, 10 January 2021.
123. Interview with a former DND official who requested anonymity, 4 November 2019.
124. Anonymous DND official, interview; DND, *Defence Intelligence and Enterprise Renewal (DI&ER), Initial Assessment of the Defence Intelligence Review, 2019*, author's copy.
125. Lt.-Col. Greg Jensen, comments on draft chapter, 7 January 2021.
126. Col. Michel Foucreault, email to author, 14 August 2020.
127. Jensen, comments.
128. For many years that was the advertising slogan of the American Express credit card.

PART II

INTELLIGENCE SUPPORT TO CANADIAN MILITARY OPERATIONS, 1970–2010

5

THE OCTOBER CRISIS

Countering Terrorism in Québec, 1970

From 5 October to 28 December 1970 the October Crisis gripped Canada. Terrorists from the Front de Libération du Québec (FLQ) had kidnapped a British diplomat and a Québec provincial cabinet minister and had killed the latter. The federal government had proclaimed the draconian War Measures Act, under whose terms nearly five hundred people were arrested. And between 9 October 1970 and 4 January 1971, thousands of troops deployed across Québec and eastern Ontario to assist the police in maintaining security and searching for the terrorists. Because the police were the lead agency during the crisis, Canadian MI played a mostly supporting role in the events of that time. Until now that story has been untold. This chapter fills that gap in the historical record.

BACKGROUND

The roots of the October Crisis can be traced to the British conquest of Québec in the mid-eighteenth century. This left under British rule a large Francophone population with an identity and culture defined by language, law, and faith. This conundrum has since defined the Canadian national political experience. By the early 1960s when the powerful idea of national self-determination was sweeping away the former colonial empires, Québec was undergoing rapid political and social change. Many Québecois were demanding an end to inequality and "English" economic dominance in the province. For some, that was not enough; they wanted an independent Québec. And a minority were prepared to fight for it. They founded the FLQ.[1]

The FLQ

The FLQ was never a single, cohesive organization. Rather, it was a movement: a loose, changing amalgam of individuals and small groups that came together over time under the FLQ's banner. They represented a cross-section of the Québec nationalist community: working class, students, intellectuals, and activists. There was little central direction; anyone could create a cell and call themselves the FLQ.[2] As such, it has been described as a "focused illusion," a wheel "minus the hub," and "amateur revolutionaries."[3]

Likewise, the FLQ does not stand out as one of the more effective or dangerous terrorist groups of the second half of the twentieth century. When compared to groups such as the Irish Republican Army and al-Qaeda, the FLQ comes up short. It lasted a mere eight years (1963–70). Each successive wave of FLQ cells carried out a handful of attacks before being arrested and jailed. Among its many weaknesses, the FLQ never tried to undermine the security of the state by, for example, attacking and undermining the police as the Irish Republican Army had done. Instead, the FLQ focused on symbolic targets, such as mailboxes marked with the royal crown. Even the victims of the October Crisis—British trade commissioner James Cross and Québec labour minister Pierre Laporte—were symbolic targets. The group killed only six people over eight years. It did, however, create a climate of fear during the crisis even within the federal government. But the FLQ was too small and too poorly organized to transform tactical success into strategic victory. There was no popular uprising or revolution, and Québec remained within Canada.[4]

The October Crisis: A Brief Chronology

The crisis began on 5 October 1970. The FLQ's Liberation cell abducted Cross from his home in Montreal.[5] Municipal and provincial police forces and the Royal Canadian Mounted Police (RCMP) responded with a massive manhunt for the kidnappers and their victim.[6] Shortly thereafter, the FLQ issued its demands: the release from prison of twenty-three convicted FLQ members, whom they called "political prisoners," and broadcast of the group's manifesto, which would explain its goals and its actions.[7] The provincial and federal governments opposed releasing the prisoners, but CKAC radio and Radio-Canada (the French-language channel of the Canadian Broadcasting Corporation) broadcast the manifesto.[8] When Cross was kidnapped, the Chenier cell was in Texas buying guns. They rushed back to Montreal, and on 10 October they abducted Laporte.[9] Two days later, the federal government requested that the CAF provide "assistance to civil authorities" in the capital region by providing armed guards for vital points and close protection for very important persons.[10] This would allow the RCMP to focus on the FLQ.

Over the next few days the FLQ cells laid low, but their spokespersons and sympathizers were rallying students and others to go on strike, and scattered walkouts and rallies occurred.[11] On 14 October sixteen high-profile figures mostly allied with the separatist provincial political party, the Parti Québecois, called for the two governments to negotiate a hostage/prisoner exchange with the FLQ. In fact, Parti Québecois leader René Lévesque went further, claiming that "Quebec no longer has a government."[12]

On 15 October the Québec government requested the deployment of troops "in Aid of the Civil Power" to relieve some of the pressure on the police in the province by taking over guard duties and assisting in searches. As required under the National Defence Act, the CAF responded immediately, and thousands of troops deployed in Montreal and across the province.[13] Early on 16 October the federal government, claiming that a state of "apprehended insurrection" existed in Québec, proclaimed the War Measures Act, which suspended many civil liberties. Acting under the provisions of the act, and its successor, the Public Order (Temporary Measures) Act, police in Québec arrested 497 people suspected of some kind of connection to the FLQ. Most, some 435, were innocent of any such association and were released after a relatively brief detention.[14] The FLQ responded in dramatic fashion. On 17 October the Chenier cell strangled Laporte after he attempted to escape. They then announced his death and left his body to be found in the trunk of a car near CFB St. Hubert.[15]

That was the apogee of the crisis. To the extent that the FLQ had gained any public support during the first two weeks of the crisis, it evaporated with the murder of Laporte. In spite of concerns about the loss of civil liberties, Québecois overwhelmingly supported the War Measures Act.[16] Since the act banned any publicity that supported the FLQ, the group lost control of the narrative. The FLQ was no longer dictating the pace of events and shaping perceptions.[17] FLQ members were simply fugitives on the run. Police, assisted in their searches by the CAF, eventually tracked down the Liberation cell. They negotiated Cross's release on 3 December. His kidnappers were flown into exile in Cuba. Twenty-five days later the Chenier cell was captured, and the crisis came to an end. A few days later the last of the troops deployed back to their bases. However, the emergency powers invoked during the crisis remained in force until 30 April 1971.[18]

Operations GINGER and ESSAY (the deployments in Ottawa and Québec, respectively) involved some 9,800 troops,[19] the largest deployment of troops for a domestic operation in Canada up to that time. The remainder of this chapter examines how the decisions were made, how the armed forces were used, and how intelligence supported their operations.

POLITICAL DECISION MAKING

The three levels of government involved have since been criticized for overreacting to the crisis and for using excessive power to break the FLQ.[20] Knowing what we know now, it is a fair criticism. Far from being a coordinated attack, the two cells had acted independently; Laporte's abduction was improvised hastily to prevent the Liberation cell from giving up prematurely.[21] The RCMP commissioner at the time, Leonard Higgitt, advised the federal cabinet that the Québec government had overestimated the size of the FLQ.[22]

But the crisis did not occur in a political vacuum. It is important to try to see it through the eyes of the decision makers at the time. Several factors probably underpinned their views, decisions, and actions. The first was the FLQ's sustained record of violence over the previous eight years. Second, in 1968 the FLQ had circulated among its members and sympathizers a treatise on insurgency, titled *Revolutionary Strategy and the Role of the Avant-Garde*, that described a step-by-step process of escalating revolutionary violence. Political kidnappings were among the last steps before a wider uprising.[23] According to scholar Michael Gauvreau, the VCDS, Lt.-Gen. Michael Dare, considered the document to be "of great significance" since it outlined a plan for the liberation of Québec.[24]

Third, by the spring of 1970, police in Québec had disrupted two FLQ kidnapping plots targeting the American and Israeli consuls.[25] In April, John Starnes, director general of the RCMP Security Service, had warned the solicitor general about this very possibility: that the FLQ would use kidnappings to force the release of its members from prison.[26] Fourth, in August 1970 *La Presse* published an interview with two FLQ members training at a Palestinian camp in Jordan. They claimed to be preparing for political assassinations and other activities along the lines of the *Revolutionary Strategy* document.[27] Fifth, after Laporte was taken, there was the appearance of political mobilization in Québec in favour of the FLQ. Add to all of that the fact that the group had kidnapped two high-profile figures within six days, and it was not wholly unreasonable for the governments to conclude that this terrorism campaign was well organized and could escalate into something worse.

This may have persuaded Prime Minister Pierre Trudeau to express concern about the emergence of a "parallel power" in Québec.[28] "The population was already being excited by people like Chartrand and Lemieux, and there would be the danger of the movement gaining many converts, resulting [in] the creation of a popular movement. In order to prevent such a development, it would be necessary for the government to act before it lost the power to act."[29] Undoubtedly, it was this line of thinking that guided Trudeau's comments to reporter Tim Ralfe, who challenged him on the deployment of troops. Trudeau stated bluntly that "there's a lot of people with bleeding hearts . . . that don't like to see people with helmets and guns. All I can say is, go on and bleed. But it's more important to keep law and order in society than to be worried about weak-kneed people who don't like the looks of a soldier's helmet."[30] Ralfe then asked, "How far would you go with that?" Trudeau replied, "Just watch me."[31]

This was brave talk, since behind the bravado the truth was more alarming. In spite of the FLQ's record and all of the warning signs preceding the crisis, the provincial and federal governments and their police forces were unprepared to handle it. In December 1969 an analysis presented to the federal cabinet showed that the federal government was not prepared to counter Québec separatism generally. The cabinet began discussing options in January 1970, including infiltration, disruption, and intelligence collection. According to historian Sean Maloney, a senior military officer briefed cabinet ministers on ACP procedures, leaving them "astonished" since none of them had ever given it much thought. Maloney goes on to say that it was not until July 1970, when the Security Service presented a threat assessment that described the FLQ as a danger to national unity, that the prime minister and his staff began to develop a counterstrategy against the FLQ. But that was not presented to the cabinet until 19 October—after the deployment of troops, proclamation of the War Measures Act, and the murder of Laporte.[32] In fact, the government's response to the Security Service's "strategic warning" was even more laggard than Maloney suggests. An internal appreciation drafted on 29 October 1970 stated that the July document "went to Cabinet level, but was not considered during August nor, indeed, had it been examined in detail by 5 October, 1970 at the time of the Cross kidnapping."[33]

Given this, it is not surprising that the records of the Cabinet Committee on Security and Intelligence—the senior federal decision-making body during the crisis[34]—show a government shaken by the kidnapping of Laporte, rendered pessimistic by the apparent deterioration of the political situation in Québec, and fearful that the FLQ would carry out more violent actions.[35] The committee was so worried, in fact, that Trudeau told the VCDS that he wanted "tanks on all the bridges in Montreal."[36] By having troops deployed in Ottawa, Montreal, and elsewhere, he essentially got what he wanted.

In addition, at the urging of A. E. Ritchie, undersecretary of state for external affairs, who was worried that the federal government was losing the information war to the FLQ, the government launched its own information operation. On 23 October it established within the prime minister's office a "Special [later Strategic] Operations Centre" to be the focal point for a single information operations strategy. The intent was to contain and preempt the FLQ's information efforts to ensure that the situation in Québec did not deteriorate further.[37]

At the outset of the crisis, the Québec government had tried to continue a "business as usual" approach. Since Cross was a diplomat, securing his release was a federal government responsibility. But the mood changed after Laporte was kidnapped. The Québec cabinet met for three days in Montreal, concluding that it could not give in to the FLQ's demands but keeping open a negotiating channel (lawyer Robert Demers) and stalling for time. According to William Tetley, then a provincial cabinet minister, Premier Robert Bourassa remained calm though his position wavered, as did those of other ministers. Tetley himself initially favoured releasing the prisoners demanded by the FLQ but later urged the premier to call in the troops and impose martial law. The Québec ministers were angry at the unyielding position of the federal government because they felt that it did not understand their feelings about Laporte. The provincial government found itself under intense pressure from not just the FLQ but also conflicting views of the provincial opposition parties, the media, and the sixteen "eminent personalities."[38]

Both levels of government contained many experienced politicians. But nothing in their experience had prepared them for the difficult legal, political, moral, and life-and-death decisions that confronted them in this crisis. Their thinking converged in the wake of Laporte's kidnapping. The Québec government wanted troops to relieve the police of some duties so they could concentrate on searching for the kidnappers. The federal government wanted a "show of force" to deliver a shock to the FLQ and its supporters.[39] These considerations led to the provincial government's decision to call for military ACP.

THE CANADIAN ARMED FORCES IN THE OCTOBER CRISIS

Although Operations GINGER and ESSAY overlapped in time (and to some degree location), they were distinct in legal and constitutional terms. GINGER, launched on 12 October and limited to Ottawa, entailed "assistance to civil authorities." That is, one federal agency, the CAF, provided "armed assistance" to another federal agency, the RCMP. Some two thousand troops from the CFB Petawawa-based 2 Combat Group relieved the RCMP from guard duties on vital points and provided close protection to very important persons. The troops also supported ACP operations in Hull and western Québec. Operation GINGER ended on 21 November.[40]

Operation ESSAY was the real "show of force" operation. Invoking provisions of the National Defence Act, on 15 October the Québec attorney general requested that armed forces be deployed in ACP. Under these terms, a provincial government has the right to request military support from the armed forces. The request went directly to the CDS, who was obligated to respond. In this case, the CDS (Gen. Frederick Sharp) was attending a NATO meeting, so the VCDS (Lieutenant-General Dare) acted on his behalf. In fact, the CAF had started moving troops as early as 9 October, when it appeared that the FLQ was planning to attack the former CAF ammunition depot at Camp Bouchard, just north of Montreal. On 15 October due to effective preplanning, deployments may have commenced before the VCDS received the ACP request. The bulk of the nearly eight thousand troops eventually deployed across Québec came from the CFB Valcartier-based 5e Groupement de Combat (Combat Group). The remainder came from troops of the 2 Combat Group not deployed in Ottawa, CFB Gagetown in New Brunswick, and the Canadian Airborne Regiment and the 1 Combat Group in Alberta. Most took over guard duties and supported police search operations. The paratroopers were the theatre reserve and the Immediate Reaction Force.[41]

C2 of the forces was complex because of the two distinct operations and the three levels of government involved. And there are differing perspectives on how it worked. Sean Maloney says that FMC headquarters at CFB St. Hubert near Montreal did not exercise command over units in Operation GINGER but does not say who did.[42] In a later interview with Douglas Bland, Dare said that he "directed the entire FLQ action from CFHQ."[43] That was true of Operation GINGER,[44] but the C2 arrangements for Operation ESSAY appear to have been more decentralized.

Interviewed by the press at the time, some army officers serving in Operation ESSAY said that "we take our orders from the police."[45] Strictly speaking, that was incorrect. The Duchaîne Report on the crisis clarifies the relationship. The Québec government had placed Maurice Saint-Pierre, head of the Sûreté du Québec (SQ), the provincial police, in charge of all security forces in Québec during the crisis, including the military. However, although he or his immediate subordinates could "direct" the military to assist the police, legally they could not issue orders to the CAF. The military chain of command had to issue any orders for military activity. That began with the FMC commander, Maj.-Gen. Gilles Turcot, who exercised operational control of all armed forces deployed during Operation ESSAY (including air units integral to FMC or under command). Under him Brig.-Gen. Jacques Chouinard commanded the 5e Combat Group, the conducting formation that comprised all of the army units deployed in Québec. FMC headquarters had to approve police requests for joint operations.[46]

But lack of experience working with the police and of established procedures for doing so hampered initial collaboration. Early in the crisis a regional direction centre had been created to coordinate the response of the three police forces. Once the military joined the fray, FMC and the 5e Combat Group assigned staff to the regional direction centre. But its role in decision making was unclear. So, Chouinard restructured it to serve as a police liaison cell to FMC, not the reverse. This way, he could make decisions on the use of his forces in consultation with the police via Major-General Turcot and the centre. However, even this arrangement did not eliminate problems, because the regional direction centre and the headquarters of 5e Combat Group (later joined by members of the Airborne Regiment) were all colocated in the SQ headquarters. The police were confused by the distinctions between these three groups and sometimes made requests to the wrong one. The federal government also muddied the waters by issuing requests for guards to FMC or to the 5e Combat Group through the regional direction centre. Likewise, the military had deployed into both operations without an internal security doctrine or rules of engagement (ROE). Deployed units solved the former problem by falling back on their standard operating procedures from UN peacekeeping operations, while CFHQ solved the latter, drafting ROE that were sent to the two brigades.[47] These problems notwithstanding, the CAF conducted itself in a quiet, professional manner that earned it credit among the media and the public.[48] That is all the more commendable given that the CAF was functioning in an unfamiliar operational environment. The CAF was structured and trained for conventional (and nuclear) warfare against mechanized enemy formations in Europe. But in this crisis it found itself in a situation where the enemy consisted of hidden individuals fighting by unconventional means and where a misstep by any soldier could have had drastic political consequences for the nation. It was an environment that cried out for timely and accurate tactical intelligence.

INTELLIGENCE SUPPORT TO OPERATIONS

Since the police were the lead agencies for operations against the FLQ, with the military acting in support, the police also took the lead in the intelligence task, developing and following up intelligence leads. However, the CAF deployed its own intelligence assets as well. Years earlier, the three police forces had created the Combined Anti-Terrorist Squad. At the time of Cross's abduction, the squad had three officers each from the Montreal force and the SQ and six from the RCMP. They followed up leads from the public, contacted their informers, made some arrests, and shadowed suspects several of whom were the kidnappers, although this was not known at the time. But the results in the first five days were disappointing.[49]

Once Laporte was kidnapped, police searches ramped up dramatically. Some 3,500 police from the Montreal and SQ forces searched homes, did snap searches at roadblocks, and processed thousands of tips from the public. The flow of information to the police began to increase after the killing of Laporte.[50] By late October the Montreal police were receiving 5,000 telephone calls per day with supposed leads on the FLQ.[51] The volume of calls was so high that SQ director St. Pierre had to issue the following plea to all Québec police forces: "Because of the large number of different types of complaints from persons who suspect (too often without good reasons) their neighbours of being sympathisers of the FLQ movement or even being members of it, it would be important to try to check by all means at your disposal, the authenticity of the information or complaints before taking action. One would eliminate by the same way, embarrassments of having the police visiting the same place several times."[52]

In this feverish milieu it is not hard to understand how Paul Rose, one of Laporte's abductors, was supposedly spotted three times in one day but evaded capture each time. Time and again, the police carried out big raids and promised results to the Québec government but failed to deliver. Moreover, some four hundred Montreal police were tied down guarding vital points. It was these concerns, at least in part, that prompted the Québec government to ask for military ACP.[53] At the time, however, Commissioner Higgitt told the Cabinet Committee on Security and Intelligence that while the police were "strained ... there was no shortage of manpower, from a police point of view."[54]

There are conflicting views on interservice police cooperation and the quality of their investigative work. According to the 1981 report of the Duchaîne inquiry, the RCMP's Strategic Operations Centre (not to be confused with the Special [later Strategic] Operations Centre in the prime minister's office), created to deal with the crisis, was poorly prepared to do so. The force had underestimated the threat, did not understand what political conditions had given rise to the FLQ, and lacked effective channels for disseminating the information it had. The report also criticized the force for not sharing intelligence with the SQ.[55]

The McDonald Royal Commission report about RCMP activities arising from the crisis, also issued in 1981, says that the directive to follow up every lead had swamped the police and that there were coordination problems among the three forces. But it also claimed that the RCMP had evidence that the FLQ had infiltrated the SQ and was reluctant to share information with the SQ for that reason.[56]

More recent scholarship, however, gives the RCMP Security Service more credit than Duchaîne had done for assessing correctly and responding more effectively to the FLQ threat. The service had advised the government on the implications of the failed kidnapping plots in the spring of 1970. Along with the Québec and Montreal police forces, the Security Service set up a contingency plan to handle any political kidnappings. In July the service had given the solicitor general a report on potential threats to internal security. During the crisis the Security Service was able to bring to bear many more human resources: some three hundred members of the service were deployed in Montreal (including those assigned to the Combined Anti-Terrorist Squad). The other forces conceded that the RCMP was the best prepared of the three to deal with the crisis. It was RCMP surveillance, prompted by a tip from the SQ, that ultimately located Cross and his kidnappers. On the other hand, the government entities could be faulted for being unprepared to evaluate the political implications of the intelligence provided by the Security Service, a classic problem of intelligence producer/consumer relations.[57] Moreover, it is clear that the RCMP did not demand the extra police powers created under the War Measures Act and had little role in drafting the extensive list of possible detainees. Both can be attributed instead to the political leadership in Québec and Ottawa.[58]

So, how did this police-driven intelligence milieu impact the ACP operations of the CAF during the crisis? Owing to limited access to original sources, it is not possible to give a definitive answer; what follows is incomplete and thus tentative. When FMC was established in 1966, its headquarters included a small intelligence staff under then director of intelligence, Lt.-Col. William Tenhaaf. While grouping a few tasks, such as air photo requests, under himself, he had set up his staff along three functional lines: operations; establishments, equipment, trial, and training; and counterintelligence. The operations section, consisting of two officers and two NCOs, would determine requirements for the FMC commander, staff, and forces under command; handle requests for information; and carry out collation, interpretation, and dissemination—all of the stages of the intelligence cycle.[59] In early November 1970 the FMC intelligence staff (plus military police) comprised fifty-eight personnel.[60] During Operation ESSAY its operations section presumably performed those same functions to support deployed CAF units.

It is likely that some FMC intelligence personnel served in the Joint Operations Centre at the SQ headquarters. Maloney also mentions a Joint Intelligence Centre (JIC), which probably was colocated with the Joint Operations Centre. A CFHQ sitrep (situation report) from late November 1970 says that the "Combined Intelligence Centre" (presumably the JIC) with members from the armed forces, the RCMP, and the SQ and Montreal police was "reestablished" at that time, presumably having been disbanded at some earlier date.[61] To the extent that there was intelligence sharing between the police and the army, it normally would have occurred at this level. As noted above, it would have flowed mostly in one direction: from the police to the army.

However, the army did have access to sources and methods that only it controlled. This started at unit level. Troops on guard duty or on patrols reported any suspicious activity up their normal unit reporting chains.[62] Within the 1st Battalion, Royal Canadian Regiment (1 RCR), deployed in Operation GINGER, that reporting structure functioned as follows. The battalion headquarters command post included an Intelligence Section under the Operations Section. When forward of the unit base, the section deployed with the command post and "performed its normal function of collection, collation, interpretation and dissemination of military intelligence and reporting to the Operations

Officers." But while in base, because of its access to a variety of sources, the section reported directly to the senior CAF liaison officer working with the RCMP, municipal police, and the SQ on matters "concerning the gathering of military information."[63] The 1 RCR and the 2 Combat Group itself conducted their intelligence liaison with the RCMP through meetings at an Ottawa subdivision, by having an RCMP officer at combat group headquarters, and by having a liaison officer from the combat group at RCMP headquarters. A police liaison centre was established at the Hull police station, with a 24/7 communications link to the battalion command post. Most of the information gained was basic intelligence about the AOR gathered through area reconnaissance and from liaison with local authorities, including police.[64]

The 1 RCR developed its own intelligence collection plan that laid out a "division of labour" between the police and the military. Under this plan, both were responsible for observing and reporting on overt signs of FLQ presence (e.g., painted slogans, hostile attitudes among the population), FLQ hideouts, and likely targets of attacks. The police would be responsible for locating arms caches and training areas and noting patterns of arms thefts and raids. They would pass information on this to the military via liaison officers.[65]

The 8th Canadian Hussars armoured regiment's intelligence officer prepared a daily intelligence summary with information from the combat group's operations and intelligence staff derived from newspapers, radio, and "small amounts from police agencies." The unit's after-action report said that "access to information with any police security value was virtually impossible."[66] Such armoured units normally would have been used for mobile reconnaissance, but with a few exceptions most were dispersed on static vital point security. According to Maloney, this "severely limited Mobile Command's ability to gather timely information on developing situations, and thus the ability to respond rapidly."[67]

One exception to this was Operation EXTEND, conducted by the B Squadron of the 8th Canadian Hussars in western Québec on 22–24 October 1970. Four six-person teams conducted a driving reconnaissance (mounted in jeeps) through a number of communities, including Gracefield, Maniwaki, and Mont-Laurier. The intent was to get to know the terrain, the communications networks, and the local population; liaise with police and civic officials; establish or confirm vital points; and seek information or follow up leads on FLQ members and activities. In one location they carried out a search at the request of the SQ and retrieved thirty-one sticks of dynamite that had been found and reported by a hunter. The postoperation report contained information on dams, roads, bridges, airfields, power stations, police, mayors, and mildly suspicious activity by a few local individuals suspected of sympathy for the FLQ.[68]

At about the same time (22–27 October), D Company of the 1 RCR carried out a similar area reconnaissance north, east, and west of Hull, Québec. Their tasks were identical to those carried out by the B Squadron. The troops detected some unusual activity, investigated, and reported it to battalion headquarters for action by the police. They found the population generally friendly, but "in isolated instances there appeared to be an underlying fear of the FLQ."[69] The after-action report concluded that the operation was too short to validate its effectiveness but also that there was sufficient evidence to show that this type of reconnaissance could provide a commander with detailed information and "can confirm intelligence obtained from various other sources."[70] What stands out from these reports, when considered within the larger context of this book, is that these patrols were virtually identical to CAF efforts to gain SA in Afghanistan.

The CAF deployed its tactical SIGINT capability: the 2 (EW) Squadron from the 1 Canadian Signals Regiment. The unit, which had been on exercise with the NATO brigade in Germany, landed in Trenton, Ontario; off-loaded its vehicles, equipment, and personnel; and moved on to Montreal after a brief stop at its base in Kingston. Operating under an RCMP warrant, the squadron monitored radio transmissions relevant to the crisis.[71]

The armed forces also deployed aerial surveillance assets. These included the CF-5 fighter jets equipped with photoreconnaissance pods. However, since the military could not access this data rapidly, it had limited tactical utility. According to confidential sources cited by Maloney, FMC was able to use two MARCOM CP-121 Tracker aircraft, equipped with infrared line-scan surveillance systems, that were on loan to the Department of Energy, Mines and Resources. In addition, the US Army loaned FMC an OV-1 Mohawk reconnaissance aircraft fitted with an infrared line-scan system and side-looking airborne radar. The aircraft flew from US bases over rural areas of the Laurentians, where the FLQ maintained some safe houses and training camps. On at least one occasion infrared line-scan data prompted an SQ raid, with backup from the Immediate Reaction Force. The reconnaissance flights also maintained a watch on sensitive sites, such as hydro stations and power lines.[72] The information gained from aerial assets would be sent to the JIC, and once it was processed the Joint Operations Centre would order the Immediate Reaction Force to respond (with the police in the lead).[73] Sources do not provide any details on how the JIC processed and shared this aerial surveillance data.

Distribution of intelligence within CFHQ was a multifaceted process. Sitreps (which are operations-focused) normally would have gone to the National Defence Operations Centre for collation and distribution to the senior leadership in NDHQ (in particular, the CDS, VCDS, and DCDS). The DGI would have been a recipient for the operational perspective. All intelligence summaries would have gone to the NDIC, would be incorporated into daily briefings to the CDS and the DCDS, and would be included as part of a DGI-generated intelligence summary for broader distribution. That included the minister and

DM of National Defence The finished products also would have been shared with law enforcement via the JIC.[74]

In the wake of Laporte's murder, DI was also drawn into the development of the information operations strategy of the prime minister's office to counter the FLQ's propaganda effort. Although this work did not directly impact CAF operations, it is worth examining since it guided high-level policy making and decision making to some degree.

The government's message themes were intended to discredit and counter the FLQ narrative by emphasizing its negative effects on Québec society.[75] The *Offensive Psywar Guidelines* put forth by the prime minister's office laid out an information operations plan to isolate, divide, and destroy the group. Wisely, this document placed intelligence at the heart of the plan. It stressed that "no campaign can be successful unless all relevant facts about the enemy are obtained, evaluated, and disseminated."[76] All agencies should ensure that all information that could be used in the propaganda campaign be made available as quickly and completely as possible. It should draw a clear distinction between proven facts and "intelligent surmise."[77] All agencies involved should fully and freely share information and intelligence. Information about individuals, organizations, techniques, strengths, and weaknesses would be of value to the campaign. But the guidelines also stressed that such information should differentiate between the FLQ and the "regular separatist," such the Parti Québecois, and "ensure accuracy of identification of P.Q. with FLQ, *if any*."[78]

The Special Operations Centre in the prime minister's office tasked Lt.-Col. Henri Chassé, the military liaison officer for the centre, and RCMP liaison officer Jules Allard with "build[ing] the most comprehensive picture of the FLQ."[79] In response, the deputy chief of intelligence and security convened a special group known as TERM that produced on 29 October 1970 an appreciation of the FLQ's likely courses of action over the forthcoming six months.[80] The following day Chassé referred to it during the centre's daily meeting, and its key findings were digested into an annex to the government's position paper titled *A Moment of Decision*.[81]

TERM's study assumed that the FLQ was guided by the doctrine espoused in the *Mini-Manual of the Urban Guerrilla* and the *Revolutionary Strategy* document but that it would not adhere rigidly to either. The TERM study argued that the FLQ's doctrine emphasized the need for popular support and that such support was lacking. This—and the deployment of the army—would force the FLQ to reevaluate its approach. Having just reached the second stage of revolutionary activity—mass mobilization—at the point when the War Measures Act was invoked, it would have to revert to the first stage: radical agitation, including internal organizing, strikes and demonstrations, bombings, kidnappings, and assassinations. The study concluded that the next six months would be relatively insignificant for the FLQ but that it would be important for the authorities to maintain rule of law and demonstrate good intentions to disarm the arguments advanced by the FLQ. Raids had disrupted the FLQ leadership and inhibited coordination, and interrogations would yield additional intelligence, but this would also reveal to the FLQ "the limits of our penetration."[82]

The TERM study went on to say that public opinion had been impressed by the government's decisive action but that such support would begin to waver. The movement would benefit from a period of reorganization through the fall and winter by drawing on a potential base of popular support. Sufficient apparatus, personnel, and logistics remained in place to sustain revolutionary activity at a lower level. But the War Measures Act, detentions, long periods of inactivity, and fear of informers was likely to lower morale. So, the FLQ had suffered a "general reversal," but those who had carried out the kidnappings had "enjoyed considerable success."[83] The report asserted that there were cells across the province but that there were not enough activists to advance the movement from stage one to stage two. The cells could cause administrative and economic dislocation but were not strong enough to organize the population for revolutionary activity. To maintain and improve morale, the movement was likely to engage in some small-scale activities. These would be carried out in areas remote from troop concentrations in order to force the authorities to disperse the security forces more thinly. Symbols of the federal government would be the most likely targets.[84] In sum, the FLQ had achieved a tactical success but had not gained a strategic victory.

The federal government took this assessment seriously and erred on the side of caution. Indeed, several incidents attributed to the FLQ in the summer of 1971 raised concerns about a possible revival of FLQ activity or actions by its sympathizers on the anniversary of the crisis. That degree of concern has since been called into question.[85] Nevertheless, in October 1971 the CAF deployed a small task force into the Montreal area. The force consisted of elements of 12e Régiment Blindé du Canada from CFB Valcartier and the 2 EW Squadron from Kingston. Operating again under RCMP warrant, the squadron (minus a detachment deployed north of Montreal) set up an EW coordination centre within the compound of FMC headquarters, whose intelligence and security section worked with the task force.[86] In any event, nothing significant occurred.

With the benefit of hindsight and access to more information, we now know that the TERM appreciation, like others that advised government leaders,[87] greatly overstated the threat posed by the FLQ in the period after Laporte's murder. TERM credited the group with greater size, cohesion, capacity, and resiliency than it had in reality. In fact, once the two cells were captured in December 1970, the FLQ all but ceased to exist. Scattered small cells continued to carry out occasional bombings and robberies during 1971, but thoroughly penetrated and compromised by the police and lacking any coordination or agreed strategy, their efforts were ineffectual.[88]

The gap between the reality of the post-Laporte FLQ and the TERM appreciation of it can be explained in several ways. First, the FLQ posed a new and unfamiliar analytical challenge for an MI organization more accustomed to counting tangible targets: tanks, troops, missiles, and ships. Second, the two active FLQ cells were not part of a larger network and had formed (and were operating) independently of each other. While not hermetically sealed, they were small and difficult to penetrate, so the police did not have a clear picture of the FLQ. The armed forces did not have alternative sources from which to draw upon to build their analysis. Third, through its actions in October, which reinforced the evidence accumulated earlier in 1970, the FLQ had succeeded in creating a deceptive illusion of strength where substance was lacking. The DND had no persuasive contrary data upon which to fashion a different picture of the FLQ.

Returning to the operational level, the army-police intelligence relationship during the October Crisis was notable in one respect. This may have been the army's first experience of intelligence-led operations. The evidence gleaned from the available sources suggests that the tactical intelligence was generally insufficient to yield success. In fact, it is clear that most of the intelligence leads came up empty simply because the larger FLQ network they were searching for did not exist. Although a few small caches of weapons and explosives were uncovered, none of the key figures in the FLQ were apprehended this way.[89] Rather, standard police investigative work led to the freeing of Cross and to the arrests of his kidnappers and the murderers of Laporte. The army and MI played no significant role in either instance. There are still gaps in the record and thus in the story. For example, existing sources tell us nothing about whether strategic SIGINT was used or whether any of Canada's Five Eyes partners shared useful information. But for all of its brevity and gaps, this chapter brings together in one place many fragments of the October Crisis MI story. Even if it is not a complete history, what we know now is more than the sum of its previously dispersed parts. But the significance of this chapter is greater than simply giving a clearer picture of this particular MI effort. Rather, in the unconventional nature of the threat, the multiagency coordination aspects of the intelligence task, and the intelligence-led operational dimension, the October Crisis experience presaged what would become the dominant paradigm of CAF operations and intelligence support to them after the end of the Cold War twenty years later.

NOTES

1. David A. Charters, "The Amateur Revolutionaries: A Reassessment of the FLQ," *Terrorism and Political Violence* 9, no. 1 (1997): 134–38; and D'Arcy Jenish, *The*

Making of the October Crisis: Canada's Long Nightmare of Terrorism at the Hands of the FLQ (Toronto: Doubleday, 2018), 5–15.
2. Charters, "Amateur Revolutionaries," 138–39. See Jenish, *Making of the October Crisis*, for a recent detailed description of the members.
3. John Oliver Dendy, "Canadian Armed Forces and the 'October Crisis' of 1970: A Historian's Perspective," in *Acta*, Montreal, 16–19 August 1988, International Colloquy on Military History 14 (Ottawa: International Commission of Military History, 1989), 322; Ronald D. Crelinsten, "The Internal Dynamics of the FLQ during the October Crisis of 1970," in *Inside Terrorist Organizations*, ed. David C. Rapoport (London: Frank Cass, 2001), 59; and Charters, "Amateur Revolutionaries," 133, 139.
4. Jenish, *Making of the October Crisis*, 19–22, 27–28, 30–31, 78, 80, 139–42, 144, 147; and Charters, "Amateur Revolutionaries," 141–43, 146–49.
5. Jenish, *Making of the October Crisis*, 205–6.
6. Louis Fournier, FLQ: *The Anatomy of an Underground Movement* (Toronto: NC Press, 1984), 220–22. The reader is cautioned that this source may include some incorrect information.
7. Crelinsten, "Internal Dynamics of the FLQ," 68, 70–73; Jenish, *Making of the October Crisis*, 239.
8. Crelinsten, "Internal Dynamics of the FLQ," 70–72; William Tetley, *The October Crisis, 1970: An Insider's View* (Montreal: McGill–Queen's University Press, 2007), 32, 35.
9. Crelinsten, "Internal Dynamics of the FLQ," 75; Jenish, *Making of the October Crisis*, 228–30, 233–34.
10. Sean M. Maloney, "'A Mere Rustle of Leaves': Canadian Strategy and the 1970 FLQ Crisis," *Canadian Military Journal* 1, no. 2 (Summer 2000): 81.
11. Jenish, *Making of the October Crisis*, 241–46; Fournier, FLQ, 241–42.
12. Tetley, *October Crisis, 1970*, 51–54.
13. Tetley, 60–61; Maloney, "'Mere Rustle of Leaves,'" 81.
14. Jenish, *Making of the October Crisis*, 209, 252, 254–56, 264, 285; and Tetley, *October Crisis, 1970*, 82.
15. Jenish, *Making of the October Crisis*, 260–63.
16. Charters, "Amateur Revolutionaries," 161–62.
17. Charters, 162.
18. Jenish, *Making of the October Crisis*, 264–69, 273–85; Tetley, *October Crisis, 1970*, 81; and Maj. Guy Morchain, "Peacekeeping at Home," *Sentinel: Magazine of the Canadian Forces* 7, no. 2 (March 1971): 3–4.
19. CFHQ, Sitrep no. 20, 2 November 1970, annexes A and B, and Chairman, Chiefs of Staff and CDS, "Exercises Operations ESSAY and GINGER," DHH, Raymond Collection, 73/1223, series 2, file 911.
20. Jenish, *Making of the October Crisis*, 257–58; and Tetley, *October Crisis, 1970*, 108–16.
21. Jenish, *Making of the October Crisis*, 229–34.
22. Canada, Cabinet Committee on Security and Intelligence, Minutes of meeting, 14 October 1970 (evening), p. 3, acquired through Access to Information by John Starnes, who was the director general of the RCMP Security Service in 1970. He shared them with the author. Estimates by those outside the RCMP varied widely from a few dozen to several thousand. See Tetley, *October Crisis, 1970*, 28–30.

23. Tetley, 21, 73, 75. The Québec government believed that the FLQ's actions showed that it was following that strategy.
24. Michael Gauvreau, "Winning Back the Intellectuals: Inside Canada's 'First War on Terror,' 1968–1970," *Journal of the Canadian Historical Association/Revue de la Société historique du Canada* 20, no. 1 (2009): 167.
25. Jenish, *Making of the October Crisis*, 190, 196–97.
26. Gauvreau, "Winning Back the Intellectuals," 165.
27. Gauvreau, 162.
28. Cabinet Committee on Security and Intelligence, Minutes of meetings, 9 and 12 October 1970; and *Montreal Star*, 13 October 1970.
29. Cabinet Committee on Security and Intelligence, Minutes of meeting, 14 October 1970 (morning), 3.
30. Quoted in Jenish, *Making of the October Crisis*, 208.
31. Jenish, 208.
32. Maloney, "'Mere Rustle of Leaves,'" 78–79; and Prime Minister, "A Strategy for Dealing with the FLQ," annex to Memorandum to the Cabinet, in Cabinet Committee on Security and Intelligence, Minutes of meeting, 19 October 1970. See John Starnes to D. S. Maxwell, Deputy Minister of Justice and Deputy Attorney General, 23 July 1970, "Report of the Strategic Operations Centre," 10 December 1970, appendix 1, LAC, Pierre Trudeau fonds, MG26-011, vol. 41, file 41-3. The Starnes letter discussed a range of threats, not just the FLQ. The place of the FLQ was discussed in the attached paper.
33. *Appreciation of Recent Events in Quebec*, 29 October 1970, LAC, Pierre Trudeau fonds, MG26-011, vol. 40, file 40-21.
34. According to Douglas L. Bland, *Chiefs of Defence: Government and the Unified Command of the Canadian Armed Forces* (Toronto: Canadian Institute of Strategic Studies, 1995), 141–42, C. R. Nixon from Treasury Board and some officials from the Privy Council Office established crisis briefing procedures and developed a response strategy.
35. See Cabinet Committee on Security and Intelligence, Minutes of meetings, 9, 12, 14, 18, 19, and 22 October 1970. A CAF document stated that the kidnappings, ransom demands, and ultimatums "have created a high state of anxiety at the federal Government level." See *2 Combat Group Operational Instruction no. 1*, 14 October 1970, DHH, 2 Combat Group fonds, file 36, released to the author under Access to Information.
36. Quoted in Bland, *Chiefs of Defence*, 190.
37. *Diary SOC*, "Terms of Reference, Information Plan, 'Special Operations Centre,'" 23 October 1970, LAC, Pierre Trudeau fonds, MG26-011, vol. 38, file 38-23; and Gauvreau, "Winning Back the Intellectuals," 170.
38. Tetley, *October Crisis, 1970*, 40–41, 51–53, 55–57, 198–99, 201–2, 203–4, 205. The latter pages are excerpts from Tetley's diary.
39. Cabinet Committee on Security and Intelligence, Minutes of meeting, 14 October 1970 (evening), 6; Maloney, "'Mere Rustle of Leaves,'" 81, citing an internal DND study; Tetley, *October Crisis, 1970*, 60–63, 65, 205; and Jenish, *Making of the October Crisis*, 250.
40. Morchain, "Peacekeeping at Home," 2; *2 Combat Group Operational Instruction 11 Operation GINGER*, 25 October 1970, DHH, 2 Combat Group fonds, file 23.

41. Headquarters, Forces Mobile Command, "Operation Essay Sitrep no. 1," 15 October 1970, and "Sitrep no. 2," 16 October 1970, DHH, Raymont Collection, 73/1223 series 2, file 911; Maloney, "'Mere Rustle of Leaves,'" 81, 82; Tetley, *October Crisis, 1970*, 60–61; Morchain, "Peacekeeping at Home," 4–6; and Bland, *Chiefs of Defence*, 190–91. Jenish, *Making of the October Crisis*, 248, describes a joint military-police planning meeting on Monday, 12 October, in which lists of buildings and people to be protected were drawn up and a determination was made as to how many units would be required for the operation. Maloney says that the VCDS issued Operation Order no. 1 on 14 October. Regarding the request and the start of troop movements, there are time discrepancies among the various sources. Ammunition operations at Camp Bouchard had ceased in 1969, but the FLQ probably did not know that.
42. Maloney, "'Mere Rustle of Leaves,'" 81–82.
43. Quoted in Bland, *Chiefs of Defence*, 209n35.
44. See annex D to *1 RCR Operational Instruction no. 7 Chain of Comd & Liaison—Western Quebec Region*, DHH, 2 Combat Group fonds, file 28.
45. Quoted in Tetley, *October Crisis, 1970*, 61.
46. Tetley, 63–64; Jean-François Duchaîne, *Rapport sur les événements d'octobre 1970* (Québec: Gouvernment du Québec, Ministere de la Justice, 1981); and Maloney, "'Mere Rustle of Leaves,'" 80–81, 83.
47. Maloney, "'Mere Rustle of Leaves,'" 83–84; and David A. Charters, "From October to Oka: Peacekeeping in Canada, 1970–1990," in *Canadian Military History: Selected Readings*, ed. Marc Milner (Toronto: Copp Clark Pitman, 1993), 371–72, 377.
48. Tetley, *October Crisis, 1970*, 64–65.
49. Jenish, *Making of the October Crisis*, 55, 226.
50. See *2 Combat Group Operational Instruction no. 6*, annex A: ("Intelligence Events," Sitrep 18–19 Oct.), 20 October 1970, DHH, 2 Combat Group fonds.
51. Municipal police sitrep, cited in 1 RCR, "Confirmatory Notes to Commanding Officer's Verbal Orders," 29 October 1970, DHH, 2 Combat Group fonds, file 28.
52. *1 RCR Operational Instruction no. 9*, annex A, 29 October 1970, DHH, 2 Combat Group fonds, file 28.
53. Jenish, *Making of the October Crisis*, 239–40; and Tetley, *October Crisis, 1970*, 201–3, 205. One SQ report placed James Cross in Rouyn-Noranda, over six hundred kilometres northwest of Montreal. See CFHQ, Sitrep 4–5 November 1970 (report of message from SQ via Ontario Provincial Police), DHH, 2 Combat Group fonds, file 19.
54. Cabinet Committee on Security and Intelligence, Minutes of meetings, 12 and 14 (morning) October 1970.
55. Tetley, *October Crisis, 1970*, 94–96; and Reginald Whitaker, Gregory S. Kealey, and Andrew Parnaby, *Secret Service: Political Policing in Canada; From the Fenians to Fortress America* (Toronto: University of Toronto Press, 2012), 286.
56. Commission of Inquiry Concerning Certain Activities of the Royal Canadian Mounted Police and David C. McDonald, *Certain RCMP Activities and the Question of Governmental Knowledge: Third Report* (Ottawa: Commission of Inquiry, 1981), 201–6.
57. Jenish, *Making of the October Crisis*, 273–76; Whitaker et al., *Secret Service*, 284–85.
58. Whitaker et al., *Secret Service*, 287–92.

59. Harold A. Skaarup, *Out of Darkness—Light: A History of Canadian Military Intelligence*, Vol. 1 (New York: iUniverse, 2005), 319–20.
60. CFHQ, Daily Sitrep no. 21, annex A, 3 November 1970, LAC, MG26-011, Trudeau fonds, vol. 38, file 38-16.
61. Maloney, "'Mere Rustle of Leaves,'" 83. See also CFHQ, Sitrep no. 41, 23 November 1970, LAC, MG26-011, Trudeau fonds, vol. 38, file 38-16.
62. See, for example, incidents reported in CFHQ, Sitreps no. 6, 19 October 1970; no. 7, 20 October 1970; no. 9, 22 October 1970; no. 15, 28 October 1970; no. 16, 29 October 1970; and no. 20, 2 November 1970, all in DHH, Raymont Collection, 73/1223 series 2, file 911. Because the army was dispersed across more than a hundred locations over thousands of square kilometres, the 1 Canadian Signals Regiment was deployed to provide long-range communications.
63. Lt.-Col. D. G. Loomis, Commanding Officer, *Report by First Battalion: The Royal Canadian Regiment on Its Operations during the Emergency in Canada Oct–Nov 1970*, DHH, 2 Combat Group fonds, section 2, file 36.
64. Loomis, *Report by First Battalion*, section 3.
65. Loomis, *Report by First Battalion*, annex A.
66. 8th Canadian Hussars, *After Action Report*, 15 January 1971, DHH, 2 Combat Group fonds, file 36. Nevertheless, Capt. Wayne Pickering, operations officer of the 8th Canadian Hussars, either authored or reproduced a history and analysis of the FLQ, "Background to the Operation" [title and date obscure] in DHH, 2 Combat fonds, file 28.
67. Maloney, "'Mere Rustle of Leaves,'" 82. But the 8th Canadian Hussars did provide two subunits to support Ottawa city police on night patrols, and the 12e Régiment Blindé conducted at least one mobile patrol along the St. Lawrence Seaway. See CFHQ, Sitreps nos. 6 and 15.
68. Lt.-Col. P. J. Mitchell, *8th CDN Hussars Phase One Operation Report*, 24 October 1970, DHH, 2 Combat Group fonds, file 12.
69. Capt. D. Robinson, *Area Reconnaissance Report*, section 5, in Loomis, *Report by First Battalion*.
70. Robinson.
71. Lt.-Col. Greg Jensen to author, email, 7 January 2020.
72. See CFHQ, Sitreps no. 29, 11 November 1970, and no. 44, 26 November 1970, LAC, MG26-011, Trudeau fonds, vol. 38, file 38-16; and *2 Combat Group, Operational Instruction 18*, annex A ("Intsum 3–4 Nov. 1970"), 5 November 1970, DHH, 2 Combat Group fonds, file 19.
73. Maloney, "'Mere Rustle of Leaves,'" 82–83. Joint SQ/Immediate Reaction Force operations are described in CFHQ, Sitreps no. 10, 23 October 1970; no. 17, 30 October 1970; no. 20, 2 November 1970; and no. 21, 3 November 1970, all in LAC, MG26-011, Trudeau fonds, vol. 38, file 38-16. The last also refers to using infrared "photography." This could refer to either the Tracker or the OV-1 aircraft.
74. See, for example, the distribution list for CFHQ, Sitrep no. 56, 8 December 1970, LAC, MG26-011, Trudeau fonds, vol. 38, file 38-17. Lt.-Col. Greg Jensen, comments on draft chapter, 8 April 2021, incorporated into the text, clarified the distribution process.
75. *Strategy Development*, "Attitudes/Images on the Offensive," 21 October 1970, LAC, MG26-011, Trudeau fonds, vol. 42, file 42-9.

76. *Offensive Psywar Guidelines*, n.d., LAC, MG26-011, Trudeau fonds, vol. 42, file 42-11.
77. *Offensive Psywar Guidelines*.
78. *Offensive Psywar Guidelines*.
79. *Diary SOC*, "Organizational Functions," 23 October 1970, p. 2, LAC, MG26-011, Trudeau fonds, vol. 38, file 38-23.
80. TERM Study Group, *Appreciation of Likely Courses of Action [of] the Quebec Revolutionaries*, 29 October 1970, LAC, MG26-011, Trudeau fonds, vol. 40, file 40-14.
81. Special Operations Centre, "Notes on Morning Meeting" and "Current Situation," 30 October 1970, LAC, MG26-011, Trudeau fonds, vol. 38, file 38-23.
82. TERM Study Group, *Appreciation of Likely Courses of Action*, 1–5.
83. TERM Study Group, 6–10.
84. TERM Study Group, 11–16.
85. *McDonald Commission: Third Report*, 211–12, 214–15, 218–19.
86. Jensen to author, email, 7 January 2020.
87. See, for example, Joint Intelligence Committee, *The Internal Threat to Canada*, JIC 1-12 (71), 19 May 1971, p. 1, LAC, MG26-011, Trudeau fonds, vol. 43, file 43-71, which described the situation in Québec as "particularly worrisome."
88. Fournier, FLQ, 265–66, 269–70, 275–77, 282–83, 287, 298–99, 301–2, 304–5, 307–8, 317, 319.
89. See CFHQ, Sitreps, nos. 5, 10, 11, 12, 20, 21, 23, 40, 43, 45, 51, 53, and 54, LAC, MG26-011, Trudeau fonds, vol. 38, file 38-16.

6

OPERATION SALON

Internal Security Operations in the Oka Crisis, 1990

On the evening of 26 September 1990, a group of Mohawk men, women, and children, along with some reporters, left a treatment centre at Kanesatake [Oka], Québec, west of Montreal. They had been confined there for weeks behind a barbed-wire cordon erected by the Canadian Army during a stand-off. The people were meant to exit through the main gate of the compound and onto buses. Instead, some breached the wire and tried to dodge the army cordon. The troops and First Nations people clashed, and a soldier seriously wounded one woman with his bayonet. It was an ugly ending to the crisis.[1]

At about the same time at the Kahnawake Reserve south of Montreal, several hundred Mohawks confronted soldiers at two locations. Scuffles broke out. The troops fired CS gas and warning shots, but the confrontation ended only after the officer in command ordered his troops to load their weapons, and issued orders to shoot the ringleaders of the group. Fortunately, cooler heads prevailed, and the Mohawks withdrew under a negotiated agreement.[2]

Those two events brought to an end a seventy-eight–day confrontation and clash between First Nations people and Canadian "forces of order": initially the SQ (the provincial police) and latterly the CAF. During Operation SALON the CAF deployed some 3,700 personnel,[3] making it the second-largest Canadian internal security operation since the October Crisis.[4] But from an MI standpoint, any comparison of the two events ends there. First, the Oka Crisis was far more volatile, involving direct clashes between troops and Mohawk dissidents, in particular the Mohawk Warrior Society.[5] Second, unlike the October Crisis, CAF intelligence personnel played a direct and significant role in supporting CAF operations and thus in shaping the course and outcome of the crisis.

BACKGROUND

The roots of the Oka Crisis lie in the European conquest and colonisation of North America. The cultural genocide of the First Nations populations by violence, disease, and displacement as a matter of policy over the course of several centuries left most of them confined to tiny "reservations" plagued by poverty, poor health, inadequate social services, and unemployment. But during the twentieth century, First Nations peoples challenged their status within Canada, primarily by reasserting claims to land taken from them. The Oka Crisis arose from one of these claims.[6]

Although the area, known to the Mohawks who lived there as Kanesatake, was not formally designated as a reservation, the federal government had approved the building of an addiction treatment centre there, lending implicit legitimacy to the claim. The land also included a Mohawk cemetery. But the town of Oka had approved the expansion of a golf course and the building of luxury condos on the same land, and the courts had ruled in the town's favour. To make matters worse, SQ actions aggravated their already poor relationship with the Mohawks. On 8 March 1990 the Mohawks of Kanesatake started their protest and a few weeks later erected their first barricade on a minor dirt side road.[7] The Oka Crisis was under way.

The crisis was accompanied in April–May by a more volatile crisis on the Akwesasne Reserve that straddled the Canadian-US border near Cornwall, Ontario. The dispute there was not just between First Nations and the authorities on both sides of the border. It was also an internal struggle among people on the reserve over control of gambling and smuggling activities and the revenues they earned. With real power at stake, the Akwesasne crisis was marked by violence. Consequently, during May and early June at least 248 CAF personnel were deployed to help Canadian and American police forces contain the situation.[8] As the Kanesatake standoff took precedence during the summer, the Akwesasne crisis receded gradually. But the potential for another flareup there remained for the duration of the Oka Crisis.

During the spring and early summer of 1990, talks between the Kanesatake Mohawks and the federal, provincial, and municipal governments failed to resolve the impasse. The town got a court injunction to remove the barricades by 9 July. The Mohawks refused to do so, and some prepared to defend the land with force. They had plenty of weapons and had constructed defensive positions. On 10 July the Oka municipal council requested the assistance of the SQ to remove the barriers and arrest those who had erected them. The SQ, in turn, requested assistance from the CAF in the form of C7 rifles, bulletproof vests, and armoured vehicles (the latter were not used). The following day (11 July) after a brief unsuccessful negotiation, the SQ mounted an armed assault on the

Mohawk positions and were driven back after an exchange of gunfire that left one SQ officer dead. The Mohawks seized an SQ front-end loader and three police cars, using them to construct barricades on Highway 344 and block traffic in and out of Oka. Even before that clash at Oka, Mohawks at the Kahnawake Reserve launched a dramatic gesture of support: blockades of three highways around their reserve, and of the Honoré Mercier Bridge, all major commuter links between the island city and its south shore suburbs.[9] Because of its impact on tens of thousands of non–First Nations residents of communities near Kahnawake, this action, more than the standoff at Kanesatake, transformed that situation into a major provincial and ultimately national crisis.

OPERATION SALON: THE CAF IN AID TO THE CIVIL POWER

Access to a body of official records allows us to reconstruct Operation SALON in considerable detail. The following sections provide a chronology of the operation and an analysis of the tactical problem that confronted the CAF, command and control issues, and the organization and conduct of intelligence support to CAF plans and actions intended to resolve the crisis.

Sequence of Events

In the wake of the clash at Oka and the blockades near Kahnawake, the SQ mounted its own barricades and checkpoints. These proved to be controversial flash points for confrontations between the Mohawks, the police, and residents of local communities. Anti–First Nations racism was rampant, and the SQ's efforts to restrict delivery of food and other essentials to the Mohawks called into question its role as an impartial agent of law enforcement. By the end of July, negotiations had failed to resolve the Oka dispute, and it was clear that the SQ could not deal effectively with the situation at either location. Consequently, on 6 August 1990 the province of Québec requested military ACP under the National Defence Act. The request went to the CDS, Gen. John de Chastelian, but as he was overseas the vice chief handled it until his return. The vice chief, in turn, asked Lt.-Gen. Kent Foster, FMC commander, to identify the forces needed for the pending operation.[10]

Since the CAF had already provided technical assistance to the SQ, the request was not a surprise. In July, CAF elements had started gathering intelligence on the Warrior Society and the lands its members were preparing to defend. At the same time, FMC headquarters and the 5e Brigade (based at CFB Valcartier, Québec) had begun discussing contingency plans, including removing the barricades by force. Training reflected that worst-case scenario.

So, when the request for ACP arrived, the army was already in a somewhat advanced state of readiness. On 9 August FMC issued orders to begin battle procedures (including briefings, reconnaissance, and establishing liaison with the SQ and the RCMP). The 5e Brigade recalled all troops from leave.[11]

On the night of 14–15 August the 5e Brigade deployed to the Montreal area, and two days later the 2nd Battalion (2 RCR) arrived from CFB Gagetown, New Brunswick. On 20 August while negotiations between the government and the Mohawks were ongoing, troops took up positions at Oka and Kahnawake between the SQ and Mohawk barricades. Talks broke down on 27 August, and the CAF was ordered to dismantle the barricades. Once the army made clear that it would remove them by force if necessary, the Mohawks agreed on 29 August to cooperate in dismantling the barricades at both locations. The last barricade at Oka came down on 2 September, reducing the Mohawk presence there to a perimeter around the treatment centre. The following day there was a brief unsuccessful attempt by Mohawks from Kahnawake to reoccupy the Mercier Bridge. It was stopped but prompted a joint CAF/SQ raid and search of the longhouse. On 6 September the bridge and the approach roads reopened to traffic. On 18 September the 2 RCR carried out an arms search on Tekakwitha Island, adjacent to Kahnawake, that ended in an ugly clash, with warning shots and CS gas being fired. The remaining Warriors and supporters at Oka surrendered on 26 September. During the first half of October troops were withdrawn, and the SQ took control of the situation.[12]

The Tactical Problems

On the face of it, the CAF mission was quite simple. The troops were to remove all barricades in the affected areas, restore freedom of movement on roads and bridges, remove all strongpoints, and restore public order and security. But the devil was in the details. The CAF faced several key limitations on the conduct of its mission: jurisdictional confusion, the absence of ROE, the undesirability of using force, and the need to ensure that operations did not disrupt ongoing negotiations.[13]

Although the CAF operated under the same ACP terms as it had during the October Crisis, Operation SALON differed from the earlier operation in one crucial respect. In 1970 the CAF had operated in support of the police, but in 1990 (in certain instances) it effectively replaced them. But the troops were not trained or equipped for policing or internal security.[14] In fact, predeployment training had been based on the premise that the CAF would be used only once all other options had failed and that they would have to remove barricades by force while meeting armed resistance.[15]

Instead, the CAF found itself conducting a stability operation, similar to peacekeeping, that entailed patrolling, mounting OPs, carrying out raids and searches, handling detainees, and negotiating with the Warriors and other First Nations members.[16] The CAF troops were subjected to constant taunting and provocation by the Mohawks and to minute-by-minute scrutiny by the news media, testing the limits of their training and discipline.[17] It was as much an information operation as one of maneuver and force if not more so. The army performed credibly under trying circumstances. Its combination of "carrot and stick"—talks and gradual pressure—succeeded; the crisis ended without further loss of life. But there were several occasions when Operation SALON nearly went terribly wrong, with potentially disastrous consequences. The operation was more of a near-run thing than many Canadians realized.

INTELLIGENCE SUPPORT TO OPERATION SALON

To what extent can this be attributed to the intelligence efforts conducted in support of the army's operations? In contrast to that during the October Crisis, the MI activities—and those of other agencies—were substantial. But were they effective? The rest of this chapter attempts to answer that question and will examine the organization of the intelligence effort as well as sources and methods, the information acquired, the analysis and production processes, and the exploitation of intelligence and its impact on operations.

Command and Control

Since Operation SALON was mounted on relatively short notice, the operational headquarters and its intelligence structure and functions had to be improvised with equal speed. The federal and Québec governments created crisis management teams to provide the strategic guidance that was intended to bring about a resolution of the crisis. The CDS and the commander of the Eastern (Québec) Region were in constant contact with these committees, providing them with military advice and keeping them informed on the results of operations. The CAF and the police set up a regional direction centre to coordinate military and police actions. It was established initially near Oka and then moved to the SQ headquarters in Montreal. At the outset FMC headquarters ran the military operation with a small staff, but as the operation expanded it required a full operations center. So, FMC headquarters eventually transferred personnel to the Eastern Region headquarters to fill out a complete operational staff. This staff translated political direction into military tasks, and once the CAF took over the operation from the police, overall direction of operations became the responsibility of the military chain of command, which relied on standing operating procedures to develop plans, orders, and instructions to be implemented by formation and unit commanders.[18]

Organization

The intelligence effort was shared among ten CAF organizations, two police forces, the Canadian Security Intelligence Service (CSIS), a civilian firm under contract, and a JIC.[19] Mounted rapidly and requiring some improvisation on the fly, it did not function perfectly. That it worked as well as it did speaks volumes for the training, experience, and professionalism of the CAF units and personnel involved.

The front line of the intelligence collection effort comprised three infantry battalions: the 2nd and 3rd Battalions of the Royal 22e Regiment (R22eR) and the 2 RCR. Their forward deployed companies and platoons were in direct contact with Mohawk activists and civilians. Two other CAF units operated behind the front lines, their collection activities reaching into those communities covertly. The Special Investigation Unit (SIU) developed clandestine sources for HUMINT, while the 2 (EW) Squadron from the 1 Canadian Signals Regiment monitored Mohawk communications. The squadron operated under the command of FMC headquarters, while the SIU belonged to the CAF Eastern Region (Québec).[20]

The RCMP had some 515 officers deployed at Oka, Kahnawake, and Akwesasne.[21] Likewise, even after being replaced by the army, the SQ still probed its own sources. Information from both forces was part of the collection matrix.

Video and still photographs came from Canadian Forces CF-5 and CP-140 Aurora aircraft, a Wescam video camera mounted on an RCMP helicopter, and a mapping and charting aircraft operated by a civilian firm under contract to the DND. HMCS *Acadian*, a small vessel belonging to the Montreal naval reserve unit, also mounted a Wescam, allowing it to conduct ground-level surveillance of Kahnawake from the St. Lawrence Seaway canal. Likewise, one more Wescam was mounted on the nearby railway bridge high enough to see into the village of Kahnawake.[22]

Information from military sources was collated and analysed at the brigade level. The 5e Brigade had its own G2 staff but also had under command the 1 Division Intelligence Company, initially attached to FMC headquarters before being chopped to the 5e Brigade.[23] At this time the company had only fourteen personnel consisting of an understaffed ICAC, a geomatics centre, a clerk, and one soldier acting as a quasi storeman, all under the command of Capt. Gordon Ohlke as of 15 July.[24] The ICAC served as a forward "joint int cell (JIC) to act as a clearing house for all the information. . . . [E]lements of 2 (EW) Sqn, the Quebec detachment Special Investigation Unit and liaison officers representing the RCMP, SQ, and Canadian Security Intelligence Service (CSIS) would report. . . . [T]his way the collection and distribution of the available intelligence could be properly coordinated amongst all interested services."[25] While the concept had been trialed in command post and field training exercises, the Oka Crisis was the ICAC's first full operational deployment.

Finally, at the apex of the CAF intelligence structure was the FMC G2 staff, which advised the FMC commander, Lieutenant-General Foster, who was responsible for the overall conduct of military activities in Operation SALON. He and his staff also kept NDHQ and the CDS informed by submitting daily sitreps to the National Defence Operations Centre (NDOC). The main JIC was located at FMC headquarters.[26]

Therefore, Operation SALON entailed a significant commitment of CAF personnel and equipment to the intelligence task. One estimate put this at 70 percent of the intelligence resources of FMC plus augmentation and some technical support from the CIS at NDHQ and from the CSE. The additional capabilities included terrain analysis and imagery interpretation elements from the Intelligence Company, a field printing section from the Mapping and Charting Establishment, and an engineer intelligence cell.[27]

Sources and Methods

Stability operations put a premium on HUMINT, and Operation SALON was no exception. The infantry units and subunits were the eyes and ears of the operation. Through their mounted and foot patrols they were in almost constant contact with the Mohawk militants and civilians observing them, meeting with them, and in some cases clashing with and detaining them. This was classic, overt HUMINT collection. Ideally, every soldier was a collector and every contact a potential source of information.[28] The Intelligence Company commander recalls that one 2 RCR officer was particularly good at developing contacts among people at Kahnawake who did not agree with the militants' agenda and were willing to talk to him. Ohlke took control of this initiative by directing questions to him. "He did wonderful work, and got a lot of information that way."[29]

The CAF supplemented overt collection with covert means. The SIU was its principal covert collection unit. The *Eastern Region After Action Report* stated that "SIU support is critical to obtaining access to police intelligence."[30] This is because SIU detachments "maintain a close relationship with police agencies" and are the only military units authorized to collect intelligence from them.[31] The Québec detachment had acquired a base of knowledge about activities at Kahnawake and Kanesatake. More important, the detachment had built up a network of informants inside the communities. For security reasons, in SIU reports the informants were identified by sequential alphabetical letters (or in some reports by numbers). Evidence suggests that the SIU had at least ten informants, not all of whom were in Québec.[32] According to Major Magee from the 2 RCR, the SIU worked so secretly that they were "operating in our sector without us knowing for quite a while."[33] In the meantime, Maj. Rusty Bassarab, who was deputy commanding officer of the 2 RCR, said that the battalion began to develop its own inside sources.[34] Likewise, the brigade G2 staff developed other sources within the First Nations communities. They were usually "interviewed by SIU investigators armed with a list of questions developed by the G2 staffs. In all cases this HUMINT product was . . . fed into the ICAC where it could be checked against data provided by other means."[35]

To conduct tactical SIGINT operations—the other covert collection means—the 2 EW Squadron deployed an intercept, jamming, and direction-finding capability. This allowed it "to take advantage of the warriors' reliance on radio and cellular phone communications."[36] The CAF acquired new direction-finding and electronic countermeasures (jamming) systems on short notice to ensure that the squadron's operations were kept secret. Due to the sensitivity of this activity, during Operation SALON the authority to use ECM was vested in the local commander, in consultation with the G3 staff and the signals/EW advisers. He, in turn, delegated ECM control to the chief of staff for operations at FMC headquarters.[37] SIGINT intercepts were conducted under RCMP warrants.[38]

Acquiring imagery entailed several distinct efforts. On 17 August the CAF announced that it would deploy two CF-5 jets with photoreconnaissance pods from CFB Cold Lake, Alberta, to CFB Ottawa. The 419 Squadron sent personnel and equipment to CFB Montreal to process aerial photos. The jets were used sparingly because their noisy low-level flights were viewed as provocative.[39] The Intelligence Company commander says that he never saw any imagery from the CF-5s, but the ICAC probably received some from CP-140 Aurora flights. HMCS *Acadian*'s Wescam could look down the roads into the Kahnawake Reserve.[40] The camera on the bridge fed live video to the 3 R22eR, whose troops checked it regularly.[41]

Lacking other imagery sources of its own, the CAF turned first to the RCMP. The force's helicopter-mounted Wescam, deployed at the request of the army, provided the Intelligence Company with "real-time imagery . . . throughout the operations. . . . This highly stabilized video camera was mounted in an RCMP helicopter flying at approximately 7,000 feet, and featured . . . real-time downlinks feeding analysts at RCMP HQ, the BN HQs, and Bde HQ. In addition, the tape produced by each mission was further exploited at the ICAC for more detailed information."[42]

The second non-CAF imagery provider was a commercial mapping and charting firm. It used a fixed-wing aircraft and an Aquarius camera to take vertical-plane photographs of the terrain and features—natural and human-made—at the two key locations. The film was sent to NDHQ, where the DIE interpreted the photos before sending them to FMC and on to the 5e Brigade and the ICAC.[43]

Information Acquired

These sources and methods yielded a bonanza of information. The data gathered included estimates of both capabilities and intentions of the Mohawks generally and of the Warriors in particular. As discussed later, the timeliness, accuracy, and utility of the resulting intelligence varied considerably.

Prior to the deployment of the 5e Brigade, the CAF's primary activity in the crisis was intelligence collection. The ICAC deployed on 18 July to help Eastern Region headquarters G2 staff build the intelligence picture. It had been overwhelmed by the volume of information.[44] The first appreciation for Operation SALON, issued that day, provided a rough estimate of the situation at Kanesatake and Kahnawake. In the absence of a comprehensive CAF collection effort, the estimate would have been based largely on information from the SQ, the RCMP, and the SIU. The appreciation started with background information: a short list of previous incidents (dating from 1988) accompanied by notes on involvement by some Mohawks in criminal activity and on the influence of militants from the Akwesasne Reserve. The report offered rough numbers of persons involved at Oka and Kahnawake, how they were organized, how motivated they were, how well-armed they were, what courses of action were open to them and which one they might choose, how they would they resist, how their defensive positions were laid out, and what their vulnerabilities were as well as terrain analysis. It also identified courses of action open to the CAF, and equipment, intelligence, and personnel needs.[45]

Based on the planning assumption that the army would have to use force to overcome defended barricades, training and intelligence in the infantry battalions focused on the physical and armed threats: what the barricades were made of and how they were defended.[46] The civilian reconnaissance flights and the RCMP's Wescam provided aerial photos of all the major barricades, obstacles, and key buildings at Kahnawake as well as of continuing defensive work. This also allowed the Mapping and Charting Establishment detachment to produce tactical maps.[47]

But the 2 RCR, which was not called up immediately, had the benefit of additional time to prepare and to consider the situation in slightly greater depth. According to Major Bassarab, familiarization training included efforts "to get some background of the crisis and the Mohawk culture.... [P]eople recognized that it was important and therefore some effort was made on that side of things. All ranks had some briefings plus what we all picked up on the news."[48] Maj. David Lambert, then battalion intelligence officer, added that "apart from following the news, we in the Int. section did provide a briefing and a small package that mainly focused on their capabilities and the threat that was there."[49] Colin Magee, then the operations officer for the 2 RCR, recalled that "we also brought in one or two people to talk about the history of the Mohawk Nation, today what we would call cultural awareness; back in 1990 it was a threat briefing. Who were the Mohawks, what was the Warrior Society, what was its historical roots, what were its cultural ties to the community, how they saw themselves, how the police saw them. They saw themselves as protectors of the Mohawk Nation; the police saw them as organized crime. . . . That meeting was for the entire battalion for a couple of hours."[50] That degree of cultural SA training was unusual at the time,[51] but it presaged the kind of preparation that since has become the norm for stability operations.

Having laid a foundation for understanding the situation, once deployed the CAF made ongoing efforts to improve its knowledge of the Mohawk communities generally and to estimate and report on their specific plans. HUMINT played the leading role in this task. According to Maj. Brad Boswell, most weapons caches were located by exploiting HUMINT. Magee noted that patrols and operations helped to build up the intelligence picture (e.g., the longhouse raid on 3 September yielded valuable documents). And Lambert said that most of their information came from troops on the front lines openly "just chatting to people."[52]

Drawing upon his psyop training, the commander of the Intelligence Company did a psychological appreciation of the people at the Kanesatake Treatment Centre. He also concluded that while some of the Warriors had some military training, most were not—as they claimed to be—Korean War and Vietnam War veterans; they were too young.[53] This meant that they had a lot of bravado but not a lot of experience, an important distinction.

Others tried to figure out who's who, putting faces to the nicknames the Warriors had given themselves.[54] A greater challenge was determining the decision-making structure of the reserves and of the Mohawk Warrior Society in particular. This was important, because it was not always clear who among the self-appointed spokespersons actually had the authority to negotiate on behalf of those at Kanesetake and Kahnawake; spokespersons seemed to change frequently. The soldiers discerned that the reserve and Mohawk Warrior Society leaderships were quite distinct, and did not always agree. The Warriors were almost a law unto themselves, quite possibly taking orders from Warriors at Akwesasne. However, it also became clear that in keeping with the longhouse tradition of the Iroquois, the Clan Mothers of the Kahnawake Reserve exerted significant influence there, sometimes even over the Warriors. If the women did not approve of an action, it either did not occur or was stopped while ongoing.[55] From a tactical perspective, the CAF learned that

> the Mohawks had a fairly sophisticated command and control network at both Oka and Kahnawake. They were equipped with a considerable array of communications equipment including cellular phones, citizen's band radio, very high frequency marine band radio and possibly a secure fax link. They also had some commercially available encryption devices for their radios and used low level codes on the air. They made extensive use of commercial telephone to protect their communications and, despite some lapses, their radio nets were generally operated in a thoroughly professional manner.[56]

The Warriors had subdivided both reserves into sectors, and intelligence suggested that they exercised tactical control through squads of ten to twenty men. They maintained constant surveillance at their barricades, monitored police radios, and had people outside the reserves reporting on police and military movements.[57] At Kahnawake they had prepared three concentric rings of field fortifications from the outer edge of the reserve to its center. But Major Ohlke, who had an opportunity to walk through them later, noted that they were not well sited and did not offer mutual support. Even so, he had mixed feelings on the challenge they would have posed to the CAF had its troops been ordered to attack. On the one hand he felt that dismounted troops would have cut through them easily. However, because of the sheer number of positions and buildings to be cleared, the need to avoid civilian casualties, and the intense political and media scrutiny that would have accompanied such action, "it would have been a significant nut to crack had they [the Warriors] tried to defend it."[58]

The initial intelligence estimate asserted that EW would have rendered the Warriors' C2 system ineffective. But that same estimate also suggested that the goal of their defensive efforts would have been to contain an assault on their position in the hope that public opinion would oblige the politicians to make concessions.[59] It was an astute observation, recognizing that "victory" was about winning the political/information rather than the military battle.

The SIU's reports derived from a variety of sources: media reporting, liaison with the police, their own OPs, and their network of informants. Consequently, the reports covered a wide range of topics with varying degrees of detail and certainty. For example, the SIU reports included "unconfirmed" sightings of heavy weapons and claymore mines in the hands of the Mohawks.[60] Backed up by rough sketches, one SIU source identified a particular Kahnawake house as a "hot place" that contained people and weapons "to defend themselves against the SQ or the army."[61]

Other reports included insider insights into changes in key Warrior personnel and in the Mohawk decision-making structure. For example, the 30 August report said that the Warrior known as "Mad Jack" (Mad Jap?), who had been in charge at Oka until 26 August, had been replaced. The new leader, known as "Eager," had been responsible for building the barricades. He was described as "a fanatic who has nothing to lose."[62] The informant debriefed on 12 September said that "The Nation Office, Tribal Council and Warrior Society all seem to have merged into a single entity ... [and] overall control is exercised fm [from] the joint Nation Office/Council. Decisions appear to be reached by a matter of consensus. Results are then passed on to pers[ons] on the barricades by [redacted]."[63] This structure was confirmed independently by a second informant.[64] But later in his debrief, the first one suggested that a person or entity (name redacted) "had either taken control away from the Warriors, or had been asked to take part by the Council primarily because of their previous military/combat experience."[65] He also added more detail to the CAF's understanding of the Mohawks' tactical organization, saying that Kahnawake was divided into nine to ten sectors with three squad leaders each, one per shift. Shifts originally were twelve hours but were reduced to eight hours once more people arrived.[66] Another report described their tactical communications net.[67]

Two separate SIU reports warned about the Warriors' intelligence collection efforts directed against the CAF. The first, on 10 September, stated that Warriors in the Oka Treatment Centre were identifying CAF "personnel, units and unit size through names, unit insignia and vehicle marking ... [and] Warrior patrols known to be operating in the Oka area have been reporting military activity to the Treatment Center." The report concluded that "this type of intelligence gathering is likely to intensify following the troop relief operation conducted on 09 Sep 90."[68] The second report, dated 23 September, quoted an unidentified source who said that "the Mohawks are actively collecting intelligence on the military and would probably obtain some warning that military action was imminent[;] however[,] they would probably unlikely be able to determine the exact time and place."[69] That the Warriors were collecting intelligence on the CAF probably was not a surprise to the SIU. But what the SIU's reports show is that it was not a haphazard effort. On the contrary, it was a concerted one guided by some knowledge of military procedures.

Because of the secrecy surrounding SIGINT operations, the evidence yields only a few brief snapshots of tactical SIGINT activity in Operation SALON. The FMC commander's postoperational briefing said that "this [SIGINT] effort, although difficult to coordinate between the three reserves, yielded a great deal of valuable information."[70] The Intelligence Company commander remarked that "often we would get tipoff's through electronic warfare."[71] On 2 September an SIU report said that "Source E" described two "intercepted communiques" in which Mohawks or Warriors threatened to blow up the Mercier Bridge.[72] The following day, a single intercept that said "Deploy 5 security teams" tipped off the CAF to the Mohawks' attempt to recapture the bridge.[73] On 9 September an SIU message included a special report from the SQ referring to what probably was a phone tap: "1934 Hrs 8 Sep 90 Lasagna to his mother."[74] Also recalled was "an intercept in Oka, they were talking with other authorities.... [T]hey seem to have had conflicting authorities, one at Cornwall Island and one at Kahnawake.... [O]ne of them at Oka [was] screaming, 'Why doesn't someone give me the order to fire?' So they were being controlled from somewhere else, or thought they were."[75]

The crisis posed a significant intelligence challenge for the CAF and its partner agencies. But their combined resources, which developed and drew upon a wide range of overt and covert sources of information integrated by the ICAC/JIC, yielded a steady flow of intelligence reports and appreciations. These were sufficient to produce a picture of the AOR and a degree of understanding of their opponent. So, how was it used to support operations?

Exploitation of Intelligence

The early intelligence appreciations had shaped the preoperation training that emphasised using overwhelming force to overcome defended barricades. Once the troops deployed, however, the nature of the operation changed. The use of heavy weapons and close combat was politically undesirable and fortunately became unnecessary. Instead, the troops found themselves conducting an operation that straddled the boundaries between internal security (including riot control) and peacekeeping.[76] The emphasis was on de-escalating tension while maintaining enough military presence to encourage a negotiated end to the blockades. In addition to patrolling and OPs, troops conducted arms searches, vehicle checkpoints, crowd control, negotiations with activists and militants, barrier removal, and briefing the media. This was not what they had trained for; internal security training had ceased in 1985. Nor did the army have riot control equipment such as visors, shields, and batons.[77] Peacekeeping practices were relevant,[78] though not all troops had served on such operations. So, the initial intelligence estimate did not support CAF operations, because largely for political reasons, the army changed its operational style from that conceived of in the initial planning.

But two operations stand out for the ways in which they were shaped by intelligence. The first of these was the longhouse search on 3 September, itself prompted by the Warriors' attempt to reoccupy the Mercier Bridge. It started with the "deploy 5 security teams" intercept. According to the Intelligence Company commander, the army understood what this meant. "We had identified that there were about five points that they needed to control access to the bridge. We had the Westcam [helicopter] going north to look at Oka, and we had it come back very quickly. There on the bridge were [a] bunch of boys, wearing webbing, holding Kalashnikovs, rebuilding the barricades. We called the brigadier.... Armand Roy and he started making preparations to deal with this."[79] The initial Mohawk move to the bridge, involving some fifteen persons, apparently was intended to be peaceful, but armed Warriors arrived, bringing the total to an estimated fifty people. However, the women intervened to prevent the incident from escalating. At the same time the army deployed troops and armoured personnel carriers, and the activists withdrew.[80]

The imagery provided by the Wescam then led to the 2 RCR raid on the longhouse. A 1991 briefing stated that "as this was happening good intelligence was received that weapons that had been with the Warriors on the Mercier bridge had been moved to the longhouse along highway 207."[81] Ohlke later told Winegard that "when they dismantled everything [the barrier on the bridge] we followed them with the Wescam and saw them stash around the Longhouse."[82]

For the first time, the army actually entered the Kahnawake Reserve. Two companies from the 2 RCR advanced to the longhouse, their progress slowed by crowds of Mohawk women. The troops eventually established a cordon around the building, and escorted the SQ officers (who had a search warrant) into it, pushing aside protesters with "Rugby-style tactics." The search yielded a haul of semiautomatic weapons and a .50-caliber Barrett sniper rifle.[83] The Intelligence Company commander recalls that "there was one lad that went into the bush with a long, heavy-barreled system. We couldn't pinpoint where he dropped it.... The RCR swept it with a fine-toothed comb but didn't find it. He probably submerged it somewhere."[84]

As is often the case, exploiting intelligence yielded more intelligence. Following the longhouse search, Brig.-Gen. Armand Roy had decided to dominate the reserve with a military presence. So, the army conducted more patrols and sweeps. A house search on 12 September yielded a "vast amount" of valuable Mohawk documents as well as confidential papers originating within the federal government.[85]

The search of Tekakwitha Island on 18 September was also intelligence-led but had both a different provenance and a different outcome. Bassarab recalls that at "0800 that morning the liaison for the SQ came to me and said, 'We have received some information which we believe to be correct, that there is a large stash of weapons on that island and we would like to search it.'"[86] Lieutenant-Colonel Magee shed some light on the source. "The SQ had an informant that tipped them of[f] to the weapons cache and illegal cigarettes on the island. The tip... was time-sensitive by the fact that he [the informant] was going to trial, and it was one of those deals that they were making with this individual and they needed to know whether the information was legit."[87] The Intelligence Company commander, however, later expressed some skepticism about that rationale: "Do you think the biggest heliborne operation in Canadian history up to that time would have been launched on something like that?"[88] He went on to point out that "we knew that Tekakwitha was significant to them in a number of ways because of their river operations."[89] So, it is more likely that the CAF and the SQ acted on multiple sources of information, not on just one source of unproven reliability.

On the planning process, Major Lambert explained that "like any opportunity . . . it is often fleeting, so your battle procedure is often condensed. You act on it as soon as possible."[90] That was the intent, but there were not enough helicopters, so the 2 RCR had to amend the plan; the operation was delayed by an hour, and fewer troops were inserted at a small bridge to the island.

Notified in advance, as was the practice in Operation SALON, the Mohawks rapidly mobilized a large crowd at the bridge. When they saw troops wearing riot gear and SQ visors, the standoff turned into a riot that injured many Mohawks as well as troops, who fired CS gas and warning shots. The arms search was only a minor success; it uncovered five illegal arms caches, but only three of the forty-eight weapons found were illegal.[91] From the SQ's perspective, they got what they needed. The results proved that their informant was reliable, although the haul was less impressive than he led them to expect. But the army was right to wonder if the results of the search were worth the bad public relations image that it earned.

Assessing the Intelligence Effort

During the operation and in after-action reports, the CAF identified a number of coordination issues that affected the performance of the intelligence assets. First, although there was a regional direction centre and a JIC, civilian agencies (the CSIS and police) were reluctant to colocate with the CAF, and police displayed a similar attitude toward sharing information.[92] The latter is a perennial, understandable problem owing to the different mandates of the police and MI. The police expect to use the information they collect to support prosecutions, so preserving chain of custody for such data is essential and sometimes precludes sharing. Furthermore, with regard to FMC's control of the SIU and EW units, Brigadier-General Roy expressed frustration at the "lack of coordination . . . observed in a number of instances due to an inappropriate choice of command relationship. . . . [I]t strikes me as essential that the detachments or subunits assigned to the operation be placed under command of the operational force, and not in location or in support. Only a command relationship such as this can prevent various agencies from taking action in the theatre of operations in support of an agenda different from that of the tactical commander."[93] This would not be the last time this issue was raised in respect of specialized intelligence units.

Second, the tempo and duration of Operation SALON strained intelligence personnel endurance. The small staff of the Intelligence Company worked twelve-hour shifts but were insufficient to maintain 24/7 operations of the ICAC for a prolonged period. Similarly, the 2 EW Squadron had to add more staff as those first deployed became exhausted.[94] This highlighted the small size of the CAF's intelligence cohort, which would be sorely tested in the years to come.

Third, the use of SIGINT and ECM highlighted a number of practical and legal issues, some of which had been raised first during Akwesasne operation in May but had not been wholly resolved by the time of Operation SALON. Major Tremblay claims that "the means to intercept were there but the information was not going to any of the tactical commanders but back to Ottawa and then would come down to the tactical level. There were legal constraints about the management and handling of that info which was very restrictive ... at that time."[95] His recollection is borne out in part by the Intelligence Company commander, who concedes that "they [the Mohawks] did pull surprises on us. An example is the retaking of the Mercier Bridge. No one was more surprised then [sic] us. Bingo, there they are. We reacted well, as we had detected it on very short notice."[96] That would seem to lend weight to Tremblay's assertion. But Ohlke insists that the Intelligence Company quickly received any SIGINT information that had immediate tactical relevance.[97]

The legal issues surrounding the use of SIGINT in domestic operations were legitimate concerns. In May 1990 NDHQ had advised FMC that Canadian courts consistently held that the originators of radio communications have no expectation of privacy. Therefore, listening to radio communications did not violate the Criminal Code. However, the Radio Act states that "no person shall intercept and divulge or intercept and make use of any radio communications." The act had been amended in 1979 to allow peace officers (i.e., police) to do so "in the administration of justice or for the purpose of a criminal investigation."[98] But it is not clear if the CAF, conducting SIGINT in support of the police, had the status of peace officers. The DND's legal adviser was researching whether cell phone users have reasonable expectation of privacy or are simply deemed other radio users. Until he gave an opinion, NDHQ suggested that information derived from cell phones should not be used or divulged. Though the sources cited here do not indicate what the legal adviser finally determined, the security forces did use cell phone–derived information during Operation SALON. But the indirect dissemination process to which Tremblay refers may have been the result of the legal advice given to NDHQ.

Likewise, the Radio Act also says it is illegal to interfere with or obstruct any radio communication "without lawful excuse." Therefore, the legal adviser was also researching what would constitute a lawful excuse to conduct ECM (jamming).[99] Again the sources cited here do not show what they found out, but the jamming issue was still controversial for both legal and practical reasons during Operation SALON. In mid-August NDHQ set out the ROE for using ECM:

> The conduct of ECM to sp [support] ops in Canada in peacetime has implications with respect to both national and international laws and regulations. It is necessary therefore that the following rules of engagement be adhered to in the event that ECM is to be used in aid of the civil authority.
> A. In all cases, the authority to use ECM rests with the local commander in consultation with G3 staff and SIGS[signals]/EW advisors. It is vital that all friendly forces, including police and other emergency agencies, be warned of the possible disruption to their command and control communications, should ECM be implemented.
> B. In case of pre-planned ECM, advise NDHQ.[100]

The practical element became apparent in late September, when the JIC that was still functioning in Cornwall, Ontario, inquired why communications in Akwesasne were being jammed. They were advised that this was not the case, but "jamming in Oka will eff [affect] Akwesasne since it will prevent Oka-Akwesasne calls."[101] These specific EW issues were symptomatic of a larger emerging problem: that rapid advances in communications technology were outpacing existing operational concepts and procedures and the legal frameworks under which the CAF applied them.

Acquiring imagery and being able to use it effectively also posed some challenges. "It took many days at the beginning of the operation to get air photos."[102] This forced the DND to contract the civilian firm. Although the DIE did excellent work enhancing and analysing those photos, processing was slow, and only vertical plane photography was possible.[103] The air photos had other limitations. "Throughout the crisis we were unable to penetrate the thick coniferous tree cover [at Kanesatake] to confirm or deny the various human source reports of a large bunker, trench, and obstacle system located within the area."[104] Equally problematic was the fact that the aerial photos did not allow interpreters and analysts to distinguish between real and fake weapons systems and sites, such as fake mortar pits.[105] Since the army did not want to underestimate its opponent and then be surprised, the tendency was to overestimate Mohawk capabilities.

In theory, troops in contact with the Mohawks should have been acting as HUMINT collectors. But there had been no HUMINT collection training up to that time. So, in practice some combat arms troops and others who had frequent opportunities to observe and meet with the militants seemed unaware of the utility of reporting such contacts.[106]

There was also some controversy over intelligence reports that aircraft had been used to extract people and weapons from Kahnawake on two occasions, in August and in September. On 3 September, FMC headquarters issued a report that said

> on 28 August 1990 an unknown number of aircraft made 15 landings and takeoffs on a roadway in Kahnewake. The incident occurred over a period... from approximately 2015 to 2136 hours. Although no positive identification was made, the aircraft were of the CESSNA or PIPER type. Observation of the flight activity was restricted because of the distance and terrain between the roadway airstrips within the reserve to the CF [Canadian Forces] observers on the perimeter barricades. Contact was reported by troops located some seven kilometers from the likely landing areas. For the most part, the troops could hear the sound of the aircraft but they were unsure of the nature of this activity, and there is some indication that they thought the aircraft were military.[107]

FMC headquarters issued a similar report on 14 September, prompting the CAF to request the deployment of radars and the Skyguard air defence system.[108] Both reports were greeted with skepticism by some officers at the time and later.[109] Lt.-Col. John Fife, then a platoon commander, told Winegard that "I had a lot of trouble believing that stuff. There were reports and we were briefed on that. On my level nothing was conclusive."[110] But the Intelligence Company commander, who had access to more information at the time, found the reports persuasive. "It is not a rumour. It occurred.... There was a Vandoo outpost that reported them too, eyewitness accounts. They were seen by an OP manned by soldiers. If they came in at treetop level they were easy to see. They came in, they came out."[111] In his interview with the author, Ohlke claimed that this was one of disputes between him and the FMC headquarters G2 staff. He opined that "I think they wanted to keep it quiet because it made us look inept." He went on to say that people at the time said the troops couldn't tell if it was "one plane five times or five planes one time.... My sense is that people were moved out, and some of the sensitive heavy weapons were moved out.... There were things we didn't find.... Can I confirm it? No. Sometimes you have to go with your gut."[112]

If some types of weapons were removed by these clandestine flights, this would explain why the initial intelligence reports appeared to have overestimated Mohawk capabilities—at some cost to the army's credibility later on. Several officers drew attention to the discrepancies. Bassarab asserted that "there is no doubt that they [MI?] over-estimated the capabilities, including the booby-traps. Was some of that because they were fed some of that information; quite possibly. By just insinuating that there were booby-traps slowed things up a lot. Did they have weapons; quite a few. Did they have as many weapons of various types? We found some .50-cals, the Barrett sniper type."[113] The Intelligence Company commander himself later acknowledged the uncertainties:

> We know they had light Barrett's [sniper rifles] as we captured one, we know they had machine guns, we heard them. We never saw anti-armour weapons or mortars. We saw something designed to look like a mock-up. We know that . . . the Mohawk Nation . . . had U.S. M-60 machine guns, they used them at Cornwall Island, they machine-gunned the customs posts, we know they did . . . how many were there? . . . More than one and less than 12. . . . We suspected LAW rockets, the old M-72's, we never saw one. We did see RPK's, the Soviet section automatic weapons. Some of those were captured. The Barrett .50-cal sniper rifle was captured. RPG was not found, we didn't capture an M-60. . . . I don't think there were any at Oka, but there probably were some at Kahnawake.[114]

The uncertainty had implications for the army's information operations and illustrated both the benefits and perils of using intelligence for public relations. Lt.-Col. Jacques Morneau told Winegard that

> the information we got was from the police forces, the RCMP and the SQ, and the informants/agents on the inside. They had been studying and watching them for years, watching the criminal activities and part of that was the picture of the weapons that were there. . . . So, we had to make plans to match and neutralize that threat. It was a surprise at first to us that they had things like a .50-cal machine gun. That is why we had to take it seriously. When we went public with that, it was also to educate the population, to make them understand why the army was deploying with so many weapon systems, armoured vehicles and so on.[115]

But Lt.-Col. D. G. O'Brien of the DGI's Military Strategic 2 section, who had served in the NDOC and briefly as NDHQ liaison officer to FMC headquarters during the crisis, was critical of how the army exploited the initial estimates. He felt that the display of Mohawk equipment for the media was impressive "and served to galvanize public opinion in favour of the military option but, as time went on, much of what was described did not materialize, or at least was not disclosed. This served to reverse, to some degree, the favourable pro-military public opinion."[116] In fact, he was critical of the overall performance of

MI, saying that "our intelligence net, using various police forces, informers and sympathizers, and SIGINT could have served us better."[117]

In short, the MI effort during Operation SALON fell short of being perfect. But it is important to recall that peacekeeping operations aside, for the CAF as a whole and the army in particular this was their first major armed operation since the October Crisis. It was politically charged, high risk, and media-intensive. The CDS himself had made it clear that the army would use force if necessary and would succeed because there was no alternative. This put a high premium on the work of the MI cohort. To defuse the crisis peacefully or otherwise, the army needed the best information MI could provide. But that cohort was understaffed and underresourced. The Intelligence Company and its ICAC were untested in an operational environment, and soldiers had received no training in HUMINT collection. In fact, the intelligence staffs had to change their concept of operations from conventional force-on-force thinking to collecting and analysing information on unfamiliar small groups and individuals. So, much of the intelligence effort had to be improvised in less than optimal circumstances.

CONCLUSION

In spite of these limitations, CAF MI provided a large measure of vital support to Operation SALON. CAF MI produced aerial maps, photos, and real-time video surveillance using an improvised mix of military and civilian assets. SIU, police forces, and some army personnel provided information from human sources, both overt and covert. SIGINT provided advance warning of some Mohawk actions. The ICAC functioned as a single point for all-source fusion and dissemination. Consequently, the army was not groping in the dark; it knew a great deal about its adversary's intentions and capabilities. This allowed the army to develop its operational plans and apply its resources skillfully in a way that defused the crisis without further loss of life. Yet, even with good intelligence support, Operation SALON was a near-run thing.

NOTES

1. Timothy C. Winegard, *Oka: A Convergence of Cultures and the Canadian Forces* (Kingston, Ontario: Canadian Defence Academy Press, 2008), 191–93.
2. Winegard, 194.
3. Winegard, 196. Elsewhere he cites a figure of 4,500 troops.
4. The security operation for the 1976 Montreal Olympics involved more troops.
5. The Warriors were a militant group within the Mohawk community. Not all Mohawks were members of the group.
6. Winegard, *Oka*, 1–2, 7, 9, 12–15, 17, 20, 22, 27–34, 37, 39–45.

7. Winegard, 65–69.
8. The total as of 3 May 1990. See Timothy C. Winegard, "The Forgotten Front of the Oka Crisis: Operation FEATHER/AKWESASNE," *Journal of Military and Strategic Studies* 11, no. 1/2 (Winter 2008): 2, https://jmss.org/article/view/57630.
9. Winegard, *Oka*, 97–110.
10. Canada, Parliament, *House of Commons Standing Committee on Aboriginal Affairs: Minutes of Proceedings and Evidence*, Issue no. 58, 19 March 1991, 34th Parliament, 2nd Session, testimony of Gen. John de Chastelain, CDS (hereafter cited as Chastelain, testimony).
11. Lt.-Col. Rusty Bassarab, interview with Timothy C. Winegard, transcript, 6 September 2005, Winegard Collection, box 1, file 2; NDOC, "Sitrep," 19 July 1990, W.C., box 1, file 5A; "Operation SALON: Briefing Given to the Infantry Conference," 18 November 1990, 2, W.C., box 1, file 1 (hereafter cited as "Infantry Conference Briefing"); and "Briefing: Operation Salon 2e R22eR LGen Coates Visit," n.d., 4, W.C., box 1, file 1 (hereafter cited as "Coates Visit Briefing").
12. Chief of Staff TF, "Commander's Conference Briefing OP SALON," 1 November 1990, 5–6, 15–19; Lt.-Gen. Kent Foster, Commander FMC, *Eastern Region After Action Report Operation SALON*, 31 January 1991, annex A; and "Infantry Conference Briefing," n.d., 4, all in W.C., box 1, file 1.
13. Winegard, *Oka*, 121; and Chastelain, testimony.
14. David A. Charters, "From October to Oka: Peacekeeping in Canada, 1970–1990," in *Canadian Military History: Selected Readings*, ed. Marc Milner (Toronto: Copp Clark Pitman, 1993), 372–74 and notes 23–30.
15. Lt.-Col. C. Magee, interview with Timothy C. Winegard, transcript, 25 October 2005; and Maj. A. Tremblay, interview with Timothy C. Winegard, transcript, 15 September 2005, both in W.C., box 1, file 2. See also "Infantry Conference Briefing," 2; Foster, *Eastern Region After Action Report*, 5; and "Coates Visit Briefing," 4.
16. Chastelain, testimony; and "OP SALON," briefing presentation text, 2nd Battalion, Royal Canadian Regiment, CFB Gagetown (1990), 10–13, author's copy.
17. Charters, "October to Oka," 383, 385, and sources cited in notes 69, 73, 74.
18. Chief of Staff TF, "Commander's Conference Briefing," 19–21.
19. Chief of Staff TF, 21–22.
20. Chief of Staff TF, 22–23.
21. Winegard, *Oka*, 115.
22. Maj. Gordon Ohlke, interview with Timothy C. Winegard, transcript, n.d., W.C., box 1, file 2; and Maj. Gordon Ohlke, interview with author, 13 June 2019.
23. Foster, *Eastern Region After Action Report*.
24. Ohlke, interview with author.
25. Chief of Staff TF, "Commander's Conference Briefing," 21–22. Ohlke, interview with author, says that the 2 EW Squadron and the SIU assigned liaison officers to the Intelligence Company.
26. These can be found in W.C., box 1, files 5 and 5A; and Ohlke, interview with author.
27. Foster, *Eastern Region After Action Report*.
28. Foster; Magee, interview; Ohlke, interview with Winegard; and Maj. David Lambert, interview with Timothy C. Winegard, transcript, 8 September 2005, W.C., box 1, file 2.
29. Ohlke, interview with author.
30. Foster, *Eastern Region After Action Report*.

31. Lt.-Col. J. F. Murphy, "Briefing on Internal Security Operations," 18 June 1991, 14, W.C., box 1, file 1; and Chief of Staff TF, "Commander's Conference Briefing," 32.
32. See SIU Detachment (CFB St. Hubert) reports, 30 August, 2 and 4 September 1990; and SIU Detachment (CFB St. Hubert), informant debriefs (transcripts), 12 and 21 September 1990, all in W.C., box 1, file 13.
33. Magee, interview.
34. Bassarab, interview.
35. Chief of Staff TF, "Commander's Conference Briefing," 22, 32.
36. FMC HQ to RCCRGQA/1CDN DIV HQ, Message, 21 July 1990, W.C., box 1, file 16; and Chief of Staff TF, "Commander's Conference Briefing," 22–23.
37. FMC HQ to NDOC Ottawa, "Re: 21 July 1990," Message, 16 August 1990, W.C., CD1, image 145654; *Statement of Requirement and Justification* [Re: 16 August 1990], n.d., W.C., CD1, image 145657; FMC Ops to RCCRGQA/1 CDN Div SIGS/Ops O, Message, 23 August 1990, W.C., CD1, image 145659; FMC HQ to RCCRGQA/1 CDN Div SIGS/Ops O, Message, 26 August 1990, W.C., CD1, image 145660; and NDHQ to FMC HQ, Message, 13 August 1990, [print copy] W.C., 2 EW SQN file.
38. Lt.-Col. Greg Jensen, comment on draft chapter.
39. "OP SALON UPDATE," 17, 24 August 1990, W.C., CD1, images 148694, 148707; and FMC HQ to NDOC, "OP SALON—SITREP," Message, 29 August 1990, W.C., CD1, image 148534. Chief of Staff TF, "Commander's Conference Briefing," 23–24, says that the jets were not used, but the FMC sitrep for 29 August (W.C., box 1, file 5A) implies that they did at least one overflight, and an SIU report from 30 August (W.C., box 1, file 14) says that "CF [Canadian Forces] air activity" revealed Warriors at Kanesetake. "Press Releases," 23 August 1990, W.C., box 1, file 10, announced the flights then postponed them.
40. Ohlke, interview with Winegard; and Ohlke, interview with author.
41. Ohlke, interview with author.
42. Chief of Staff TF, "Commander's Conference Briefing," 23.
43. Chief of Staff TF, 23; and Foster, *Eastern Region After Action Report*.
44. See NDOC, "Sitreps," 19 and 20 July 1990, W.C. box 1, file 14; and Foster, *Eastern Region After Action Report*.
45. FMC Headquarters, *Appréciation de renseignement* [Intelligence Appreciation] *Opération SALON* [no. 1], n.d. (annex A is dated 18 July 1990); "List of Weapons Purchased by Warriors," n.d.; and "Overview of Native Weapons Purchase" [post-December 1990], all in W.C. box 1, file 14.
46. Magee, interview; Tremblay, interview; and "Operation SALON: Briefing Given to Infantry Conference," 2, 4, and *Operation SALON: Lessons Learned*, 29 January 1991, 4, W.C., box 1, file 1.
47. Chief of Staff TF, "Commander's Conference Briefing," 12; and Foster, *Eastern Region After Action Report*. Copies of the aerial photos can be found in file 11A.
48. Bassarab, interview.
49. Lambert, interview.
50. Magee, interview.
51. The 2 R22eR did not get similar training before it deployed. "Coates Visit Briefing."
52. "Coates Visit Briefing"; Lambert, interview; Lt.-Col. Bradley Boswell, interview with Timothy C. Winegard, transcript, 8 September 2005, W.C., box 1, file 2; Foster, *Eastern Region After Action Report*; and "Coates Visit Briefing." A typical

frontline report is "SITREP," 30 August 1990, W.C., box 1, file 13: "Troops in visual contact" reported the "first reliable sighting" of an M-72 Light Anti-Tank Weapon at a specific location at Kahnawake (target # and grid reference provided).
53. Ohlke, interview with Winegard. He had taken a psyops course in the United Kingdom.
54. See "Int Coy SUPINTREP," 6 September 1990, W.C., box 1, file 14, listing people at the treatment centre and the nicknames by which they identified themselves.
55. Bassarab, interview; Boswell, interview; Ohlke, interview with Winegard; and FMC Headquarters, *Appréciation de renseignement*. See also "Structure Politique de Kahnawake" [a three-page schematic diagram of the power structure there], n.d., W.C., box 1, file 15; Chief of Staff TF, "Commander's Conference Briefing," 6; and Winegard, *Oka*, 5–6, 68, 100.
56. Chief of Staff TF, "Commander's Conference Briefing," 10–11.
57. Chief of Staff TF, 11.
58. FMC Headquarters, *Appréciation de renseignement*; Ohlke, interview with Winegard; and Maj. Gordon Ohlke to author, email, 21 February 2020.
59. FMC Headquarters, *Appréciation de renseignement*.
60. SIU Detachment (CFB St. Hubert), reports, 30 August, 10 September 1990, W.C., box 1, file 14.
61. SIU Detachment (CFB St. Hubert), report, 19 September 1990, W.C., box 1, file 14 (heavily redacted).
62. SIU report, 30 August 1990.
63. SIU Detachment (CFB St. Hubert), "Debrief 002—SIU Informant," debrief, 12 September 1990, W.C., box 1, file 14.
64. SIU Detachment (CFB St. Hubert), "SIU Source Meeting PM," debrief, 21 September 1990, W.C., box 1, file 14.
65. SIU Detachment, "Debrief 002."
66. SIU Detachment.
67. SIU Detachment (CFB St. Hubert), report, 24 September 1990, W.C., box 1, file 14, identified the location of the radio control center and four outstations that correlated to checkpoints plus another twenty-two call signs on that net.
68. SIU report, 10 September 1990.
69. SIU Detachment (CFB St. Hubert), report, 23 September 1990, W.C., box 1, file 14.
70. Chief of Staff TF, "Commander's Conference Briefing," 23.
71. Ohlke, interview with Winegard.
72. SIU report, 2 September 1990. It does not identify the source or explain how Source E intercepted the messages. This may have come from an SQ wiretap.
73. Ohlke, interview with Winegard.
74. Maj. J.-G. Plante, Commandant du détachement [SIU], "Sensitive Info Include the Following SpecRep 110/90-111/90-112/90," Message, 9 September 1990, box 1, file 14. The content was redacted.
75. Ohlke, interview with Winegard.
76. *Agenda of Policy Issues Operation SALON*, annex B to 1000-1 (DCDS), 22 March 1991, item iii; and Foster, *Eastern Region After Action Report*, 4–6, 7–8, 21–22.
77. "Coates Visit Briefing," 4; and Charters, "October to Oka," 383, 384.
78. One soldier mentioned the similarities between this operation and UN peacekeeping in Cyprus: *Montreal Gazette*, 23 August 1990.
79. Ohlke, interview with Winegard.

80. Ohlke; Winegard, *Oka*; and SIU report, 4 September 1990.
81. "Coates Visit Briefing."
82. Ohlke, interview with Winegard.
83. Winegard, *Oka*, 164.
84. Ohlke, interview with Winegard.
85. "Coates Visit Briefing."
86. Bassarab, interview.
87. Magee, interview.
88. Ohlke, interview with author.
89. Ohlke.
90. Lambert, interview.
91. Bassarab, interview; "OP SALON Update," 19 September 1990, W.C., CD1, image 145716; and SIU report, 19 September 1990. The troops and police also seized a lot of ammunition and military/paramilitary equipment.
92. Foster, *Eastern Region After Action Report*, 10.
93. Maj.-Gen. Armand Roy, Commander LFQA, to Commander LFC, *Summary of the Principal Lessons Learned during OP SALON 1990*, annex A to *Comments on Armed Assistance to Civil Authorities*, 8 February 1994, W.C., box 1, file 1.
94. Foster, *Eastern Region After Action Report*, 11; FMC HQ to NDHQ, Message, 16 August 1990, W.C., box 1, file 16; and Ohlke, interview with author.
95. Tremblay, interview.
96. Ohlke, interview with Winegard.
97. Ohlke, interview with author.
98. NDHQ to RCESCGA/FMC HQ, "Subj: Use of 2 Sqn—OP FEATHER," Priority message, 7 May 1990, W.C. box 2, file 1.
99. NDHQ to RCESCGA/FMC HQ.
100. DCEOT/NDHQ to FMC HQ SSO/OPS and SSO/SIGS, Message, 13 August 1990, W.C., box 1, CD1, image 145661. If there is more to this message it either was not copied or had been redacted.
101. [Originator redacted], "Communications Log, Ser. 17, 1445 Hrs.," 25 September 1990, W.C., box 1, file 16.
102. "Briefing Given to Infantry Conference; Lessons Learned," 3.
103. Foster, *Eastern Region After Action Report*, 12.
104. "Briefing Given to Infantry Conference; Lessons Learned," 13.
105. Lambert, interview.
106. Ohlke, interview with author; and Foster, *Eastern Region After Action Report*.
107. FMC Headquarters, "Int Report Light Aircraft Activity—Kahnawake 28 August 1990," 3 September 1990 [second page not included], W.C., CD1, image 147290. The document refers to maps that are not included.
108. FMC Headquarters, "OP SALON OPERATIONS UPDATE," 14 September 1990, image 145738; and FMC HQ to NDOC, Message, 14 September 1990, image 145741, both in W.C., CD1.
109. Bassarab, interview.
110. Lt.-Col. John Fife, interview with Winegard.
111. Ohlke, interview with Winegard.
112. Ohlke, interview with author.
113. Bassarab, interview.

114. Ohlke, interview with Winegard.
115. Lt.-Col. Jacques Morneau, interview.
116. Lt.-Col. D. G. O'Brien (D Mil Strat 2), "OP SALON—LESSONS LEARNED," 29 January 1991, W.C., box 1, file 1.
117. O'Brien.

7

OPERATION FRICTION

Naval and Air Operations in the Persian Gulf War, 1990–1991

Four days before the Québec government requested military ACP to deal with the Oka Crisis, Iraq invaded Kuwait. Pursuant to a UN Security Council resolution calling on Iraq to withdraw, a military and diplomatic coalition assembled to confront it. On 17 January 1991 following five and a half months of fruitless negotiations with Iraqi dictator Saddam Hussein, the military coalition, acting under the authority of Security Council Resolution 678, launched Operation DESERT STORM to drive Iraqi forces from Kuwait. Forty-three days later after an air, naval, and ground campaign, Kuwait was liberated.

Canada joined the military coalition at the outset. Within days of the Iraqi invasion the naval staff at NDHQ began planning to deploy a naval task force to the Persian Gulf. The task force sailed in mid-August and was joined a month later by a squadron of CF-18s. The CAF later stood up a theatre headquarters, Canadian Forces Middle East (CANFORME). During the war the aircraft took part in combat operations over Iraq and Kuwait, while the naval task force commanded the coalition's Combat Logistics Force.[1] Concerns about field formation readiness and potentially high casualties quickly ruled out deploying a substantial ground force.[2] So, Canada's navy and air force dominated Operation FRICTION.

Given the scale and scope of the planned military campaign and the sizable Iraqi forces occupying Kuwait, the coalition's MI effort was massive. By contrast, the Canadian MI contribution was small. During the Persian Gulf War the CAF and the DND were consumers of intelligence generated almost exclusively by others, in particular the US intelligence community. This was true both at NDHQ and in theatre. Indeed, they are almost two separate intelligence stories.

STRATEGIC OBJECTIVE

Under UN Security Council Resolution 678, the strategic objective of the war was clear: the use of military force to end the Iraqi occupation of Kuwait and restore the legitimate government of Kuwait.[3] US president George H. W. Bush adhered strictly to the letter of the resolution and directed the American commanders of the coalition to prosecute the war within those parameters.

CONCEPT OF OPERATIONS

Although this was a coalition effort, the US military dominated it in numbers and resources and imposed its combined-arms AirLand Battle concept of operations on the coalition. It planned and conducted the war through four phases: a strategic air campaign against Iraqi C2 structures, an air supremacy campaign in the Kuwait theatre of operations, which included much of southern Iraq; preparation of the battlefield; and a ground offensive. The first three overlapped with each other and with the ground war.[4]

COMMAND AND CONTROL

Overall command of the coalition in theatre rested with US general Norman Schwarzkopf, commander of US Central Command (CENTCOM), the conducting formation headquarters. He took direction from Secretary of Defense Dick Cheney through Gen. Colin Powell, chairman of the US Joint Chiefs of Staff. Although national command authority rests with the president as commander in chief of US armed forces, Bush and Cheney largely delegated command decisions to Powell and Schwarzkopf.[5]

Schwarzkopf exercised C2 of the coalition forces through a joint Saudi/coalition headquarters and a series of component (service) commands. The two applicable to CAF operations were the Air Component Command, led by US Air Force lieutenant general Charles Horner, commander of US Central Command Air Forces (CENTAF), and the Naval Component Command, headed by US Navy admiral H. H. Mauz, commander of US Naval Forces Central Command (NAVCENT). CENTCOM also created mechanisms to coordinate actions with the Arab forces and other non-NATO coalition members.[6] CAF liaison officers served in both component commands and within CENTCOM headquarters itself to facilitate coordination of Canadian and coalition forces' plans and activities.[7] This was not something unique to this conflict; CAF members routinely serve in other national and multinational headquarters under bilateral, UN, or NATO arrangements.

Canada did not surrender all national control of its deployed forces to the coalition. But retaining some degree of control was challenging, requiring consultation within the Canadian government, between the CAF theatre commanders and NDHQ, and with CENTCOM and its component commanders.[8] Moreover, the overlap of Operations SALON and FRICTION generated "a frenzy of activity just short of a full mobilization of NDHQ."[9] While it was mostly an administrative organization, the rapid and growing demands, costs, and political sensitivity of the two operations meant that NDHQ was increasingly drawn into managing them. Maj.-Gen. Jim Gervais, who was FMC commander during Operation FRICTION, recalled later that the CDS Gen. John de Chastelain "kept a tight grip on military activity."[10] But the defence and crisis management structure was quickly shown to be inadequate to deal with rapid C2 decision making required by the two crises.[11]

According to Todd Fitzgerald and Michael Hennessy, the crises provided the impetus for NDHQ to begin implementing an emergency plan that the CDS had been developing before they broke out. Designating certain NDHQ staff positions as joint staff "in effect transformed NDHQ into an operational command organization."[12] But the heavy lifting was done by a smaller Crisis Action Team (including the newly designated J2) working under the direction of the DCDS. However, as the CAF's role in Operation FRICTION grew, complications relating to command authority over deployed forces showed that planning, direction, and C2 arrangements were inadequate and unclear. This forced the CDS to issue an order in mid-October meant to ensure that Cmdre. Ken Summers, designated the commander of CANFORME, had authority to make operational decisions, while the existing commands (e.g., FMC) would retain responsibility for force generation and sustainment. So, his headquarters, located ashore in Manamah, Bahrain, was responsible for "operational planning, communications, intelligence analysis and dissemination, along with supply and logistics for all Canadian Forces serving in the Gulf.... [M]ost importantly, [the CANFORME headquarters] provided Commodore Summers with a single line of communication to the J-Staff working in NDHQ."[13] Once the NDHQ and theatre J staffs were in place, C2 worked more smoothly.

Missions assigned to the naval task force and the air task group were negotiated with the relevant CENTCOM component commanders and with NDHQ, with the latter exercising the final say on what missions CAF could undertake, in which AORs, in which circumstances, and under what ROE.[14] Adjusting the AOR of the naval task group to allow it to operate in support of the USN vessels in the more dangerous northern part of the Persian Gulf was one of the cases that required consultation or advance clearance.[15] However, some discretion was granted to on-scene commanders to allow for unanticipated short-notice situations. For example, on 30 January the US Navy requested that two CF-18s divert temporarily from their assigned combat air patrol mission box to attack a fleeing Iraqi naval vessel in the northern Persian Gulf.[16]

Although the fighter squadron, designated Canadian Air Task Group Middle East (CATGME) was initially expected to be integrated into the coalition air units operating under CENTAF, Commodore Summers argued successfully that the task group should be assigned to NAVCENT. His logic was twofold: first, the CF-18s were identical to those flown by the USN and US Marine Corps units protecting the fleets in the Persian Gulf, allowing shared logistic support, and second, since the naval task group was operating under NAVCENT, this would keep the two Canadian formations together, with the jets directly providing top cover to the ships. And once the CAF established the CANFORME headquarters, this allowed Commodore Summers to retain command of all CAF units in theatre. But he took direction from US rear admiral William Fogarty, who coordinated what became known as the Maritime Interdiction Force (MIF) from USS *Lasalle*. He was berthed at Manamah alongside USS *Blue Ridge*, the command ship of NAVCENT's Adm. Mauz (succeeded by Vice-Adm. Stanley Arthur in December 1990).[17]

However, mission assignment for CATGME was more complex than this suggests. Summers had operational command of all CAF units in-theatre, but senior coalition commanders exercised operational control of them. Although in theory CENTAF would control all air missions over land and NAVCENT those over water, separation of domains required some compromise. Ultimately, CENTAF coordinated all air missions through its Tactical Air Control Center in Riyadh, Saudi Arabia, which issued the daily air tasking orders that assigned specific missions to all coalition aircraft in theatre. The CAF had assigned three liaison officers to the center. Officially, the CATGME received its air tasking orders through the formal chain: CENTAF-NAVCENT-MIF-CANFORME. But owing to poor communications with the NAVCENT cell in the Tactical Air Control Center, the liaison officers informally bypassed that cumbersome chain, so CATGME received its orders directly and sooner, allowing it to be more responsive.[18]

CANADIAN ARMED FORCES OPERATIONS

The operations of the two CAF task groups varied over time and in location and mission. These differences and changes naturally influenced their intelligence requirements and tasks.

Naval Task Group

Under Security Council Resolution 665 (approved 25 August 1991), the Canadian naval task force initially joined the MIF, whose mission was to monitor the sanctions imposed on Iraq after its invasion and "to use measures commensurate with the circumstances to halt all inward and outward maritime shipping in order to inspect and verify their cargoes."[19] The Canadian ships were assigned to patrol designated sectors in the central Persian Gulf. HMCS *Athabaskan* and HMCS *Terra Nova* took up station on 1 October, conducting their first hailings and boardings that day. Notwithstanding the navy's experience with Canadian offshore fisheries patrols, this was a new and unfamiliar task. And for the task group and the MIF, HMCS *Protecteur* carried out its traditional task: replenishment at sea.[20]

Even while MIF operations continued, coalition and Canadian commanders had begun planning for the roles the task group might play in war.[21] As the coalition transitioned to war in January 1991, the task group was given command of the Combat Logistics Force, the supply train that supported coalition naval, naval air, and amphibious combat operations in the maritime Kuwait theatre of operations.[22] Naval control of shipping was a task for which the RCN was trained and equipped (especially in communications),[23] so for the duration of the war the task group coordinated logistics for coalition combat and supporting vessels in the Persian Gulf.[24]

Air Task Group

Prime Minister Brian Mulroney announced on 14 September 1990 that Canada would deploy a squadron of CF-18 fighter aircraft to provide air defence for the naval task group. Planning actually had begun a month earlier, and once a base was secured in Qatar and the logistical and air transport infrastructure was in place, the planes deployed from Canada's base in Germany. By 12 October, eighteen CF-18s had arrived at their base at Doha.[25]

Like the naval task group, the CATGME AOR and missions varied over time. They started familiarization patrols in the central Persian Gulf sector (designated Whiskey-2) in October but later moved to the northern sector (Whiskey-1). Being closer to the Kuwait theatre of operations, Whiskey-1 was tactically more significant. But as early as 14 October while on station in Whiskey-2, two CF-18s chased two Iraqi jets that had flown out from Kuwait. Similar incidents occurred later that month, with the Canadians blocking Iraqi attempts to probe coalition naval defences. By the end of November, CATGME jets were flying patrols in Whiskey-1 without US Marine Corps F-18 escorts. They flew nearly 2,400 sorties before the war started. Operational training with other coalition aircraft continued into December, but ROE were not settled until the eve of the war.[26] One point that emerged from this period is that the CAF aircraft would be providing top cover for any coalition naval units sailing within CATGME's patrol areas, not just for Canadian vessels.

As the situation in the Persian Gulf transitioned from peace to war, the DCDS, Lt.-Gen. David Huddleston, briefed the defence minister, William McKnight, on the optional roles for CATGME if war broke out. These included air defence patrols, sweep and escort missions into Kuwait and Iraq, and bombing missions. On 2 January 1991 the government gave tentative approval for the CAF aircraft to escort coalition bombers.[27]

On D-1 (16 January 1991) the CDS ordered Commodore Summers to transfer tactical control of the two task forces to Admiral Arthur. The CF-18s began flying operational combat air patrols in the Whiskey-1 sector that day, although back in Canada the House of Commons did not officially approve Canadian participation in the war until 22 January. The jets flew one hundred patrol hours on the first day of the war (16–17 January), bearing the brunt of fleet air defence until 19 January. On 17 January, Prime Minister Mulroney authorized CATGME to take part in bomber escort missions into the Kuwait theatre of operations. Their job was to protect bombers from attack by Iraqi fighters and confirm the locations of Iraqi surface-to-air missiles (SAMs). The CF-18s would flush out the fighters or provoke the SAM units to turn on their radars. They were meant to fly their first two escort missions on 20 January but due to bad weather did not do so until 24 January.[28]

Despite concerns about excessive flying hours and the risks from Iraqi air defences during the escort missions and in the new combat air patrol sector (Whiskey-4) much closer to Kuwait, CATGME roles did not change until late February. On 20 February even though aircrew training and other preparations were not yet complete, the minister of national defence announced that the Canadian jets would take part in bombing missions inside Iraq and Kuwait. The CAF carried out its first bombing mission on 24 February, the opening day of the ground offensive. Two formations of CF-18s bombed an artillery concentration in southern Kuwait. Between 24 and 28 February, when hostilities ceased, the CAF carried out fifty-six bombing missions. These were all directed against fixed, predetermined targets and did not provide close air support to advancing coalition ground troops. The ground war moved so quickly, with the Iraqis withdrawing just as fast, that it was not possible to do a damage assessment of the effectiveness of CAF bombing.[29]

Other CAF Elements

Several other CAF units bear mentioning. The 1st Canadian Field Hospital, which did not deploy fully until late February, was fully operational for only the final day of the war. After treating Iraqi and British casualties, it began redeployment to Canada only days after arriving.

Three more comprised the CANFORME headquarters defence platoon at Manamah, the base defence company protecting the airfield at Doha, and another company assigned to protect the hospital. All had to be prepared to deal with a range of possible threats. None of them engaged in hostile action, although the hospital protection company was used to guard Iraqi prisoners held nearby at the British prisoner-of-war camp.[30]

INTELLIGENCE SUPPORT TO CAF OPERATIONS

None of these CAF formations or units could operate safely and effectively in theatre in an information vacuum. The remainder of this chapter examines their intelligence requirements, their collection and analysis efforts, and the impact of intelligence on their operations.

Canadian Intelligence Requirements

The Persian Gulf crisis and war involved the standing conventional armed forces of nation-states. This simplified the intelligence requirements of the coalition. Generally, during the crisis phase and the early stages of the war the armed forces needed to know Iraq's capabilities to strike coalition deployment areas in Saudi Arabia, using its ground, air, naval, or missile forces. Just as important, the coalition needed to know whether Iraq intended to do so—to put the coalition forces on the defensive, inflict major casualties on them, and delay or prevent efforts to liberate Kuwait. If Iraq did not attempt to preempt a coalition offensive, then coalition forces had an extensive menu of intelligence requirements.

Canada's naval task group was concerned about several specific threats to its operations: ballistic missiles aimed at harbours used by the task group (possibly using chemical warheads), attack by antiship missiles launched from Iraqi aircraft, a similar attack from Iraqi naval ships, and fixed or drifting sea mines. And there was fear of terrorist, Iraqi SOF, or paramilitary attacks on Canadian bases.[31] Thus, they needed tactical indications and warning of the various aircraft/missile threats and the ability to detect mines, submarines, suspect boats, and vehicles and persons displaying suspicious behaviour.

But commanding the Combat Logistics Force imposed broader intelligence requirements for the task group. Dr. Richard Gimblett, who served as combat officer on HMCS *Protecteur* during the war, explained that because the Canadian ship operated all over the Persian Gulf and the Gulf of Oman fulfilling supply and coordination duties for the Combat Logistics Force, it needed to have awareness of the larger operational situation, not just the tactical area (within thirty miles of the vessel). So, the *Protecteur* maintained "a general operations plot. Which would sort of go out a 500 nautical mile radius around the ship that you knew what was going on."[32]

The air task group had to consider the possibility that its base could be hit by a ballistic missile or an air-to-surface missile fired from Iraqi aircraft. Canadian combat air patrols were vulnerable to attack by Iraqi air-to-air missiles (at the outset of the air campaign, there also was a high risk of blue-on-blue incidents). Escort and bombing missions exposed the CF-18s to Iraqi SAMs and antiaircraft artillery (AAA). Thus, like their naval counterparts, they needed indications and warning of surface-to-surface and air-to-surface missile launches that might hit their base. In addition, for escort and bombing missions they needed to know the locations of the many SAM and AAA sites. Finally, for their own bombing missions, they also required target intelligence.[33]

CANFORME headquarters needed SA of the theatre generally and of the AORs of its formations specifically. Like the latter, CANFORME headquarters required indications and warning of ballistic missile attacks. The base defence units were unlikely to face direct attack by Iraqi ground forces, but they had to be prepared to face possible attack by Iraqi SOF or terrorists acting on behalf of the regime.[34]

Coalition Intelligence Collection

At the strategic level, a great deal could be learned about Iraq's military capabilities from open sources. Iraq had spent most of the previous decade engaged in a war with Iran. Western media had covered the war extensively, and Western militaries and think tanks had observed the combat performance of both sides. The Iraqi order of battle, equipment holdings, and arms purchases were public knowledge.[35] Except for its weapons of mass destruction programs (whose scale and scope were discovered only after the war),[36] there were few major gaps in what coalition and Canadian leaders and their deployed forces needed to know.

However, to conduct operations effectively required more specific location- and time-sensitive tactical information. The CAF formations had limited capability to collect this on their own. For self-defence, the ships had air defence radars, submarine- and mine-detecting sonars, and some electronic support measures sensors. Their helicopters also had the ability to detect threats and targets.[37] For seeing the bigger threat picture, such as ballistic missile warning, and for air threat and air-to-ground targeting by the CF-18s, they depended on the coalition's (mostly American) technical collection systems and platforms. Fortunately for the coalition and Canadians, there was no shortage of these.

For the first time in war, space-based systems played a major role in intelligence collection. The United States relied on a range of previously deployed satellites for imagery intelligence, SIGINT and ELINT, and ballistic missile launch detection. The latter task was the responsibility of the Defense Support Program satellites, one of which was positioned in geo-synchronous orbit 22,000 miles above the Indian Ocean. It could detect Iraqi Scud missiles once they reached an altitude of 50,000 feet. Within a few minutes US Space Command and NORAD in Colorado could validate the launch, verify the trajectory and likely impact area, and send a threat warning to CENTCOM headquarters in Riyadh, which would in turn warn the likely targets and alert the Patriot antimissile batteries in Saudi Arabia and in Israel (also a target of Iraqi ballistic missile attacks). Several were launched in the general direction of Canadian naval forces in the Persian Gulf but missed.[38] Lt.-Gen. (ret.) David O'Blenis, who at the time commanded the Canadian NORAD Region and Fighter Group, explained that when Defense Support Program satellites detected Scud missile launches,

> We were seeing those in Colorado Springs and we had to invent a way to get that information into theater.... We could get it to Washington and to Ottawa, but... the Americans had to Jerry rig [sic] a way to connect the right folks in theater in the Middle East.... [B]ecause of the time lines, we had to get straight into Saudi, into Riyadh, and into Doha, where we were, and Bahrain.... And, of course, into Israel, within seconds[,] because the flight time was very, very short. So there were some interesting times making that work properly. It also gave our folks time to don their nuclear, chemical, biological, warfare gear because we were concerned that some of those Scuds could have those kinds of warheads on them. And it also gave some cueing time for the Patriot missile batteries that were placed in certain places to try to forestall... a missile actually landing there.[39]

The United States tasked portions of its constellation of intelligence-gathering satellites to collect data on Iraqi forces and infrastructure in the Kuwait theatre of operations. Operated by the National Reconnaissance Office, the array of satellites, the KH-11/12, CHALET/MAGNUM, VORTEX, and LACROSSE among them, deployed a range of sensors, including long focal-length high-resolution cameras, radar imaging systems, infrared/near infrared cameras, and electronic eavesdropping sensors to map the theatre of war. Their collection targets included Iraqi bases, equipment, air defence weapons and radars, troop movements and fighting positions, road networks, bridges, obstacles, C2 nodes, communications, military-industrial complexes, and suspected weapons of mass destruction sites. Imagery, SIGINT, and ELINT were downloaded either directly to the CENTCOM JIC or to analysis offices in the Central Intelligence Agency, the Defense Intelligence Agency, and the National Security Agency (for SIGINT). To meet shortfalls in demand that exceeded military satellite capacity, the United States also used NASA's LANDSAT and purchased imagery from the French satellite operator SPOT Image. In the period prior to the outbreak of fighting, satellites produced hundreds of thousands of images.[40] CANFORME J2 headquarters and the fighter squadron intelligence staff received imagery as needed. It was essential for developing and disseminating the bombing mission target packages.

The Joint Reconnaissance Center controlled and assigned missions to the in-theatre reconnaissance aircraft. These included the U-2R and TR-1, which conducted high-altitude aerial photography flights and could carry other sensor packages. Other assets included the RC-135 RIVET JOINT, whose sensors could gather SIGINT and ELINT, and the USN's P-3 Orion (one variant carried an over-the-horizon radar directed against naval surface targets) and S-3B Viking, the USAF's RF-4C Phantom, and the Royal Air Force's Tornado, Jaguar, and Nimrod aircraft. The CATGME CF-18s probably interacted most with the E-3A AWACS, which exercised airspace control of coalition aircraft and, in tandem with the radars of the USN's Aegis-class cruisers, provided surveillance of Iraqi aircraft movements; the E-8 Joint STARS, which could direct bombers onto fixed or moving ground targets at ranges up to 150 miles; and the Airborne Battle Command and Control Center (ABCCC), an EC-130E aircraft crewed and equipped to coordinate coalition air strikes. All three C4I systems worked in collaboration with each other. Coalition reconnaissance aircraft flew about seventy-five missions per day.[41]

This massive, complex technical collection effort was the first battle test of the ISR fusion concept. It was made possible by the US military's ability to exploit the many advances in camera, sensor, radar, space systems, and communications technologies that are associated with and attributed to the RMA. Of course, this process did not function perfectly. Demand for imagery exceeded capacity to deliver, and collection could not keep pace with the tempo of operations. However, it worked well enough to give the coalition an unprecedented ability to "see" the open desert battlefield and the enemy forces arrayed on it.[42]

Coalition Intelligence Coordination

The CENTCOM J2 staff, led by US brigadier-general Jack Leide, was responsible for advising General Schwarzkopf and his planning and operations staff. The J2 staff also managed the coalition intelligence collection, analysis, production, and dissemination effort through the JIC. Some seven hundred strong, the JIC included American and coalition intelligence analysts and operators. In addition to the JIC staff, the JIC housed the Joint Reconnaissance Center and the Joint Imagery Processing Center. The JIC also served as the conduit to and from the US national intelligence agencies and the assets they controlled and as a clearinghouse for intelligence from non-US sources. The Joint Reconnaissance

Center comprised "reconnaissance and intelligence platform managers, collection managers, theater-level intelligence analysts, and focused on meeting near-real time needs."[43]

Canadian National-Level Intelligence Support

At an early stage, to support planning for the Persian Gulf deployment, the Current Intelligence section within the DGI created a Gulf Desk, which generated a brief on the Kuwait situation. The Current Intelligence section also contributed to the operational intelligence picture. For example, on 6 September 1990 NDHQ passed to MARCOM headquarters a report from the Department of External Affairs (DEA) Kuwait Task Force about "some evidence of Iraqi arming of aircraft with anti-shipping missiles."[44]

The overlapping operations (SALON and FRICTION) and the related command changes had a significant impact on the functioning of the DGI. In fact, one study asserts that intelligence coordination "posed a challenge for NDHQ."[45] One complicating factor was that while the crises were occurring, NDHQ was in the midst of the "Functional Review" discussed in chapter 3. The CIS, Rear Adm. John Slade, managed to persuade NDHQ to postpone the proposed changes to DGI until after the war.[46]

In early January 1991 the branch stood up a J2 staff to handle intelligence support for the CAF's war operations. Some sixty-seven members of the DGI comprised the Persian Gulf War J2 staff.[47] Toward the end of January Slade asserted that "it is now apparent, after only one week of war, that my whole branch will be fully engaged in support of the operations."[48] But James Cox, relying on postwar interviews, says that the J2 staff did not have much to do. In Ottawa and in theatre, the CAF consisted mainly of recipients and consumers of intelligence, but CAF intelligence personnel were able to add value through additional analysis and tailored production. CANFORME headquarters received most of its intelligence from the vast resources of the United States and CENTCOM, whose products were more voluminous and detailed than anything that could be produced in Ottawa. The main role of the J2/DGI "was to keep senior DND/CF [Canadian Forces] decision-makers informed of events and his intelligence was coming mainly from [CANFORME headquarters].... They provided much good 'situational awareness' information."[49]

Lt.-Cmdr. Andrea Siew arrived at Maritime Command Pacific headquarters to be senior staff officer for intelligence there just as the Persian Gulf crisis began. She worked with the DGI to prepare the deployment intelligence package for the naval task group. Siew had a USN exchange officer on her staff and worked closely with her counterparts at the USN's commander of the Pacific Fleet headquarters in Hawaii to develop that package. But once the ships were deployed, her staff did not support them directly. That was the responsibility of MARCOM's intelligence office, which was staffed 24/7. Still, by operating under extended hours during the crisis and the war, the intelligence staff maintained constant situational awareness in order to keep the Maritime Command Pacific commander informed of developments. They received daily intelligence summaries directly from the ships as well as intelligence from allies. Siew and her staff would alert the admiral to specific threats to the Canadian ships, such as reports of missile attacks.[50]

Intelligence Support in Theatre

Establishing a forward-deployed theatre headquarters with a complete joint battle staff also meant creating a J2 (intelligence) cell. The headquarters became operational on 6 November. But the J2, Lt.-Cmdr. Darren Knight, began his regular twice-daily briefings to Commodore Summers on 1 November. They continued for more than four months.[51] Summers, who knew Knight, had chosen him to be the J2. The posting confronted Knight with several challenges. First, this was a joint headquarters, which was new to the CAF, so everyone was learning and adapting on the fly. The second was staffing. NDHQ had put a cap on the number of troops deployed to the Persian Gulf, so the J2 cell had only ten people. Two of them had just finished working the Oka Crisis when they were posted to CANFORME. Knight developed a 24/7 watch schedule (with two people always on duty) but had to work around this to meet the need to provide briefers.[52]

Canadians also served at CENTCOM headquarters in Riyadh. In December 1990, NDHQ approved the dispatch of a team of eight imagery analysts who were deployed in January to the CENTAF "Black Hole," where they did highly regarded work on bomb damage assessment. Also in early January, Maj. Jerry Mayer, Capt. Linda Knie, and Lt. Dave Canavan were sent to serve in the coalition JIC. They each worked daily twelve-hour shifts. Mayer and Canavan served on the army intelligence day and night shifts, respectively, and Knie served on the air intelligence night shift. Mayer and Canavan stayed until early April monitoring the postwar uprisings in Iraq.[53]

Knight's third challenge was communications and networking, both physical and interpersonal. At that time in the CAF, military messages had to be typed at the analysts' desks and then retyped for transmission, which was very slow and labour-intensive. A lot of data, such as imagery and maps, could not be sent easily or quickly by the means available to the CAF at the time. This opened Knight's eyes to the potential of computers.[54]

At the personal contact level, the Americans were very supportive of meeting Knight's intelligence requirements through either existing liaison channels via Ottawa or new linkages developed in theatre. If Knight needed to contact the Defense Intelligence Agency, he talked to it from USS *Blue Ridge*. He could also go aboard USS *Lasalle* or talk to the shore-based staffs when he wanted to connect with other US intelligence organizations. Command of the Combat Logistics Force, familiarity with USN procedures, and membership in the Five Eyes network conferred on the Canadians senior partner status in the coalition. Moreover, their shipboard C2 systems were interoperable with those of the USN. So, they were able to drink from the fire hose of US intelligence as needed to support CAF operations. Knight also had access to a liaison aircraft, which allowed him to visit the fighter squadron and CENTCOM headquarters. Reachback to Ottawa for intelligence was largely minimal because he had access to more timely and detailed in-theatre sources. In fact, the flow was one way, from theatre to national, to support the intelligence requirements of decision makers. There were two exceptions to this where Ottawa had high-quality niche capabilities: SIGINT and imagery analysis.[55] Those were the roles of the CSE and the DIE, respectively.

Because of the possibility that Iraq might rely on SOF or terrorist attacks by supportive groups to disrupt coalition activities, Knight also spent a fair amount of time on force protection and counterintelligence. However, those threats never materialized for the CAF in theatre.[56]

The CANFORME J2 staff was not involved in providing targeting intelligence for the air campaign. Instead, CATGME headquarters (wing level, between the theatre headquarters and the fighter squadron) had its own intelligence staff, led initially by Capt. Wayne Nightingale and then by Capt. Sean Bruyea and Warrant Officer Matt McCann, whose job was to advise the CATGME commander and the headquarters staff on the Iraqi threat and to support the requirements of the squadron intelligence section. They did this by exploiting their coalition contacts and giving daily formal (and many informal) briefings. In addition, the fighter squadron had its own nine-person intelligence section (led initially by Capt. Michel Foucreault, then on the next rotation by Lt. William Glenfield) that received route, tactical, and targeting intelligence directly from CENTAF. According to the squadron history, prior to each mission the CF-18 pilots would visit the section to be briefed on the air and ground threats and on mission planning, such as which air corridors to use. On returning from their missions the aircrews were debriefed by the section on any hostile activity they encountered as well as on their assessment of any damage they inflicted on targets during bombing missions. The mission reports would be included in the daily sitreps that the squadron sent to the CANFORME J2 and to Canadian and multinational intelligence services.[57]

The foregoing shows that the CAF in-theatre intelligence effort during the Persian Gulf War entailed what would become a familiar refrain thereafter. A relatively small number of CAF intelligence personnel were required to perform a wide range of tasks to the high standards expected by Canada's coalition partners while constrained by limited qualified personnel and technical resources. So, how did the Canadian intelligence effort measure up overall? Sources available to the author do not provide sufficient information to give a definitive answer. Success or shortcomings at one level (tactical vs. strategic) do not necessarily translate into a similar result at others. Moreover, it is difficult to disentangle the Canadian role and contribution from that of the coalition as a whole.

Strategic Assessment

So far as we know, the coalition had no high-level HUMINT sources inside the regime, so throughout the crisis and the war Saddam Hussein's intentions remained somewhat opaque. Given that his invasion of Kuwait was prompted by Iraq's desperate economic situation brought on by the eight-year war with Iran, it was hard to believe that Hussein wanted another war. It was equally hard to believe that he thought he could defeat the coalition militarily. His only hope was to divide it politically. The ballistic missile attacks on Israel were undoubtedly intended to achieve that and failed when Israel declined to respond. If Hussein had expected to undermine domestic support for the war in coalition countries by inflicting massive casualties on their forces, that failed too; his forces were unable to do so. After those two setbacks, his only concern may have been to survive.[58]

The apparent ease with which the coalition defeated the Iraqi forces might suggest that they were nothing more than a paper tiger. But that was not the prevailing opinion at the outset of the crisis or even on the eve of the war. At that time, Iraq had deployed forty-three divisions in Kuwait and southern Iraq, on paper more than three hundred thousand troops. They were equipped with thousands of modern Soviet tanks and artillery pieces. An additional twenty-three divisions were stationed in the rest of Iraq. The Iraqi ground forces were dug in behind extensive defensive works, protected from air attack by a relatively dense air defence network. The Iraqi air force had some seven hundred mostly Soviet combat aircraft.[59]

And the Iraqi military had recent combat experience. After initially poor performance at the start of the war with Iran, the Iraqi military demonstrated increasing competence in both defensive fighting and combined-arms offensive operations. Most ominously, Iraqi forces had used chemical weapons repeatedly in combat against Iranian forces and against perceived domestic enemies.[60] Western punditry at the time presented the Iraqis as a formidable force.[61]

However, the Iraqi forces were less formidable than they appeared. About one-quarter of their divisions were manned at levels barely above 50 percent. The best troops and most modern weapons were concentrated in the dozen Republican Guard divisions, leaving the remainder poorly equipped. Even before the fighting began, poor morale and leadership and inadequate logistic support had demoralized and depleted the ranks of the frontline units. The coalition air campaign, which gained complete air superiority within the first forty-eight hours, compounded those problems. So, when the ground war began, Iraqi resistance dissolved rapidly. US intelligence had not adequately analysed the qualitative problems of the Iraqi forces. While their equipment and personnel strength were known quantities, the political and military leadership were less capable than they should have been to conduct a modern war of maneuver.[62]

Iraqi units that did fight were simply no match for the coalition ground forces, most of which comprised the best from the US military and the NATO alliance. They had been preparing for decades to fight against the Soviet Union and the Warsaw Pact. They were highly trained, experienced, professional forces equipped with the latest-generation weapons systems, guided by a combined arms AirLand Battle doctrine, and supported by cutting-edge C2 and by a massive logistics train that spanned the globe by sea and air. In so many respects, it was an unfair fight. But given what was known (or estimated) about Iraqi forces at the time, it would have been irresponsible for General Schwarzkopf and his staff to underestimate their opponent. So, the coalition planned for a large-scale prolonged and potentially bloody conventional campaign, possibly exacerbated by the use of chemical weapons.[63] Indeed, even though pundits expected the coalition to prevail, they predicted high coalition casualties.[64] So did the US intelligence community.[65]

Canadian intelligence assessments were similar to those of the United States and other coalition members. A DEA report from 2 August 1990 stated what became the conventional wisdom about Iraq's motive for the invasion of Kuwait: that it was primarily economic/financial.[66] Another DEA assessment later in August by its Gulf Assessments Group assessed—correctly—that a blockade would not induce Iraq to withdraw from Kuwait and that the United States would not have the patience to maintain a static military presence there indefinitely. The assessment group was skeptical that an air campaign alone could achieve the desired objectives and was even more doubtful about the prospects for a successful ground attack. "The option of driving the Iraqi army out of Kuwait by a counter-invasion on the ground would be ... difficult to accomplish, and far too costly in American lives.... [W]ith the Iraqi defensive buildup now in place in Kuwait, the window of opportunity for the United States may also be closing. A ground invasion would only be a last resort. We do not believe the US administration intends to send in ground forces to repossess

Kuwait, although contingency plans are undoubtedly being made."[67] The report concluded correctly that at that point the US preferred to seek a diplomatic solution but was not optimistic about those prospects. Iraq's plans and capabilities remained uncertain.[68]

Once the Gulf War was under way, the DEA recirculated an Australian DI report on Iraq's options for using chemical weapons, a matter of considerable interest to the deployed Canadian forces. It stated that "at some point in the ground battle, Iraq will use CW [chemical warfare]."[69] The report argued that CW was now integrated into Iraqi offensive and defensive battle doctrine, so its use should be expected. However, the report regarded the strategic use of CW, such as in a Scud ballistic missile attack on Israel, as more problematic for Iraq, suggesting that even if such an attack provoked an Israeli counterattack that would not necessarily split the coalition. Without adding any Canadian analysis, the Gulf Assessment Group stated flatly that "we agree with the assessments contained therein."[70] Iraq never used CW on a major scale during the war, although it may have been used sporadically on a small scale. But even that is in dispute.[71]

Another DEA assessment, issued just before the ground war, attempted to interpret Saddam Hussein's mindset and what actions might arise from it. The report drew upon open and sensitive sources, Canadian and foreign, but without sources inside the regime its value could be challenged. The assessment correctly suggested that Hussein would try to manage the war in a way that ensured his survival, which he would see as a victory. But it completely missed the mark when trying to predict his last-ditch military options. "If necessary, he will undoubtedly use, with attention to maximizing the benefits of unexpected timing, new weapons in his arsenal, including suicide attacks, chemical weapons, fuel air explosives, and possibly bacteriological agents. He will abet and encourage terrorism. If the apparent rejection of the latest Soviet proposals leads to a ground war, all stops will be removed. He has said as much, and thus far has been remarkably true to his word."[72]

None of those predictions came to pass, although they were consistent with public worst-case thinking. Moreover, the distribution list shows that document was for DEA consumption: for the minister, senior officials, and the embassies. The DND and NDHQ were not on the list, although they may have been briefed on it at a meeting of the interdepartmental Intelligence Advisory Committee. Whether any of the deployed intelligence personnel ever saw it (or the Australian document) is unknown. That said, from the earliest stages of the deployment, the CAF units and personnel understood the CW threat implicitly, trained for it, and donned protective gear when the situation warranted (twenty-one times for the air task group). The forces also were constantly aware of the possibility of SOF and terrorist attacks, though none materialized.[73]

It should be noted that during the MIF phase in December 1990, the naval task group contributed to the coalition intelligence picture. HMCS *Athabaskan* intercepted two tugs outbound from Iraq. Under questioning, the crews provided details of the "increasingly desperate" conditions inside the country. The Canadians quickly shared this information with their coalition partners.[74]

Indications and Warning

In the absence of access to original sources such as war diaries, it is difficult to assess the quality and value of the intelligence available to the deployed CAF units. Secondary sources provide only episodic glimpses into the intelligence picture. None of the Canadian units and headquarters appear to have been deliberately targeted by Iraqi actions, such as Scud missile launches, although several came close. In all cases, the ships and bases seem to have received warning of impending attack.[75] This suggests that the improvised ballistic missile threat warning system that NORAD devised was effective. But whether that would have been sufficient to take protective measures had the missiles been more accurately aimed at the Canadians is another question.

Tactical/Targeting Intelligence

Even before the naval task group arrived in theatre in October, it carried out an appreciation to determine which AOR in the Persian Gulf it would be best suited for. "Item by item, they undertook a realistic threat assessment, compared their findings with the capabilities of the Canadian and Coalition ships and evaluated communications inter-operability and available logistics support."[76] In the appreciation forwarded to MARCOM headquarters, Commodore Summers concluded that the task group could play "a high profile, meaningful, and professionally challenging role" by operating in patrol area Charlie in the central Persian Gulf.[77]

In spite of the impressive intelligence capabilities available to the coalition, they fell short in some respects. According to a study by a major think tank, one of these was the absence of an effective targeting system for the air/airland campaign. The US intelligence community "could not provide either air or land commanders with timely or accurate targeting data."[78] Consequently, air commanders bypassed the intelligence community. The study added that the C4I system could not keep up with the tempo of the air and airland campaigns, and the bomb damage assessment process was plagued by coordination, organizational, and technical limitations. Intelligence support for targeting was overcentralized in the Joint Forces Air Coordination Center and CENTAF "Black Hole." Dissemination of imagery was a problem; systems could not meet demand, especially from air units, for imagery that would help them refine follow-on attacks after initial strikes.[79] According to the *Gulf War Air Power Survey*, the demand for target imagery from air units was "well-nigh insatiable."[80] Likewise, the intelligence staffs were unprepared in terms of personnel and procedures for the "enormity" of the bomb damage assessment task. The number of attack sorties outstripped their capacity to handle the data.[81]

The intelligence problems identified in those two studies barely scratch the surface. Although these issues might have had an impact on CATGME operations, the sources available tell us little about their effects. The one bombing mission described in the squadron history indicates that the four-aircraft flight launched on 25 February had been prebriefed on a specific target: an artillery concentration in Kuwait. However, en route an ABCCC advised them that the fire support coordination line had now advanced faster and closer than expected to their designated target. They were handed off to a forward air controller (possibly on an E-8 Joint STARS), who redirected them to a new target: a column of Iraqi armoured vehicles ninety miles farther on. The new targeting data was programmed into the planes' computers and took them to the right area, where radar-imaging gave the pilots a visual of the target, allowing them to release their bombs with some expectation of hitting it. But the results were not known because the situation on the ground was changing so fast that the bomb damage assessment could not keep pace.[82] In this case, preflight intelligence did not support the attack.

CONCLUSION

The Persian Gulf War was the CAF's first expeditionary combat operation since the Korean War. It was also the CAF's first joint services command and first coalition operation outside of UN peacekeeping missions. In addition, this was the first time since the Korean War that CAF intelligence personnel had been deployed in a wartime operation. As such, the war resulted in a steep learning experience for everyone.

The intelligence challenge was significant. The intentions of Iraq's leader were unknown throughout the crisis and the war. The coalition intelligence picture of Iraq's military capabilities was comprehensive but incomplete. Owing to the uncertainties about those forces and to the limitations of US and coalition intelligence collection and analysis, there was a tendency to overestimate Iraqi capabilities and overlook their qualitative shortcomings. Canadian strategic assessment shared these problems.

In addition to the uncertain threat, CAF in-theatre intelligence confronted a range of challenges: limits on the number of personnel and consequent high demands on their time and skills; creating hybrid intelligence units by integrating personnel from the different services, who had not worked together previously; inadequate technological support, especially for messaging and for receiving and disseminating imagery; and changing missions and AORs. For the naval task group this included shifting from blockade enforcement to coordinating coalition seaborne logistics to escorting a damaged US cruiser out of a minefield. For the CF-18 squadron, this sometimes meant being directed to new targets for which they had not been briefed preflight. That they appear to have accomplished these tasks effectively speaks to the skill, flexibility, and professionalism of the CAF personnel, including those providing intelligence support.

One year after the Persian Gulf War, the CAF embarked on a series of peacekeeping and peace-enforcement missions that would tax the capacity of the forces to the limit over a decade and would present new intelligence challenges. Those missions could not be foreseen in 1991. Nevertheless, the war provided some pointers toward that future. First, it showed that the CAF intelligence community was underresourced in terms of personnel and equipment. Second, the war made clear that the CAF and its intelligence enterprise were not keeping pace with RMA-related changes. If Canada was going to be in coalitions in the future, it would have to up its game and invest in intelligence technology.

Third, the DGI and the deployed intelligence staffs interacted but had not functioned as an integrated, mutually supporting effort. They were two distinct activities that served different purposes: in Ottawa, strategic assessment and high-level decision making, and in theatre, operational planning. The latter provided a steady stream of intelligence to the former, but the reverse was not the case. Simply put, Ottawa could not compete with the deployed forces' access to coalition assets and products. There were two exceptions to this: SIGINT products from CSE, and imagery analysis from the DIE, which supported national-level decision makers and the Five Eyes. Although the home-based American national intelligence agencies were not oriented to support war fighting, they were forced to adjust to do so, however imperfectly. This is not to suggest that the American intelligence experience could be transposed exactly on the CAF and the DGI. Rather, it could be seen as a signpost toward a possible intelligence future.

As the following chapters show, the DND and the CAF did take steps to increasingly integrate intelligence tasking and product-sharing between NDHQ and deployed intelligence staffs. Starting in the Balkans, this came to full fruition in Afghanistan. But two things did not change. CAF intelligence had to support those missions with insufficient personnel and had to improvise and adapt budget-limited intelligence-collection technologies to unintended tasks and unanticipated, unconventional targets.

NOTES

1. Jean H. Morin and Richard Howard Gimblett, *Operation Friction, 1990–1991: The Canadian Forces in the Persian Gulf* (Toronto: Dundurn, 1997), 21, 29–30, 97–98, 215–16, 222–23.
2. Sean Maloney, "'Missed Opportunity': Operation Broadsword, 4 Brigade and the Gulf War, 1990–1991," *Canadian Military History* 4, no. 1 (1995): 36–46.
3. United Nations Security Council (45th Year: 1990), "Resolution 678 (1990) / Adopted by the Security Council at Its 2963rd Meeting," United Nations Digital Library, 29 November 1990, https://digitallibrary.un.org/record/102245.
4. United States, Department of Defense, *Conduct of the Persian Gulf War: Final Report to Congress, Pursuant to Title V of the Persian Gulf Conflict Supplemental Authorization and Personnel Benefits Act of 1991 (Public Law 102-25)* (Washington, DC: Department of Defense, 1992), 97–101; and Anthony H. Cordesman and Abraham R. Wagner, "The Gulf War," prepublished manuscript (1994; revised 2013, 2016), first published 1996 by Westview Press (Boulder, CO) as *The Lessons of Modern War*, Vol. 4, *The Gulf War* (1994; Washington, DC: Center for Strategic and International Studies, 2016), chap. 1: 11, chap. 3: 124–25, 152, 162, 164, 169–70, 606, 633–34, https://www.csis.org/programs/burke-chair-strategy/lessons-war/gulf-war. Note: page numbering in Cordesman and Wagner is not consistent in each chapter.
5. Cordesman and Wagner, "Gulf War," chap. 3: 168, chap. 4: 252; and US Department of Defense, *Conduct of the Persian Gulf War*, 55.
6. US Department of Defense, *Conduct of the Persian Gulf War*, 55–58.
7. Morin and Gimblett, *Operation Friction*, 104–7; and Cordesman and Wagner, "Gulf War," chap. 4: 247–48.
8. Cordesman and Wagner, "Gulf War," chap. 4: 245, 251; and Morin and Gimblett, *Operation Friction*, 114, 134, 158, 180, 182, 205.
9. Morin and Gimblett, *Operation Friction*, 36.
10. James Cox, "The Transformation of Canadian Defence Intelligence since the End of the Cold War" (master's thesis, Royal Military College of Canada, 2004), 53–54, CFIHP; VCDS to Comd MARCOMHQ, "Re: OP FRICTION Resource Implications," Message, 31 August 1990, W.C., OP FRICTION file, box 3, file 1.
11. Morin and Gimblett, *Operation Friction*, 36–37.
12. Michael A. Hennessy and Todd Fitzgerald, "An Expedient Reorganization: The NDHQ J-Staff System in the Gulf War," *Canadian Military Journal* 4, no. 1 (2003): 25. On the efforts to change NDHQ's role in war and other emergencies, see also Douglas L. Bland, *Chiefs of Defence: Government and the Unified Command of the Canadian Armed Forces* (Toronto: Canadian Institute of Strategic Studies, 1995), 191–97.
13. Hennessy and Fitzgerald, "Expedient Reorganization," 25–27; Bland, *Chiefs of Defence*, 201–2.
14. Duncan E. Miller and Sharon Hobson, *The Persian Excursion: The Canadian Navy in the Gulf War* (Clementsport, Nova Scotia: Canadian Peacekeeping Press and Canadian Institute of Strategic Studies, 1995), 89–90.
15. Miller and Hobson, 86–88.
16. Morin and Gimblett, *Operation Friction*, 169–70.

17. Morin and Gimblett, 58, 60, 73, 104–7; and Miller and Hobson, *The Persian Excursion*, 94.
18. Morin and Gimblett, *Operation Friction*, 106–7.
19. Morin and Gimblett, 59, 60.
20. Morin and Gimblett, 76, 79, 89.
21. Morin and Gimblett, 133–34, 137–39.
22. Morin and Gimblett, 180–82. The name was later changed to Combined Logistics Force.
23. Miller and Hobson, *The Persian Excursion*, 92; and Marc Milner, *Canada's Navy: The First Century* (Toronto: University of Toronto Press, 1999), 298–99.
24. For detailed discussions of the Combat Logistics Force's operations, see Miller and Hobson, *The Persian Excursion*, 157–59, 162–80; and Morin and Gimblett, *Operation Friction*, 184, 187–88, 190–97, 199–210.
25. Morin and Gimblett, *Operation Friction*, 97–104.
26. Morin and Gimblett, 109–11, 132.
27. Morin and Gimblett, 152, 158. Air Command—the air force headquarters—deployed six more CF-18s, bringing the Canadian total to twenty-four.
28. Morin and Gimblett, 160, 163, 167–69, 175.
29. Morin and Gimblett, 170–75.
30. Morin and Gimblett, 108, 153, 155, 213–32.
31. Miller and Hobson, *The Persian Excursion*, 69–77, 159, 167, 169–70, 179.
32. Lt.-Cmdr. [Dr.] Richard Gimblett, interview, 7 January 2004, Canadian War Museum Oral History Program.
33. Morin and Gimblett, *Operation Friction*, 154–55, 163–64, 165–66, 170–71, 175. See also David N. Deere, *Desert Cats: The Canadian Fighter Squadron in the Gulf War* (Stoney Creek, Ontario: Fortress Publications, 1991), 80.
34. Morin and Gimblett, *Operation Friction*, 153; United States, Office of the Secretary of State and Office of the Coordinator for Counterterrorism, "Patterns of Global Terrorism: 1991; Middle East Overview" (April 1991), https://irp.fas.org/threat/terror_91/mideast.html.
35. See, for example, Stephen C. Pelletiere, *Iraqi Power and US Security in the Middle East* (Carlisle Barracks, PA: Strategic Studies Institute, US Army War College, 1990); the entries for Iraq in International Institute for Strategic Studies (IISS), *The Military Balance, 1989–1990* (London: IISS, 1989); and International Institute for Strategic Studies, *The Military Balance, 1990–1991* (London: IISS, 1990).
36. Frank Ronald Cleminson, "What Happened to Saddam's Weapons of Mass Destruction?," *Arms Control Today* 33 (September 2003), https://www.armscontrol.org/act/2003-09/features/what-happened-saddams-weapons-mass-destruction (sections on successes by the UN Special Commission and the UN Monitoring, Verification and Inspection Commission). See also Cordesman and Wagner, "Gulf War," 963–67, 993–1006.
37. Miller and Hobson, *The Persian Excursion*, 12, 23–25, 31–32, 34, 38, 54–55, 73; and Morin and Gimblett, *Operation Friction*, 40, 44, and appendix C (268–69).
38. Cordesman and Wagner, "Gulf War," chap. 5: 7; and Morin and Gimblett, *Operation Friction*, 207.
39. Lt.-Gen. (ret.) David O'Blenis, interview, 19 October 2006, Canadian War Museum Oral History Program.

40. Cordesman and Wagner, "Gulf War," chap. 3: 151, chap. 4: table 2, 282–83, and chap. 5: 6–8.
41. Cordesman and Wagner, 5, 9, 11–12; and Morin and Gimblett, *Operation Friction*, 167, 175.
42. Cordesman and Wagner, "Gulf War," chap. 5: 1, 3–5.
43. Cordesman and Wagner, chap. 5: 24.
44. NDHQ to MARCOM COMD/Chief of Staff Operations, "Re: Political Sitrep," Message, 6 September 1990, W.C., OP FRICTION file, box 3, file 1.
45. Hennessy and Fitzgerald, "Expedient Reorganization," 27.
46. CIS, Memorandum, "Functional Review Implementation vs. the Gulf War—CIS Branch," 25 January 1991, LAC, RG24, BAN 2005-00285-2, box 12, file 1901-1, part 5.
47. J2 (Rear Admiral Slade), Memorandum, "NDHQ Joint Intelligence and Security Intelligence Organization—J2—Persian Gulf Crisis," 11 January 1991, LAC, RG24, BAN 2008-00172-5, box 10, file 1901-CIS, part 11.
48. CIS, "Functional Review Implementation."
49. Cox, "Transformation of Canadian Defence," 60. See for example, "Defence Executive Meeting Agenda," 24 September 1990, W.C., OP FRICTION file, box 3, file 1. The agenda included intelligence briefings on Operations SALON and FRICTION.
50. Capt. (N) Andrea Siew, interview with author, 7 November 2019.
51. Morin and Gimblett, *Operation Friction*, 113–16, 120–23.
52. Lt.-Cmdr. Darren Knight, interview with author, 6 November 2019.
53. Morin and Gimblett, *Operation Friction*, 154; and Jerry Mayer, email to author, 11 January 2021.
54. Knight, interview; and Lt.-Cmdr. Darren Knight, email to author, 22 February 2020.
55. Knight, interview; Knight, email to author; and Jensen, comments on draft chapter, 21 November 2021.
56. Knight, interview; Knight, email to author; and Jensen, comments.
57. Knight, interview; Knight, email to author; Deere, *Desert Cats*, 80, 82, 88; and Col. (ret.) Michel Foucreault, email to author, 25 August 2020. Scud missile launch warnings came into the Air Operations Centre rather than to the Intelligence Section.
58. Lawrence Freedman and Efraim Karsh, "How Kuwait Was Won: Strategy in the Gulf War," *International Security* 16, no. 2 (1991): 15, 18, 26–27, 27n73.
59. Cordesman and Wagner, "Gulf War," chap. 3: 127, table 3.1, 135, 139, 140–43, 148–49; and US Department of Defense, *Conduct of the Persian Gulf War*, 55–56.
60. US Department of Defense, *Conduct of the Persian Gulf War*, 9–11, 18.
61. "Who Will Stop Saddam?," *The Economist*, 4 August 1990; "Saddam's Army No Pushover," *The Guardian*, 12 August 1990; Frank Greve, "It Won't Be Easy to Dislodge Iraqis from Kuwait," *Montreal Gazette*, 1 November 1990; and John J. Fialka and Andy Pasztor, "The Attack against Iraq: A Pushover or a Stalingrad?," *Wall Street Journal*, reprinted in *Globe and Mail*, 16 November 1990.
62. Cordesman and Wagner, "Gulf War," chap. 3: 129–33, table 3.3, chap. 5: 29–33, 8, 622–24; and observation by Foucreault, email to author.
63. Cordesman and Wagner, "Gulf War," chap. 3: 150–52, 163–64, table 3.10, 167–72, and chap. 8: 614, 619–20, 624; H. Norman Schwarzkopf and Peter Petre, *It Doesn't Take a Hero: General H. Norman Schwarzkopf, the Autobiography* (New York: Bantam Books, 1992), 300, 356, 381, 385.

64. Jack Cahill, "Grim Forecast for Gulf War: 10,000 Dead," *Toronto Star*, 13 November 1990.
65. Cordesman and Wagner, "Gulf War," chap. 5: 3–4.
66. Canada, Department of External Affairs (DEA), *Intelligence Report Iraq: Invasion of Kuwait*, 2 August 1990, LAC, RG25, BAN 2017-00434-0, box 12, file 29-2-23, part 9.
67. Canada, DEA, *Intelligence Report Iraq/Kuwait: U.S. Intentions and Options*, 24 August 1990, in DEA, *Intelligence Report Iraq: Invasion of Kuwait*, LAC, RG25, BAN 2017-00434-0, box 12, file 29-2-23, part 9.
68. Morin and Gimblett, *Operation Friction*, 137.
69. Canada, DEA, *Intelligence Report—Chemical Warfare (CW) and Saddam's Next Move*, 29 January 1991, LAC, RG25, BAN 2017-00440-5, box 29021, file 29-2-31.
70. Canada, DEA, *IR—Chemical Warfare*. There is no distribution list, so we don't know if the DGI or deployed intelligence staffs saw it.
71. See Jonathan B. Tucker, "Evidence Iraq Used Chemical Weapons during the 1991 Persian Gulf War," *Nonproliferation Review* 4, no. 3 (September 1997): 114–22; "Gulf War Non-Use of Chemical Weapons—Iraq Special Weapons Facilities," Federation of American Scientists, 4 November 1998, https://nuke.fas.org/guide/iraq/cw/non-use.htm.
72. Canada, DEA, *Current Assessment Oil and Water, Fire and Ice: Saddam Hussein and the War in the Gulf*, 20 February 1991, LAC, RG25, BAN 2017-00434-0, box 29021, file 29-2-31.
73. Morin and Gimblett, *Operation Friction*, 23, 154–55, 162, 165–66, 184, 207; and Miller and Hobson, *The Persian Excursion*, 73–77.
74. Morin and Gimblett, *Operation Friction*, 140.
75. Note that on twenty-one occasions CATGME personnel donned their CW protective gear. See also Morin and Gimblett, *Operation Friction*, 165–66, 207; Miller and Hobson, *The Persian Excursion*, 69, 180.
76. Morin and Gimblett, *Operation Friction*, 63.
77. Morin and Gimblett, 63.
78. Cordesman and Wagner, "Gulf War," chap. 5: 4.
79. Cordesman and Wagner, 18, 39.
80. Thomas A. Keaney and Eliot A. Cohen, *Gulf War Air Power Survey*, summary report (Office of the Secretary of the Air Force, 1993), 135.
81. Keaney and Cohen, 139.
82. Deere, *Desert Cats*, 41–43; and Morin and Gimblett, *Operation Friction*, 175.

8

PEACEKEEPING IN THE BALKANS

The UN Years, 1992–1995

It was in former Yugoslavia that the CAF first confronted the chaos of the post–Cold War era. The country forged out of the remnants of the Austro-Hungarian Empire had been consolidated under personalist communist rule of Josip Broz Tito after World War II. But when he died in 1980, the system he had created began to unravel. Within a decade the economy was in a shambles, and power had shifted to ambitious regional leaders who exploited local fears by appealing to ethno-nationalist identities. Slovenia and Croatia declared their independence in June 1991, and Bosnia-Herzegovina followed suit in March 1992. The Serb-dominated Yugoslav government tried to prevent secession by force. This plunged the country into a vicious civil war that lasted until the autumn of 1995, when the United States and European allies brokered a peace deal, commonly referred to as the Dayton Accords.[1]

The Yugoslav civil war was characterized by the worst fighting seen in Europe since World War II. This included indiscriminate bombardment of cities and communities; mass murder, rape, and scorched-earth tactics to cause ethnic cleansing of areas dominated by rival ethnic groups; concentration camps; and the deliberate generation of a massive internal and external refugee problem.[2]

UNPROFOR: THE UN PEACEKEEPING MISSION

Because the Yugoslav civil war started out as an internal Yugoslav crisis, the UN played no role in preventing the outbreak of fighting. But once the international community recognized the independence of Slovenia, Croatia, and Bosnia, the war became an international conflict.[3] Consequently, the UN was drawn into efforts to end or contain it. To that end it deployed peacekeeping forces, first in Croatia and shortly thereafter in Bosnia. But not since its ill-fated mission in the Congo in the 1960s had the UN confronted a more difficult challenge with a capability so unsuited to the task. There was no peace to keep. Cease-fires that took days or weeks to negotiate collapsed within hours. The combatants, who were mostly undisciplined irregulars, refused to recognize the UN's authority or legitimacy and sometimes deliberately targeted the peacekeepers to intimidate them or to force the UN to accede to their demands. Aid convoys were delayed, hijacked, and looted. The militias ignored and violated the protocols of UN Protected Areas (UNPAs), capturing or killing people sheltering therein and carrying out attacks from within. The UN civilian and military chains of command proved unwieldy, unable to deal with the realities, and the peacekeeping forces—lacking the numbers, resources, and mandate—were mostly unable to prevent the worst excesses. The mandates and tasks of the UN forces changed with the shifting situation on the ground.[4]

The May 1991 Croatian vote for independence was accompanied by the first clashes between Croats and Serbs. Croatia's formal declaration of independence on 25 June was followed by the outbreak of a civil war inside the country. The worst fighting took place in the Serb-dominated areas: the Krajina and eastern and western Slavonia. According to Sabrina Ramet, by the end of October Serb militias controlled about one-third of Croatia. By the end of the year some three thousand people had been killed, and more than five hundred thousand had been forced from their homes, many of them fleeing to other European countries.[5]

Following prolonged and difficult negotiations to reach a cease-fire (as part of an intended broader settlement of the conflict), in February 1992 the UN Security Council passed Resolution 743, which authorized the creation of the United Nations Protection Force (UNPROFOR) for Croatia. The bulk of the force did not arrive until after the Security Council passed Resolution 749 in April. The UN role rested on three conditions: that the Yugoslav People's Army (JNA) would withdraw fully from Croatia, that the UNPAs would be demilitarized, and that local authorities and police would continue to function. UNPROFOR's mandate was to ensure that those conditions were upheld.[6]

UNPROFOR was to control access to the UNPAs, ensure that they remained demilitarized, and "ensure that all persons living in them are protected from fear of armed attack."[7] While this was defined as a peacekeeping mission, Lt.-Col. Glenn Nordick, who commanded the 3rd Battalion, Princess Patricia's Canadian Light Infantry (PPCLI) in Sector West in 1992–93, explained that his unit's role in that UNPA straddled the line between keeping the peace and enforcing it.[8]

In March 1992 shortly before fighting broke out in Bosnia, the UN decided that UNPROFOR headquarters would be located in Sarajevo. Canadian brigadier-general Lewis MacKenzie—recently appointed UNPROFOR chief of staff—advised UN undersecretary for special political affairs Marrack Goulding, responsible for peacekeeping operations, that Sarajevo was a poor choice for the headquarters for sound operational considerations but also for risky political reasons: "once we put the UN flag up in front of our headquarters, it will be a lightning rod for every problem in and around Sarajevo; yet we'll have neither mandate nor resources to deal with the inevitable requests for help."[9]

MacKenzie's warnings were ignored but proved prophetic. The Serb bombardment of the city that began in April was followed in quick succession by a series of incidents that drew the UN into the Bosnian war: the JNA's kidnapping of the Bosnian president on 3 May, a subsequent Bosnian attack on a JNA convoy attempting to leave Sarajevo, attacks on UN convoys on 18 and 22 April, and the "breadline massacre" of 27 May in which seventeen civilians were killed.[10]

Three days later, the UN imposed comprehensive sanctions on the former Yugoslavia, demanded that all parties to the conflict ensure that humanitarian aid could be delivered unimpeded, and established a security zone around Sarajevo, including the airport. On 8 June Security Council Resolution 758 expanded UNPROFOR's mandate and strength to include the deployment of "military observers and related personnel and equipment to Sarajevo to supervise the withdrawal of anti-aircraft weapons and the concentration of heavy weapons at agreed locations in the city."[11] Still, with fighting ongoing, it took another three weeks of negotiations, an ultimatum from the UN secretary-general, a visit to Sarajevo by French president Francois Mitterand, and the deployment of a Canadian battalion and a French commando company to the airport to finally give force to the UN's intent. Sarajevo became an UNPROFOR sector, with MacKenzie (promoted to major-general) in command. By early July the airport was open to receive humanitarian aid flights.[12]

But fighting continued in and around Sarajevo, complicating efforts to receive and deliver that aid. So, on 14 September 1992 the UN Security Council passed Resolution 776, further expanding UNPROFOR's strength and mandate. It would "support efforts by the United Nations High Commissioner for Refugees (UNHCR) to deliver humanitarian relief throughout Bosnia and Herzegovina."[13] At the request of the UNHCR, UNPROFOR would provide protection for those aid deliveries. At the request of the Red Cross, troops also could be used to protect convoys of released civilian detainees. The larger force would be deployed in four or five new zones, each consisting of an infantry battalion group, with civilian staff filling political and information functions and liaison with the UNHCR. UNPROFOR had normal UN ROE, which authorized it to use force in self-defence "including situations in which armed persons attempt by force to prevent them from carrying out their mandate."[14]

That mandate expanded more than a dozen times in two years. UNPROFOR took on the following tasks: greater peacekeeping functions in the UNPAs in Croatia; security for and running of the Sarajevo airport; delivery of humanitarian aid through the airport into Sarajevo and the rest of Bosnia-Herzegovina; protection of the UNHCR convoys delivering the aid; monitoring of the Pink Areas (mostly Serb areas close to the UNPAs) in Croatia; monitoring of military withdrawals, removal of heavy weapons, and demilitarization of the Prevlaka

Peninsula in Croatia; establishment of a preventive deployment in the former Yugoslav Republic of Macedonia; passively monitoring and (by NATO) actively enforcing the no-fly zone over Bosnia-Herzegovina; establishing Sarajevo, Srebrenica, and four other Bosnian towns as safe areas; and authorizing use of NATO airpower to defend them.[15]

John Hillen identified the problems with this constantly expanding mandate. The UN Security Council approved the expansions "with apparent disregard" for the forces available, the will of the international community to provide more, and the environment in which the force operated.[16] Moreover, UNPROFOR's mandates were fraught with contradictions. First, as Mats Berdal notes, UN secretary-general Boutros Boutros-Ghali told the Security Council in November 1992 that although troops protecting delivery of relief supplies were "pioneering a new dimension of UN peacekeeping," this did not require new ROE. But, Berdal argues that the principal military lesson from Bosnia is that in the midst of a civil war "any kind of support operation by the military is exceptionally difficult." To secure routes from artillery and mortar fire would require more troops and equipment and more liberal ROE. UNHCR officials, responsible for aid delivery, argued that absent enforcement provisions, armed escorts were no substitute for negotiations.[17]

Second, the use of NATO airpower, however sparingly (only eight airstrikes out of some thirty-six thousand sorties), proved problematic. The UN's process for requesting air support from NATO was slow and cumbersome.[18] Some NATO member states that had forces on the ground opposed the use of air strikes out of fear of the risk to their troops. Those fears were real. In response to air strikes in May 1995, Serb forces seized several hundred UN troops as hostages.[19] Yet even before that happened, NATO secretary-general Willi Claes said in November 1994, "I do not believe ... that we can pursue decisive peace enforcement from the air while the UN is led, deployed, and equipped for peacekeeping on the ground.... [W]e cannot mix these two missions."[20]

The conflict continued almost unabated in the fashion described until the autumn of 1995. The problems posed by the nature of the fighting, its impacts on the civilian population, and the self-inflicted limitations and contradictions of the various UN missions were never resolved before the conflict was brought to a halt by the Dayton Accords. This, then, was the situation into which Canada deployed as many as 2,300 troops at any one time over a period of four years.

THE CANADIAN ARMED FORCES IN THE BALKANS, 1992–95

The Canadian commitment to the Balkans evolved by stages over time as a result of both Canadian and UN decisions and the shifting situation on the ground. Under Operation HARMONY in 1992, Canada committed a battle group

(BG)—an infantry battalion and an engineer unit—designated Canadian Battalion (CANBAT) 1 to Croatia's Sector West then later to Sector South. The 1st Battalion, Royal 22nd Regiment (1 R22eR), commenced operations in April but at the end of June was diverted to Sarajevo temporarily to secure the airport. CANBAT 1 remained in Croatia for the duration of the conflict. Over the next three years six more BGs, drawn from all three Canadian infantry regiments and other units, cycled through the CANBAT 1 AOR on six-month tours of duty.[21]

The deployment to Sarajevo evolved into an ongoing UN commitment in the rest of Bosnia, UNPROFOR 2. The Canadian portion was designated Operation CAVALIER, and the assigned BGs became known as CANBAT 2. This formation remained in Bosnia until the end of the UN mission in the autumn of 1995, by which time six more BGs had served there. In sum, more than a dozen CAF BGs served in the Balkans between 1992 and 1995. In addition, Canada provided a combat engineer unit to support UNPROFOR headquarters, forward air controllers, four logistics battalions, and EW detachments.[22]

The BG tasks in Croatia included force protection, fixed and mobile checkpoints, patrolling (on foot, in vehicles, or in helicopters), mine clearance and explosive ordnance disposal, searches for illegal arms, assistance to local authorities, and protecting mass grave sites.[23] To be prepared for the full spectrum of operations, the 3rd Battalion, Princess Patricia's Canadian Light Infantry (3 PPCLI), which succeeded 1 R22eR, had robust ROE that allowed the BG to use its heavy weapons in the event of an attack on the UNPA. So, the 3 PPCLI had deployed with its full complement of subunits (four rifle companies, signals, reconnaissance, engineers, headquarters, and supporting elements) and warfighting vehicles and equipment, including tube-launched, optically tracked, wire-guided (TOW)–under-armour (TUA) antitank missile launcher vehicles; .50-caliber heavy machine guns; and 81mm mortars.[24]

On three occasions the BG had to bring some or all of its subunits to battle-ready status to deal with hostile local forces that seemed intent on confronting the UN forces. The 3 PPCLI also carried out a major successful search for illegal arms caches in response to an attack on one of its vehicles during a confrontation incident.[25] Displaying this combat power and the intent to use it if necessary, combined with prolonged negotiations, defused the standoffs and allowed the search operation to proceed unhindered. Then in Sector South in September 1993, peacekeeping shifted briefly but dramatically into open combat. The 2 PPCLI (with French troops attached) was tasked to enforce a cease-fire and occupy a zone of separation in an area known as the Medak Pocket. Croatian forces resisted their advance and engaged the UN force in a fifteen-hour firefight before negotiations ended the confrontation.[26]

In Bosnia, CANBAT 2 troops carried out many of the same tasks but (with the exception of the Medak Pocket) in an even less permissive atmosphere. The first rotation of CANBAT 2—the 1,200 strong 2nd Battalion, Royal Canadian

Regiment (2 RCR) BG—arrived in the region in November 1992, but the Bosnian belligerents prevented it from deploying to its intended base in Visoko (west of Sarajevo) for four months. In January 1993 while it was still waiting in Sector West, the BG deployed a company to Macedonia to prevent its neighbours from stirring up trouble there. Finally, in April 1993 the BG had barely settled in at Visoko when it had to detach a company to protect the newly declared safe area of Srebrenica.[27] The initial 2 RCR presence there consisted of two sections (eighteen soldiers and two armoured personnel carriers from Golf Company that had accompanied UNPROFOR commander French general Philippe Morillon to the town in late March, when he had declared it a UNPA. The rest of the company arrived ten days later.[28]

Golf Company's mission was to establish the Srebrenica UNPA as a demilitarized zone. It was not a simple task, since armed Bosnian troops were inside the perimeter. The Serbs were shooting at them, and they returned fire. They also left the UNPA to fight the Serb forces. The company set up checkpoints around the town, and anyone returning was searched and had to surrender their weapons. Similarly, the company took control of several tanks, armoured personnel carriers, and a howitzer. In addition, the company mounted OPs and carried out patrols. Golf Company deployed TUA detachments to show determination to defend the UNPA. Even so, the force came under frequent sniper fire, suffered casualties, and returned fire in self-defence as their ROE allowed. In late April while the 2 RCR was starting to rotate home, Golf Company was relieved in place by a smaller company group from the 2 R22eR.[29]

The BG from 12th Régiment Blindé [Armoured] du Canada (12e RBC), consisting of 780 soldiers with infantry and engineers attached (250 soldiers fewer than the previous one), served in Bosnia from November 1993 to May 1994. Its intended mission was to provide convoy escort to UNHCR. However, it carried out a number of additional tasks and was dispersed over a large portion of the Bosnian theatre. The infantry company that would have performed camp guard, traffic checkpoints, and other tasks was reassigned to the Srebrenica UNPA. With support elements, that took 160 troops out of the BG's roster of subunits and personnel from November through mid-March and forced the commander, Lt.-Col. David Moore, to divert one of his armoured squadrons to the camp security role, leaving only one for convoy duty and reconnaissance patrols. In addition, at any one time about one-quarter of the troops were on leave. As Moore explained, "We weren't tasking sub-units or sub-sub units or sub-sub-sub units we were tasking people by name to do things. Plugging holes in the dam, from November ... to the middle of March, until we got the company group back from Srebrenica."[30]

All of this limited the BG's ability to perform its primary function. Even so, it escorted over 135 aid convoys that delivered over eight thousand tons of food.

This was in spite of human blockades that stopped the convoys and raided the supplies and having to cope with long, frustrating negotiations to get convoys through the various factions' checkpoints. When the Washington Peace Accord was signed in February 1994, creating the Muslim-Croat federation, the 12e RBC was called upon to arrange the disengagement and withdrawal of Croat and Muslim forces from their confrontation lines in BG's AOR. This entailed more difficult negotiations, during which 16 of its soldiers were taken hostage for a week, and assigning some of the BG troops to establish OPs, supervise the withdrawals, and start the demining process.[31] Such experiences were common to all of the Canadian contingents that served in UNPROFOR.

Often overlooked in the attention devoted to the battlegroups was the role of the Force Engineers, who were the first UNPROFOR troops deployed into Bosnia. Lt.-Gen. (ret.) Michel Gauthier, who commanded the 4 Combat Engineer Regiment there in 1992, explained that their mission was to ensure that the UN troops could move safely throughout the country. This meant identifying which roads and bridges could handle heavy vehicles and locating minefields and sites with unexploded ordnance.[32] This important intelligence task will be discussed below.

There also was a separate but parallel naval operation intended to contain the conflict. From 1993 through 1996, acting under Security Council Resolution 820, NATO and the Western European Union jointly mounted a naval blockade in the Adriatic Sea to enforce an arms embargo and economic sanctions against former Yugoslavia. Warships and aircraft from fourteen nations, including Canada, participated in Operation SHARP GUARD. Over nearly four years the enforcement ships challenged some 74,000 vessels, boarded 5,900, and diverted 1,480 to ports for closer inspection. But of those, only 6 were blockade-runners carrying embargoed cargos.[33] Over the duration of the operation, Canada contributed 9 ships on eleven rotations: 2 modernized Tribal Class destroyers, 6 Halifax-class frigates, an operational support ship, and 2 CP-140 Aurora maritime patrol aircraft. The CAF ships operated as part of NATO's Combined Task Force 440, under the commander of Allied Naval Forces, Southern Europe. An American admiral exercised operational command of the maritime patrol aircraft. The tasks carried out by Canadian ships were common to those of all Combined Task Force 440 ships, including patrols, surveillance, hailing merchant vessels, and mounting boarding parties for inspections.[34]

INTELLIGENCE SUPPORT TO THE CANADIAN UNPROFOR CONTINGENTS

If the missions described above were not difficult enough, they were made even more so by problems in acquiring intelligence to plan and support operations.

That in turn can be attributed in large measure to the UN's enigmatic approach to intelligence.

The double entendre quote "the UN has no intelligence" contains more than a grain of caustic truth.[35] But it might be fair to say that the UN took a cautious approach to intelligence. Out of deference to its members' political sensitivities, in peacekeeping operations it used the term "military information," which seemed less intrusive or threatening.[36] This was reflected in Canadian peacekeeping doctrine that used the term "information gathering."[37]

But the UN's caution went beyond terminology. It also prohibited its peacekeepers from using secret and intrusive information collection methods.[38] This too was written into Canadian doctrine, which stated that "information is primarily gathered through surveillance of the area of operation . . . by using observation posts, patrolling, and maintaining close contact with the belligerents and the civil population."[39] That said, as Walter Dorn shows, the prohibition was not absolute. During the Congo crisis in the 1960s, which was as chaotic as was former Yugoslavia, UN peacekeepers had used prohibited sources and methods.[40] Similarly, a closer examination of the UN's and the CAF's approaches to intelligence in UNPROFOR yields a less clear-cut picture: absolute in theory but pragmatic in practice and evolving over time.

Sarajevo and Sector West

The experiences of Lt.-Col. Michel Jones in Sector West and Brig.-Gen. Lewis MacKenzie in Sarajevo in 1992 provide a useful baseline. Their common starting point was insufficient predeployment information and thus limited understanding of the situation within the country. This was not their fault. The Canadian Department of Foreign Affairs and International Trade had been monitoring developments in Yugoslavia but considered unthinkable Canadian involvement in some kind of international intervention there.[41] So, the DND had not begun to prepare for possible deployment there until January 1992. At that time the intelligence officer for the 1 R22eR had started to work up a small book on the historical background and the political, economic, and cultural conditions.[42] Once the battalion, which was based in Germany, was formally designated in February 1992, the intelligence section at the 4 Brigade headquarters in Lahr scrambled to bring Jones and his officers "up to speed on the situation."[43]

Fortunately, they had some inside help. Jones was able to draw upon the firsthand knowledge of CAF colonel Donald Ethell, who was serving on the European Community Monitoring Mission in Yugoslavia. Ethell sent his senior intelligence NCO to brief Jones. Furthermore, Jones's own battalion intelligence officer, Captain Turcotte, was also serving on the mission. He returned to the unit and helped to draft the operation estimate. Jones had one other internal asset. A sergeant of Yugoslav origin in his intelligence section "built us a memory aid ... at the language level[,] ... a few pages on the most used terms then how to pronounce them and then on the military equipment that existed in the former Yugoslavia."[44] Jones and his senior staff also did their own reconnaissance to familiarize themselves with their AOR and adjusted his deployment plan accordingly.[45] But there remained one significant gap: maps of Yugoslavia. The NDHQ had none. So, Jones's team exploited a contact, a US Air Force intelligence sergeant in Ramstein, Germany. "My intelligence sergeant went down there to get the maps," but the officer was not certain he could hand them over, "so he called the Pentagon right away and within the ... hour they got the answer. ... 'Yes, give it to the Canadians.'"[46]

The only hitch was that they couldn't take the maps with them to former Yugoslavia. Once deployed in Sector West, patrolling allowed the battalion to build up an "order of battle" picture of the two belligerent forces. This in turn allowed the UN troops to effectively monitor the withdrawal of those forces during the demilitarization phase in the sector.[47] So, intelligence was central to that.

Jones also created twelve liaison teams to operate on both sides of the conflict to keep him informed and to develop working relationships that would facilitate negotiations. But apart from his intelligence sergeant, who spoke Serbo-Croat and was assigned to the Serbian side, Jones's teams had to rely on hired interpreters to overcome the language barriers. Once his BG started patrolling, Jones insisted that they always drive with "hatches open" so that "everyone would have an eye to observe what was going on, to be able to report information ... right now."[48] However, to avoid causing incidents owing to misidentification in darkness, they patrolled only in daylight.

MacKenzie's introduction to Yugoslavia came via the news reporting in the summer of 1991 after the fighting had broken out in Slovenia and Croatia. In March 1992 as newly appointed chief of staff to UNPROFOR, he spent a day at NDHQ reading briefing materials. Since the DGI division did not have a Yugoslavia desk at this time, much of the material that MacKenzie read probably came from the Department of Foreign Affairs and International Trade, which was keeping a watching brief on the situation there. That material left him skeptical of the UN's plans for dealing with the conflict. And the planning sessions that followed at UN headquarters in New York did little to dispel his concerns.[49]

Arriving in Sarajevo less than a week before hostilities broke out there, MacKenzie quickly realized that until UNPROFOR could figure out what was happening, there was little it could do except offer its "good offices."[50] It was not a matter of trying to ignore what was going on because the UN had no mandate in Bosnia, as Carol Off alleges,[51] but rather in large measure because there was an intelligence gap. Whatever information he had received in Ottawa and New York had not prepared MacKenzie adequately for what was about to unfold in theatre. The UN was not privy to any discussions or decisions taking place behind closed doors within either the Bosnian government or the Serb dissident regime in Pale. In addition, the UN did not intercept communications, and neither MacKenzie nor the other senior international officials spoke the local languages. The UN was not just flying blind; it was flying deaf as well. MacKenzie recognized the limits of his understanding, and to rectify that he "assigned a couple of locally hired observers to monitor the radio and TV, and to keep him at least superficially briefed."[52] At the same time, he could not lose sight of his primary mission: ensuring that the force in Croatia could do its job in spite of poor UN administration.[53]

Others helped keep MacKenzie sensitized to the evolving situation. An example of indications and warning came on 11 April, when JNA general Milan Aksentijevic drew his attention to a "mass exodus" of the Jewish community from the city. He told MacKenzie that "this is not a good sign. The Jewish community is an excellent barometer on which to base predictions of the future. If they are leaving Sarajevo in large numbers . . . I fear it is the beginning of the end." MacKenzie reflected later that he turned out to be "dead right."[54]

Strategic warning was one thing; tactical warning was another, and in Bosnia it was rare. Instead, tactical surprise was the only constant. The irregular forces operated unpredictably, often in defiance of orders from higher authorities. To have been able to anticipate their actions would have required an intrusive intelligence capability that UNPROFOR did not have. So, MacKenzie, his staff, and his troops were frequently caught by surprise, the incidents in May being cases in point. Nor did UNPROFOR have the ability to accurately monitor the terms of the agreement reached in early June 1992 to open and secure Sarajevo airport. The UN was making commitments and extracting promises that it had no means to guarantee or verify. Consequently, the airport was not opened for weeks.

That is not to say that they did not try. Col. John Wilson's UN military observers kept watch on the city from the roof of the UN's downtown headquarters, from which they "could pretty well see the entire city. Their job was to determine who was doing the firing and at what targets."[55] But given that the weapon of choice on both sides was the mortar, which is relatively quiet when fired, it was hard to determine who was to blame for incidents. Neither side readily admitted firing, "and on the rare occasions when they did, they would claim that they had been provoked."[56]

This made two points clear: first, that intelligence alone is not sufficient to guide decision making or negotiations in complex political-military conflicts, and second, that even if the intelligence is incomplete, it is still indispensable.

With the approval of both sides, MacKenzie had asked UN headquarters to approve the acquisition of satellite or reconnaissance aircraft imagery so he could prove who was cheating on agreements. But the UN denied the request. This left him feeling frustrated that he "had to get my intelligence from the BBC. The UN was still following its outdated rules that precluded our even saying the word 'intelligence,' let alone producing it. . . . [W]e scarcely had the foggiest notion what was going on around us."⁵⁷

Unofficially, however, he occasionally acquired intelligence from unattributable sources. For example, on 2 July he received "a classified message from a non-UN source" indicating that Croatian forces were getting "dangerously close to Sarajevo."⁵⁸ There were only a few countries (mostly the Five Eyes) that had either the "national technical means" providing SIGINT or a covert observation capability to gather that kind of information and the means to send it to MacKenzie securely. Since Canada is a Five Eyes member, MacKenzie was able to receive sensitive intelligence (even if the UN did not know). But other UN commanders were not so fortunate. Walter Dorn mentions an instance when a Canadian officer with a NATO clearance was able to receive and use American satellite photos but could not share them with his UN commander, a French officer who was not similarly cleared.⁵⁹ Like the UN, the United States, NATO, and the Five Eyes had not yet adjusted their intelligence-sharing protocols to the new operating environment.

While the global media's attention was focused on Sarajevo, the original UNPROFOR mission continued in Croatia. For the Force Engineers this meant "relating terrain-based information . . . to enemy or belligerent forces and what they're doing to affect our job as engineers on the ground."⁶⁰ They had to understand what fighting had occurred and where unexploded ordnance and minefields might be at a time when the belligerent forces "were not that professional" and "their record-keeping was a challenge."⁶¹ The engineers had to create their own minefield maps from scratch. "We had to gather that . . . by physical ground recce on the one hand, by negotiating with the parties, building a relationship with them . . . to get that information, and that's what we did."⁶² Mine awareness became the focus of Gauthier's small intelligence cell of five to six people. "They became expert in anything to do with mines and minefields in particular, as well as unexploded ordnance. A big part of what they ended up doing—it's sort of a variation on intelligence products—[was] briefing our forces, all of the battalions that were deploying. It became a mine awareness campaign.⁶³

From September 1992 to April 1993 in Sector West, Nordick's BG was responsible for an AOR of roughly six hundred square kilometres. He divided it into three company sectors, with the fourth company acting as battalion reserve. Even if it was not described as such, intelligence gathering was central to their daily routine. The BG intelligence section had three tasks: indications and warning, situation development, and threat assessment. In each sector, two platoons manned permanent checkpoints and maintained contact with the population through vehicle and foot patrols. The reserve platoons in each company sector carried out mobile patrols and mobile checkpoints. The reserve company provided two platoons (one each) for day and night patrols, while the battalion reconnaissance platoon conducted patrols in more remote areas and to assist the Jordanian and Nepalese battalions assigned to Sector West. That platoon also regularly carried out random mobile checkpoints, covert observation of suspected illegal weapons caches, and surveillance of likely mortar base plate locations.[64] In short, the 3 PPCLI saturated its AOR with constant observation and intelligence collection. This helped to determine whether the local belligerents were adhering to negotiated agreements and also contributed to force protection. Sector West remained relatively stable and quiet and when the 3 PPCLI handed the sector over to Lt.-Col. Jim Calvin's 2 PPCLI, the incoming BG initially conducted the same tasks.[65]

Sector South

Sector South was a whole different story. The Croatians had carried out an offensive in January 1993, recapturing some vital ground. The Serbs felt that the UN had let them down, so they had taken their heavy weapons out of storage, reigniting Serb-Croat fighting. French general Jean Cot, the UNPROFOR commander, negotiated a deal to create buffer zones between the two and required additional troops to secure those zones. In mid-July he ordered the 2 PPCLI to deploy to Sector South. On arrival in what was a hot zone of constant skirmishes and artillery duels, the battalion made intelligence collection its primary task. The troops conducted reconnaissance and patrols and mounted OPs to observe military activity in the disputed areas. Prior to the Medak Pocket battle, one OP manned by a single Canadian sergeant was for twenty-four hours the UN's only source of information on the Serb-Croat fighting in that area. He passed his observations up the reporting chain to BG headquarters. The 2 PPCLI sent it to UNPROFOR headquarters in Zagreb, which in turn faxed it to UN headquarters in New York. Capt. David McKillop recalled that two local Serbs who spoke English regularly talked with Canadian troops at one of the checkpoints. "We got all sorts of good information out of these guys. None of it really useful, just good information to have."[66] That was one effect of the Canadians standing firm against the Croatians and also showed the value of maintaining contact with the population.

However, it is not clear how well informed the BG was about the disposition and intentions of Croatian forces. An UNPROFOR intelligence report issued as the 2 PPCLI arrived in the sector had suggested that the area would be quiet for the next few days.[67] The constant fighting the BG encountered, even before its own battle, put paid to that notion. Its OPs were able to observe the Croatian troops' positions and track their movements. But lacking access to

Croatian planning or communications, the UN forces probably underestimated the willingness of the Croats to resist by force their advance into the buffer zone on 15 September. The result was the unexpected battle of the Medak Pocket. This highlights a common intelligence problem: that determining intentions is harder than identifying capabilities. Units such as the 2 PPCLI were very good at the latter but were not able to do the former.

UN Intelligence Support

By this time both the UN and the DND were making efforts to cope with the changing character of peacekeeping operations. The UN had formally established the Department of Peacekeeping Operations in 1992 to coordinate its many ongoing missions. But it was not until April 1993 that it set up the Situation Centre, whose mandate was

> to speed up, complement, and amplify the information flows generated in the field to facilitate timely decisions by the Under-Secretary General for Peacekeeping Operations. Its role is to maintain communication links with all missions, to solicit information from the field, as well as to process and analyze raw incoming information. Its staff, organized in teams to provide coverage around the clock, will screen incoming information, respond immediately to factual queries, judge when to contact senior decision makers and summarize incoming information.[68]

The Department of Peacekeeping Operations staff consisted of twelve to fifteen duty officers working on rotation to allow 24/7 coverage, plus a team of four analysts. Between 1993 and 1997–98 the United States provided the Situation Centre with a joint deployable intelligence support system: a computer workstation with communications capability. The United States used it to pass less-sensitive information to the centre; high-grade intelligence was hand-delivered at UN headquarters and in the field. The centre's primary purpose was to support the UN Secretariat in New York rather than operations in the field.[69] It was not a "comprehensive intelligence unit" per se and could not on its own fulfil "the need for a proper analysis and assessment capability to serve the policy-makers" or "provide the Secretary General and the Security Council with a UN overview."[70]

There was a small Military Information Office at UNPROFOR headquarters in Zagreb, Croatia, whose main function was to produce daily intelligence summaries for the mission commander. But it did not have a collection plan and did not task collectors. Rather, according to Lt.-Col. Rhe Probert, the information it produced came mostly from soldiers, units, and sectors that contributed daily summaries from their AORs. Some units were more generous in their reporting details than others. Manned by individual MI officers rather than a proper G2 or J2 staff, the office was not adequately formed to provide assessments of future situations. It reported regularly to UN headquarters but "received little guidance and no strategic intelligence in return." The cell was criticized for being "all suck and no blow."[71]

The Military Information Office suffered from other limitations. The staff drew its officers from the armed forces of many countries, not all of whom were equally qualified to contribute to the task. Some had considerable understanding of the AOR and had experience with intelligence- or information-sharing procedures, while others did not. So, the latter's contribution was necessarily less substantial. Moreover, given the national caveats on intelligence sharing, Probert found that in a UN environment, developing military information products and assessments to which all of the member nations had access "was challenging and at times limiting."[72] By contrast, he found the corresponding structure at UNPROFOR headquarters in Sarajevo to be "a more capable organization." Even so, it lacked the complete range of resources and staffing of a "full-up" intelligence structure, such as an intelligence staff or unit as might be found in a NATO military force.[73] Not surprisingly, the CAF's Army Lessons Learned Centre concluded that "United Nations–generated intelligence support was virtually non-existent and of no use to units."[74]

Canadian National-Level Intelligence Support

In 1993 NDHQ's DGI supported CAF operations in the Balkans by creating the YCC within the NDIC. As of 1994 it had seven to nine watch officers.[75] They were responsible for preparing and sending daily intelligence reports to the MI officer at Canadian Contingent UNPROFOR headquarters. The reports also were distributed widely within the DND/CAF intelligence network and shared with selected allied headquarters. They also would have been sent to the CDS, the deputy CDS, and the minister and assistant deputy minister of national defence. The reports consisted of a mix of military and political intelligence covering the fighting and the diplomatic and political developments, in particular efforts to reach a negotiated settlement.[76] There were also special supplementary reports on specific topics, including a September 1993 report on Bosnian Serb irregular forces such as Arkan's Tigers.[77]

While sources were not identified, content ranged from unclassified to secret, probably gleaned from a mix of open sources, diplomatic reports, UN reporting, contingent and unit sitreps, and intelligence shared by allies. The UN rules that prevented its forces from gathering intelligence by clandestine means themselves did not prevent them from receiving information gathered by such means from organizations outside the UN. As a member of both the Five Eyes and NATO alliances, the CAF was in a privileged position when it came to sharing the take from its allies' sensitive sources and methods.

The NDIC's reports did not necessarily represent an agreed view across government—marginal notes (probably from Department of Foreign Affairs and International Trade personnel) on one document lamented unspecified inaccuracies.[78] Interestingly, the reports for 16, 17, and 20 September 1993 made no mention of the CAF/Croatian battle in the Medak Pocket. This raises the possibility that the reporting was suppressed. However, a threat assessment issued on 22 September clearly drew upon that incident to highlight new risks to Canadian troops in the area: "The move of CANBAT 1 to a sector where both factions have recently been fighting has required a reevaluation of the threat to Canadian Forces. Although the risk level remains relatively unchanged . . . it is assessed that . . . the Croats are the more likely threat."[79] The assessment went on to place the threat within the context of Croatian political expectations and suggested that "UNPROFOR may be perceived as an obstacle to Croatian aspirations." It concluded that "if, and when, a deliberate attack upon UNPROFOR troops where [sic] to occur it is likely to originate from Croat forces."[80] It was a sound assessment for the benefit of those outside the area, but the Canadian troops in the Medak salient already knew that. Indeed, two weeks later that area experienced the highest number of cease-fire violations.[81]

On 1 November 1993 the NDIC issued its weekly assessment of threats to Canadian forces in UNPROFOR, focusing on "strategic intentions" rather than "tactical capabilities." Circulated widely as unclassified, it assessed the risk to CAF positions in both Croatian and Bosnia as "low with potential to rise rapidly to medium." Not surprisingly, Sector South was deemed the "most likely Canadian area in the former Yugoslavia for a rapid escalation of the threat level." If the Croats decided to launch even a limited offensive, it probably would take place in the Canadian area "and could occur with little or no strategic warning."[82]

Although the DGI did not anticipate any major military activity in the Srebrenica area, where Canadian troops were based in the fall of 1993, it felt that this was the locale in Bosnia most likely to escalate to a medium threat level. This could occur if tensions increased between Bosnian Muslims and Serbs in the area or if the Muslims in the enclave feared that the UN force was going to be reduced. The threat level could rise with "little or no strategic warning."[83] As if to reinforce that point, heavy fighting was reported north of the town the very next day. And by 8 November, the DGI had raised the threat level there to medium, with the potential to escalate rapidly being high.[84] These assessments demonstrate how volatile the situation was inside former Yugoslavia at that time and how quickly it could worsen. Thus, it made sense for the analysts to err on the side of caution and pessimism.

The NDIC also tried to keep Canadian UN forces and NATO abreast of the belligerents' intelligence and EW capabilities. For example, in November 1993 the NDIC circulated a report on a Croatian air force initiative. It had modified an AN-2 Colt biplane to conduct passive ELINT operations using a Lockheed-Sanders SR-200B electronic support measures system. The AN-2 would be able to detect radars at long distance as well as the launch of FROG-7 missiles and would allow the Croatians to build an "electronic order of battle" of Serb forces in the Krajina.[85] The source was not revealed, but since the work undoubtedly took place in secret away from the combat areas, the information probably was acquired through non-Canadian clandestine means. An April 1994 NDIC study of Bosnian Serb tactics included a brief discussion of their EW and communications security capabilities.[86]

On 19 November 1993 the NDIC circulated a statistical analysis of data compiled by the US Defense Intelligence Agency of "hostile acts" against international forces in the Balkans. The DGI did its own analysis and interpretation of the data before circulating it, making clear to the reader that this represented a Canadian perspective, not one from any allied agency. Covering a thirteen-month period from October 1992 to October 1993, it showed over nine hundred attacks, of which more than five hundred occurred in the most recent five months. The incidents were correlated with specific campaigns of fighting, including the Croat Medak offensive. UNPROFOR troops were the most frequent targets, with British forces targeted most (9% of attacks on UNPROFOR) and the French and the Canadians next (5% each). The DGI pointed out that this made sense since these were the largest contingents, deployed in the least stable areas.[87] As a useful follow-on to this study, the threat assessment for the last week of November noted that the contingent in Srebrenica was the most exposed CAF unit in the area. Presciently, the report also warned that "in the event of air strikes, we assess that the Bosnian Serb Army will most likely intentionally target UN/NATO forces in retaliation. Strategic warning of this will likely be available."[88] In reality, this report itself *was* strategic warning. No one who saw it could legitimately claim to have been surprised when UNPROFOR troops were taken hostage after NATO air strikes in 1994 and 1995.[89]

As the commitment lengthened, the Canadian contingent increasingly received reports from the NDIC that originated (or may have) from sensitive sources and methods. For example, in December 1993 the NDIC told the Canadian Contingent UNPROFOR that "a Bosnian Muslim soldier is reported to have said that 3,000 Muslim troops have moved into the area of Novi Travnik. He claimed that this area would be the main point of effort for the next Muslim offensive."[90] The report does not indicate how this source conveyed the information or who was the original recipient. And while this kind of HUMINT normally requires multisource corroboration to determine its reliability, in this case subsequent intelligence reports detailing Bosnian Muslim forces' attacks in that area lent credibility to this source reporting.

At the end of January 1994, an NDIC report on Croatian regular forces operating in Bosnia identified specific units and subunits, reorganized tactical groupings, equipment, and locations. The level of detail in this report suggests that it likely was based on fused intelligence from multiple source reporting from patrols and OPs, UN military observers, the European Community Monitoring Mission in Yugoslavia reporting, NATO aerial reconnaissance, SIGINT, and overt and covert HUMINT (possibly including Croat defectors).[91] A few days later, an NDIC report noted the presence west of Zvornik of 160 troops from 389th Signals Battalion of the JNA 1st Army, which it interpreted as an indication of growing JNA support for Bosnian Serb forces. The very specific details suggest that it relied on more than just routine patrol reports.[92]

Two days after that, the NDIC issued an extended analysis of the Markela Market attack in Sarajevo that killed sixty-eight people on 5 February. Due to the complex incident scene, investigations thus far had been inconclusive, so the UN had been unable to assign responsibility for the attack. The Western media roundly condemned the Serbs for it, although given the political situation at the time they had nothing to gain from ordering such an attack. The NDIC report states that "Special Intelligence indicates that they were unaware of the incident before it occurred."[93] The source likely was SIGINT, probably from NATO members, since the US National Security Agency apparently did not have good coverage of eastern Bosnia.[94]

On 11 February the DND's DIE circulated a US Defense Intelligence Agency report that identified weapons, vehicles, and other equipment at specific locations by grid reference, noting troop movements, battlefield changes, and usage in seven selected areas of Bosnia. The report was based on "all source reporting," including some from "sensitive intelligence sources and/or methods" (it specified imagery acquired on 25 January and 1 February). It was not to be released outside Canadian-UK-US eyes,[95] but the Canadian Contingent UNPROFOR could access this high-grade intelligence without having to violate the UN's ban on covert collection.

Similar reports, circulated on 15 and 21 February, identified (for possible aerial targeting purposes) field and AAA artillery positions around Sarajevo. Like the preceding documents, the first carried a warning that it contained "material derived from single source reporting. . . . Some of the material . . . may have been derived from sensitive sources and/or methods and therefore this report shall not/will not be released to non-NATO organizations."[96] In fact, the latter report was based on "all NATO tactical reconnaissance sources as well as theatre and national sources."[97] Theatre sources may have included British-based U-2s, while satellites probably comprised the national ones.[98] Some of these reports (such as the one of 11 February) were generated by the NDIC or the DIE at the request of the Canadian Contingent UNPROFOR. Access to such sources was a value-added complement to the limited capabilities UNPROFOR deployed on the ground.[99] But there were instances—probably due to weather conditions—when they could not provide usable imagery.[100] And the factions objected to this kind of surveillance.[101] On 12 February 1994 the NDIC had circulated an estimate, requested by the DCDS, on the forces and equipment available to the factions in Bosnia. The drafters of the report conceded that "current all source intelligence available is accounting for only a fraction of the heavy equipment available to factional forces in Bosnia. A rough estimate of current coverage with strategic assets is, at best, one third of the estimated total forces present. The data in this document is an estimate based on the Yugo Crisis Cell draft orders of battle.... Confirmed or reported data is available for one third of factional units. The remainder have been templated, based on an average of known units."[102] The authors noted that where the estimates offered a range of numbers, the higher figures were more likely for the Bosnian Serb forces and the lower for the Bosnian government forces.

The DGI also handled requests for information from NATO itself. On 18 February the NDIC had passed along a request for information from Supreme Headquarters Allied Powers Europe (SHAPE) for specific types of intelligence on the Tuzla, Srebrenica, and Mostar areas (the cities themselves and up to 30 kilometres outside). The NDIC wanted terrain analysis; lists of all artillery, air defence, and defensive positions; updated ground order of battle; biographies of local commanders; and the reactions of local factions to the UN presence. The DGI assigned the first task to the Directorate of Geomatics Operations, the second to the DIE, and the remainder to the YCC. In its reply on 28 February the DGI was able to supply detailed information only on the Srebrenica area. For Tuzla and Mostar the DGI had data only on terrain, weapons, and local commanders.[103]

Since NATO had issued an ultimatum to the factions after the market attack, this request for information clearly reflected its anticipation that it might become more deeply involved whether through air strikes or other means. Thus, it is probably no coincidence that during 1994 the United Kingdom and several other European countries created a covert team to collect terrain and infrastructure intelligence inside Bosnia. Operating under the cover story of a "tourist association" interested in postconflict development, the team collected the intelligence openly. But the UN did not know about this covert operation.[104] Presumably, the SHAPE Intelligence Division was the intended recipient.

In response to another request for information from SHAPE, on 16 March the NDIC provided a forecast of political and military activity in former Yugoslavia for the next two months. The assessment covered the peace negotiations, the cease-fire agreement between the Bosnian government and the Croats, renewed military activity by all factions, and the reactions and positions of Serbia and Croatia. Overall, the NDIC offered a cautious, even pessimistic prognosis on all of the topics.[105] The SHAPE Intelligence Division would have collated reports such as this with those of other NATO members, then integrated the content into an agreed NATO assessment. That would be used by NATO planners responsible for enforcing the no-fly zone and other possible actions.

The following month in the wake of the Serb defeat of Bosnian forces in the UNPA of Gorazde, the DGI offered a blunt, grim assessment of its implications. "Strategically, they have given a graphic demonstration of their continuing supremacy on the battlefield, and have achieved a major psychological victory over the Muslims, NATO, and UNPROFOR.... Politically, the Serbs have shown sufficient resolve to successfully defy NATO and the UN. Their relationship with both agencies has been irrevocably changed in their favour."[106] The report added that "Karadzic has won, and is not going to let the UN off the hook all at once." The Bosnian Serb Army still held 135 UN personnel as hostages and were unlikely to rescind the implicit threat to UN forces until they were certain they would get what they wanted from the UN. But a rapprochement with the Serbs would not bring respite to the UN forces, since the Bosnian Muslims felt betrayed by them. So, the UN forces would remain at risk of attack from both sides. The DGI regarded this as "a new and potentially explosive phase" for the UN mission.[107]

In Gorazde itself, the cease-fire was holding at the end of April, and UN military observers were reporting that "virtually all" Bosnian Serb Army heavy weapons had been withdrawn from the twenty-kilometre exclusion zone around the UNPA. But the DGI stated that UN forces lacked the means to "thoroughly monitor" the zone. The DGI noted that the Serbs could have moved those weapons into buildings, caves, and other concealed positions and that the UN's inability to check withdrawals would "further encourage the Serbs non-compliance with the agreement."[108] This highlights the impact of having insufficient personnel to cover a large politically complex and geographically challenging AOR and of the limits imposed on collection sources and methods. It is clear from this report alone that UNPROFOR could not always count on NATO or Five Eyes assets to offset the deficiencies in its own collection capabilities.

Naval Intelligence Support

The NDIC/YCC also reported regularly on the disposition, activities, and movements of former Yugoslavian naval units. The navy consisted of some fifteen surface combatants, a roughly equal number of minesweepers, several submarines, and fixed artillery, all optimized for coastal defence.[109] The Serbian forces held the Prevlaka peninsula, which protected the main Yugoslav naval base at Kotor. While these forces had no capacity to alter the situation on the ground in Bosnia, they could have impacted the conduct of Operation SHARP GUARD temporarily had they chosen to do so. However, apart from the occasional exercise, they rarely ventured from port. Nevertheless, the NDIC kept its distribution list in the loop on naval activity. That list included the intelligence staffs at Canadian naval headquarters and at key NATO and allied offices: the assistant chief of staff for intelligence at SHAPE, the Joint Analysis Centre in the United Kingdom, the intelligence staff and Canadian liaison officer at Allied Forces Southern Europe, and the US European Command headquarters, among others.[110] They would have had access to the same intelligence and similar assessments from NATO, Five Eyes, and other national agencies.

The reports do not say how the information was collected, but this is not hard to deduce. The NATO naval vessels carried sensors that could detect ship movements and intercept the communications of vessels that might be putting to sea. HMCS *Algonquin*, the first ship in the Canadian rotation, monitored the air box over the sector closest to the Yugoslav coast and collected electronic support measures and EW data. Its primary targets were shore-based Styx missile batteries and their radars. *Algonquin*'s Serbo-Croat–speaking linguists monitored Yugoslav VHF communications. All such data was shared among the SHARP GUARD forces.[111]

From August 1993 to January 1994 two CAF CP-140 Aurora aircraft, operating out of the NATO base at Sigonella, Sicily, flew one-third of the ten-hour patrol missions every day. They carried a surface search radar; had stabilized infrared tracking, sonobuoys, magnetic detection, electronic support measures; and could do night photography, a rare capability among the NATO forces (figure 8.1). Each CP-140 was data-linked to the surface task group in its sector, liaising with the Air Control Unit, which during their tour was either *Algonquin* or its successor, HMCS *Iroquois*.[112]

These Canadian efforts were part of a larger coordinated naval and air intelligence operation that was supporting enforcement of the embargo. Writing several years later, Stephen Prince and Kate Brett put that operation in perspective, noting that one of the main challenges of SHARP GUARD was "achieving constant situational awareness of shipping movements in the busy Adriatic waters and then choreographing the tracking, challenging, inspection, and diversion of suspect vessels as required."[113] They assert that the recognized air and surface picture) "had been good from an early stage . . . largely due to the almost universal distribution of the Link-11 data-sharing system as a minimum standard for NATO surface ships participating in Sharp Guard."[114] Even so, it fell short of perfect. The ships could not send data to Allied Naval Forces, Southern

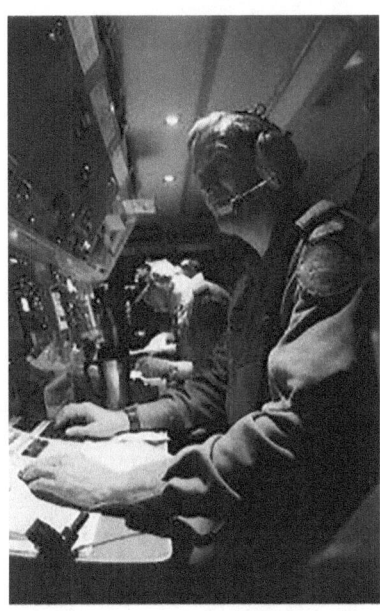

FIGURE 8.1. The tactical compartment on a CP-140 Aurora maritime patrol aircraft operating out of Sigonella, Italy, in 2004 on a NATO antiterrorism operation. *Department of National Defence*

Europe headquarters. Sensor coverage of the blockade areas was limited to the range of shipborne sensors and was never complete in the Strait of Otranto. So, the Allied Naval Forces Southern Europe recognized air and surface picture was usually twelve to eighteen hours out of date. Blockade-runners were able to exploit this gap.[115]

These problems eventually were overcome through two related initiatives. The first was the designation of a "Red Crown" ship (usually a USN Aegis cruiser) that would develop a "theatre-wide Link-11 picture" that fused data from the task groups working in both sectors. When this data was combined with greatly increased coverage by maritime patrol aircraft that "filled the gaps in surface surveillance," it yielded a more complete picture of the operational theatre. The second initiative was to have a USN officer in the Red Crown ship use its Tactical Command Information Exchange Subsystem (a satellite data system) to transmit this picture to Allied Naval Forces Southern Europe, where the United States "had donated the necessary receiving equipment."[116] The Red Crown ship also sent the data to the USN Fleet Ocean Surveillance Information Facility in Rota, Spain, which then added other American information and data from any non–Link-11 NATO ships. The Fleet Ocean Surveillance Information Facility then sent the enhanced data to "all ships participating in Sharp Guard."[117] The result was a kind of virtuous circle of intelligence that began with raw data from the sensors of individual ships and returned to them as an enhanced all-source intelligence product. The operational impact of this process was to create a nearly watertight naval embargo.

CONCLUSION

The NDIC reports from 1993–94 shed considerable light on the intelligence support provided to the CAF contingents in UNPROFOR and SHARP GUARD and on that being circulated at the highest levels in the DND/NDHQ. First, it is clear that the contingent headquarters were keeping NDIC well informed of events and changes in theatre that its units and personnel observed. They also reported on incidents that posed risks to CAF personnel so that Ottawa would not be caught by surprise by media reporting. So, they were contributing directly to the situational awareness picture of the conflict and the operations being seen at NDHQ.

Second, the main value of NDIC's reports for CAF in UNPROFOR and for the senior leadership in NDHQ probably was their strategic perspective that could correlate political shifts and trends with actual or anticipated changes (escalation, de-escalation) in the situation on the ground (and vice versa). NDIC's analysis also showed that while the conflict involved many irregular activities and excessive, gratuitous violence, there was some strategic coherence to the fighting. All sides were using largely conventional weapons, tactics, and operations to seize and hold ground for strategic purposes: to consolidate territory for their entities.

Third, they illustrate how precarious was the position of UNPROFOR troops and how constrained was their ability to influence events or even report on them. Finally, the reports reveal the extent to which Five Eyes and NATO intelligence collection and analysis assets were harnessed to assist the UNPROFOR mission. They could observe things that were denied to the UN forces by either their own rules, their insufficient numbers, obstruction by the belligerents, or even the challenges posed by difficult terrain. This data was also useful for NATO planners tasked with preparing for air strikes or other contingencies. But they also show the limits on the utility of such assets: time delays between collection, analysis, and distribution and the gaps imposed by intelligence-sharing protocols and weather.

In short, better intelligence could not make UNPROFOR more effective. For a whole array of reasons, success—defined as either containing or ending the fighting—was beyond its grasp. UNPROFOR contingents, including the Canadians, could not even protect their own personnel from harassment, threats, attack, and capture. The nature of the conflict, the attitudes, the goals and actions of its belligerents, and the overly ambitious goals coupled with the insufficient resources of the UN mission, unrealistic ROE, and their dispersed vulnerability doomed UNPROFOR to failure. No amount of good intelligence was going to change that.

NOTES

1. Sabrina P. Ramet, *Balkan Babel: The Disintegration of Yugoslavia from the Death of Tito to the Fall of Milošević*, 4th ed. (Boulder, CO: Westview, 2002), 5–9, 15, 18–20, 26–27, 50–51, 56–60, 66–69, 163, 203, 205–7, 211–12, 216–17, 230–39; and Steven L. Burg and Paul S. Shoup, *The War in Bosnia-Herzegovina: Ethnic Conflict and International Intervention* (London: Routledge, 2015), 20, 40–45, 46–61, 65–68, 81–84, 118–20, 129, 131–36, 140–59, 164–69, 324, 328–29, 331, 348–53, 355–77.
2. Ramet, *Balkan Babel*, 67–69, 163; and Burg and Shoup, *War in Bosnia-Herzegovina*, 119–20, 137, 140, 145, 169–81, 324–25.
3. Burg and Shoup, *War in Bosnia-Herzegovina*, 190–91.
4. Mats R. Berdal, *Whither UN Peacekeeping? An Analysis of the Changing Military Requirements of UN Peacekeeping with Proposals for Its Enhancement* (London: Brassey's, for the International Institute for Strategic Studies, 1993), 22, 28–29, 31; and John Hillen, *Blue Helmets: The Strategy of UN Military Operations* (Washington, DC: Brassey's, 1998), 158–62, 167, 169.
5. Ramet, *Balkan Babel*, 59–60, 64, 66–69.
6. Department of Public Information, United Nations, "Former Yugoslavia— UNPROFOR: United Nations Protection Force, Background," United Nations Peacekeeping, September 1996, https://peacekeeping.un.org/mission/past/unprof_b.htm.
7. Department of Public Information.
8. Brig.-Gen. (ret.) Glenn Nordick, interview with author, 11 June 2019.
9. Lewis MacKenzie, *Peacekeeper: The Road to Sarajevo* (Vancouver: Douglas & McIntyre, 1993), 106–7.
10. Burg and Shoup, *War in Bosnia-Herzegovina*, 129, 131, 165–66.
11. Department of Public Information, "Former Yugoslavia."
12. Department of Public Information; Burg and Shoup, *War in Bosnia-Herzegovina*, 132. MacKenzie, *Peacekeeper*, 198–278, explains the chaotic and dangerous process of reaching a cease-fire and securing the airport. But Carol Off, in *The Lion, the Fox and the Eagle: A Story of Generals and Justice in Yugoslavia and Rwanda* (Toronto: Random House, 2000), provides an unflattering view of MacKenzie's efforts.
13. Department of Public Information, "Former Yugoslavia."
14. Department of Public Information.
15. Hillen, *Blue Helmets*, 169.
16. Hillen, 169.
17. Berdal, *Whither UN Peacekeeping?*, 22.
18. Hillen, *Blue Helmets*, 142–43, 161–62.
19. Burg and Shoup, *War in Bosnia-Herzegovina*, 329.
20. Quoted in Hillen, *Blue Helmets*, 176. The DGI had reached this conclusion in April 1994. See *DGINT Assessment—The Aftermath of Gorazde*, 21 April 1994, LAC, RG25, vol. 28210, file 21-14-7-UNPROFOR-1, part 8.

21. National Defence, "United Nations Protection Force (UNPROFOR)," Government of Canada, 11 December 2018, https://www.canada.ca/en/department-national-defence/services/military-history/history-heritage/past-operations/europe/canengbat-mandarin-harmony-cavalier-medusa-panorama.html.
22. National Defence.
23. Glenn W. Nordick, *Battalion Command: UNPROFOR (Sector West) Croatia, September 1992 to April 1993*, Personal Experience Monograph (Carlisle Barracks, PA: US Army War College, 1999), 20.
24. Nordick, 5, 26.
25. Nordick, 20–27.
26. Lee A. Windsor, "Professionalism under Fire: Canadian Implementation of the Medak Pocket Agreement, Croatia 1993," *Canadian Military History* 9, no. 3 (2000): 23–35. Carol Off, *The Ghosts of Medak Pocket: The Story of Canada's Secret War* (Toronto: Vintage, 2005), provides a detailed journalistic analysis.
27. Sean M. Maloney and John Llambias, *Chances for Peace: Canadian Soldiers in the Balkans, 1992–1995: An Oral History* (St. Catharines, Ontario: Vanwell, 2002), 11.
28. Scott Taylor and Brian Nolan, *Tested Mettle: Canada's Peacekeepers at War* (Ottawa: Esprit de Corps Books, 1998), 100–101.
29. Taylor and Nolan, 101–9; and Maloney and Llambias, *Chances for Peace*, 48–49. Both sources rely on the personal recollections of the 2 RCR soldiers who served in the enclave.
30. Maloney and Llambias, *Chances for Peace*, 221–22, 223–24, 260–61.
31. Maloney and Llambias, 223, 226–37, 261–67, 273–74. The squadrons also had to protect the BG's own convoys moving supplies and personnel.
32. Lt.-Gen. (ret.) Michel Gauthier, interview with author, 5 November 2019.
33. "NATO/WEU Operation Sharp Guard—IFOR Final Factsheet," NATO/OTAN North Atlantic Treaty Organization, 2 October 1996, https://www.nato.int/ifor/general/shrp-grd.htm; and Stephen Prince and Kate Brett, "Royal Navy Operations off the Former Yugoslavia: Operation Sharp Guard, 1991–1996," in *You Cannot Surge Trust: Combined Naval Operations of the Royal Australian Navy, Canadian Navy, Royal Navy, and United States Navy, 1991–2003*, ed. Gary E. Weir and Sandra J. Doyle (Washington, DC: Department of the Navy, 2013), 63.
34. Sean M. Maloney, *The Hindrance of Military Operations Ashore: Canadian Participation in Operation Sharp Guard, 1993–1996* (Halifax, Nova Scotia: Centre for Foreign Policy Studies, Dalhousie University, 2000), 14, 23–25, 28, 31–32, 35, 40–49, 56, table 1.
35. Cited in Hugh Smith, "Intelligence and UN Peacekeeping," *Survival* 36, no. 3 (1994): 174.
36. A. Walter Dorn, "The Cloak and the Blue Beret: Limitations on Intelligence in UN Peacekeeping," in *Intelligence in Peacekeeping*, Pearson Papers 4 (Clementsport, Nova Scotia: Canadian Peacekeeping Press, 1999), 1. See also Sir David Ramsbotham, "Analysis and Assessment for Peacekeeping Operations," in *Intelligence Analysis and Assessment*, ed. David A. Charters, Anthony Stuart Farson, and Glenn P. Hastedt (London: Frank Cass, 1996), 162.
37. Canadian Armed Forces and NDHQ, *CFP 301 (3) Peacekeeping Doctrine* (first draft, Ottawa, June 1992), 21.
38. Dorn, "Cloak and the Blue Beret," 6; and Nordick, interview.

39. *CFP 301 (3)*, 21. Patrolling was the major collection task. Michael Anthony Staples, *Combat Ready: Travelling with Canada's Peacekeepers in the Former Yugoslavia*, 2nd ed. (Fredericton, New Brunswick: Unipress, 2000), 17, says that in 1994 in Sector South 1 RCR's quick-reaction force was conducting between eight and fourteen patrols per day.
40. Dorn, "Cloak and the Blue Beret," 8–12.
41. *INP Intelligence Report Eastern Europe: Difficult Roads to Democracy*, FIB 90-39, 90-05-08 (8 May 1990) and *INP/INE Intelligence Report Yugoslavia: Challenges to the Federation* FIB 90-64, 90-09-17 (17 September 1990), both LAC, RG25, BAN 2017-00434-0, box 12, file 29-2-23, part 9; and *INP Current Assessment Yugoslavia: Tensions Increase as Deadlines Approach*, FAB (CA) 91-50, 91-05-07 (7 May 1991), LAC, RG25, BAN 2017-00440-5, box 29021, file 29-2-31.
42. Maloney and Llambias, *Chances for Peace*, 25.
43. Taylor and Nolan, *Tested Mettle*, 42.
44. Lt.-Col. Michel Jones, interview, 22 September 2005, Canadian War Museum Oral History Program.
45. Jones.
46. Quoted in Maloney and Llambias, *Chances for Peace*, 25.
47. Maloney and Llambias, 27–28.
48. Jones interview.
49. MacKenzie, *Peacekeeper*, 94–97, 100, 105–7.
50. MacKenzie, 137.
51. Off, *The Lion, the Fox and the Eagle*, 139.
52. Off, 139.
53. MacKenzie, *Peacekeeper*, 143.
54. MacKenzie, 145.
55. MacKenzie, 217.
56. MacKenzie, 217.
57. MacKenzie, 281, 284–85.
58. MacKenzie, 278–79.
59. Dorn, "Cloak and the Blue Beret," 13.
60. Gauthier, interview.
61. Gauthier.
62. Gauthier.
63. Gauthier.
64. Nordick, *Battalion Command*, 18–19. These were routine peacekeeping tasks. See David A. Charters, "Out of the Closet: Intelligence Support for Post-Modernist Peacekeeping," in *Intelligence in Peacekeeping*, Pearson Papers 4 (Clementsport, Nova Scotia: Canadian Peacekeeping Press, 1999), 57, 67, and note 56.
65. Off, *Ghosts of Medak Pocket*, 106.
66. Off, 128, 132, 153, 155–56; and Maloney and Llambias, *Chances for Peace*, 115–18, 140, 160.
67. Taylor and Nolan, *Tested Mettle*, 124.
68. NDHQ, "Briefing to Mr. John Richardson, Parliamentary Secretary to the Minister of National Defence, Concerning the UN Situation Centre, New York," 22 July 1997, 1, author's copy.
69. NDHQ, 2–5. See also additional sources cited in Charters, "Out of the Closet," 51–52n36.

70. Ramsbotham, "Analysis and Assessment," 169.
71. Charters, "Out of the Closet," 56n55; "1994–1995, Canadian Intelligence in the Former Yugoslav Republic: Article by Col C. S. Hamel," in Harold A. Skaarup, *Out of Darkness—Light: A History of Canadian Military Intelligence*, Vol. 2 (New York: iUniverse, 2005), 273–74; and Lt.-Col. (ret.) Rhe Ap Probert, interview with author, 12 June 2019.
72. Probert interview.
73. Probert.
74. DND and Army Lessons Learned Centre, *Operations in the Former Republic of Yugoslavia*, Dispatches 4.1 (Kingston, Ontario: DND and Army Lessons Learned Centre, September 1996), 25.
75. Col. Victor Ashdown, "DDI Reorganization," Memorandum, 6 July 1994, LAC, RG24, BAN 2005-00285, box 15, file 1920-1, part 12. See also NDIC to distribution list, "Subj: Yugo Crisis Cell (YCC) Schedule/Manning Amendments," Message, 28 March 1994, LAC, RG25, vol. 28210, file 21-14-6-UNPROFOR-1, part 7.
76. See, for example, DND, "Former Yugoslavia Int Report," 25 August 1993, and "Former Yugoslavia Intrep," 21 January 1994, LAC, RG25, vol. 28210, file 21-14-6-UNPROFOR-1, parts 1 and 5, respectively. Unless otherwise indicated, all DND intelligence reports and messages cited below are from the same record group, volume, and file—LAC, RG25, vol. 28210, file 21-14-6-UNPROFOR-1—differing only by date and part (where given).
77. DND, "Subj: RSK Irregular Forces," Message, 2 September 1993.
78. DND, "Former Yugoslavia Int Report," 8 September 1993.
79. DND, "Subj: Threat to Canadian Forces in Former Yugoslavia," Message, 22 September 1993.
80. DND, "Threat to Canadian Forces."
81. DND, "Former Yugoslavia Int Report," 30 September 1993.
82. DGI, "Former Yugo Weekly Threat Assessment," 1 November 1993.
83. DGI.
84. DND, "Former Yugoslavia Intreps," 2 and 8 November 1993.
85. DND, "Former Yugoslavia Intrep," 9 November 1993.
86. NDIC, "Bosnian Serb Tactics," 18 April 1994, part 8.
87. *Hostile Acts against UN/International Forces Oct 92 to Oct 93*, 19 November 1993.
88. DGI, "Former Yugo Weekly Threat Assessment," 22 November 1993.
89. See NDIC, "Former Yugoslavia Intreps," 12 and 18 April 1994.
90. DND, "Former Yugoslavia Intrep," 10 December 1993.
91. NDIC, "Current Intelligence Report Croat Forces (HV) Deployment in Bosnia–Hercegovina," 31 January 1994, part 5.
92. DND, "Former Yugoslavia Intrep," 4 February 1994.
93. DND, "Sarajevo Situation Update," 6 February 1994.
94. See Bob de Graaff and Cees Wiebes, "Fallen off the Priority List: Was Srebrenica an Intelligence Failure?," in *The Role of Intelligence in Ending the War in Bosnia in 1995*, ed. Timothy R. Walton (Lanham, MD: Lexington Books, 2014), 157.
95. DIE to CCMIO Camp Polom [and rest of distribution list], "Subj: DIE Imagery Highlight Intrep (IHREP) 007/94," Intrep, 11 February 1994.
96. DIE, "Subj: Special Sarajevo Artillery/AAA Baseline," Message, 14 February 1994. The data was compiled by US European Command's Joint Analysis Center at RAF Molesworth, United Kingdom. The JAC had been opened in October 1991.

It included a new built-to-purpose facility for processing long-roll wet film from U-2 image intelligence missions flown out of RAF Alconbury. See Col. USAF (ret.) Robert G. Stiegel, "The Origin and Evolution of the Joint Analysis Center at RAF Molesworth," *Studies in Intelligence* 62, no. 1, Extracts (March 2018): 29, 31, 32–35.

97. DIE to CCMIO Camp Polom, "Subj: Special Sarajevo Artillery/AAA Baseline," Message, 21 February 1994.
98. DIE, "Imagery Highlight Rep (IHREP) 013/94," Intrep, 25 March 1994, notes the use of radar imaging on 18 March to track vehicle movement at Udbina airfield. This probably was carried out by U-2/TR-1 or by satellite. DIE, "Imagery Highlight Rep (IHREP) 018/94," Intrep, 25 April 1994, also cites use of radar and electro-optical imagery.
99. For example, DIE, "Imagery Highlight Rep (IHREP) 011/94," Intrep, 14 March 1994, includes overhead imagery and UNPROFOR reporting on the air order of battle at Udbina airfield, but the former had not confirmed the latter.
100. DIE, "Imagery Highlight Rep (IHREP) 009/94," Intrep, 25 February 1994.
101. A Krajina Serb commander protested to UNPROFOR about NATO overflights of his area on "intelligence collection missions": DND, "Former Yugoslavia Intrep," 10 March 1994.
102. NDIC to distribution list, "Subj: Former Yugoslavia—Estimate of Bosnian Factions Affected by NATO Ultimatum of 09 Feb 94," Message, 12 February 1994, part 7.
103. NDIC, "Subj: NATO Request for Info," Message, 28 February 1994.
104. Dorn, "Cloak and the Blue Beret," 9.
105. NDIC, "Subj: Former Yugoslavia Assessment Update," 16 March 1994, in response to SHAPE request on 15 March.
106. NDIC, "Former Yugoslavia Intrep," 18 April 1994.
107. NDIC; DGI, *Aftermath of Gorazde*.
108. NDIC, "Former Yugoslavia Intreps," 27 and 29 April 1994.
109. Maloney, *Hindrance of Military Operations*, 13–14, 17–18.
110. See, for example, NDIC, "Former Yugoslavia Int Reports" for 25 and 30 August, 3, 15, 16, 24 September, and 13, 29 October 1993; DGI, "Former Yugo Weekly Threat Assessments," 1 and 8 November 1993. The naval portion in the assessment of 31 January 1994 was no different from those cited in the fall of 1993. Many 1994 reports included no reference to naval forces.
111. Maloney, *Hindrance of Military Operations*, 25.
112. Maloney, 33–35, 38.
113. Prince and Brett, "Royal Navy Operations," 55.
114. Prince and Brett, 57.
115. Prince and Brett, 57.
116. Prince and Brett, 57–58.
117. Prince and Brett, 57–58.

9

PEACE ENFORCEMENT IN BOSNIA

The NATO Years, 1996–2004

A sequence of events brought the Bosnian war to an end in 1995: Croatia's Operation STORM, which forced the Serb forces out of many areas they had captured; NATO air strikes, which coincided with the Croatian offensive; and the partly negotiated, partly imposed settlement, the General Framework Agreement for Peace, commonly referred to as the Dayton Accords, which the leaders of all three belligerent entities signed in December 1995. The accords comprised eleven articles and annexes meant to promote a permanent military cease-fire and disengagement and political and social reconstruction within the framework of a multiethnic, bicameral federation of Bosnia-Herzegovina. This would be secured by NATO forces, the initial Implementation Force (IFOR) and its successor, the Stabilization Force (SFOR).[1]

But this agreement could not resolve the underlying sources of the conflict, so the political and social reconstruction was not wholly achieved. With nationalist leaders in control, political positions remained rigid. Major fighting had stopped, but there was a strong undercurrent of low-level intimidation and violence. Moreover, the Dayton Accords did not address the fate of rump Yugoslavia (Serbia, Vojvidinja, Kosovo, and Montenegro). That state remained in crisis, which came to a head in 1997–99 when a Kosovar insurgency and Serb military repression created yet another political and humanitarian crisis. This prompted another NATO intervention, which is discussed in chapter 10.[2]

The CAF participated in the peace enforcement efforts in Bosnia and Kosovo. Those operations offered a stark contrast to those conducted under UNPROFOR. First, those in Bosnia were carried out within the framework of the Dayton Accords. The security pillar of the accords (Annexes 1 A and B) underpinned all other efforts, since without security nothing else could be achieved.[3] Second, the UN had authorized this security mission but had subcontracted the task to NATO, simplifying the C2 process with a single chain of command and decision making. Third, the NATO mission in Bosnia was a peace-enforcement operation, operating under UN Chapter Seven guidelines. This meant that NATO could use force to ensure that the partners to the accords adhered to its terms.[4] Fourth, NATO deployed a substantial force (initially, some sixty thousand troops) to show that it had the power to enforce the security provisions. NATO's IFOR operated there from December 1995 to December 1996, when it was replaced by the smaller (initially thirty-five thousand and then reduced gradually) SFOR that remained until December 2004.[5] Finally, the CAF missions required and mostly received modestly robust intelligence support.

THE OPERATING ENVIRONMENT

The operating environment varied considerably over time and location. In Bosnia, cities and towns had been severely damaged or destroyed, and unmarked minefields and booby traps had rendered the countryside and roads unsafe. Hundreds of thousands of people had been driven from their homes and wanted to return, but in many cases their areas were held by their enemies. The economy had collapsed, and the fighting had damaged or destroyed critical infrastructure. Political reconciliation was paralyzed by the fact that strong nationalists remained in power in Bosnian- and Serbian-controlled entities within the federation created under the accords.[6]

The nature and level of the threat had changed dramatically from the UNPROFOR era. Major factional fighting had ceased, and the risk of attacks on NATO troops was almost nil. The IFOR/SFOR were sufficiently powerful forces that none of the local factions had the means or will to challenge it. Even so, the US military—the dominant force in the IFOR/SFOR—did not take any threats lightly and gave high priority to "force protection."[7] Most of the low-level violence was directed at displaced minorities trying to return to their homes. One such incident in the Canadian sector in April 1998, which led to rioting and attacks on the UN's International Police Task Force, is discussed below.[8]

The principal threat in Bosnia was from as many as one million mines dispersed in marked or unmarked minefields. This imposed limits on the mobility of IFOR/SFOR troops and locals. Assisted by the SFOR, civilian nongovernmental organizations and entity military demining teams carried out the painstaking clearance task so that road and cross-country movement could be safely assured.[9]

CANADIAN ARMED FORCES COMMITMENT

Just as it had in UNPROFOR, the Canadian commitment evolved over time. First, under Operation ALLIANCE it deployed two six-month rotations of one thousand or more troops each to Bosnia from December 1995 to December 1996. This included a brigade headquarters and a small BG consisting of an infantry company, a reconnaissance squadron, and an engineer squadron, with a Czech mechanized infantry battalion under command.[10] Canada also committed naval and air assets to maintain the maritime arms blockade and the no-fly zone.

Second, when the IFOR shifted into the longer-term SFOR in 1997, Canada contributed a larger battalion-based BG until 2004 under Operation PALLADIUM. In March 1998 the Canadian contingent consisted of 1,285 troops: the 1st Battalion Royal Canadian Regiment (1 RCR) BG of about 900 troops (three mechanized infantry companies, a reconnaissance squadron, an engineer squadron, and headquarters and support) under a contingent headquarters that had administration, logistics, signals, military police, and a medical unit. Two other units were assigned directly to the SFOR: an engineer company and the new CANIC. The CAF contingent was part of the Multi-National Division South West (MND-SW), which had five additional BGs (British, Czech, Dutch, and Malaysian) under command of a joint headquarters. The MND-SW was British-led until Canadian major-general Rick Hillier commanded it from September 2000 to September 2001.[11]

OPERATIONS ALLIANCE AND PALLADIUM

The remainder of this chapter examines the CAF mission, its intelligence requirements, the intelligence support provided, and its impact on operations.

Missions, Tasks, and Intelligence Requirements

The mission of the IFOR/SFOR—to enforce the security pillar of the Dayton Accords—committed the NATO-led forces to maintaining the zones of separation between former belligerent forces, overseeing and securing the cantonment of heavy weapons and demobilization of forces, and supervising and assisting demining.[12] This brief summary simplifies what were at times challenging and politically fraught activities. They required the CAF contingent to be prepared to employ the full range of its combat capabilities as well as its skills at diplomacy, negotiation, and crisis de-escalation learned through decades of peacekeeping experience.

C2 technology and the unique features of modern war—both conventional and unconventional—have combined to blur the lines between the strategic, operational, and tactical levels of war and between the intelligence requirements of each level. Nevertheless, the commander's critical intelligence requirements format provides a useful lens through which to view the intelligence requirements of the CAF units deployed in IFOR and SFOR, in light of the tasks they had to perform.[13]

Since the CAF had been operating in Bosnia since 1992, it and NDHQ were already familiar with many of the commander's critical intelligence requirements that normally would accompany an entirely new mission in a new theatre. Intelligence reporting during 1993–94 showed considerable understanding of military-strategic intelligence on the belligerents: leadership and chains of command, orders of battle, major equipment holdings and capabilities, bases and deployments, training, doctrine, intelligence, and logistics. Likewise, the CAF had spent several years becoming familiar with topography, climate, critical infrastructure, ports of entry, lines of communication, and sustainment factors. All of these were relevant as well to mission planning at the operational level. In addition, IFOR units would need to know the intentions of the former belligerent forces toward the cease-fire agreement and toward the IFOR itself, their deployments after withdrawal from the zones of separation, whether they had placed all heavy weapons into cantonment, the extent of their compliance with de-mobilization, and whether those units and former soldiers retained small arms that could pose a threat to the IFOR or to persons from rival factions.[14] The IFOR/SFOR would have to find out much of this information through its theatre-level intelligence collection efforts.

Finally, at the tactical level within its AOR, the Canadian BG would need to know cantonment sites, barracks, and bases of local regular (and irregular) forces; minefields and booby-trapped buildings and obstacles; police and other security services; persons, sites, and routes to be secured, protected, patrolled, and monitored; local black market and arms trade activities; the local official and unofficial power structures and their opposition; family/clan relationships; normal patterns of life; and any changes that could indicate potential trouble.[15] In sum, to meet its intelligence requirements, the BG would require a full-spectrum intelligence capability.

Intelligence Assets

In that respect, the deployed CAF intelligence assets were minimalist but covered the essentials. The IFOR brigade G2 cell headquarters (July–December 1996) consisted of a Field Intelligence Support Team from the 1 Division Intelligence Company led by Capt. J. V. Gilles Clairoux. His job was to brief the brigade commander and staff as well as do personal reconnaissance and analyse the information gained therefrom. The remainder of the Field Intelligence Support Team consisted of two tactical analysts (noncommissioned members) monitoring implementation of the accords' political aspects, two more focusing on the former combatant forces, and a collator/personalities analyst. In

FIGURE 9.1. The Canadian National Intelligence Centre, Bosnia, 1997. This truck-mounted box was the work space for half of the six-person unit, headed by an Intelligence Branch major. Here Canadian Armed Forces intelligence is entering the computer age. *Major (ret.) Harold A. Skaarup*

addition, one senior noncommissioned member was attached to brigade headquarters to coordinate with the G2 cell for administrative and support functions, liaise with other units and external agencies (with access to almost every possible source), and prepare "collection plans, patrol task tables and intelligence requests."[16] But reporting from units initially was "marginal at best ... [,] the single weakest link in the intelligence function."[17] Under Operation PALLADIUM (SFOR), the brigade headquarters was disbanded, and an intelligence section was created for the battle group headquarters; in 1997 it consisted of nine personnel under the command of a captain. The BG's subunits and personnel were its organic collection assets. However, during both operations the BG received additional support in the form of the CANIC (figure 9.1). The unit, initially six strong and based in Sarajevo, had a mission to support the IFOR/SFOR, the Canadian contingent commander, and national decision makers. As such, it was not a collection unit but rather one for liaison, analysis, and reporting (to/from NDHQ). It had an analysis section and a SIGINT team from the CFIOG. Prior to deployment the first CANIC commander, Maj. W. A. Rennett, "sought and received very clear guidance on his role" and got permission to liaise directly with all agencies in Ottawa. In theatre, he conducted "ruthless liaison with the other intelligence staffs ... building personal and professional relationships."[18] But as communications researcher Chief Warrant Officer Susan Bastien explained later, "there were only select countries that would share information or work closer than others."[19] In the Canadian case, this meant primarily the Americans and the British.

One of the CANIC's jobs was to ensure that NDHQ and the Canadian government were not caught by surprise by events in the Canadian AOR. To that end, the CANIC sent weekly sitreps to NDHQ. For its part, the DGI had rebadged its Yugoslav Crisis Cell as the Balkans Intelligence Response Team. Its job was to act on reach-back requests from the theatre and push information out to them.[20] In spite of the internal DND reorganization efforts and budgetary limits explained in chapter 3, the DGI treated such support as its first priority.[21]

The MND-SW was multinational but initially had a British-led headquarters (based in Banja Luka) that had a UK intelligence company and a Joint and Combined Intelligence Centre, with representatives from all of the national contingents in the division. The division had its own collection assets (aviation and UK SOF) and analytic capacity. It received reports from the BGs and from SFOR headquarters and undoubtedly received analytic products from the UK DI staff and SIGINT support from Government Communications Headquarters. But that material may not have been shared with all of the partner contingents. When Major-General Hillier took command of the division, a three-person detachment from the CANIC relocated to his headquarters so that he had direct secure access to any Canadian intelligence products and communications systems that he required.[22]

Operating in the Balkans as part of NATO may have enhanced the CAF's collection and intelligence-sharing capabilities. Initially, however, NATO intelligence efforts in support of the IFOR were somewhat constrained. First, NATO's Intelligence Division had long been hampered by organizational weaknesses and the limits imposed by separate and unique sharing arrangements with and among its member states.[23] Second, deployment of the IFOR coincided with a major reorganization of NATO's command structure. So, the IFOR J2 headquarters initially consisted of only seven members drawn from several countries. There were, however, three intelligence officers on the J3 (operations) staff, which ensured that intelligence was integrated into operational planning. Two other NATO structures provided additional support: the Joint Analysis Centre at Molesworth, United Kingdom (which had provided imagery to UNPROFOR), and the Allied Forces South headquarters intelligence directorate, located in Naples, Italy. With sixty personnel, it became the split-based rear support for the IFOR J2. While the latter focused on indications and warning and current intelligence, the Allied Forces South team concentrated on collection management, long-term assessments, counterintelligence, briefings, and staff actions. NATO intelligence support improved once the IFOR morphed into the SFOR at the end of 1996. The United States provided a military intelligence battalion to support SFOR headquarters, thereby expanding the J2's capabilities while taking some of the load off of Allied Forces South. In addition to the CANIC, a dozen other NATO and allied nations established national intelligence centers, and a number of other intelligence services deployed in theatre. These units were colocated with SFOR headquarters in the Sarajevo suburb of Ilidza. Known colloquially as the "NIC Village," their close proximity facilitated both formal and informal information sharing.[24]

Since the Balkans lay outside NATO's long-planned operational area, NATO had to create a new communications and information architecture to provide C4I support to operations in this theatre. This entailed knitting together a large hybrid mix of NATO, UN, national, civilian, and commercial networks, systems, and components. NATO's years of investment in the standardization of C4I paid off, as the various headquarters were able to connect and to transmit voice, fax, data, and imagery. However, this ad hoc system had to be upgraded significantly during the rollover from IFOR to SFOR. Nor was the whole system high-tech. The Linked Operation-Intelligence Centers Europe system, which provided near real-time order of battle and situation data, was difficult to use and did not operate below division level in the IFOR/SFOR. As one writer put it at the time, "The information Age has arrived for NATO but largely stops at the division level."[25] In fact, none of the CANIC members deployed in 1996 had been trained on the Linked Operation-Intelligence Centers Europe system prior to deployment.[26]

Collection

Just as under UNPROFOR, patrolling was at the heart of BG activity and its intelligence collection efforts. This included mounted or dismounted proactive and reactive framework patrols, roving patrols at night, and long-range patrols to deal with specific concerns. Short patrols could be six to twelve hours in duration, while long ones could be thirty to ninety hours away from base. Every patrol was debriefed on return. In addition, civil-military cooperation (CIMIC) and psyops teams also gathered information throughout the AOR. Contact with the local population and liaison with local government, key figures, the International Police Task Force that monitored local police activity, and nongovernment organizations helped to generate SA. In her thesis, Capt. Lisa Elliott aptly referred to these activities as "social patrolling."[27]

Maj.-Gen. Dean Milner, who had commanded a BG there from September 2003 to April 2004, put a form of social patrolling at the heart of his formation's activities:

> I realized that... we needed to live amongst the community. So, we developed these—what we called these MOST teams—monitoring observation surveillance teams—that actually moved out into the community to live in houses so... they could speak to the individuals on a more casual—they

could eat lunch with them. They could find out—that was my main source of info gathering from my info ops cycle that I created, because I never did anything unless I, you know, found out things and then I'd deploy my guys.... We adopted the whole structure within the battle group, but we were really the first ones to push it. I actually became ... the MOST Commander.... I was responsible to the Brigade Commander for establishing these teams throughout our area of responsibility, connecting in with the ... civil authorities and the police and all that. It was amazing how critical these teams became in providing us the feedback and the information that we were looking for, right across, you know, the spectrum of operations.[28]

The BGs' forward observation officers, forward air controllers, and TUA vehicles provided surveillance capability for close observation of specific targets. Taken together, these efforts allowed the BG to monitor the weapons cantonments, entity military training, order of battle, and compliance with the Dayton Accords and to locate minefields, the latter being a focus of the engineer squadron's collection task.[29]

SFOR headquarters had at its disposal a number of collection assets whose results might be shared with the SFOR divisions and their battle groups. These included the US MI battalion, which had both collection and analysis capabilities, and aerial reconnaissance systems: P-3 Orion and Joint STARS aircraft, UAVs, and the gun cameras of Apache attack helicopters. However, since the collection targets were mostly political and social, the former belligerent forces were largely inactive, and the physical terrain was mountainous, the Joint STARS aircraft was limited mostly to maintaining surveillance on large fixed military targets, such as cantonment sites and entity garrisons, and on mass graves. SIGINT provided by NATO member countries was criticized for being consistently "a day late and a dollar short."[30]

Of potentially greater value in probing the human/social/political target were the Joint Commission Observer teams. Created by the British during the UNPROFOR era, from 1997 the teams consisted of American SOF operating under command of the SFOR's Joint Special Operations Task Force. Given that the Joint Commission Observer teams were meant to generate a flow of information "from the streets" and to "influence the behavior" of the former belligerents, their mandate straddled the intelligence/psyops boundary within a larger conception of information operations. Although considered an American asset as much as an SFOR one, they did operate within the Canadian AOR. They reported only to the commander of the Special Operations Task Force but probably shared some of their intelligence with the Canadian BG via liaison channels.[31]

Using the CANIC as a conduit, the Balkans Intelligence Response Team likely was able to forward some imagery and geomatics products to the BG (which had a geomatics team in its headquarters). Similarly, the CANIC's CFIOG detachment probably served as the BG's source for tactical SIGINT (and for reports and analytic products from CSE and from its Five Eyes partners).[32]

Production (Collation and Analysis) and Dissemination

The BG intelligence staff would collate and analyse intelligence received from unit reports and from any higher-level sources. The G2, the staff, or both would brief the BG commander and his operations staff daily and were responsible for providing intelligence input to any specific operation planning. They also would prepare regular summaries to be sent to MND-SW headquarters, the IFOR J2, and the CANIC for forwarding to the DGI and its NDHQ customers.

Exploitation

In a mission such as this, the line between intelligence collection and exploitation was often blurred. Information gained on one patrol might determine the aim, location, and collection targets and requirements of the next one. Cantonment site inspections were both security operations and intelligence-collection efforts. Any discrepancies found during an inspection would become part of an intelligence report and would guide the next inspection or bring about more intensive observation. But the author does not have access to mission records that would allow for comment on any specific operations, with two exceptions.

The first exception relates to the rioting in Drvar in April 1998. Since riot control was not part of the SFOR mandate and the CAF BG (based on the 1 RCR) was not equipped or trained for it, its performance during that incident will not be addressed here. The only question relevant to this chapter is whether the BG had warning of the likelihood of trouble or whether it was taken by surprise. The answer is that it had strategic warning and acted on it. The UN's plan to push Bosnian refugees and internally displaced persons back to their home communities—calling 1998 "The Year of the Returnee"—was well-publicized official policy. Equally well known was the resistance to that plan by those who now occupied areas where returnees were due to arrive. Drvar, once a predominantly Serb city, was by 1998 dominated by Bosnian Croats, who were opposed to Serbs returning to live there. That resistance manifested itself in widespread arson. Since November 1996 more than 150 buildings had been burned in the area, 30 of them since January 1998. Following the murder of an elderly Serb returnee couple in mid-April and the failure of the local police to investigate the crime properly, the UN fired the chief of police, and the BG deployed a company into the town, mounting patrols to enhance security. So, the BG's intelligence staff was well aware of the sources of trouble and the potential for violence. The staff so advised the BG commander, and he acted on the advice by deploying much of the BG into the Drvar area until 24 April.[33]

What they did lack was tactical warning that Bosnian Croats would deliberately instigate a major riot on *that* day[34] and that the BG would be forced to respond because the local police were unable or unwilling to contain the rioting. (The International Police Task Force contingent had no authority or capacity to respond to a riot.) The Canadian troops succeeded in doing so without taking any lives, but the rioters had already inflicted much damage and political chaos.[35] NDHQ was kept informed about the rioting and the actions of the Canadian troops to contain it.[36]

Three years later the CAF BG—this one based on the 3 RCR—conducted an operation probably unique in the annals of CAF peacekeeping history: the "bank raid" of Tomislavgrad. In this instance, strategic-level SA, enhanced by SFOR counterintelligence, led to a tactical operation meant to help contain a political crisis that could have unraveled the federation.

The background to this lay in one aspect of the unfinished business of the Dayton Accords: its failure to accommodate Bosnian Croat aspirations within the new federation. The accords had given "entity" status to the Bosnian Muslims and the Serbs, but not to the Bosnian Croats. Yet, it was the Bosnian Croats and the Croatian military's 1995 offensive that had liberated most of Bosnia from the Serbs. Moreover, Croatia was funding Bosnia's public-sector employees and its armed forces. Bosnian Croat calls for the creation of a "Third Entity" within the federation had gone unanswered. By 2001 Bosnian Croat anger had boiled over into secession. Their leaders in the political party the Croatian Democratic Union of Bosnia and Herzegovina declared autonomy and withdrew from Bosnian institutions. The party intended to set up self-governing structures, financed by taxes and donations from businesses, and also ordered Bosnian Croat soldiers serving in the Bosnian armed forces to leave their barracks.[37] This posed a political (and potentially military) threat to the federation and, by extension, to the SFOR mission.

To complicate matters further, there was an organized crime dimension to the crisis.[38] Running parallel to the overt Bosnian Croat efforts to assert their demands was a sophisticated covert operation to delay or subvert the implementation of the accords. This entailed money laundering and a related political influence operation that had penetrated the Bosnian political structure and its police and military.[39] The SFOR's counterintelligence operation WESTAR, which took place in the Multi-National Division South East sector in October 1999 had revealed the scale of this joint Bosnian Croat/Croatian effort. SFOR troops seized thousands of documents, dozens of computers, and hundreds of floppy discs and CDs that directly implicated the Croatian Intelligence Service and its Bosnian Croat counterpart in espionage against the International

Criminal Tribunal for Yugoslavia and other international organizations, including the SFOR. The illegal activities included identity theft, credit card fraud, pornography, impersonation of police officers, forcible confinement of women, and recruitment via "special means," including intimidation, of Bosnian Croats and members of the international community to spy on behalf of Croatia, the Bosnian Croat underground, or both.[40]

The Bosnian Ministry of the Interior had intelligence that identified seven branches of the Hercegovacka Banka engaged in criminal activity related to the Third Entity dispute[41] including the one in Tomislavgrad, which was within the Canadian AOR. The Office of the High Representative, the international civilian body in charge of implementing the accords, issued instructions to the SFOR commander to seize control of those banks as part of the wider effort to stop the Bosnian Croat secession. The SFOR ordered the MND-SW, then under Hillier's command, to execute the operation. He in turn assigned the Tomislavgrad target to the 3 RCR BG, commanded by Lt.-Col. Denis Thompson. Since the BG was dispersed across the AOR, the task fell to Maj. Don Haisell's Para Company, which was based on the outskirts of the town and maintained an OP inside it.[42]

According to Haisell, the bank operation was mounted on short notice. Hillier said that he wanted to launch it "the day after tomorrow," although the Para Company had been in theatre less than a week.[43] The need for speed was understandable. The Office of the High Representative and the Bosnian government had to be concerned about preservation of evidence and the risk of leaks if action was delayed.

There was no time to do a detailed plan. Intelligence preparation of the battlefield consisted of a night patrol to the target by Haisell and his platoon commanders. Since such patrols through the town were routine, this would not have attracted undue attention. To conduct the raid, Haisell had a company group of about 135 soldiers—consisting of his soldiers, two platoons from the BG, an armoured reconnaissance troop from the Royal Canadian Dragoons, a platoon of Italian Carabinieri from the Multinational Support Unit (crowd control force), HUMINT collection resources from MND-SW headquarters, and a covert photo/video surveillance team.[44]

On 6 April 2001, Haisell's company group was ready by 7:15 a.m. A dismounted patrol confirmed that the bank was open. Military police established traffic control at key intersections. The force deployed at 7:35, and by 7:45 the bank was secured for entry. The CAF troops provided a sealed outer cordon, and the Multinational Support Unit provided the inner one. This allowed Office of the High Representative members, Interior Ministry forensic accountants, and the federation police to enter the bank undisturbed. The International Police Task Force was asked to notify local police and direct them to assist with traffic and crowd control. However, the local police did not cooperate, and at times they actually helped to stir up the small crowd of fifty to one hundred protesters. There was no serious violence, and there were no casualties. By 9:05 a.m. the investigators had secured the bank records, computers, and money and had loaded it onto CAF vehicles, which the Multinational Support Unit escorted back to the company camp outside town. Shortly thereafter, the evidence was sent to Sarajevo under escort of the Royal Canadian Dragoons troop.[45]

The operation achieved complete surprise and success in spite of a number of problems. The Office of the High Representative and federation police participants were not well prepared. They had met only hours before the operation started, having missed the coordination meetings and rehearsal. During the action, one of the auditors insisted on making computer-printed labels for the boxes they seized. Only the growing rowdy crowd outside the cordons persuaded him to abandon that task. The information operations were ineffective. People threw back without reading the handbills the troops had distributed, and local radio commentary was very hostile to the operation. Finally, the operation's HUMINT collection effort was poor; the photos were too hazy to be useful in identifying people, and information was slow to filter down to company level after the operation was done.[46]

While this unfolded in Tomislavgrad, SFOR troops carried out simultaneous raids on seven other bank branches across Bosnia. The one in Mostar ended in violence, with eighteen soldiers injured.[47] In his memoir, General Hillier claimed that "the amount of intelligence we gathered [from the raids] allowed us to break the back of the Bosnian Croat resistance and led to much of the progress Bosnia has made in the past few years."[48] This is not an idle boast. Scholars writing since have credited these efforts with decisively blocking the Bosnian Croat attempt at self-rule.[49]

In two related operations in mid-April and early May, Major Haisell's company seized Bosnian military weapons and ammunition at seven locations within its AOR. They then consolidated them under CAF control and supervision at two locations, Livno and Kupres, until such time as the Bosnian military could establish a reliable chain of command over the sites. This ensured that any Bosnian Croat effort to create its own army was stopped in its tracks.[50]

It would be an exaggeration to describe the bank raid as an intelligence-led operation. At the tactical level, Major Haisell had relatively little intelligence on which to act. He and his subordinates had eyes on the target and its surroundings but little else. For the job they had to do, that was sufficient. But clearly their operation was prompted and informed by a surfeit of intelligence from other sources that designated the Tomislavgrad bank as the correct target. That the raid achieved tactical surprise and achieved its goals should be attributed to the ability of the Canadian troops to professionally execute a hasty operation based on minimal intelligence.

CONCLUSION

Maj. Harold Skaarup, who commanded the CANIC in the second half of 1997, commented to the author in 1999 that during the SFOR period the Canadian BGs benefited from "the best intelligence support we've ever had."[51] He may have been right; his is a well-informed but necessarily self-interested view. Moreover, the author's analysis, limited by the scant sources available, offers only a narrow snapshot of intelligence support to operations in this theatre at the time. So, it is difficult to draw a firm conclusion on the quality of that support and its impact on Canadian peace enforcement operations in Bosnia. A definitive analysis must await a future historian with access to a more complete range of original sources.

What we can say is this. A relatively small number of CAF intelligence personnel initially confronted a challenging multifaceted intelligence task without all of the tools and the people they needed: an all-too-familiar refrain in the Canadian MI experience in this era. Maintaining an intelligence footprint, a learning curve, and institutional memory was hampered by short tours and rapid turnover. Yet, it is also clear that the IFOR/SFOR intelligence mission represented a qualitative improvement from that of UNPROFOR. The BGs and their intelligence staffs benefited from a clearly defined mandate and task list and a less volatile operational environment. The intelligence targets were largely a known quantity: identifiable persons and groups and measurable items at fixed locations.[52] Even if NATO's high-tech systems were not well suited to some of these targets and the terrain, tried-and-true methods such as social patrolling, learned from earlier peacekeeping operations, yielded the kind of situational awareness of the AOR that the battle groups needed. Later, HUMINT training, link-analysis software, and digital cameras were introduced.[53] And there was structural innovation: the CANIC gave the BGs and the CAF contingent commander a direct conduit for strategic and operational intelligence to and from the DGI. The contrast with the UNPROFOR experience could not be more obvious and speaks for itself.

NOTES

1. See the terms of the Dayton Accords laid out in its annexes. *The General Framework Agreement for Peace in Bosnia and Herzegovina, Also Known as the Dayton Peace Agreement (DPA)*, Organization for Security and Co-operation in Europe, 14 December 1995, https://www.osce.org/bih/126173.
2. Dana H. Allin, *NATO's Balkan Interventions* (Abingdon, UK: Routledge, 2002), 47–49, 63–64, https://doi.org/10.4324/9781315000664.
3. United States, General Accounting Office, National Security and International Affairs Division, *Bosnia Peace Operation: Mission, Structure, and Transition*

Strategy of NATO's Stabilization Force, Report to the Chairman, Committee on Foreign Relations, US Senate (Washington, DC: GAO, 1998), 5, https://www.gao.gov/assets/nsiad-99-19.pdf. Jane M. O. Sharp, "Dayton Report Card," *International Security* 22, no. 3 (1997): 113–14, 117–19, offers a critical view of the security aspects of *The General Framework Agreement for Peace in Bosnia and Herzegovina*.

4. See *The General Framework Agreement for Peace in Bosnia and Herzegovina*, annex 1-A, "Agreement on the Military Aspects of the Peace Settlement," article 1, parts 1–3. This and subsequent articles gave the IFOR/SFOR the authority to use "all necessary measures" to enforce the terms.
5. See R. Cody Phillips, *Bosnia-Herzegovina: The U.S. Army's Role in Peace Enforcement Operations 1995–2004* (Washington, DC: Center of Military History, 2005), 16, 19. He gives a figure of fifty-seven thousand military personnel for IFOR at its inception. By 2004, the SFOR consisted of only seven thousand troops.
6. On these interwoven challenges, see Lenard J. Cohen, "Whose Bosnia? The Politics of Nation Building," *Current History* 97 (March 1998): 103–12; and Sharp, "Dayton Report Card," 102, 115, 117–19, 123–25, 128.
7. Jonathan Smith, "The Impact of Intelligence on DOD Perceptions of the Bosnian Conflict, 1995," in *The Role of Intelligence in Ending the War in Bosnia in 1995*, ed. Timothy R. Walton (Lanham, MD: Lexington Books, 2014), 142.
8. See NATO/SFOR, "Transcript: Joint Press Conference," NATO, 16 April 1998, https://www.nato.int/SFOR/trans/1998/t980416a.htm, and 17 April 1998, https://www.nato.int/SFOR/trans/1998/t980417a.htm; and United Nations Mission in Bosnia and Herzegovina, Sarajevo, *A Summary of Recent Violence against Serb Returnees in Drvar and the Response of the Local Authorities*, 14 July 1998, Gregg Centre Archive, Bosnia IFOR folder.
9. "Mine Awareness Briefing," Security and Defence Forum (SDF) Field Excursion to Bosnia, Camp Black Bear, Velika Kladuša, 14 March 1998, Gregg Centre Archive, SDF Field Excursion Briefing Binder. See also Col. John Dawson, SFOR Chief Engineer, "Entity Demining Briefing," 18 March 1998, Gregg Centre Archive, SDF Field Excursion Briefing Binder, tab F.
10. J.A.E.K. Dowell, *Intelligence for the Canadian Army in the 21st Century: "Enabling Land Operations"* (Kingston, Ontario: DLCD, 2012), 26.
11. Col. Ray Romses, Commander Canadian Contingent SFOR, "Briefing from Canadian Contingent SFOR," 14 March 1998, Gregg Centre Archive, SDF Field Excursion Briefing Binder, tab E. Romses gave a figure of 881 for the BG, while an oral briefing gave 905. By 2004, the division had been reduced to a brigade.
12. In annex 1-A, article 4, the signatory parties were responsible for demining, but owing to their lack of capacity and of cooperation, overseeing and training demining teams fell to the IFOR/SFOR.
13. Lt.-Gen. Sir David Ramsbotham, "Analysis and Assessment for Peacekeeping Operations," in *Intelligence Analysis and Assessment*, ed. David A. Charters, Anthony Stuart Farson, and Glenn P. Hastedt (London: Frank Cass, 1996), 165; Canada, Chief of the Defence Staff, *Land Force*, Vol. 1, *Conduct of Land Operations: Operational Level Doctrine for the Canadian Army, B-GL-300-00/FP-000* (Ottawa: DND, Chief of the Defence Staff, 1996), chap. 7 ("Information Operations"), 3–5.
14. Ramsbotham, 165–67; Hugh Smith, "Intelligence and UN Peacekeeping," *Survival* 36, no. 3 (1994): 175–76; Maj. R. C. Fountain, "Intelligence versus Information:

The United Nations Dilemma" (1997), 4–5, Douglas Dearth, "Information and Intelligence: The United Nations Conundrum" (10 October 1995), 6–7, Pär Eriksson, Nils Marius Rekkedal, and Wegger Strømmen, *Intelligence in Peace Support Operations: A Joint Report by the Swedish and Norwegian Defence Research Establishments* (Stockholm: National Defence Research Establishment, Department of Defence Analysis, 1996), 12–13, 44–46; US Army, *FM 100-23: Peace Operations* (Washington, DC: Department of the Army, 1994), 44–47; Charles M. Ayers, *Peacekeeping Tactics, Techniques, and Procedures* (Langley Air Force Base, VA: Army–Air Force Center for Low Intensity Conflict, 1989), 6–8; Andrei Raevsky, *Managing Arms in Peace Processes: Aspects of Psychological Operations and Intelligence* (Geneva: UN Institute for Disarmament Research, 1996), 21–22; and Cameron Graham and James D. Kiras, "Intelligence and Peacekeeping: Definitions and Limitations," *Peacekeeping & International Relations* 24, no. 6 (1995): 3.

15. Smith, "Intelligence and UN Peacekeeping," 176; Fountain, "Intelligence versus Information," 6; Graham and Kiras, "Intelligence and Peacekeeping," 3; and CAF and NDHQ, CFP 301 (3) *Peacekeeping Doctrine* (Ottawa: NDHQ, 1995), chap. 6, 16.

16. Extracts from an article by Warrant Officer John Paul Michael Parsons, in Harold A. Skaarup, *Out of Darkness—Light: A History of Canadian Military Intelligence*, Vol. 2 (New York: iUniverse, 2005), 339–40.

17. Capt. Robert Martin [Martyn], "Trends in Tactical Intelligence: Global Conflict and the Canadian Forces," *Army Doctrine and Training Bulletin* 1, no. 2 (1998): 75, http://publications.gc.ca/collections/Collection/D12-9-1-2E.pdf.

18. Lt. Jim D. Godefroy, "1996, CANIC, Sarajevo, Observations," in Skaarup, *Out of Darkness—Light*, 2:342–43, and Skaarup's own report as CO of the CANIC (387–88). Maj. Gordon Ohlke, interview with author, 13 June 2019, said the SIGINT team was from the CSE, but the CFIOG was more likely.

19. Chief Warrant Officer Susan Bastien, interview, 5 September 2007, Canadian War Museum Oral History Program.

20. Skaarup, *Out of Darkness—Light*, 2:384; and Ohlke, interview with author.

21. *Military Intelligence Priorities 1997–1998*, annex A to *DG INT/J2 Memorandum Defence Intelligence Priorities 1997*, 2 May 1997, LAC, RG 24, BAN 2005-00285-2, box 11, file 1901-1 part 3.

22. Ohlke, interview with author; and Harold A. Skaarup, *Out of Darkness—Light: A History of Canadian Military Intelligence*, Vol. 3 (New York: iUniverse, 2005), 398–99. On Government Communications Headquarters support to the MND-SW and its limitations, see John Robert Ferris, *Behind the Enigma: The Authorised History of GCHQ, Britain's Secret Cyber-Intelligence Agency* (London: Bloomsbury, 2021), 685–86.

23. Brig.-Gen. (ret.) James S. Cox, interview, 22 June 2004, Canadian War Museum Oral History Program. See chapter 10 for additional insights on NATO intelligence at this time.

24. Lt.-Col. George K. Gramer Jr., "Operation JOINT ENDEAVOR: Combined-Joint Intelligence in Peace Enforcement Operations," *Military Intelligence Professional Bulletin* 22, no. 4 (1996): 11, 13; Capt. Angus Matheson, "The Evolution of NATO Intelligence Structures" (paper presented, War Studies Course 536, Royal Military College of Canada, November 1998), 8–9, 11–12, 14; and Skaarup, *Out of Darkness—Light*, 2:378, 380, 389.

25. Gramer, "Operation JOINT ENDEAVOR," 12; Larry K. Wentz, "NATO Command, Control, and Communications in Bosnia," in *NATO 1997: Year of Change*, ed. Lawrence R. Chalmer and Jonathan W. Pierce, 145–51 (Washington, DC: National Defense University Press, 1998); C. Kenneth Allard, *Information Operations in Bosnia: A Preliminary Assessment*, Strategic Forum, no. 91 (Washington, DC: National Defense University, Institute for National Strategic Studies, 1996), 1; "Linked Operational Intelligence Centers Europe [LOCE]," Global Security, n.d., https://www.globalsecurity.org/intell/systems/loce.htm.
26. Lt. Jim Godefroy, quoted in Skaarup, *Out of Darkness—Light*, 2:343.
27. This summary was compiled from notes taken during a series of briefings at the 1 RCR BG headquarters and "Platoon House" in Bihac and by C Squadron Royal Canadian Dragoons and D Company during the Security and Defence Forum visit to the Canadian AOR in March 1998.
28. Maj.-Gen. Dean Milner, interview, 15 November 2005, Canadian War Museum Oral History Program. He was a colonel at the time of the interview.
29. See the schematic in Matheson, "Evolution," fig. 3, "3 RCR Battle Group Intelligence Architecture"; and Skaarup, *Out of Darkness—Light*, 3:322.
30. Adam B. Siegel, "Intelligence Challenges of Civil-Military Operations," *Military Review* 81, no. 5 (9 October 2001): 47; and David A. Charters, "Out of the Closet: Intelligence Support for Post-Modernist Peacekeeping," in *Intelligence in Peacekeeping*, Pearson Papers 4 (Clementsport, Nova Scotia: Canadian Peacekeeping Press, 1999), 59–60, notes 66 and 68. In his Canadian War Museum interview, Colonel Milner mentions that his BG was involved in at least one operation that involved information from Joint STARS aircraft but provides no details.
31. Robert F. Baumann, "IFOR, SFOR, and Civil Implementation," in *Armed Peacekeepers in Bosnia*, ed. Robert F. Baumann, George W. Gawrych, and Walter E. Kretchik (Fort Leavenworth, KS: Combat Studies Institute Press, 2004), 203. The Joint Commission Observer teams are shown on the 3 RCR BG schematic.
32. *Military Intelligence Priorities 1997–1998* states that support is provided by imagery exploitation and SIGINT assets but does not mention geomatics. However, the 3 RCR BG schematic shows the J2 Geomatics as a national asset that supported the BG.
33. UN Mission in Bosnia and Herzegovina, *Summary of Recent Violence*, 1–3. See also Lt.-Col. Howard Coombs, "Keeping Peace and Freedom in Bosnia: Drvar 1998," in *On the Front Lines of Leadership: Sub-Unit Command on Operations*, ed. Bernd Horn (Winnipeg: Canadian Defence Academy Press, 2006), 72–73, 76; Skaarup, *Out of Darkness—Light*, 3:319; and briefing notes from Security and Defence Forum tour to the CAF AOR (SDF Field Excursion Briefing Binder, Gregg Centre Archive).
34. Coombs, "Keeping Peace," 76, notes that the riot began "without warning." He was at that time the commander of C Company, 1 RCR, assigned to Drvar.
35. Coombs, 80–85. See also his detailed and dramatic verbal account of the events: Lt.-Col. Howard Coombs, *"I'm a Canadian. Come with Me!": Around the World with the Canadian Infantry*, interview by David Siry, video, 20 June 2016, The West Point Center for Oral History, https://www.westpointcoh.org/interviews/i-m-a-canadian-come-with-me-around-the-world-with-the-canadian-infantry.
36. Information provided privately to the author.
37. Denisa Kostovicova and Vesna Bojicic-Dzelilovic, "Ethnicity Pays: The Political Economy of Postconflict Nationalism in Bosnia-Herzegovina," in *After Civil War:*

Division, Reconstruction, and Reconciliation in Contemporary Europe, ed. Bill Kissane (Philadelphia: University of Pennsylvania Press, 2015), 200–201. According to Lt.-Col. Don Haisell, whose company carried out the bank raid, the would-be new entity was promising the soldiers $500 a month if they resigned from the federation military and joined the new force. Interview with author, 16 December 2020.

38. Kostovicova and Bojicic-Dzelilovic, "Ethnicity Pays," 201.
39. Rick Hillier, *A Soldier First: Bullets, Bureaucrats and the Politics of War* (Toronto: HarperCollins, 2009), 228–29.
40. NATO/SFOR, "Transcript: Op Westar Special Press Conference and Information Packet for Journalists," NATO, 17 December 1999, https://www.nato.int/Sfor/trans/1999/t991217a.htm.
41. See Kostovicova and Bojicic-Dzelilovic, "Ethnicity Pays," 202–3.
42. Hillier, *A Soldier First*, 229; and Haisell, interview.
43. Haisell, interview; Karina Roman, "Newly Arrived Canadian Troops Hit the Ground Running: Play Key Role against Hardliners," *Ottawa Citizen*, 7 April 2001, copy in Haisell, private papers.
44. Roman, "Newly Arrived"; and Capt. Rob Calhoun, "Operation ATHENA 6 April 2001," *Bulletin*, Army Lessons Learned Centre, 9, no. 1 (January 2003): 2, copy in Haisell, private papers. "Op ATHENA," *Petawawa Post*, 1 May 2001, 10, Haisell, private papers, also mentions Engineers from the 24 Field Squadron.
45. Calhoun, "Operation ATHENA," 2; and "Op ATHENA."
46. Calhoun, "Operation ATHENA," 3; "Op ATHENA"; and Haisell, interview.
47. "Peacekeepers Hurt in Croat Riot," CNN, 6 April 2001, http://www.cnn.com/2001/WORLD/europe/04/06/croat.bank/.
48. Hillier, *A Soldier First*, 229–32.
49. Kostovicova and Bojicic-Dzelilovic, "Ethnicity Pays," 201.
50. Haisell, interview; Capt. Guy Turpin, "Canadians Control Bosnian Weapon Storage Sites," *Maple Leaf*, 30 May 2001; and Capt. Phil Millar, "Weapon Storage Site Consolidation in Peace Support Operations," (no publication details), both in Haisell papers.
51. Quoted in Charters, "Out of the Closet," 59.
52. By 2004, the entity armed forces were no longer seen as threats but instead as "Blue" partners. Skaarup, *Out of Darkness—Light*, 3:274.
53. Skaarup, 3:153.

10

PEACE ENFORCEMENT IN KOSOVO

Air and Ground Operations, 1999–2000

From late March until mid-June 1999, CAF CF-18 fighter-bombers (designated Task Force Aviano) engaged in combat with Yugoslavia under NATO's Operation ALLIED FORCE. This CAF effort, code-named Operation ECHO, entailed 678 sorties by eighteen aircraft.[1] When the Yugoslav military and security forces withdrew from the disputed province of Kosovo, a NATO-led multinational force, the Kosovo Force (KFOR), entered the contested area to enforce the postconflict peace. As part of KFOR, the CAF deployed a BG and command and support units.[2] Under the designation Operation KINETIC, the Canadian troops operated as part of a British brigade for two rotations, from June 1999 to June 2000. Because they were small parts of larger coalition operations and because NATO exercised operational control of the Canadian task forces, the CAF role will be examined within that wider strategic and operational context. That applies as well to the intelligence dimension, since CAF operations depended heavily on coalition collection and production assets.

BACKGROUND

The Kosovo-Serbia conflict and the NATO operations that followed shared the same origins as their counterparts in Croatia and Bosnia: the collapse of the Yugoslav federation. Those successful but costly secessions inspired ethnic Albanians in Kosovo to follow suit. Just as in Croatia and Bosnia, the separatist movement encountered fierce resistance from the Serb-led Yugoslav government, which regarded Kosovo as historically sacred territory. Starting in 1997, this clash led to a cycle of insurgency and repression that created yet another political and humanitarian crisis in the Balkans. That in turn prompted the NATO interventions.[3]

OPERATIONS ALLIED FORCE AND ECHO

The following sections address the key features of the air campaign, then delve into the intelligence dimensions: requirements, collection and analysis efforts, and impacts on air operations.

NATO Air Assets and Command and Control

At the start of the air strikes, NATO deployed a force of 344 combat aircraft in Europe augmented by several B-1 bombers that flew from bases in the United States. Of these, 130 were from non-US NATO members including the Canadian CF-18 fighter aircraft. Quickly realizing that these numbers were insufficient, the United States added more aircraft over the next few weeks. The NATO air component eventually totalled 829 combat aircraft from fourteen countries. In addition to these were reconnaissance, refueling, and search and rescue aircraft. US general Wesley Clark, NATO's Supreme Allied Commander Europe, exercised overall command of the operation. Adm. James Ellis (commander of Allied Forces Southern Europe, headquartered in Naples) exercised overall operational control of the NATO air component. Under his direction, USAF lieutenant general Michael Short (commander of Allied Air Forces Southern Europe, headquarters at Aviano, Italy) controlled all aircraft except the specialized US bombers and reconnaissance aircraft. Short grouped his planes into three wings, two at Aviano and one at Mildenhall in the United Kingdom. Ellis directed conventional aircraft through air tasking orders prepared at the CAOC at Vicenza, Italy.[4]

Strategic and Operational Planning

NATO's strategic objective, simply put, was "to stop the [Serbian regime's] violence against Kosovar Albanians."[5] That entailed three related goals: demonstrate NATO's serious opposition to Serbian repression, deter the regime from continuing and escalating its attacks on Kosovar civilians by inflicting costs for those actions, and damage the ability of Yugoslav Serbian forces to do so in the future "by seriously diminishing its military capabilities."[6] So, the strategy was one of coercion and attrition.

American military planning had begun in June 1998, when the violence in Kosovo was escalating. The preferred US option was to hit the Serbs hard at the outset. However, because NATO had to approve a plan that all members could accept and they were not united in their perspectives on the Kosovo crisis, the result was a compromise. The North Atlantic Council approved Operation Plan 10601, which took a graduated, incremental approach to the application of force. NATO's final plan was meant to inflict "just enough pain" to persuade Yugoslav Serbian leader Slobodan Milošević to give in.[7]

Gen. Klaus Naumann, head of the NATO Military Committee before and in the early weeks of the war, later commented that NATO had created a plan designed to get Milošević to the negotiating table, but "we faced an opponent who had accepted war, whereas the NATO nations had [just] accepted an operation."[8] This was similar in intent to the US Operation ROLLING THUNDER during the Vietnam War: airpower was to be used as leverage or as a bargaining tool that could be scaled up or down.[9]

The plan laid out three phases: phase 1, fifty-one suppression of enemy air defence attacks and forty "punishment" ones out of 169 in NATO's Master Target List; phase 2, attacks on military targets in the southern half of Serbia, including its forces in Kosovo; and phase 3, attacks on military and strategic targets all over former Yugoslavia, including those in Belgrade. The North Atlantic Council had approved all three phases in October 1998 and had given approval to execute them to NATO secretary-general Javier Solana on 30 January 1999. Following the collapse of negotiations with the regime and expecting only a short air campaign, on 24 March 1999 the North Atlantic Council approved execution of phase 1 only.[10] But four days later it authorized phase 2. Then on 1 April, NATO planes began to strike Yugoslav infrastructure.[11]

At this point, there was a divergence of views on targeting between the Supreme Allied Commander Europe and Lieutenant-General Short. Clark directed Short to allocate more attacks against Serbian ground forces in Kosovo. Clark considered them to be the "center of gravity" for Milošević, who could not afford serious military losses. Clark was also "keenly aware of political pressure to show results against these forces."[12] Short, however, preferred to hit fixed targets (infrastructure and C2 sites, including leadership) across former Yugoslavia for two reasons. First, he did not believe that air attacks were going to stop the ethnic cleansing in Kosovo, because it was too difficult to hit the dispersed Serbian forces in the rugged terrain. It also put his aircraft and crews at greater risk. Second, he felt that "it made more sense to attack the head of the snake in Belgrade than the tail in Kosovo."[13]

This dispute eventually was resolved in Short's favour. Arguably, the issue should have been settled before the air strikes began, but it seems fair to concede that the relative coercive and attritional values of the two approaches could not be proven in advance. Operations would be the only valid test, and it would take time to assess the results and their effects both on the ground and on the decision makers in Belgrade. To its credit, NATO adjusted its campaign once it was clear that its initial approach was not working, but it still overestimated its effects and underestimated Milošević's resolve.

Air Operations

Operation ALLIED FORCE opened on 24 March 1999 with two waves of cruise missile attacks launched from surface ships, submarines, and B-52 bombers.[14] This was followed by aircraft attacks: some 400 sorties on the first night, including 120 strike missions against forty targets. There were heavier attacks on the second night. During the first two nights only 20 percent of the attacks were directed against Serbian forces in Kosovo. On the third night that grew to 40 percent.[15]

Over the entire seventy-eight-day campaign, NATO aircraft (excluding cruise missiles) flew 38,004 sorties, including 10,484 strikes on strategic and tactical targets and 3,100 for suppression of enemy air defence. US and British forces also fired 308 cruise missiles. NATO forces fired or dropped 28,236 weapons of all types, expending a total of some twelve thousand tons of munitions. American forces accounted for the vast majority of these; in fact, a mere twenty-two US heavy bombers delivered 12,000 of the actual weapons. About 70 percent of the bombs were dropped in the final three weeks of the war. Up to that point, NATO's bombs-dropped average was only 150 per day.[16]

On the opening night four CF-18s flew as part of a sixteen-plane strike package. Of the 678 total Canadian sorties, 120 were for combat air patrol, some of which were assigned as the aircraft were returning from strike missions. The remaining 558 sorties were flown on 167 bombing missions. They dropped 532 bombs (361 of them precision-guided), totalling almost 250 tons, on targets in Kosovo and the rest of Yugoslavia. One hundred seventy-six sorties were cancelled due to bad weather, 85 for unspecified operational reasons, and 6 for serviceability.[17]

To put this in perspective with regard to the whole NATO effort, with only 2 percent of the aircraft available to NATO, Task Force Aviano flew about 4 percent of the strike missions.[18] That was a much higher proportion of sorties than the CAF air task force had flown during the Persian Gulf War nine years earlier. And the CF-18s were now almost a decade older.[19]

Effects

The air campaign eventually achieved its goal. It—and the NATO decision made late in the campaign to intervene with ground forces—forced the Serbian regime to end the repression in Kosovo by withdrawing its forces.[20] But the air operation suffered from a number of self-inflicted wounds. NATO had not planned for a long war and had not considered that possibility. Its member states were risk-averse with regard to collateral damage and to casualties on all sides, leading to highly restrictive ROE and a complex and slow target approval process. For domestic political reasons the United States took the threat of a ground attack off the table at the outset, leaving NATO without a plan B if the air campaign did not succeed. The postoperation review conducted by Admiral Ellis concluded that NATO had lacked a coherent campaign plan and target set and also lacked the staff needed to generate a detailed plan. Finally, the operation was launched with insufficient aircraft to achieve the stated goals.[21]

The Yugoslav armed forces posed two distinct challenges to the air campaign. First, they had enough SAMs and AAA to make low- and medium-level air strikes—the ones likely to be most effective—highly risky. That and NATO's desire to limit its casualties led to strike missions being carried out mostly from fifteen thousand feet or higher. Second, the Yugoslav ground forces, operating as relatively small dispersed battle groups, were often mingled with civilian vehicles and proved adept at concealment and deception. These two factors, further aggravated by poor visibility due to bad weather, rendered many of the air strikes ineffective. Post-conflict on-site target analysis seemed to show little damage to the Yugoslav military deployed inside Kosovo.[22] Consequently, as Ivo Daalder and Michael O'Hanlon explained, NATO never achieved air supremacy, the ability to carry out air operations of any type "with impunity at any altitude."[23]

INTELLIGENCE SUPPORT TO AIR OPERATIONS

Intelligence support to air operations proved to be a complex, difficult task, involving multiple organizations and systems and legal and political constraints complicated by challenging terrain, poor weather, robust enemy air defences, and dispersed ground forces skilled at concealment and deception.

Intelligence Requirements

Task Force Aviano shared the same intelligence requirements as its coalition partners. For both suppression of enemy air defence targeting and defensive purposes they needed to know the type, location, numbers, and operating parameters of the SAM and AAA systems (and their associated radars) deployed in Kosovo and across the rest of former Yugoslavia.[24] For battlefield interdiction within Kosovo, they had to be able to locate, identify, and track army and special police units, vehicles, weapons and other equipment. They needed knowledge of how these forces conducted operations: doctrines and tactics. NATO forces also had to be able to distinguish as much as possible military and paramilitary activity from that of noncombatants, a constantly changing challenge since they often were intermingled by chance or by design. Intelligence for strategic bombing included a broad spectrum of targets: critical infrastructure such as bridges, power generating stations, and transmission grids; defence-related targets such as military bases, arms factories, and weapon storage facilities; and C2 targets that included buildings where Serb leaders developed and implemented plans for military operations. This also included the communications systems that transmitted orders and those that broadcast propaganda for domestic and international audiences.

In addition to these, NATO targeters and strike planners needed geomatics data (terrain, road, and urban area maps and imagery) and weather forecasts, especially cloud cover and visibility over the target areas. At the level of strategic planning, since the air strikes were intended to coerce the regime into changing its behavior, NATO analysts would need to assess the impact of the campaign on the Serbian leadership's policies and decisions. Finally, they would want to understand how the civilian population of former Yugoslavia was reacting to the air campaign: was it weakening or increasing their support for the regime and its policies?

Intelligence Operations

Task Force Aviano was a hybrid formation that had not existed in the CAF Air Command order of battle. Created specifically for the Kosovo mission, it combined an enhanced fighter squadron with a task force headquarters drawn from several units across Canada.[25] The headquarters included a small A2 intelligence staff, whose primary task was to brief aircrews preflight with targeting, threat, and weather information and to debrief them postflight about their strikes and enemy air defence activity. They would also collect data from onboard sensors. The A2 staff had four daily reporting tasks: to the task force commander; to the NATO targeting and intelligence staffs in the CAOC, which included several CAF staff officers; to Air Command headquarters; and to the DCDS via J2/DGI. The latter, specifically the Balkans Intelligence Response Team, could also push down to the task force any relevant intelligence it had collected through its normal channels and any analyses it had prepared in-house, though tactical intelligence support for air operations was not its focus. However, since air squadrons have no organic collection capabilities, Task Force Aviano relied primarily on US and other coalition collection and production assets assigned to higher headquarters to meet its intelligence needs. This was consistent with air operations intelligence practice, which, as explained in chapter 4, tends to be top-down rather than bottom-up.

Collection

On the face of it, NATO went into the Kosovo air campaign with an overwhelming intelligence advantage. CAF brigadier-general James Cox, who served as deputy to the NATO assistant chief of staff for intelligence during the air campaign, later explained the intelligence architecture at SHAPE that supported the Supreme Allied Commander Europe. It had two major staff components: strategic intelligence and current intelligence. The latter, responsible for monitoring ongoing activity and NATO operations in the Balkans, worked in SHAPE's Joint Operations Centre. Beyond these two, there was a geomatics staff, a security branch, and a counterintelligence organization. The United States assigned liaison officers from the National Security Agency and the Defense Intelligence Agency. Likewise, the United Kingdom posted liaison officers from Government Communications Headquarters and from the DI staff. Altogether SHAPE's intelligence staff totalled about 118, but it expanded during the air campaign.[26]

Supporting this staff were two unique units. One was the Special Handling and Evaluation Detachment, which was responsible for receiving and selectively disseminating highly sensitive SIGINT. Led by an American officer on loan from the National Security Agency, the Special Handling and Evaluation Detachment had a staff of eighteen to twenty personnel from several NATO countries, including Canada. The second was the US Joint Analysis Centre at Molesworth in the United Kingdom. With a staff of about one thousand, it received, collated, and disseminated imagery received from the reconnaissance aircraft and satellites surveilling the Balkans. Because the air campaign was a joint American/NATO operation, the Supreme Allied Commander Europe (General Clark) received two briefings every morning: from the US forces and from NATO intelligence. The US colonel who ran the Joint Analysis Centre would brief him first by video link on the targets that had been hit since the last briefing and on those that were going to be struck.[27]

SHAPE also had its own targeting staff. Starting as a two-person office, it expanded to forty-eight as the crisis escalated. Cox says they were not involved in targeting or bomb damage assessment at the operational level. But since Clark had to explain to NATO leaders and to the media why certain targets had been bombed and with what effects, the SHAPE targeters were involved in "managing the information ... [and] keeping General Clark up to speed on what was going on."[28] So, from Cox's perspective they performed a dual function: strategic-level intelligence for decision support to the senior commander and input to NATO's information operations that accompanied the air campaign. But as shown later, a RAND Corporation analyst credited SHAPE and General Clark with more direct active targeting roles.

Since SHAPE had been observing the crises in Yugoslavia for a decade, neither Milošević nor his forces were unknown quantities. The Kosovo Liberation Army (KLA) was a relatively new combatant, but it was not NATO's target. For strategic-level assessment, NATO could draw upon data, analysis, and experience already gained as well as information from embassy reporting, national-level SIGINT, security and intelligence services, and open sources including the news media, which had been reporting extensively on events in the region. But such assessment was less relevant to aircrews, whose intelligence needs lay in the tactical domain.[29]

At the operational/tactical level, NATO could rely on an impressive array of collection assets for targeting and air MI. US reconnaissance satellites were employed to locate, identify, observe, and monitor both deployed forces and fixed targets. Some could download imagery directly to National Reconnaissance Office data-reception hardware installed at the 31st Air Expeditionary Wing's Tactical Integrated Planning Centre at Aviano. The centre shared that imagery with Five Eyes members and certain NATO partners cleared to receive it. The Defense Meteorological Support Program satellites provided weather imagery, while the Defense Support Program satellites contributed near real-time information in support of the bomb damage assessment process. According to RAND analyst Benjamin Lambeth, the tasking of satellites included input directly from the CAOC in a manner not seen in previous operations.[30]

Within the theatre, at the start of the operation the United States had deployed ten ISR aircraft. By the end, they had flown 1,038 sorties; UAVs flew another 496 missions. The American aircraft included U-2, RC-135 RIVET JOINT, RC-12, and E-8 Joint STARS. The UAVs included the Pioneer, the Hunter (based in Macedonia), and the new RQ-1A Predator, which flew out of Tuzla in Bosnia.[31] Some American F/A-18D fighters carried the Advanced Tactical Airborne Reconnaissance System.[32] NATO members such as Britain, France, and Germany also contributed reconnaissance-capable aircraft and UAVs, but the United States conducted some 90 percent of the ISR and EW sorties.[33] Between them these ISR platforms (including the satellites) provided a multispectral (SIGINT, photo, radar imaging, infrared, and near real-time video) capability to conduct 24/7 surveillance of the battle space. In reality, bad weather hampered observation during much of the campaign.[34]

Lambeth offers some insights on how NATO used these collection systems. He says that although the Yugoslav army tried to avoid detection by maneuvering its forces in small units, during the last two weeks of the air war the Joint STARS aircraft and other sensors could identify troop movements.[35] "UAVs offered commanders and planners the frequent advantage of real-time video imagery without any accompanying danger of aircrew losses. Some . . . were flown as low as 1,000 ft above . . . troop positions to gather real-time imagery, which, occasionally enabled prompt and effective attacks . . . against the often fleeting targets."[36]

The Predator had twenty-four-hour endurance and carried a synthetic aperture radar that enabled it to track targets through clouds. It augmented the two Joint STARS aircraft that were flying near but not over Kosovo airspace. This

UAV also could collect SIGINT, since it could fly closer to threat emitters than manned aircraft and could monitor low-power transmissions, such as those from cell phones and portable radios operated by the Serb forces.[37]

The Hunter UAV could loiter over targets under air attack and provide real-time bomb damage assessment. It initially downloaded its imagery to ground controllers at the base in Skopje, where it was forwarded to the CAOC and to NATO headquarters and the Pentagon if needed. Alternatively, it could upload imagery to a military communications satellite, which downlinked the images to the Joint Broadcast System in the United States, which sent it to the CAOC. With a time delay of only one second, this gave the CAOC virtually real-time visualization.[38] As another analyst explained, UAVs proved to be versatile intelligence collectors. They provided almost nonstop surveillance of Serbian forces in Kosovo, monitored the expulsion of ethnic Albanians, probed air defence sites, identified targets and attack and escape routes, and conducted bomb damage assessment and SIGINT.[39] However, since they flew lower and slower, a number of them were shot down.[40] Their flights were also weather-dependent.

One of the most valuable contributions to NATO's intelligence knowledge base may have come from Operation EAGLE EYE. Launched in November 1998, it provided aerial surveillance to verify compliance by all parties in Serbia and Kosovo with the provisions of the October 1998 agreement, which was meant to defuse the emerging crisis. The overall aim of the operation was to provide NATO headquarters a clear picture of the situation in Kosovo. It carried out three critical tasks: verification, assessment, and reporting. Manned and UAV surveillance platforms sent imagery to NATO processing offices, such as the Joint Analysis Centre. NATO analysed the information, and shared its assessments with the Kosovo Verification Mission, led by the Organization for Security and Cooperation in Europe, and with the UN. These surveillance flights gave NATO unrestricted access to Kosovo's airspace for almost five months until Operation ALLIED FORCE began.[41]

Finally, NATO had ground-based radars and human sources.[42] The latter included the KLA, which in spite of denials of cooperation, began supplying NATO with target and other battlefield intelligence in May. The KLA chief of staff passed information to NATO officers based in northern Albania.[43] Some Stabilization Force units in Bosnia had SIGINT systems that could be tuned in to intercept Serb forces' communications. SOF troops were used to collect intelligence in Serbia and Kosovo. Cox asserts that "although we had American... and... British Special Forces in on the ground, there wasn't a lot of them.... [T]hey weren't everywhere, and they weren't all the way into the country."[44]

So, NATO was well equipped with cutting-edge intelligence-gathering systems. Nevertheless, these systems also exhibited some limitations, yielding less than perfect collection. First, intelligence collection and targeting were pulled simultaneously in two contradictory directions: toward the need for eyes on target, which normally would be achieved by low-level flying to ensure precise strikes and to minimize the likelihood of civilian casualties, and toward the need for NATO aircraft to observe and attack from higher altitudes in order to minimize aircraft/aircrew losses.[45] While certain advanced collection systems could offset this problem to some degree, it degraded the precision that those systems promised. Second, poor weather and difficult terrain hampered collection that relied on visual identification of targets. Third, the Serb forces did not present attractive hard targets. Moreover, they proved adept at using cover, concealment, decoys, and deception.[46]

Lambeth has identified a host of other collection problems. For example, the Predator UAV had a top speed of only seventy miles per hour. This meant that it took a long time to reach its search area, by which time any Serb forces that had been there might have moved.[47] Then, "because of the mountainous terrain of Kosovo, the moving target indicator and synthetic aperture radar aboard the E-8 Joint STARS could not detect targets at oblique look angles, although the sensors carried by the higher-flying U-2 often compensated for this shortfall."[48] Lambeth goes on to say that the USAF did not fully appreciate the E-8's capabilities (it had been included in the aircraft roster at the request of the US Army) and delayed its inclusion in the air tasking orders. Once it was deployed the USAF regarded the E-8 as a surveillance platform for the intelligence community rather than as a "strike support asset" that could provide "direct and immediate assistance to NATO aircrews conducting flexible targeting missions." Gen. John Jumper later remarked that the air campaign planners and operators soon learned that "they had to make forward air controllers out of what previously had been intelligence collectors."[49] Moreover, high demand for the Joint STARS combined with low availability (there were only two in theatre) imposed long-duration flights (seventeen to twenty-one hours) and the need for backup aircrews.[50]

As impressive as American space-based collection systems were, they had limitations. The Defense Meteorological Support Program satellites could not provide continuous weather reporting, which led NATO to cancel some strike missions. The photoreconnaissance satellites could not provide the right kind of imagery, and the best target identification-to-strike timeline the National Reconnaissance Office's ELINT and SIGINT satellites could provide was three to four hours.[51] Just as in the Persian Gulf War, the American space-based systems were not optimized for supporting dynamic combat operations.

Production (Collation and Analysis) and Dissemination

If the collection problems were not enough to impede the intelligence process, production suffered from an "excessively lengthy information and intelligence cycle time."[52] Aircrews and commanders were "repeatedly frustrated" by the lengthy "sensor-to-shooter" cycle that hindered the ability to strike targets of opportunity.[53] A flexible targeting cell had been created at the end of the first month, but it did not have a "sufficiently high-volume data link with enough channels to quickly get the information where it needed to go."[54] In intelligence production, timeliness is second only to accuracy. This is particularly essential in war fighting, since the combatants operating in the battle space usually are not static. Locations of units, concentrations, composition, and capabilities can change by the hour.

Lambeth suggests that the air campaign suffered from an inefficient targeting process that involved too many players participating from the Pentagon, SHAPE, the CAOC, and other entities. The process began at the Joint Analysis Centre, which served as NATO's all-source collation and fusion centre. The centre would send targeting data to the planners at SHAPE and the US European Command, which would start creating target folders. Lawyers would vet them to ensure that they were valid targets in conformity to the laws of armed conflict. From there the proposed targets would be reviewed for approval by the Joint Targeting Coordination Board, then by Admiral Ellis and his staff, next by General Clark and back to Ellis, and on to the USAF's 32nd Air Operations Group (at Ramstein air base, Germany) and the US Navy's 6th Fleet command ship, both of which prepared final target folders. Some NATO allies had input into the process, and the CAOC maintained separate processes for specialized US aircraft (B-1s, B-2s, B-52s, F-117s, and cruise missiles) assigned by the US European Command and those operated solely by NATO. Cox says that since it relied on national sources to provide intelligence, NATO was always "a pace slower" than those national systems.[55] The strikes had been under way for thirty-seven days before there was "a smoothly running target development and review mechanism" and another ten days before there was a joint integrated prioritized target list. Prior to that, the Master Air Attack Plan Team had been assigning only targets that had been politically approved. So, for the first half of the operation NATO had not attempted to create a consistent targeting strategy, which would not have been possible anyway.[56] Had NATO troops been attacking only fixed targets the processes probably would have been sufficient, but they could not respond nimbly to constantly moving ground forces.

Furthermore, because NATO had not planned for an air campaign lasting more than a few days, the CAOC initially was understaffed, lacking the critical planning cells needed for a prolonged campaign. Later it became overburdened with personnel (some 1,400) and with bureaucratic "gridlock." Since the bomb damage assessment process involved multiple agencies inside and outside of NATO and at least two sources were needed to confirm a target destroyed, this delayed assessment past the time needed to do mission planning and retargeting.

So, some targets were restruck without actual need. That and the fact that records of flexible targets hit inside Kosovo were not being kept meant that the bomb damage assessment of attacks on Serbian forces contained a large margin of uncertainty. Moreover, there was constant tension between the demands on the limited ISR assets to support attack operations and to use them to inform the bomb damage assessment process.[57]

Finally, there was the inevitable bugbear of coalition operations: intelligence sharing and classification problems. Most of the collection systems were American, so sharing their products was complicated by a maze of cross-cutting (and sometimes conflicting) arrangements governed by bilateral and multilateral agreements within the NATO and Five Eyes networks. Sharing was slowed by these bureaucratic hurdles, by the time needed to reclassify materials, and by technical problems such as a lack of computer interoperability at different security levels.[58] Again, this obstacle precluded timely production and dissemination.

Exploitation

However, there is (and was) a world of difference between the work of mission planners and bomb damage assessment analysts in the CAOC and that of the forward air controllers directing strike aircraft onto their targets in hot airspace. Bruce Nardulli et al. described the latter process: "An EC-130E/J Airborne Battlefield Command and Control Center [ABCCC] would designate areas within Kosovo for attack using a grid system. As strike aircraft entered Kosovo airspace . . . they would contact the EC-130E/J for instructions. Controllers on the EC-130E/J would brief the pilots and hand them off to forward air controllers, usually flying OA-10A aircraft. The EC-130 would also provide updated intelligence to the forward air controllers, who would then direct their strike aircraft to their targets."[59] What Nardulli and his coauthors do not make clear is whether this procedure applied only to preplanned and predesignated targets or to all strikes. Lambeth suggests that a similar process was applied to flexible targeting. "When targets of opportunity presented themselves on rare occasions, sensor platforms that detected ground vehicular movement would pass the coordinates and target characterization information to the EC-130 ABCCC, which, in turn, would vector NATO attack aircraft into the appropriate kill box, first to confirm that the targets were valid and then to engage them."[60]

Nardulli and colleagues go on to say that during the last two weeks of the war, the Joint STARS and other sensors were usually the first to pick up Serb forces' movements. They would send the coordinates of those troop concentrations to the forward air controllers, "who, in turn, directed both unmanned aerial vehicles (UAVs) and fighters in for closer looks, and ultimately for attacks."[61]

Although NATO strove to avoid the appearance of being the KLA's air force, there was some cooperation, and it was difficult to distinguish NATO air strikes on predetermined interdiction targets from close air support to the insurgents. To prevent such strikes from hitting the KLA, the CAOC issued orders directly to the ABCCC and to the attacking aircrews.[62] And, "One new procedure demonstrated for the first time in Kosovo entailed... fusion of UAV sensor and specialized command and control procedures, in which two Predators... would provide electro-optical and infrared identification of mobile targets and a third Predator would then use its laser designator and mapping software to provide geo-location, after which orbiting A-10s or F-16s could be called in on the detected target."[63] Even with all of these targeting aids, about 25 percent of Task Force Aviano's laser-guided bombs missed their targets, a rate consistent with that of other NATO allies. Bergen attributes this to insufficient training with the targeting pods, which were too few in number in Canada.[64]

The Impact of Intelligence on Air Operations

Even the harshest critics of Operation ALLIED FORCE are compelled to concede that in the end it succeeded. The Milošević regime was forced to withdraw its troops from Kosovo, cease its repression of Kosovar Albanians and allow the return of refugees, and allow an international peacekeeping force to replace Serb rule in the former Yugoslav territory. To the extent that there is debate, it is about the relative impacts of the bombing, the threat to intervene with ground forces, and the role of diplomacy in persuading Milošević to accept the outcome.[65] Moreover, the air campaign failed to prevent the ethnic cleansing of Kosovo, which actually accelerated during the bombing.[66] Worse still, postwar on-site target analyses concluded that the NATO campaign had inflicted minimal losses on Serb forces, which withdrew in good order.

The foundation for this was laid by campaign planning, which in turn had been shaped by the political constraints imposed on the plans by national leaders and by NATO's collective reluctance to resort to force or to accept casualties on all sides. The result was an air campaign plan that was flawed from the outset. Effective attacks against Serb forces in Kosovo would have required low-level air strikes. Likewise, NATO wanted pilots to have eyes on target to reduce the likelihood of collateral damage or casualties. But its members' insistence on minimizing risks to aircrews ruled that out. NATO bombers had to release munitions from higher altitudes, almost ensuring that such strikes would be less effective against Serb forces (and more likely to cause civilian casualties). Moreover, NATO had expected the strikes to last only a few days, and when Serb resistance stiffened, NATO was forced into a longer campaign for which it had not prepared.

The contrary demands of the campaign plan compromised the ability of intelligence systems, staffs, and processes to support the air strikes effectively. But a poor plan does not absolve the intelligence effort of fault for its own limitations, technical or human. NATO's intelligence assets and processes should have conferred an overwhelming advantage. Yet in crucible of combat, it suffered from an intelligence deficit that could not provide the kind of support the air campaign needed.

On the technical side, in the years since the Persian Gulf War little had been done to make US space-based reconnaissance systems more responsive to the needs of dynamic war fighting.[67] The E-8 Joint STARS surveillance systems, which had performed so well in the Iraqi/Kuwait desert, had difficulty observing forces tucked into the rugged terrain of former Yugoslavia. The Predator UAV's low airspeed meant that it took a long time to reach its search areas, by which time Serb forces might have moved or hidden. The UAVs' ability to fly low was very useful for close-up imagery of enemy forces, but this also led to some being shot down.

These collection limits were compounded by process problems, including the convoluted target approval process and the lack of a flexible targeting system during the first half of the campaign. Furthermore, the sensor-to-shooter chain was lengthy. These constraints imposed a degree of rigidity on strike mission planning and on the aircrews, who could not respond quickly to targets of opportunity until much later in the war. This also affected the bomb damage assessment process, since missions, including some restrikes, had to be planned before the assessment task was complete. The CAOC went from being understaffed at the outset to having too many people inserting themselves into assessment and other tasks. Finally, data classification and interoperability hurdles hindered intelligence sharing among the allies.

In the absence of original source material, we cannot say definitively how and to what degree these intelligence issues affected Canadian fighter operations. Bashow's article briefly discusses the target selection and validation process but says nothing about either the utility or limits of intelligence support. However, since Task Force Aviano relied on coalition collection and production capabilities, it is hard to imagine that the force was immune to the intelligence problems affecting the rest of the NATO air contingents.

OPERATIONS JOINT GUARDIAN AND KINETIC

When KFOR deployed into Kosovo, it confronted a threat environment similar to that in Bosnia: widespread destruction of housing and infrastructure as well as population displacement but within a smaller area. However, there was no peace agreement comparable to the Dayton Accords and no accepted local authority able to exercise power. The UN Mission in Kosovo (UNMIK), which was to provide interim civil administration and policing, was slow to stand up. In this vacuum, armed extremists and criminal elements continued to wield influence; "ethnic tensions remained high and vengeful Kosovar Albanians attacked Serbs and other minorities."[68]

KFOR MISSION AND CONCEPT OF OPERATIONS

The leading elements of the CAF's Task Force Kosovo deployed into Kosovo on 12 June 1999 under the terms of UN Security Council Resolution 1244. That resolution provided for the withdrawal of Serbian forces from Kosovo, the creation of UNMIK, and the deployment of an international security force, KFOR. Its mission was to oversee the withdrawal of Serb forces, deter the resumption of hostilities, demobilize the KLA, and create a secure environment that would allow refugees and other displaced persons to return to Kosovo.[69] The Canadian portion of NATO's Operation JOINT GUARDIAN was named Operation KINETIC.[70]

In the immediate aftermath of the cease-fire, two factors shaped the KFOR mission. First, there was widespread disorder. Second, UNMIK was not able to generate the planned international police force as quickly as it was needed. In fact, it was not able to recruit to full strength and had to revert to rebuilding and training a new local force. Consequently, KFOR had to take on the policing task for the short term.[71] Task Force Kosovo units also performed CIMIC activities.[72]

The commander of KFOR, British lieutenant-general Sir Mike Jackson, defined his intent and concept of operations as follows:

> My intent is to establish a stable and secure environment throughout Kosovo, while operating in a firm, fair and even-handed manner.... Our role is principally one of creating the conditions within which UNMIK can bring about political, economic, and humanitarian renewal.... We will achieve success by synchronising our work along complementary lines of operation, coordinating deep, close and rear operations.... Deep operations will focus on the will and perceptions of the people in order to maintain popular support for KFOR and the renewal process. Close operations will be directed at establishing and maintaining a stable and secure environment. Rear operations will ensure force protection and assistance to UNMIK ... and NGOs.[73]

Historian Sean Maloney says that this formed the basis for all CAF actions over the next year. In the UK multinational brigade (MNB) this translated into three major tasks: security, preventing the return of Serb forces; compliance, demilitarizing the KLA; and CIMIC, including intelligence gathering and information operations.[74] Significantly, Jackson stated that "KFOR must have a thorough understanding of the complex situation in Kosovo."[75] Therefore, intelligence work would be central to its peace enforcement efforts and to the operations of Task Force Kosovo. Over the next twelve months the two rotations of CAF troops carried out essential intelligence tasks: indications and warning, reconnaissance patrols, collecting and reporting on paramilitary groups and activities, situational awareness, covert and overt surveillance (urban and rural), border surveillance, and counterintelligence.

TASK FORCE KOSOVO: ORGANIZATION AND MISSION

Planning for a CAF ground force in Kosovo had begun while the NATO-Yugoslav talks were under way in March 1999, with a warning order issued on 4 March. While detaching and reassigning all or some of the Canadian SFOR contingent in Bosnia would have simplified planning and preparations, weakening SFOR was not an option. So, the CAF contribution to KFOR had to come from Canada. On 1 April the DCDS (Lt.-Gen. Ray Hennault) told the Land Staff to plan for the training and preparation of an infantry battle group of 1,400–1,500. At that point it was not clear whether NATO troops would be making a forced or permissive entry into Kosovo. Clearly, if NATO had to fight its way in on the ground, that would have major implications for planning, force structure, logistics, and so on. After considerable debate over force structure and the capabilities needed, the government approved a compromise contingent, described in detail below. Col. Mike Ward exercised command of Task Force Kosovo from the National Command Element based in Skopje, Macedonia, but the reconnaissance squadron and helicopters were under operational control of the United Kingdom's 4 Armoured Brigade. KFOR and the brigade's intelligence staff viewed Task Force Kosovo's new Coyote light armoured vehicles (LAVs) in particular as an asset vital for its operations.[76]

The Serb withdrawal of its forces and the consequent sudden end to the air campaign on 10 June caught the Canadians only partly ready to deploy. Government approval allowed the CDS (Gen. Maurice Baril) to issue the warning order for the entire BG on 11 June. But the reconnaissance squadron and helicopters were already en route and were able to join the UK brigade advance into Kosovo on 12 June. The remainder of the BG arrived in late July.[77]

Under command of Brig. Bill Rollo, the British brigade initially consisted of an armoured regiment, an armoured reconnaissance regiment, and two mechanized infantry battalions plus the CAF units: the armoured reconnaissance squadron from the Lord Strathcona's Horse and part of the 408 Tactical Helicopter Squadron. By late July the BG from the 1 PPCLI, commanded by Lt.-Col. Steve Bryan and then Shane Brennan, joined them. The second rotation, commanded by Lt.-Col. Bruce Pennington, comprised a BG from the 1 RCR with elements of the Royal Canadian Dragoons. The BGs were pared down to six hundred personnel from the normal eight hundred to nine hundred. They had two rifle companies instead of three, with smaller platoons and sections. Their combat support companies included a troop of five Leopard tanks, a reconnaissance platoon of six Coyotes, and mortar, antiarmour, and pioneer platoons along with a combat engineer troop. The BGs also had an expanded intelligence section and a sniper section. Both were augmented by specialists as needed.[78]

KFOR consisted of five brigades dispersed through five separate AORs, with Russian troops assigned to three subsectors attached to the United States, French, and German AORs. The MNBs operated within a single KFOR chain of command under Jackson's direction. However, at least initially there was little coordination between them; each operated according to its own plans. For example, there were six information operations plans: the KFOR plan and five devised by the MNBs. Furthermore, Jackson found that although there was a mechanism for mutual assistance, he could not order forces from one MNB to aid another.[79]

The Canadian troops were responsible for an AOR that included the vital Drenica Valley and the area around Pristina airport (which was controlled by Russian troops). The valley consisted of open farmland in the north and rugged, forested hills in the south. The Task Force Kosovo base was at Donja Koretica, south of the major town of Glogovac. The valley was about 90 percent Albanian, but during the conflict it had been a heavily contested area. As the Serb forces entered from the north, many of the locals had fled to the hills to hide or keep fighting. The hills were heavily mined. After the war, the area remained a KLA stronghold.[80]

The BG's task was to prepare the ground for a successful UN administration, UNMIK.[81] The BG had to apply KFOR's rules and guidelines for the KLA strictly and consistently. The main challenge confronting the BG in the first few months was to create a secure environment where there was no law and order, no official civic government (but several shadow ones), and no UN civil authority and where criminal gangs were extorting payoffs. So, the Canadians had to fill the void in internal security and policing. The BG therefore would have the dual roles of stabilization and deterrence on the one hand and coordinating humanitarian assistance and reconstruction on the other,[82] a familiar combination for Canadian troops with recent peacekeeping experience.

INTELLIGENCE REQUIREMENTS

The initial intelligence target for the Task Force Kosovo reconnaissance and helicopter squadrons in late June was the Serb military: monitoring its withdrawal from Kosovo. That was not peaceful; there were nightly Serb/KLA clashes. But that task also served to confirm the limited effects of the air campaign. Then Lt. Christopher Hunt, commanding a Coyote LAV troop, personally observed the withdrawal of two Serb tank battalions, each still retaining over fifty tanks.[83]

Once the withdrawal was completed, the Canadians' attention shifted to other groups and organizations. Although the KLA had disbanded in theory, because of its high profile and political ambitions it was KFOR's most important target to ensure that its behaviour didn't change without being noticed. So, the squadrons monitored KLA orders of battle and boundaries; any non-compliance regarding weapons caches; its attitudes toward the undertaking to disband and toward KFOR, including indications and warning of an impending attack on KFOR; and the long-term intentions of individual KLA members. In addition, KFOR needed to be aware of local government activities administered by the KLA as well as political parties and their size, leaders, aims, funding, and relationship to the movement. But the KLA was not the only player that warranted observation. On the Serb side, the squadron had to monitor any Serbian Interior Ministry police, special forces, and stay-behind presence as well as any unsanctioned Serb paramilitary presence, structures, and leaders and their intentions. They also had to keep a watch on isolated Serb populations, who were vulnerable to Kosovar revenge attacks. This also meant identifying and observing any Albanian paramilitary structures or presence, along with the activities of organized crime groups, which tended to overlap with paramilitaries of all stripes. There was an ongoing potential for terrorist attacks that could not be attributed to any specific group or community. The sites of alleged war crimes had to be kept under observation to ensure the integrity of investigations. Finally, in the realm of SA, KFOR troops needed to understand local attitudes toward different political parties as well as communities, infrastructures, religious sites, and key leaders. These requirements eventually applied to the entire BG.[84] Their implications were profound. Out of necessity, the BG had to invent a new concept of operations: intelligence-driven peace enforcement.

Task Force Kosovo Intelligence Staff

According to Colonel Ward, during the initial deployment intelligence support consisted of a single warrant officer, which left the formation in the dark until a fully staffed intelligence cell arrived in mid-July.[85] The 1999 *Intelligence Branch Newsletter* stated that eight branch personnel were serving in army intelligence positions in Kosovo. A later issue provided details. The Roto 0 intelligence cell, led by J2 Maj. Hugh Fergusson, comprised seven staff. Roto 1 had fourteen, with the J2, Maj. Daniel Villeneuve, also heading the CANIC. His staff included a J2 Operations, a J2 Analysis, a collator, two photo technicians, and a linguist fluent in Serbian from Canadian Forces Station Leitrim. One officer was assigned to the National Command Element. In addition, the 1 RCR BG had two intelligence officers as well as two noncommissioned member operators, while the helicopter squadron (from December 1999, the 430 Squadron) had three intelligence noncommissioned members.[86]

Even with the larger establishment given the wide range of intelligence targets and tasks and with the assets described below, that number was hardly sufficient. So, although the mission clearly was going to be intelligence-driven, the human resources to make that a reality could not be provided by the branch alone; they had to be augmented by secondments from other branches and services. For example, the Royal Canadian Dragoons used two of their soldiers (who had received combat intelligence training) as their analysts.[87]

Collection Assets

The reconnaissance Sabre squadron consisted of three troops of five Coyotes (each with a crew of four) plus two for the squadron headquarters, a total of seventeen vehicles. For each troop, there was a command vehicle, two with surveillance masts and two with remote sensors (deployed away from the vehicles). They normally operated in two-vehicle patrols: one with a mast and the other with the sensors (figure 10.1). The squadron also had an assault troop (forty-seven solders) that could carry out combat engineer tasks or operate as an infantry platoon. Often sections were attached to the Coyote troops to reinforce their patrols in urban and other higher-threat areas. They were mounted in five Bison armoured vehicles equipped with machine guns, mortars, and antitank missiles. There was also a four-person combat engineer section with a Bison engineer vehicle.[88]

The Kosovo Rotary Wing Air Unit, drawn initially from the 408 and then the 430 Tactical Helicopter Squadrons, was equipped with eight CH-146 Griffons and ten three-person aircrews plus a headquarters, ground support vehicles, and an airfield security force. The Griffons could be equipped with a forward-looking infrared thermal imaging sensor linked to a VHS recorder, a 3.8-million candle-power Nightsun spotlight, GPS, and night-vision goggles for the crew. When a sensor package was added, a mission specialist was attached to the aircrew to run the system. The helicopters operated under the control of the brigade commander.[89]

The BGs' primary intelligence assets were their infantry companies. They also had a reconnaissance troop with six Coyotes equipped with remote sensors only, and their TUA vehicles had night-vision capability. In addition, the sniper section was used to collect intelligence.[90] According to Capt. Todd Hisey, who served on the 1 PPCLI G3 staff, on arrival in theatre the BG concluded that at

FIGURE 10.1. A Coyote light armored vehicle reconnaissance patrol of the Lord Strathcona's Horse armoured regiment serving as an observation post, with surveillance mast deployed, Kosovo, 1999. *Colonel Christopher Hunt*

KFOR and brigade headquarters there was an information vacuum regarding the Drenica Valley, which seemed to be the center of everything linked to the KLA. To fill that information vacuum, the BG "really became an intelligence battalion. Every soldier was a collector on the ground" focused primarily on the KLA's leadership and its capacity to exercise influence.[91]

Notwithstanding the truncated scale of each of the CAF units, had they been used in concert they would have been a powerful intelligence team that could be focused on targets. However, because of the demands on the brigade, they were often used piecemeal, effective individually for the given task but unable to exploit their combined capabilities to their fullest. Still, as will be shown, what they did accomplish was impressive enough.

Of course, the Canadian task force was not solely dependent on its own resources. First, it could reach back to the Balkans Intelligence Response Team in the DGI. The task force also was part of a brigade that had assets such as SOF. Moreover, as a member of NATO and the Five Eyes network, Canada had access to sources and products generated by other alliance members either through direct sharing via their national intelligence centres or via the Joint Analysis Centre. The United States deployed the most collection and analysis assets within KFOR. Their organization for Task Force Falcon (MNB East) included the G2, an analysis control element, a National Intelligence Support Team, and a special operations coordination and control element. They interacted with the KFOR J2 and the US national intelligence centre and had reach-out ability to Europe-based US intelligence bodies as well as reach-back to US national agencies. They shared intelligence with the British brigade and the Canadians. There was close cooperation at the tactical level in SIGINT collection and sharing. According to a study by Larry Wentz, the National Security Agency "was quite cooperative in sharing U.S. signals intelligence with KFOR and the other MNBs."[92]

The Americans deployed a wide range of collectors, including Predator and Hunter UAVs, U-2, RC-135 RIVET JOINT and RC-12 GUARDRAIL aircraft, remote sensors, and ground surveillance radars. The United States also deployed HUMINT teams. That said, intelligence reaching the Task Force Falcon G2 was stovepiped from the various US tactical, theatre, and strategic/national collection sources, and the volume was enormous. The analytical tools and systems were insufficient to process and analyse the data, leading to information overload on the commander and staffs.[93] So, it is not clear how effectively the Task Force Falcon intelligence apparatus was able to share with its coalition partners.

COLLECTION ACTIVITIES

Given the aim of the mission, the nature of the AOR, and local political culture dominated by the KLA, Maj. Jerry Walsh, the BG G3 operations officer, and his staff felt that it was essential to give priority to intelligence collection. They decided to focus on the KLA, because they felt that KFOR had not devoted enough attention to the Drenica Valley. Walsh's successor, Maj. Omer Lavoie, devised a concept of operations that prioritized dominating the AOR through patrolling, vehicle checkpoints, and surveillance operations. The need to support UNMIK was the driving force behind intelligence collection.[94]

As a brigade collection asset, the Task Force Kosovo reconnaissance squadron carried out a range of collection missions across the AOR against a variety of targets. This included route and area reconnaissance, overt and covert surveillance of former KLA members and of the border with Serbia, surveillance while the assault troop conducted patrols, working with helicopters to observe locations where mines could be planted at night, covert surveillance of suspected Russian-Serbian smuggling operations across the border in the MNB-East sector, surveillance and patrolling directed specifically to the Russian forces at Pristina airfield, observing KLA splinter insurgent activity and Serb counterinsurgency actions in the Presevo Valley area of Serbia, monitoring a Serb EW site, and intercepting and analysing their electronic traffic that responded to KFOR maneuvers along the border.[95]

Prior to deployment of the helicopters, three limitations had been identified. First, the British brigade staff had not fully thought out how to use them in the surveillance/reconnaissance role. Second, the forward-looking infrared system was unreliable and had inadequate magnification. Finally, the aircrews had limited knowledge and experience with the surveillance/reconnaissance role, which the Air Command had effectively abandoned when the light observation helicopter was scrapped. So, the Griffons were used mostly to transport troops, conducting reconnaissance tasks as add-ons. They supported ground patrols by doing covert or overt overwatch, flying blacked out and using the forward-looking infrared and night-vision goggles for the former or activating the Nightsun for the latter. At times they did surveillance flights five nights per week, providing support to vehicle checkpoints after inserting the troops. The Griffons maintained a watch on certain KLA members who shot at KFOR patrols or were involved in smuggling weapons from Albania. They did border surveillance to track infiltration by Serbian SOF, sometimes working with the Coyote troops, who could not observe everything from their ground positions. Finally, the Griffons used imagery and other sources to search for mass graves.[96]

Before deploying, the BG operations staff had gathered information on Kosovo from the internet and from intelligence sources. They put together biographies of all the key players who were linked to the valley. Once in theatre, they set up vehicle checkpoints and tracked those people. BG companies deployed into KLA-dominated areas, familiarizing themselves with the population and influential figures. The effort was multifaceted. "CIMIC, psychological operations, public affairs," and other efforts overlapped and were mutually reinforcing.[97]

Although the CAF had done CIMIC activities on previous peace support operations, it had no CIMIC doctrine. So, Maj. Douglas Delaney (who commanded the combat support company) was put in charge of CIMIC, and his two teams improvised on the fly, drawing on their experiences. They collected and collated information on community needs and on what nongovernment organizations were doing to address those needs. There was so much information, in fact, that the teams' warrant officer and a clerk had to create and maintain a database to keep track of it. While CIMIC was not in itself an intelligence task, it built relationships with the local population and became a source of information for the BG. The CIMIC and J2 staffs exchanged information each had collected that would be useful to the other. When combined with other sources, CIMIC data contributed to the larger intelligence picture.[98]

In addition to these intelligence collection efforts, the BG carried out a range of other collection activities. OPs watched illegal policing by Kosovar police and video-taped them: "we knew who was who, what cars they used."[99] The BG also maintained a watch on the Russians and their clashes with the KLA, observed KLA funerals, did counterintelligence operations against KLA espionage efforts, and used its snipers and TUA vehicles for surveillance, and infantry sections conducted two or three four-hour foot patrols daily through the villages. Those generated a lot of so-called white SA: photos with names, employment histories, etc.[100]

CAF units also played an intelligence role during a major crisis in the city of Mitrovica in February 2000. A series of attacks by ethnic Serbs and Kosovar Albanians, attacks on KFOR troops, and major demonstrations raised concern that any further escalation of the violence could provoke Serb military intervention. KFOR troops, including Canadian, were temporarily deployed from their regular AORs to Mitrovica. With the approval of the DCDS, Col. Ivan Fenton (Ward's successor) directed the 1 RCR BG to dispatch one company (with snipers, reconnaissance troops, and Pioneers attached), along with Royal Canadian Dragoons Coyotes and helicopters. Over a period of about three weeks the Coyote troops and snipers did surveillance independently and in collaboration with British snipers and UK and Swedish EW detachments. The BG infantry did covert night patrols in downtown Mitrovica and also did overt social patrolling, which generated a flow of white SA.[101] One of the platoon commanders told Maloney that this generated an "amazing" amount of intelligence: patrol reports that were "inches thick.... Photos and disks full of digital photos."[102] Maj. Pat Koch conceded that they overloaded the BG intelligence staff and possibly the brigade level as well. But he felt that they provided "a running commentary on what was going on."[103]

PRODUCTION (COLLATION AND ANALYSIS)

Turning this raw data into processed intelligence was the responsibility of the Task Force Kosovo J2 intelligence cell. Except for the one officer at the National Command Element, it was colocated with the BG at the Donja Koretica base. Its principal role was to provide timely intelligence to the Task Force Kosovo commander, and as the CANIC it would assist the commander in consulting with the NDHQ and making decisions with national implications, such as deploying Task Force Kosovo elements to MNB-East or to Mitrovica. To that end, the J2 cell developed and maintained close liaison with other intelligence organizations in theatre to ensure good SA. That included KFOR main headquarters and the other national intelligence centres. The J2 cell passed along pertinent and Canadian-eyes-only information to all Canadian units in theatre and answered requests for information from Ottawa, in addition to the daily and weekly reports the CANIC sent to the Balkans Intelligence Response Team.[104] The J2/CANIC was also the focal point for receiving imagery (probably via the DIE) from allied space-based assets that could then be used to generate maps for the BG, the reconnaissance squadron, and the helicopters.[105]

Maj. Pat Koch impressed upon his soldiers the potential analytical value of data in the patrol reports, saying "you might come back with one little tidbit of information: this particular person there, for example, which to you doesn't really mean anything, but when we bring that in and we put them with a bigger picture ... all of a sudden it becomes very, very important."[106]

Section leader Sgt. Kevin Earl recognized the utility of that kind of social network link analysis. Noting problems in distributing aid in certain areas, he focused his attention on the locals who seemed to control it, identifying them and the others to whom they were connected. "We built a big data-base. We could type in license plate numbers and it would go back to this person and all their known links. Everything from fuel to people who owned fuel stations. ... It was all linked together in a big, big clique of military-oriented people. ... It all revolved around who was who before."[107] This network controlled who got what. They distributed aid from nongovernmental organizations, and a large portion of it ended up in KLA training camps. Earl went on to say that knowing this allowed the task force to address problems such as the drug trade and graft. Solid analysis of this kind of problem started with the soldiers on patrol asking the right questions, such as "Did you just buy this auto parts store? Who owned it before you? Has this always been an auto parts store? Where do you get your auto parts?"[108] That kind of information allowed the BG to generate a picture of these complex networks that in some cases might lead back to a single individual.[109]

This kind of analytical approach was not new to stabilization operations or to the CAF. They had used it in Somalia and more recently in Bosnia. The British had done it in Northern Ireland. It required a different mindset from intelligence support to conventional war operations. The evidence suggests that the CAF had adapted to it quite well. The BG and the J2 staff did some of this analysis, although neither had sufficient personnel and other resources required to do all the work. The task force had access to computers, but the computer revolution and the internet were still relatively new to the CAF. Signals detachments ran several local area networks at the task force headquarters level to distribute secure information, but it is not clear if the BG had its own such network. The task force headquarters did have satellite uplinks via Inmarsat to communicate with NDHQ.[110]

DISSEMINATION AND EXPLOITATION: IMPACT ON OPERATIONS

The intelligence collection and production processes were considerable for the relatively small Canadian contingent. So, what impact did they have on Task Force Kosovo operations and on their operating environment?

First, intelligence defined the nature of CAF operations within KFOR. They were not only driven by intelligence but also driven to gather, analyse, and exploit it. Working together but even used individually, Task Force Kosovo's ISR capabilities created a virtuous circle of intelligence and operations supporting each other. With the possible exception of the Oka Crisis, no CAF operation up to this point had so clearly displayed a closer intelligence/operations nexus.

Second, Task Force Kosovo actions did exert some influence on the operating environment. The presence of CAF and other KFOR troops ensured that Serbian military and Interior Ministry police forces did not return to Kosovo in force, though it is not clear that they intended to do so. So, the most that can be said in that regard is that deterrence *appeared* to work. CAF intelligence efforts contributed to that by maintaining surveillance on the border and on Serb forces in close proximity to it.[111]

KFOR could not prevent all low-level conflict between Kosovar Albanians and Serbs. But echoing the British Army's Northern Ireland experience, KFOR could limit it to "an acceptable level of violence" and prevent it from escalating out of control. Sometimes covert surveillance allowed troops to capture former KLA troops engaging in intimidation or criminal activity. On other occasions, the presence of the Coyotes with their masts up was enough to deter would-be attackers. CAF troops deploying video cameras while overwatching market days had a similar effect, thus blurring the line between intelligence and operations.[112] However, Lt. Christopher Hunt noted one limitation on the Coyotes. He felt that deploying them on covert surveillance at standoff ranges of four to five kilometres reduced their ability to identify suspicious nonmilitary vehicles. Instead, the handheld colour camera with zoom, microphone, and tripod, employed from a closer dismounted OP, was more effective than the Coyote's monochrome day camera.[113]

Using the helicopters for surveillance and overwatch had a similar effect. The analysts kept track of the crime rate in Pristina. When the helicopters were there at night the crime rate dropped, and when they stopped the crime rate rose noticeably. By using forward-looking infrared along the border, the helicopters could track infiltration by Serbian military and Interior Ministry police forces, and then British troops could deal with the intruders.[114]

The BG's CIMIC operations and intelligence were interwoven and mutually supporting; neither could work effectively without the other. After some delay, KFOR decided to shut down illegal KLA policing operations. Task Force Kosovo Operations WOLVERINE and QUARTERBACK stopped at least two of these. Both were preceded and informed by overt and covert surveillance. But a covert sniper OP inserted after they ended revealed a counterintelligence problem: KLA surveillance of the Canadian BG. The actual KLA threat was to the Russians, who moved supply convoys through the Canadian AOR. This led to a BG raid on an arms cache at Komorane, where they seized six truckloads of mines and weapons. The impact on the local KLA brigade was significant; they shifted their arms stockpiles to another sector because Task Force Kosovo was too effective in controlling their area.[115]

Finally, the deployment to Mitrovica began with reconnaissance squadron providing ISR support to British troops doing arms searches. The Kosovar march there had been anticipated, though the scale was drastically underestimated. The result was that the Canadians were caught up in a riot. But after that, intelligence-based searches continued in the city.

Task Force Kosovo operations in Kosovo during 1999–2000 were crucial to KFOR efforts to implement its objectives: deterrence, containment, and stabilization. That was possible only because Task Force Kosovo developed a significant process synergy between intelligence and operations. In fact, Colonel Ward—not a disinterested observer, of course—felt that in the intelligence field the Canadians more than held their own. "Our information operations doctrine, operations planning procedures and intelligence preparation of the battlefield enabled the execution of operations with better-equipped Allies, and in fact we were ahead of many of them in terms of emerging intelligence, surveillance, target acquisition and reconnaissance concepts."[116]

NOTES

1. David L. Bashow et al., "Mission Ready: Canada's Role in the Kosovo Air Campaign," *Canadian Military Journal* 1, no. 1 (Spring 2000): 55.
2. National Defence, "Operation Kinetic," Government of Canada, 22 July 2013, https://www.canada.ca/en/department-national-defence/services/operations/military-operations/recently-completed/operation-kinetic.html.
3. Dana H. Allin, *NATO's Balkan Interventions* (Abingdon, UK: Routledge, 2002), 63–64.
4. Benjamin S. Lambeth, *NATO's Air War for Kosovo: A Strategic and Operational Assessment* (Santa Monica, CA: Rand, 2001), 24–27, 31, 33; William M. Arkin, "Operation Allied Force: 'The Most Precise Application of Air Power in History,'" in *War over Kosovo: Politics and Strategy in a Global Age*, ed. A. J. Bacevich and Eliot A. Cohen (New York: Columbia University Press, 2001), 21.
5. Bruce R. Nardulli et al., *Disjointed War: Military Operations in Kosovo, 1999* (Santa Monica, CA: Rand, 2002), 21–22, citing the public statements of the NATO secretary-general and US president Bill Clinton.
6. Nardulli et al., 22, quoting President Clinton.
7. Lambeth, *NATO's Air War*, 11, 13.
8. Quoted in Ivo H. Daalder and Michael E. O'Hanlon, *Winning Ugly: NATO's War to Save Kosovo* (Washington, DC: Brookings Institution Press, 2000), 104–5.
9. Lambeth, *NATO's Air War*, 28.
10. Lambeth, 13; Nardulli et al., *Disjointed War*, 4.
11. Nardulli et al., *Disjointed War*, 32–33; Lambeth, *NATO's Air War*, 24.
12. Nardulli et al., *Disjointed War*, 34.
13. Nardulli et al., 24; Arkin, "Operation Allied Force," 10–11.
14. Nardulli et al., *Disjointed War*, 24.
15. Lambeth, *NATO's Air War*, 20–23.
16. Arkin, "Operation Allied Force," 21.

17. Bashow et al., "Mission Ready," 55, 57, 59; Bob Bergen, *Scattering Chaff: Canadian Air Power and Censorship during the Kosovo War* (Calgary, Alberta: University of Calgary Press, 2019), 232.
18. Bashow et al., 59, says that Task Force Aviano flew 10 percent of the battlefield interdiction missions in Kosovo.
19. Bergen, *Scattering Chaff*, 179, says that six of eighteen CF-18s were cannibalized for parts to keep the other twelve flying.
20. Nardulli et al., *Disjointed War*, 1; Daalder and O'Hanlon, *Winning Ugly*, 184.
21. Daalder and O'Hanlon, *Winning Ugly*, 103–5; Nardulli et al., *Disjointed War*, 2–3, 12, 19–20, 24, 27.
22. Nardulli et al., *Disjointed War*, 3–4, 27–30, 48; Lambeth, *NATO's Air War*, 38.
23. Daalder and O'Hanlon, *Winning Ugly*, 118.
24. Capt. Paul D. Johnston, "2002, A Tactical Fighter's Perspective on Intelligence," in Harold A. Skaarup, *Out of Darkness—Light: A History of Canadian Military Intelligence*, Vol. 3 (New York: iUniverse, 2005), 162.
25. From 3 Wing and 4 Wing.
26. Brig.-Gen. (ret.) James S. Cox, interview, 22 June 2004, Canadian War Museum Oral History Program.
27. Cox.
28. Cox.
29. Skaarup, *Out of Darkness—Light*, 3:162.
30. Lambeth, *NATO's Air War*, 97–99. During the 1991 Persian Gulf War, the National Reconnaissance Office managed satellite surveillance.
31. Lambeth, 19, 56, 64, table 3.4, 94–97, 99, 157.
32. Lambeth, 127. ATARS provided digital and electro-optical images generated by synthetic aperture radar that could be downlinked in real time to ground stations.
33. Daalder and O'Hanlon, *Winning Ugly*, 150.
34. Nardulli et al., *Disjointed War*, 44.
35. Lambeth, *NATO's Air War*, 56.
36. Lambeth, 94.
37. Lambeth, 94–95.
38. Lambeth, 96.
39. Michael G. Vickers, "Revolution Deferred: Kosovo and the Transformation of War," in *War over Kosovo*, ed. Bacevich and Cohen, 194.
40. Lambeth, *NATO's Air War*, 94.
41. Nardulli et al., *Disjointed War*, 13.
42. Nardulli et al., 49.
43. Lambeth, *NATO's Air War*, 55.
44. Sean M. Maloney, *Operation Kinetic: Stabilizing Kosovo* (Lincoln, NE: Potomac Books, 2018), 106; Cox, interview.
45. Nardulli et al., *Disjointed War*, 27–28.
46. Nardulli et al., 30, 48; Lambeth, *NATO's Air War*, 37.
47. Lambeth, *NATO's Air War*, 96n27.
48. Lambeth, xvi.
49. Lambeth, 95–96, 124.
50. Lambeth, 160, 175.
51. Lambeth, 164–65.
52. Lambeth, 100.

53. Lambeth, 102; Nardulli et al., *Disjointed War*, 48. For example, the CAOC had to approve pop-up air defence system targets detected by the RC-135 or other sensors, resulting in missed chances to attack such targets.
54. Lambeth, *NATO's Air War*, 159–60.
55. Lambeth, 186–89, 187n22; see also 189, fig. 7.1, which illustrates the complex targeting, attack planning, and air tasking order process; Cox, interview.
56. Lambeth, 214.
57. Lambeth, 213–14, 216–17.
58. Lambeth, 215–16.
59. Nardulli et al., *Disjointed War*, 31–32.
60. Lambeth, *NATO's Air War*, 52–53. The ABCCC also exercised airspace control and de-confliction.
61. Lambeth, 56.
62. Lambeth, 56–57.
63. Lambeth, 95. Several confirmed hits on Serb tanks were achieved this way.
64. Bergen, *Scattering Chaff*, 161, 163, 176, 201, 206.
65. Nardulli et al., *Disjointed War*, 1–2; Daalder and O'Hanlon, *Winning Ugly*, 178, 183–84; Arkin, "Operation Allied Force," 26.
66. Nardulli et al., *Disjointed War*, 49–51; Lambeth, *NATO's Air War*, 23; Arkin, "Operation Allied Force," 8–9.
67. Lambeth, *NATO's Air War*, 166.
68. Nardulli et al., *Disjointed War*, 105–10.
69. UN Security Council (54th Year: 1999), "Resolution 1244 (1999)," 10 June 1999, https://digitallibrary.un.org/record/274488.
70. Maloney, *Operation Kinetic*, 79–80.
71. Maloney, 134–35; Dana H. Allin, *NATO's Balkan Interventions*, 84–85.
72. Maj. Douglas E. Delaney, "CIMIC Operations during Operation 'Kinetic,'" *Canadian Military Journal* 1, no. 4 (Winter 2000/2001): 29–34.
73. Quoted in Maloney, *Operation Kinetic*, 135.
74. Maloney, 147–50.
75. Maloney, 135.
76. Maloney, 78, 80, 82, 86, 93–94, 98–100, 107, 110–11; Col. Michael Ward et al., "Task Force Kosovo: Adapting Operations to a Changing Security Environment," *Canadian Military Journal* 1, no. 1 (Spring 2000): 67–68. The National Command Element, including intelligence and the National Support Element, remained under CAF control.
77. Maloney, *Operation Kinetic*, 116, 118–20, 124.
78. Maloney, 140, 258–63.
79. Nardulli et al., *Disjointed War*, 94–95, 99.
80. Maloney, *Operation Kinetic*, 264–68.
81. Maloney, 285.
82. Maloney, 257, 284.
83. Lt.-Col. Christopher Hunt, comments on draft chapter, 7 March 2021.
84. Maloney, *Operation Kinetic*, 173–74, 287.
85. Ward et al., "Task Force Kosovo," 68. Hunt suggests that there was also a CAF Intelligence Warrant Officer serving in the British brigade headquarters.
86. Skaarup, *Out of Darkness—Light*, 3:33, 73–74.
87. Skaarup, 3:74.

88. Maloney, *Operation Kinetic*, 161–62; Hunt, comments on draft chapter.
89. Maloney, *Operation Kinetic*, 218, 222–24, 229.
90. Maloney, 260, 263.
91. Maloney, 288.
92. Larry K. Wentz, ed., *Lessons from Kosovo: KFOR Experience* (Washington, DC: DOD, 2002), 451–52.
93. Wentz, 452–54.
94. Maloney, *Operation Kinetic*, 285, 342.
95. Maloney, 181, 186–89, 193–96, 197–98, 202–4, 206–13; Hunt, comments on draft chapter.
96. Maloney, *Operation Kinetic*, 238–89, 241–52.
97. Maloney, 288.
98. Maloney, 288, 289, 291, 295–96; Delaney, "CIMIC Operations," 30–31.
99. Maloney, *Operation Kinetic*, 305–6.
100. Maloney, 305–7, 322–23, 325–27, 344, 345, 350, 360, 368–69.
101. Maloney, 371, 377–81, 396–97, 399–400, 404.
102. Maloney, 345.
103. Maloney, 347.
104. Skaarup, *Out of Darkness—Light*, 3:74–75; J.A.E.K. Dowell, *Intelligence for the Canadian Army in the 21st Century: "Enabling Land Operations"* (Kingston, Ontario: DLCD, 2012), 32; Maloney, *Operation Kinetic*, 408.
105. Maloney, *Operation Kinetic*, 413.
106. Maloney, 347.
107. Maloney, 346.
108. Maloney, 346.
109. Maloney, 346.
110. Maloney, *Operation Kinetic*, 409–11.
111. Maloney, 193–98, 250.
112. Maloney, 179–81, 184–85, 189.
113. Lt. Christopher Hunt, "Observations and Lessons from Reconnaissance Squadron: Lord Strathcona's Horse (Royal Canadians) in Kosovo," *Army Doctrine and Training Bulletin* 3, no. 1 (Spring 2000): 66; also, his comment on the draft chapter.
114. Maloney, *Operation Kinetic*, 243, 250–51.
115. Maloney, 305–11, 327–30.
116. Ward et al., "Task Force Kosovo," 69.

11

KANDAHAR AND KABUL

Stabilizing Afghanistan, 2001–2005

War can be a driver of change and innovation within armed forces. The experience of Canadian intelligence in Afghanistan was no exception. At the outset, it played a modest role. But once the CAF was deployed in strength, first in Kabul and then in Kandahar, it expanded dramatically in size and scope and eventually drove CAF operations.[1]

In spite of warnings over the summer of 2001, no one anticipated a direct terrorist attack on the continental United States.[2] And on the eve of 9/11 no one was expecting that within a few months Canada would be at war—in Afghanistan.[3] Stephen Saideman wrote that prior to the attacks, Afghanistan had played "no role in Canadian foreign policy history."[4] In response to 9/11, NATO invoked Article Five of its treaty, which required its members to come to the defence of any member attacked by a foreign enemy. The Canadian government, however, hesitated to commit militarily to a war against al-Qaeda. Canada's economy depends on trade with the United States, so the government's first priority was to keep the border open. And it was not inclined to suddenly spend more on defence.[5] Latterly, it wanted to find a way to contribute to the emerging coalition against al-Qaeda that balanced support for Canada's most important ally with what it thought Canadians might find acceptable. The government was buffeted by conflicting views of what Canada's role should be: war fighters alongside the Americans, or neopeacekeepers, with its European allies. Some in the CAF, concerned about overstretching a small military already committed to several peacekeeping operations, were inclined to recommend only a token naval task force. So, the first phase of Canada's involvement in Afghanistan emerged by stages.[6]

OPERATION APOLLO: THE CAF IN THE AFGHANISTAN WAR, 2001–3

The first stage began on 1 October 2001, when the CAF began to set up a theatre support base near Dubai. The second began on 7 October, two days after the United States formally requested a CAF contribution to the fight, when Prime Minister Jean Chretien announced that Canada would contribute land, sea, and air units. The following day Defence Minister Art Eggleton announced Operation APOLLO, which committed some two thousand personnel to the campaign until October 2003. These comprised six Navy ships to two locations, the Arabian Sea and the Persian Gulf; two Aurora maritime patrol aircraft; and four transport planes. The naval contingents, assisted by the maritime patrol aircraft, were tasked to intercept al-Qaeda members fleeing Afghanistan and its neighbouring states by sea. From October 2001 to April 2002, Cdre. Jean-Pierre Thiffault commanded this operation through Joint Task Force South West Asia (JTFSWA) headquarters, which was colocated with US CENTCOM headquarters at MacDill Air Force Base, Tampa, Florida. But the Canadian ships and planes were under operational control of the local US commanders.[7]

The third stage began in December, when forty Canadian SOF troops from Joint Task Force 2 (JTF2) were deployed to join other coalition SOF troops hunting al-Qaeda and Taliban in Afghanistan. A chronology of the CAF in Afghanistan suggests that the government had decided in October to deploy the SOF troops.[8] Their arrival in December probably was due to the need for environment-specific and operational readiness training.

Finally, in February 2002 the CAF deployed a BG from the 3 PPCLI to Kandahar airfield. Over the next six months the BG, under the command of Lt.-Col. Patrick Stogran, carried out a variety of actions: airfield security, humanitarian operations, sensitive site exploitation, and combat operations alongside US forces. The BG returned to Canada at the end of July 2002.[9]

Arriving on station 26 November 2001 and remaining until December 2003, the naval task force engaged in an array of operations related to both the Afghanistan War and maintaining UN sanctions against Iraq (dating from the 1991 Persian Gulf War). These included protection of the USN amphibious-ready groups off the coast of Pakistan, escorting commercial vessels and US and British naval replenishment ships through the Strait of Hormuz, and surveillance of tanker fleets operating in and out of the Persian Gulf to contribute to the recognized maritime picture (figure 11.1). Other tasks included leadership interdiction operations to intercept and capture fleeing al-Qaeda and Taliban members, tracking and turning back a Pakistani submarine operating near

FIGURE 11.1. Combat Operations room on a Canadian Patrol Frigate Program vessel, where intelligence, surveillance, and reconnaissance systems and products inform operations. *Department of National Defence*

the American fleet during an India-Pakistan standoff, command of the mixed fleet of coalition naval vessels supporting USN operations, interception and boarding of suspicious vessels, and replenishment at sea of Canadian, USN, and other coalition ships.[10]

Due to operational security reasons, there is little public information about JTF2's activities. One source says that by the end of its tour the unit had carried out "42 reconnaissance and surveillance missions as well as 23 direct action missions."[11] The latter involved combat and other close engagement with the enemy: "snatching senior Taliban officials, manning high altitude observation posts and combing mountain cave complexes."[12] According to journalist Peter Pigott, JTF2 teams killed at least 115 al-Qaeda and Taliban members and captured 107 Taliban leaders.[13] The US forces came to rely on JTF2 for direct-action (DA) missions against these high-value targets (HVTs).[14] Likewise, except for a tragic friendly fire incident that killed four members of the unit, the 3 PPCLI BG deployment has not attracted a lot of attention. But during Operation HARPOON in March 2002, it did engage in combat.[15]

INTELLIGENCE SUPPORT TO DECISION MAKING AND OPERATIONS, 2001–2

In 2003 Dr. Kenneth Calder, DND assistant deputy minister of the policy branch, remarked with respect to Afghanistan that "we don't know anything about this country."¹⁶ Strictly speaking, that was an overstatement. By that time, through CAF operations in the country and intelligence sharing from Canada's allies, the CAF and the DND must have accumulated a considerable amount of information about Afghanistan. But prior to 9/11 there was no substantial knowledge base on it within the DND, the CAF, or elsewhere in government. This reflected the challenge of developing intelligence priorities among competing interests within government and then deciding how to allocate Canada's limited collection and analytical resources to fulfil those priorities. In the Afghan case, leaders became engaged in the problem only after it became clear that Canada would be involved in the conflict.¹⁷

Before 9/11, there was no Afghanistan desk in the NDHQ DGI division; it was part of the section that handled the rest of the world. When the Privy Council Office was drafting Canada's intelligence priorities for 2000–2001 in late 1999, the DGI ranked Afghanistan as a Category C priority: one of thirty-five countries of "potential" significance to Canada. Afghanistan was not seen as one that could threaten Canada or its allies (Category A) or could destabilize a major region (Category B).¹⁸ Of course, the threat to the United States and its allies, including Canada, came not from the Afghan state itself but instead from the al-Qaeda terrorist movement that had found sanctuary in that country and was using it as a base to prepare for attacks elsewhere.¹⁹ Within the Canadian government, the CSIS was responsible for monitoring terrorist threats such as that posed by al-Qaeda. The CSIS assessments went to the Privy Council Office's International Assessments Secretariat but not directly to the DGI.

Therefore, it seems unlikely that the DGI played a major role in the cabinet's deliberations on Canada's response to 9/11. But it had to ramp up rapidly its support for the DND's decision making. If CAF personnel or units were going to deploy to Afghanistan, then the DGI had to be able to backstop the senior DND/CAF leadership with information that was relevant to operational planning. The DGI's input would have been funnelled into discussions within the DCDS group.²⁰ Supported by the DGI, the DCDS group would have to identify possible base locations in the region to support CAF operations there and requirements for overflight permissions among countries where existing arrangements were not already in place. The DGI would have to start identifying potential targets for military operations in Afghanistan. And all of this was, of course, purely hypothetical until the prime minister and his cabinet decided whether Canada would commit forces—when, where, how many—and defined the mission.

There is little in the public domain to explain how this process worked during this period. What follows is a best guess. The J2/DGI—at that time Brig.-Gen. Patricia Samson—probably assembled a team of analysts to focus on support to DND decision making. That team would have turned to a variety of sources for additional information: the Department of Foreign Affairs and International Trade for political reporting from embassies in Pakistan, India, and other countries in the region; the CSIS for background and its latest updates on al-Qaeda; the CSE and its Five Eyes partners for SIGINT data and assessments; the Mapping and Charting Establishment for geomatics support; and the DIE for imagery, which would have to come from allies. It is likely that the DGI team was burning up the phone and fax lines to their counterparts in Washington and London. The Canadian forces intelligence liaison officers and defence attachés in those capitals were knocking on every door, tapping every personal contact, and calling in every favour they could.[21] All of this was meant to extract any intelligence that could help the DND and the CAF prepare for a possible war in a country virtually unknown to them.

Once Operation APOLLO was under way, however, the picture at the operational and tactical level became much clearer. The Canadian commitment to the campaign against al-Qaeda dramatically increased the flow of information and intelligence from the United States.[22] Lt.-Gen. (ret.) Michel Gauthier, who commanded the JTFSWA from April to October 2002, came to appreciate that from the US perspective, "if you're sharing in the risk, they will open the tent flaps wide open. So, getting access to their intelligence was not a problem at all . . . and the intelligence they were able to bring to bear was massive."[23] Some in the DGI division and the DCDS group had access to top secret special access intelligence (SIGINT and imagery) shared by Canada's Five Eyes allies. But for CAF personnel not normally accustomed to receiving it, the experience was an eye-opener.

The JTFSWA headquarters initially included a five-person J2 staff (one being a SIGINT specialist) and a SCIF to handle top secret special access material. They provided intelligence support to the commander "by plugging into the vast intelligence resources of CENTCOM."[24] The J2 also had one officer assigned to the Coalition Intelligence Center; he eventually became its operations officer. In his study of post–Cold War Canadian DI, Brig.-Gen. (ret.) James Cox says this was important for maintaining CAF access to most if not all intelligence from its allies in the coalition.[25] Just as important if not more so was Canada's direct access to the head of CENTCOM. During the daily briefings, Gauthier and his predecessor, Commodore Thiffault, sat beside CENTCOM commander Gen. Tommy Franks. Thiffault also sent a liaison officer to CENTCOM's naval command, NAVCENT, in Bahrain and another one to the USN carrier *John C. Stennis* on station in the region.[26] From Gauthier's perspective, perhaps more important than access to the intelligence flow was the fact that every morning he was at the table with Franks for the meetings first with the larger coalition and then with the more exclusive Four Eyes group. "Based on that relationship, I was getting a lot more than I was giving." So, JTFSWA headquarters was able to feed up to the Canadian strategic-level insights that were helpful to them. "We gave more than we got to our national headquarters."[27]

However, once CENTCOM moved its headquarters into the region to prepare for war in Iraq, JTFSWA headquarters remained behind and had less access to firsthand intelligence.[28] Furthermore, once the Canadian government decided that the CAF would not participate in the Iraq War, Cmdre. Roger Girouard, then commander of the Canadian naval task group, "noticed an immediate and perceptible cut-off of access to certain elements of intelligence, which came as quite a shock after decades of close operational exchanges with the USN."[29]

The BG deployed to Afghanistan with a five-person intelligence section whose capability, according to Cox, looked little different from what had existed in the Army fifteen years earlier. Moreover, the Army's pool of regular force intelligence personnel had declined from over one hundred in the early 1990s to only seventy-four in 2001; almost half would be deployed by the end of the year. But the BG had a Coyote LAV reconnaissance/surveillance squadron (from the Lord Strathcona's Horse armoured regiment), an EW section from the 2 EW Squadron that worked with its US counterparts in a combined SIGINT/EW Operations Center, and a SCIF staffed from the CFIOG. However, the BG intelligence officer found it difficult to work with the SCIF team, which tended to bypass the intelligence section and present SIGINT to the BG commander "separately from other multi-source intelligence products."[30]

Although the BG functioned under operational control of a US Army brigade (Task Force Rakkasan), they received little tactical intelligence from US sources.[31] But Sean Maloney asserts that it was thanks to the Canadian EW detachment, whose equipment was newer than that of the US force, that Task Force Rakkasan was able to blanket the Kandahar AOR with EW and SIGINT, thereby helping to secure the Kandahar airfield base. Even so, the 2001–2 campaign highlighted the limitations of technical systems originally optimized for tracking mechanized conventional forces when deployed against insurgents. "Technical systems are not well suited for fixing people in time and space," Maloney says.[32] He adds that SIGINT units learned that they needed to direct their collection procedures against cell phones and email rather than HF/UHF combat network radios.

By contrast, the JTF2 SOF "by virtue of what they were doing and the activities they were involved in, very focused [counterterrorist operations] . . . , lived and breathed intelligence-driven operations."[33] Apparently, in 2003 a Geomatics and Imagery Support Team was deployed to support them.[34] According to Maloney, JTF2 detachments worked with local forces to establish remote safe houses from which they could collect intelligence,[35] thereby expanding the range of the intelligence picture.

OPERATION ATHENA, PART 1: KABUL 2003-4

In the wake of defeat of the Taliban regime in late 2001, the UN had authorized the creation of a security force, ISAF, to stabilize initially Kabul and then the rest of the country. This was intended to prevent the descent into chaos that followed the Soviet withdrawal from Afghanistan in 1989 and led to the Taliban's rise and seizure of power. In its first iteration (2002-3) the ISAF comprised mostly European forces, and Canada was not part of it.[36] But ISAF was too small, outnumbered, and outgunned by the Northern Alliance that, with help from American airpower and SOF, had defeated the Taliban and was the real power in Afghanistan. ISAF could do little more than patrol Kabul and protect itself.[37]

That changed somewhat in 2003 when NATO took charge of ISAF and Canadian brigadier-general Peter Devlin took command of the Kabul Multi-National Brigade (KMNB). Rotation (Roto) 0 of the CAF contingent, which deployed in the summer, included a brigade headquarters from the 2 Brigade, a battalion BG from the 3rd Battalion Royal Canadian Regiment (3 RCR), a reconnaissance squadron from the Royal Canadian Dragoons, an artillery battery, a troop equipped with the Sperwer UAV, an ASIC, and supporting elements. The KMNB also included German and French BGs. In 2004 Lt.-Gen. Rick Hillier took command of ISAF, Brig.-Gen. Jocelyn Lacroix succeeded Devlin in command of the KMNB, and the brigade headquarters and BG, the 3rd Battalion Royal 22e Regiment (3 R22eR, or "Vandoos"), were drawn from the 5 Brigade. After those first two rotations, Canada relinquished command of ISAF, and the CAF contribution was scaled back to an infantry company, the reconnaissance squadron, the ASIC, and an engineer squadron with explosive ordnance disposal capability. The KMNB helped to secure the Loya Jirga reconciliation meeting and carried out cantonment of heavy weapons from militias such as the Northern Alliance. Those two efforts alone stabilized Afghanistan sufficiently to allow national elections to proceed in 2004.[38] In the meantime, however, according to Lt.-Col. Donald Denne, who commanded the 3 RCR BG, the Canadians "definitely considered the threat environment in Kabul to be much more dangerous than in Bosnia. . . . The enemy could not be identified at all. . . . The enemy completely blended in with everybody else in Kabul. So they had a significant advantage on us in the sense they could see us but we couldn't see them."[39]

INTELLIGENCE SUPPORT TO OPERATION ATHENA, PART 1

For Operation ATHENA the CAF deployed with a robust and technologically advanced intelligence cohort of eighty people, including an ASIC and an ISTAR company.[40] The ASIC consisted of an All-Source Cell, a Geomatics and Imagery

FIGURE 11.2. The All-Source Intelligence Centre, Camp Julien, Kabul, Afghanistan, 2004. *Canadian Forces Intelligence Command*

Support Team, a SIGINT Support Element, a Field HUMINT Team (FHT), a counterintelligence team, and a SCIF. The RCMP and the CSIS also attached some staff. The ASIC's primary customer was the KMNB headquarters, but it also supported the brigade's three BGs, the SOF, and the ISTAR company and served as the CANIC (figure 11.2). The ASIC received information from the ISTAR company, the BGs, and the SIGINT/EW Operations Center and from reach-back to the DGI. Brigadier-General Devlin explained that the ASIC carried out long-term intelligence analysis, document exploitation, and targeting. With regard to the latter, the ASIC served as the brigade's HVT fusion center for planning SOF DA missions to capture insurgents and seize/neutralize weapons and explosives caches. As might be expected with a new hybrid unit and capability, the ASIC experienced a learning curve complicated by multinational rivalries, national caveats, and legal constraints over the use of German and French intelligence assets.[41]

The ISTAR company consisted of the Canadian armoured reconnaissance squadron (two five-vehicle troops of Coyote LAVs), an artillery counterbattery targeting radar, a troop from the 2 EW Squadron, an FHT (detached from the ASIC), and a German UAV detachment. The CAF deployed its Sperwer UAV in November 2003, but it proved unreliable, so the CAF continued to rely on the Germans. The Coyotes carried impressive and useful radar, video, and infrared night vision sensors, but they were not ideal for tracking individuals or small vehicles in urban environments. So, the BGs' forward observation officers and forward air controllers added their eyes and ears to the ISTAR's capabilities.

Then Maj. Andrew Zdunich, who commanded the ISTAR company from February to August 2004, also had under his command a well-trained and well-equipped fourteen-man SOF unit from Slovenia that he used on its own or attached to his Coyote LAV patrols. The ISTAR Control Centre (ISTAR CC)—linked to the brigade G2 staff—synchronized the company's capabilities with those of the BGs to plan the tasks that would be assigned to it. In the summer of 2004 Canada scaled back its intelligence cohort to the ASIC and the reconnaissance squadron. The counterintelligence, EW, and FHT detachments were folded back into the ASIC.[42] In its full format the ASIC represented an evolution of the Army's ICAC, which had performed well during the Oka Crisis. Unfortunately, it disappeared when the 1 Division Intelligence Company was disbanded in 1999–2000.[43]

Zdunich's interview sheds some light on the challenges of coordinating use of the EW troop. He describes it as having a "split personality" because it was both a KMNB and a CAF task force asset. So, although the troop was under his command, either of those headquarters could assign tasks to it; their requirements could take precedence over his. The static element remained at Camp Julien (the CAF base in Kabul), while the maneuver element could deploy but only with one of his patrols. Their equipment was too sensitive for the troops to go out on their own. However, since they knew all of the reconnaissance squadron's operations, they would attach themselves "to whatever patrol . . . would fit into their own surveillance plan."[44]

Similarly, all of the Sperwer UAV missions were flown on behalf of the brigade (figure 11.3). Any of its national contingents could request a UAV mission. Zdunich says that "on a few occasions, they flew oversight of some sensitive site exploitation missions from different countries and provided real time feed data that was . . . communicated by a liaison officer who was there, on to the troops that were on the ground."[45]

There is relatively little information in the public domain on the collection, processing, and exploitation of intelligence during this phase of CAF operations in Afghanistan. But a few observers have provided snapshots of intelligence at work in this phase. Zdunich says that patrol reporting was constant. He received information from the reconnaissance elements in all of the national sectors and from other assets. This allowed him to do "first level fusion" and generate a picture of what was going on across the brigade AOR.[46]

Maj. Mike Purcell, who was chief of the brigade SIGINT/EW Operations Center in 2004, wrote that during his tenure KMNB forces conducted thirty-two DA operations: fifteen against weapons caches and the remainder intended to detain persons deemed to be a threat to ISAF or to the interim Afghan government.[47] Sean Maloney briefly describes one operation from 2004 in which the ISTAR squadron used the cameras on their Coyotes to track a would-be suicide

FIGURE 11.3. A Sperwer Tactical UAV, the first UAV used in operations by the Canadian forces in Afghanistan, shown here on exercise in Canada, 2007. *Canadian Forces Joint Imagery Centre*

bomber across Kabul, leading to his capture by SOF.[48] In this case, the high-tech systems were able to follow a single person. But this account leaves a lot unsaid: how did they identify that man as a potential threat, and how did they decide to capture him? Some targeting originated with ISAF headquarters, which had at its disposal a number of HUMINT teams, including the ISTAR company's FHT.[49] What follows is a summary of Purcell's description of the brigade-level DA targeting process.

First, Afghan security forces were the lead agency, with KMNB forces working in support of and in coordination with them. But with access to its full range of sources, including HUMINT, SIGINT/EW, patrol reports, liaison officer reports, and imagery in some cases, the KMNB often initiated the targeting process. Second, once a target was identified, either the brigade or the ASIC would refine and develop a target package on the target by tasking Canadian assets and asking for KMNB assets to be assigned. Although unavoidable in some cases, "every effort was made to ensure that wherever possible, target folders did not rely on single source intelligence."[50] In fact, the majority were based on HUMINT and SIGINT, both of which were integrated with imagery from the Canadian and German UAVs.

Third, the ASIC initially sent target packages to the ISAF Command HUMINT staff for finalization and assignment to the brigade's forces. During Purcell's tour this step changed, owing to a shortage of ISAF Command HUMINT staff officers in relation to the volume of possible targets and because of the need to put the targets through the brigade's new validation process.

Moreover, existing targeting doctrine dealt with kinetic operations but did not address "the sensitive and complex issues surrounding targeting of individuals."[51] So, the proposed DA target folder would be brought before a new Brigade Target Approval Board, consisting of the brigade commander and his senior staff. Based on a thorough examination of the file and discussion (including dissenting views), they would decide if the target was both valid and worth the effort, given the current operational context. Finally, the brigade commander would make a go/no-go decision for DA against the target. Once a "go" decision had been made, the operational planning process followed, then orders were issued to the unit tasked to conduct the operation. "There was always a concerted effort to link the tasked Commanding Officer ... directly with the source or at least the handler of the source (assuming a HUMINT source) to reduce the length of the sensor to shooter chain."[52]

Lieutenant-Colonel Denne shed some additional light on the DA targeting process. The operations were conducted "against specific targets that had become the subject of a certain amount of surveillance by us and/or the Kabul City Police or the National Directorate of Security."[53] The CAF input originated with the BG's "patrol commanders. The master corporals and the sergeants that were out on the streets ... doing the patrols and who were meeting the people and doing patrol reports and gathering information. All that ... allowed us to build an intelligence picture that would allow us to incorporation [sic] with the Kabul City Police or the National Directorate of Security."[54] The ASIC then did the analysis that turned the surveillance and other information into target intelligence that could lead to a DA operation. Denne recalled that his BG planned and prepared five and carried out three and that only one yielded success: Operation WHIRLWIND, 26 January 2004. "We had developed a certain amount of intelligence that led us to believe there was [a] fellow who had a compound probably very close to our camp.... He was a bad guy and we pulled the National Directorate of Security into this fairly quickly."[55] The Canadians suspected that it was "a terrorist hideout or a base for terrorist operations," and they were proven correct. The sensitive site exploitation that followed the raid yielded "an amazing amount of rockets, projectiles, missiles, mines, grenades, small arms ammunitions, you name it was all hidden in floor boards and in walls. But it takes that gathering of intelligence to be able to do that with some degree of certainty that you're going to find something."[56]

However, because ISAF put a premium on having Afghan forces lead the DA operations, the follow-through on this intelligence and targeting process was not always wholly satisfactory. Afghan units were not always trained and equipped for the task or willing to go through preraid rehearsals. Confirmation of the captured target's identity was often difficult, especially at night. Local priorities and loyalties sometimes prevailed. The Afghan force might set the target free after capture and occasionally denied the KMNB forces the opportunity to do sensitive site exploitation, probably to protect the target from incrimination by material evidence.[57]

Purcell's essay offered advice for future DA planners: the need for sensitive site exploitation teams to accompany each operation and the need to consider the information operations aspects of any DA action, since these operations were disruptive and frightening to families at the target locations. Finally, he issued a plea for patience in handling HUMINT sources. They are often risking their lives, so delays, mix-ups, and cancellation of meets are normal. In the Afghan case most could not read maps, so they could not direct the operations to the right location. Some would lose patience with the lengthy ISAF planning process.[58] Such agent-handling challenges would be familiar to secret intelligence services, but for military HUMINT collectors they were part of the learning curve.

Drawing upon CAF experience in the Balkans and, to a more limited extent, Afghanistan, Capt. Lisa Elliott devoted her Royal Military College of Canada thesis to a study of the utility of HUMINT in asymmetric conflicts. Like Purcell, she identified it as a key collection discipline for operations in that environment. According to one of Elliott's sources (a Canadian former KMNB G2), the CAF's specialized HUMINT teams arrived in theatre too late in 2004 to produce usable intelligence. So, her study emphasised the role and value of the individual soldier as a HUMINT collector. A postoperation report from Roto 1 of Operation ATHENA stated that BG operations "were triggered and guided by HUMINT," which was seen as "the greatest source of actionable intelligence."[59]

But as valuable as it was, HUMINT collection presented the CAF with a serious ethical problem. Canadian policy acknowledged Afghan sovereignty. This meant that Afghan forces should, wherever feasible, take the lead on operations, with the CAF acting in support. Anyone detained would be handed over to the Afghan police or the National Directorate of Security. This was also a practical matter; the cultural and language barriers forced the CAF to rely on Afghans to help question captives. However, the Afghan forces were suspected of abusing detainees in their custody. This raised two problems. First, it implicated by association the CAF in that mistreatment, thereby violating Canadian and international law. Although an investigation by the Military Police Complaints Commission ultimately cleared the CAF of any wrongdoing, the controversy outlasted the war.[60] Second, from an intelligence perspective it also was a cautionary tale, since it forced the CAF to question the reliability of HUMINT derived from Afghan security forces' interrogations.

For the Canadian Army in particular, operations in Afghanistan yielded both familiar and new intelligence experiences. Intelligence sharing with American and NATO forces and collecting intelligence through patrolling were familiar activities that had been conducted in the peace support operations in the

Balkans and Somalia. Likewise, the ASIC concept was not entirely new. What was new was the ISTAR company and the UAV detachment: a new unit and a new capability that had not existed before. The army had to adapt to using these in active operations within a multinational coalition, including support to DA SOF tasks, without the benefit of a lengthy period of peacetime testing and training. This forced everyone into a steep learning curve that yielded effective results in some operations.

In the summer of 2005 the residual Canadian contingent, including the ASIC, deployed to Kandahar Province, where the CAF took on what became a full-blown counterinsurgency mission. Canada's first five years in Afghanistan provided a baseline of useful experience that would serve subsequent rotations well. But this next phase posed its own unique challenges that would require the CAF to acquire and adapt to new intelligence capabilities and processes.

NOTES

1. David A. Charters, "Canadian Military Intelligence in Afghanistan," *International Journal of Intelligence and CounterIntelligence* 25, no. 3 (2012): 470–507.
2. National Commission on Terrorist Attacks upon the United States, *The 9/11 Commission Report: Final Report of the National Commission on Terrorist Attacks upon the United States* (Washington, DC: US Government Printing Office, 2004), 254–63.
3. Janice Gross Stein and J. Eugene Lang, *The Unexpected War: Canada in Kandahar* (Toronto: Viking, 2007), 7, 20, 21, 129, 185–87, 196, 289–90.
4. Stephen M. Saideman, *Adapting in the Dust: Lessons Learned from Canada's War in Afghanistan* (Toronto: University of Toronto Press, 2016), 10.
5. Stein and Lang, *Unexpected War*, 6–7.
6. Stein and Lang, 2–3, 11, 14–17. See also Richard Howard Gimblett, *Operation Apollo: The Golden Age of the Canadian Navy in the War against Terrorism* (Ottawa: Magic Light for DND, 2004), 14–15.
7. Stein and Lang, *Unexpected War*, 2–3; Nancy Teeple, *Canada in Afghanistan: 2001–2010; A Military Chronology*, contract report (Ottawa: Defence Research and Development Canada, Centre for Operational Research and Analysis, December 2010), 5–6; Gimblett, *Operation Apollo*, 81; and Lt.-Gen. (ret.) Michel Gauthier, interview with author, 5 November 2019.
8. Teeple, *Canada in Afghanistan*, 6.
9. Peter Pigott, *Canada in Afghanistan: The War So Far* (Toronto: Dundurn, 2007), 91.
10. Gimblett, *Operation Apollo*, 47–51, 54, 65–67, 73, 77, 147–48.
11. Media report quoted in Bernd Horn, "The Canadian Special Operations Forces' Legacy," in *Special Operations Forces: A National Capability*, ed. Emily Spencer (Kingston, Ontario: Canadian Defence Academy Press, 2011), 46–47.
12. Horn, 47.
13. Pigott, *Canada in Afghanistan*, 86–87.
14. Col. Bernd Horn, *No Ordinary Men: Special Operations Forces Missions in Afghanistan* (Toronto: Dundurn, 2016), Kindle.
15. Pigott, *Canada in Afghanistan*, 89–91.

16. Quoted in Stein and Lang, *Unexpected War*, 21.
17. I am grateful for the insights on this from Lt.-Col. James Godefroy, comments on draft chapter, 23 April 2021. He served as the J2 for Task Force Kandahar in 2009.
18. *Ministerial Recommendation 1999–2000 Defence Intelligence Priorities*, annex D to *Memo J2 Plans and Pol, FY 2000–2001 Canadian Intelligence Priorities*, 4 November 1999, LAC, RG24, BAN 2005-00285-2, box 11, file 1901-1 part 3.
19. National Commission on Terrorist Attacks upon the United States, *9/11 Commission Report*, 63–67.
20. Godefroy, comments on draft chapter.
21. Confirmed by the officer who had served as the Canadian forces intelligence liaison officer in London at the time of 9/11 and immediately after.
22. James Cox, "The Transformation of Canadian Defence Intelligence since the End of the Cold War" (master's thesis, Royal Military College of Canada, 2004), 155, Canadian Foreign Intelligence History Project. According to Gimblett, *Operation Apollo*, 58–59, this intelligence support included classified equipment and codes (ciphers).
23. Gauthier, interview.
24. Gauthier; Cox, "Transformation of Canadian Defence," 154–55; and Teeple, *Canada in Afghanistan*, 6, 13.
25. Cox, "Transformation of Canadian Defence," 155.
26. Gimblett, *Operation Apollo*, 130–32.
27. Gauthier, interview. At this time New Zealand was excluded from the intelligence alliance inner circle, making it four instead of five "Eyes."
28. Cox, "Transformation of Canadian Defence," 156. The J2 staff was reduced to one by 2003.
29. Gimblett, *Operation Apollo*, 116.
30. Cox, "Transformation of Canadian Defence," 162–64; Daniel Villeneuve, "A Study of the Changing Face of Canada's Army Intelligence," *Canadian Army Journal* 9, no. 2 (Summer 2006): 23; and Sean M. Maloney, *Enduring the Freedom: A Rogue Historian in Afghanistan* (Washington, DC: Potomac Books, 2007), 59.
31. Lisa Elliott, "Finding a Balance: A Study of the Canadian Army's Approach to Human Intelligence in an Asymmetric Environment" (master's thesis [extracts], Royal Military College of Canada, 2005), reprinted in Harold A. Skaarup, *Out of Darkness—Light: A History of Canadian Military Intelligence*, Vol. 3 (New York: iUniverse, 2005), 393.
32. Maloney, *Enduring the Freedom*, 55, 59.
33. Gauthier, interview. They also served as intelligence collectors, conducting many reconnaissance and surveillance missions. See Horn, "The Canadian Special Operations Forces' Legacy," 47.
34. J.A.E.K. Dowell, *Intelligence for the Canadian Army in the 21st Century: "Enabling Land Operations"* (Kingston, Ontario: DLCD, 2012), 34.
35. Maloney, *Enduring the Freedom*, 59.
36. David P. Auerswald and Stephen M. Saideman, *NATO in Afghanistan: Fighting Together, Fighting Alone* (Princeton, NJ: Princeton University Press, 2014), 32; and Stein and Lang, *Unexpected War*, 2–3, 15–17.
37. Sean M. Maloney, *Confronting the Chaos: A Rogue Military Historian Returns to Afghanistan* (Annapolis, MD: Naval Institute Press, 2009), 44.
38. Maloney, 7–8, 27.

39. Lt.-Col. Donald Denne, interview, 4 December 2009, Canadian War Museum Oral History Program.
40. Cox, "Transformation of Canadian Defence," 164–65.
41. Charters, "Canadian Military Intelligence," 478–79; Maloney, *Confronting the Chaos*, 28–29, 50; and details from a retired CAF intelligence officer.
42. Charters, "Canadian Military Intelligence," 479–80.
43. Adrienne Hubble, "Retrospective of an Afghanistan Deployment," in Harold A. Skaarup, "Out of Darkness—Light: A History of Canadian Military Intelligence," [Vol. 4] (unpublished manuscript, 2018, author's copy), chap. 3, 66. See also Lt.-Col. Andrew Zdunich, interview, 10 July 2006, Canadian War Museum Oral History Program.
44. Zdunich, interview.
45. Zdunich.
46. Zdunich.
47. Mike K. Purcell, "Considerations in the Planning of Direct Operations from the Experience of the Kabul Multinational Brigade," in Skaarup, *Out of Darkness—Light*, 3:239, 248. Thirty-one were deemed successful.
48. Maloney, *Confronting the Chaos*, 28.
49. Purcell, "Considerations," 242; and Zdunich, interview. The CAF HUMINT team was attached to Zdunich's squadron for administration purposes.
50. Purcell, "Considerations," 240–41.
51. Purcell, 241.
52. Purcell, 241–43.
53. Denne, interview.
54. Denne.
55. Denne.
56. Denne.
57. Purcell, "Considerations," 243–46.
58. Purcell, 246–48.
59. Elliott, "Finding a Balance," 386, 388.
60. "Tories Reject Call for Afghan Torture Inquiry," CBC News, 19 November 2009, https://www.cbc.ca/news/politics/tories-reject-call-for-afghan-torture-inquiry-1.801848; Robin Rowland, "Knowing about War Crimes," CBC News, 23 November 2009, https://www.cbc.ca/news/canada/knowing-about-war-crimes-1.864189; "Afghan Officials Beat Detainees 'on a Whim': Military Inquiry," Canadian Press, *Toronto Star*, 7 May 2010, https://www.thestar.com/news/world/2010/05/07/afghan_officials_beat_detainees_on_a_whim_military_inquiry.html; Laura Payton, "Afghan Detainee Records Still Hold Questions, MPs Say," CBC News, 22 June 2011, https://www.cbc.ca/news/politics/afghan-detainee-records-still-hold-questions-mps-say-1.980794; and "Military Police Complaints Commission Releases Report in Afghan Detainee Case—MPCC," press release re: MPCC 2008-042, Military Police Complaints Commission of Canada, 27 June 2012, http://mpccwet4.imatics.com/03/afghan/2012-06-27-eng.aspx?=undefined&wbdisable=true. In 2015, another allegation surfaced of Canadian military police abusing prisoners. See David Pugliese (for *Ottawa Citizen*), "Military Police Watchdog Gears Up for Investigation of Alleged Detainee Abuse in Afghanistan," *National Post*, 4 August 2016, https://nationalpost.com/news/politics/military-police-watchdog-gears-up-for-investigation-of-alleged-detainee-abuse-in-afghanistan.

12

RETURN TO KANDAHAR

Counterinsurgency in Afghanistan, 2005–2010

To counter a resurgent Taliban and to stabilize the country to a greater degree, in 2004 NATO had begun extending the writ of the ISAF outside of Kabul, starting first in the north and then in the west, with Regional Command-South (RC-South) being established in Kandahar in 2006.[1] The Canadian decision in 2005 to accept responsibility for development and security in Kandahar province was and remains controversial, since it committed Canadian forces to a major combat role there. But the debate over the political reasons for doing so lie outside the scope of this book.[2]

THE TALIBAN INSURGENCY

By 2005, the Taliban had recovered from its defeat four years earlier and was rebuilding its combat and political capacity, particularly in the southern provinces of Helmand, Uruzgan, and Kandahar. With its leadership (the Quetta Shūrā) safe from attack in Pakistan, it was conducting a classic insurgency: a strategic battle for legitimacy and a tactical battle for control.[3] Because it had violently repressed non-Pashtun minorities during the 1990s, the Taliban was not a truly national liberation movement. Nor was it a single, unified organization. But as a Pashtun movement led by religious figures, the Taliban could appeal to traditional tribe and local clan loyalties and to their faith in Islam in the Pashtun heartland of Kandahar. In its battle for legitimacy, the Taliban combined political action and Islamic-themed information operations designed to mobilize support for them, undermine support for the central government and its local representatives, and sow distrust of the foreign (ISAF) forces. In tandem with its information operations, the Taliban's tactical battle for control was designed to replace Afghan government and ISAF control of the population with its own. The insurgents mounted guerrilla and bomb attacks on ISAF and

Afghan security forces and used intimidation and terror attacks against those suspected of collaborating with the government or with ISAF. Moreover, most of this was carried out in clandestine fashion. The Taliban had good security and the means to ensure it.[4] This process was already well established by the time the Canadian troops arrived in Kandahar. So, rolling back this insurgency presented a daunting task.

OPERATION ATHENA, PART 2: THE CANADIAN ARMED FORCES IN KANDAHAR, 2005–10

The Canadian role in Kandahar started modestly and narrowly focused: the deployment of a Provincial Reconstruction Team (PRT), a hybrid unit meant to assist Afghan communities in developing improved facilities such as wells, clinics, and schools. NATO saw the PRTs as the key pillar of the strategic battle for legitimacy within its counterinsurgency program. Their "good works" were intended to weld the loyalty of the population to the government in Kabul. The PRT was an American concept and did not exist in the CAF. So, it had to be improvised. The CAF PRT combined military engineers, civilian police, government experts on justice and political reform, and medical and development projects along with troops to protect them. It was announced in February 2005 and became operational in Kandahar City in June.[5]

The PRT was followed in quick succession by more units and an expanding role for the CAF. In March 2005 CDS General Rick Hillier announced that Canada would send a battalion-based BG to Kandahar to protect the PRT and expand its security perimeter outside the city. The ASIC and its protection company moved there from Kabul in June, and the following month the CDS announced that CAF SOF would deploy there to fight the Taliban.[6] Over the next four years the CAF presence, based at Kandahar Airfield (KAF), expanded to a brigade-size force that included: JTF-A headquarters; an air wing with transport aircraft, UAVs, and helicopters; a National Support Element (logistics); medical support; an engineer regiment; a CIMIC team; a signals squadron; and an Operational Mentor and Liaison Team to work with the Afghan National Army (ANA). From 2008, two US battalions and an armoured cavalry squadron were placed under JTF-A command. At its peak the Canadian contingent totalled just over 3,000 troops and civilians,[7] with the attached American troops adding about 2,500 more.

In the early years the CAF role was wide-ranging and ambitious. The PRT was responsible for consulting with villagers about their needs and responding by helping the Afghans to help themselves, facilitating political negotiations that would extend and legitimize the writ of the central government, and reforming and rebuilding the police and the prison system.[8] The PRT concept was sound in theory but was criticized then and later for problems in practice. The strategic plan—the National Solidarity Program—set out the goals that the Afghan government and the ISAF had agreed to achieve, but it was not applied uniformly across the country. Each contributing nation ran its own PRT program separately and differently, not in coordination with efforts in neighboring provinces. Moreover, many PRTs were too small to achieve their goals or were unable to operate outside their secure bases.[9]

The Canadian BGs carried out stability and security patrols, combat operations against Taliban units, and operations against improvised explosive devices (IEDs), while SOF conducted DA operations against HVTs: Taliban leaders. The Operational Mentor and Liaison Team trained and assisted the ANA *kandak* (battalion) operating within the Canadian AOR. Creating a capable and reputable Afghan army was central to the effort to legitimize an Afghan government that would be accepted by the population. Most of the Canadian actions initially were focused in and around the city of Kandahar, the agrarian belt of villages to the west, and the Dhala Dam to the northeast. The intent was to put into practice the fundamentals of counterinsurgency doctrine—to "clear, hold, and build" and protect and aid the population. But in the first few years, this effort fell short. Although JTF-A itself grew in size and capability, its BG task forces lacked the capacity to exert the full range of political and security influence over a province of fifty thousand square kilometres. CAF troops had to clear repeatedly because they could hold only in some areas for limited periods. When they moved elsewhere, the Taliban kept returning. So, the PRT and its Afghan partners were unable to build in a sustainable way. It was only from 2009 on, when US troops reinforced JTF-A, that the Canadian AOR could be reduced to an area small enough to allow the troops to concentrate in numbers sufficient to protect the population.[10]

CAF OPERATIONS AND INTELLIGENCE REQUIREMENTS

The kind of nonkinetic activities the CAF undertook in Kandahar province were not unprecedented or wholly unfamiliar. They had been part of daily activity in the Balkans, essential for trying to contain sectarian violence (mission goal) and to minimize the threat to the peacekeeping units (force protection). Lt.-Col. Christopher Hand, who had commanded an infantry company from the 2nd Battalion Royal Canadian Regiment (2 RCR) in Bosnia and then ran the Tactics School at the Combat Training Centre, noted that the 2 RCR–based task force Rotation (Roto) 1-07 command team all had some experience from the Balkans, Haiti, or elsewhere. He saw such experience as useful in Kandahar. "Collectively, those missions provided a body of knowledge that informed the way TF [Task Force] 1-07 prepared for its Afghan mission. LCol Hand . . . says, 'for those who don't think the Balkans are relevant, because Afghanistan is not peacekeeping, think again.'"[11] That was undoubtedly true insofar as tactics, techniques, and procedures are concerned, but the Balkans and Afghanistan had entirely different cultures, so mission-specific knowledge was essential.

Attending key leader engagements and village *shūrās* (consultations) were a regular feature of PRT and CIMIC operations. The intention was to help communities either build new capacity or enhance existing ones. Key leader engagements and *shūrās* emphasised identifying needs, determining what things would get done, and mobilizing the population to work on projects once funding and resources were available. They also served as a forum for airing grievances about government corruption and neglect, police brutality, and missteps, collateral damage, and use of excessive force by the ANA and the CAF.[12]

Running parallel to this activity and the BG's kinetic operations were the nonkinetic information operations. The messages and the means to deliver them were important, separately and in combination. The campaign in Kandahar was "Canada's first information age war in which both sides employed cellular phones, laptops and the Internet as tools and weapons."[13] Like the PRTs, information operations were population-centric; the people were the key strategic battleground in the counterinsurgency campaign. Winning, keeping, or losing their support would ultimately decide the outcome.

To influence them, the CAF deployed its new tactical psychological warfare teams. Their task was to reach out to the population with messages to counter the Taliban's antigovernment, anti-ISAF information operations narratives. Using a variety of media but especially radio, the tactical psychological warfare teams would explain Afghan government programs and actions and CAF and ANA activities that were intended to benefit the population and would also try to show the disconnect between Taliban claims and their actions that harmed the community. This was a challenging task, since the Taliban were already embedded in the population, spoke their language, understood the culture, and often could get the Taliban message out faster than the tactical psychological warfare team. The Taliban were quick to exploit CAF/ANA mistakes, since those reinforced their narratives. ISAF and the CAF often found themselves on the defensive, giving the Taliban the information operations advantage.[14]

What all of these nonkinetic activities had in common was a fundamental requirement to understand the human environment in which they were operating. Anthropologist Alexei Gavriel, who had field experience in Afghanistan, refers to this understanding as "cultural intelligence[,] ... an intelligence discipline that analyzes cultural knowledge to assess or interpret the impact it has on the operating environment, adversary, and operational planning considerations. It has strategic-, operational-, and tactical-level implications."[15] This is more than just having a basic grasp of the local "who's who" and the "do's and don'ts." Rather, it is HUMINT collection and analysis at its most granular and intimate. Ideally, an ethnographic intelligence process will produce in-depth cultural knowledge. This effort tries to learn what is going on in the group being examined and how its culture affects the operating environment and thus influences the decisions and actions of the counterinsurgency forces. But being able to do this requires knowledge and understanding of that group's "perceptions, attitudes, mind-set, and beliefs" that stem from values and behaviors.[16]

Dr. Emily Spencer, an analyst for Canadian Special Operations Forces Command, described cultural intelligence as having "the ability to see reality through the eyes of others."[17] Gavriel asserts that this kind of cultural knowledge can support strategic intelligence by yielding "a comprehensive understanding of the social structures, ideologies and narratives insurgents use to organize their networks and mobilize segments of the population."[18] Effective "cultural intelligence preparation of the operational environment" can aid operational intelligence in understanding the factions and groups in the AOR and what factors may be fueling parts of the conflict. CIMIC units can benefit from understanding how local values are represented in dispute resolution. Tactical psychological warfare teams would benefit from cultural knowledge in developing information operations that "speak to locals in a manner they would be receptive to."[19] Gavriel adds that "indoctrinating soldiers with cultural knowledge during pre-deployment training" could benefit tactical operations by making soldiers more "inter-culturally effective": showing respect to local customs, thereby "minimizing the possibility of turning potential friends into enemies."[20] So, cultural intelligence can be used to "assess the effectiveness of adversary and coalition information operations, assess local reaction or fallout from proposed coalition courses of action, and understand how local social organization can have an impact on operations, how local dynamics may fuel conflict, or even how local values and perceptions shape local actors' views of coalition forces and operations."[21]

It is hard to dispute Gavriel's logic, but the ethnographer's methods are problematic for military forces. He stresses the need for specialized teams already trained in the discipline and that in-depth cultural knowledge can be gained only from spending months if not years immersed in the group/culture.[22] The CAF did not have the luxury of being able to dedicate personnel to spend months or years studying Afghan culture before reporting to the intelligence staffs on what they had learned. The commitment to Kandahar came on relatively short notice. So, whatever cultural knowledge and situational intelligence the CAF gained had to be acquired, absorbed, and exploited on the fly and thus could not meet Gavriel's exacting standards.

Kinetic counterguerrilla operations, on the other hand, presented more familiar intelligence requirements: the who, what, where, when, and how questions. These were vital for the tactical battle for control. But the strategic and tactical tasks were not separate; they were closely related. If gaining "human terrain" intelligence[23] allowed the CAF to "think like the enemy"[24] and get inside their decision-making cycle, then developing trust and sources among Afghan communities would also help them build a tactical intelligence picture that could lead to effective kinetic operations and prevent actions that would undermine the strategic battle.

In British experience, counterinsurgency was a platoon commander's war.[25] But CAF operations in Kandahar did not always bear this out. BG-size operations were common,[26] even though they were complex, slow to generate, and too visible and noisy to achieve tactical surprise. Operation MEDUSA, conducted by the 1st Battalion Royal Canadian Regiment (1 RCR) BG and Afghan and coalition forces in September 2006, is the best known of these, but it was not the only one.[27] The majority of BG operations involved one or two companies or subunits, coalition and ANA troops, often supported by enablers such as artillery, tanks, the reconnaissance squadron, and air assets. These operations took the form of regular presence patrols (often mounted at night), sweeps and searches, key leader engagements in villages, and CIMIC activity. Though the BG operated out of KAF and a number of forward operating bases, it never was confined to them. The Canadians operated throughout their AOR.

Much less has been said publicly about Canadian SOF DA operations, which were carried out in greater secrecy.[28] The CAF's SOF units were assigned to the Coalition Joint Special Operations Task Force–Afghanistan, and they did not always operate in conjunction with regular JTF-A forces. But, both they and SOF units conducted DA operations against Taliban HVTs. Most reports do not specifically refer to SOF, Canadian or otherwise, so it is difficult to determine which units were responsible for which actions; it has to be inferred from the data. Over time, the CAF's AOR got smaller, while the SOF ranged over all of the RC-South AOR. The information now available is incomplete,[29] so what follows should be read with that caution in mind.

Col. Bernd Horn's study of Canadian SOF in Afghanistan, *No Ordinary Men*, notes that JTF2 was back in-theatre in late 2005 conducting DA missions against IED cell and other tier 1 Taliban commanders. By 2006 the new Canadian Special Operations Regiment had been formed; it was later deployed to Afghanistan. Horn's book provides detailed accounts of several Canadian SOF missions from 2005 to 2011 based on information provided by the participants. In many cases the CAF SOF teams were supported by other coalition SOF and by air assets and enablers. These operations were not all successful against HVTs but almost always yielded detainees and captured equipment, both of which had intelligence value. They disrupted Taliban bases, lines of communication, and safe houses and kept them off balance. By 2007, the SOF efforts were degrading the Taliban's ability to coordinate operations.[30]

NATO/ISAF news releases that were accessible in 2011 indicated that in the 2008–10 period there were at least twenty-three targeted (DA) operations in the Kandahar AOR. SOF probably carried these out, although the data does not indicate which missions involved Canadian and/or coalition SOF. Maj. Gordon Ohlke recalled that during his tour on the RC-South J2 staff (2009–10) SOF operators reported regularly when they had eliminated HVTs, disrupted networks, or apprehended individuals who were on the HVT list.[31]

Finally, it is essential to say something about counter-IED (C-IED) operations, since IEDs posed the greatest threat to CAF; they caused 71 percent of Canadian casualties. Dealing with them was a high priority for both "force protection and mission success."[32] The C-IED effort entailed two parts: (1) technical, or "defeat the device," involving locating, disarming, and destroying IEDs before they exploded, and (2) offensive, "attack the network" (ATN), involving the removal of the Taliban's capability to finance, acquire, and deploy the devices. By 2009 offensive ATN operations had become the main C-IED effort, and intelligence was central to this task.[33]

According to Lt.-Col. James Godefroy, who was the Task Force Kandahar J2 in 2009, the C-IED campaign introduced some duplication of intelligence efforts. The problem, in his view, was that it "attempted to function as a parallel enterprise."[34] IEDs were central to insurgents' operations—their weapon of choice—but IED-related activity was not separate from the overall insurgent mission. "The networks of insurgents who moved IED parts also moved weapons, people, and ammunition. . . . Because almost all insurgent networks were engaged in IED-related component movement, production, or use, when the ASIC was tracking and analyzing insurgent activity, this inherently included everything related to IEDs."[35]

Nonetheless, the CAF combat engineers, "who adopted the American C-IED methodology, expanded their efforts to include ATN concepts, which resulted in them developing a separate analytical effort using the same intelligence that the ASIC was generating and handling."[36] Godefroy argues that characterizing some insurgent teams as IED networks "was simply a way to attract resources to C-IED–focused organizations." This was done with the best of intentions; "the operators involved seemed to genuinely believe that they were filling an intelligence gap and that their focus and methodology was appropriate."[37] Nevertheless, "having a parallel intelligence activity running alongside the J2 staff and ASIC's production efforts created a risk of stove-piping of any intelligence they might receive or develop through their activities; to avoid this, their analyst was 'virtually' integrated into the ASIC. Despite this effort, the ambition of C-IED squadron leaders to be seen to be generating effects resulted in competition, including demand for additional resources."[38]

This was one of many efforts by nonintelligence elements to generate competitive intelligence that could capture the commander's attention and provide perceived value. For example, the J5 (strategy, policy, and plans) staff datamined historical data about IED emplacement trends in an attempt to predict hotspots.[39]

INTELLIGENCE ASSETS AND ARCHITECTURE IN AFGHANISTAN, 2005–10

This phase saw the largest overseas deployment of Canadian intelligence personnel, resources, and new capabilities since World War II. The eventual result was that the CAF in Afghanistan was able to exploit a full-spectrum intelligence effort that was increasingly effective at the tactical and operational levels. This effort was notable for intelligence fusion from different sources and methods, multiple levels of collection and analysis, and multiple producers, Canadian, coalition, and Afghan. Finally, as a result of this multifaceted effort, intelligence-led operations (ILOs) eventually became the dominant paradigm for CAF operations in Afghanistan.

In early 2006 the Canadian Special Operations Forces Command deployed an SOIC to support Canadian SOF operations. It included an FHT, a geomatics and imagery support team, a counterintelligence team, CSIS operators, target development analysts, and a deployable SIGINT support team. The geomatics and imagery support team and the deployable SIGINT support team had reach-back capability to the CF Joint Imagery Centre and the CFIOG, respectively.[40] Prior to this, Canadian SOF probably relied heavily on American intelligence assets.

Horn's discussion of an SOF operation in the Shah Wali Kot area in December 2005 offers some insights on their intelligence support structures and their limitations. The Canadian SOF operation began when a conventional unit under the command of US Combined Joint Task Force 76 passed a target intelligence package to JTF2, asking them to use it to conduct a capture/kill operation against a level II target (Taliban leader Mullah Abdul Ghafour). The American intelligence officer briefed the target intelligence package to the commander of JTF2 and his staff. But the planning and conduct of this operation, carried out in collaboration with other coalition SOF, revealed the shortcomings of the existing intelligence architecture. The CAF SOF operations centre did not have direct access to all of the coalition intelligence feeds that provided information on the battle space. And the Canadian SOF had problems communicating with non-Canadian units. At the tactical level, "all intelligence or planning products, flowing either way, were pushed through the CANSOF KAF liaison officer, who physically walked the products to the various units. This proved to be extremely time-consuming. . . . As a result, passage of information was slow, which affected the ability of various units to plan effectively."[41]

A Canadian SOF DA operation in the Tarin Kowt area of Uruzgan province in July 2006 was launched at the request of a coalition SOF partner that provided "a comprehensive and well-developed target intelligence package."[42] This target intelligence package allowed the SOF analysts and planners to prepare the operation without burdening the SOIC with "additional target development work" at a moment when it "was busy focusing on . . . the disruption of threats to Canadian Armed Forces in the Kandahar City/Zhari/ Panjawayi sectors."

In February 2006 Canada deployed to KAF Task Force AEGIS, a Canadian-led multinational brigade headquarters commanded by Brig.-Gen. David Fraser. He had his own J2 staff plus the ASIC and a Sperwer UAV troop. His headquarters also received input from US sources and from the Afghan Intelligence Response Team within the CDI (formerly the DGI) division in Ottawa.

The ASIC based at KAF was similar to its KMNB counterpart but eventually had a staff some one hundred strong. By 2011 it included a command team; a collection coordination intelligence requirements management cell; an operations cell to synchronize and plan ASIC actions; an all-source (fusion) cell, responsible for developing targeting information for the whole JTF-A AOR; a collation team whose role was to meet the ASIC's knowledge and information management requirements; a geomatics and imagery support team; a tactical SIGINT support team from the CFIOG; a HUMINT team; counterintelligence teams; from 2009 a forensic lab to exploit captured equipment and documents; and an attached EW troop under operational command or control if needed. The ASIC's job was to turn the JTF-A commander's priority intelligence requirements into collection and analysis tasks. The ASIC also served as the CANIC.[43] While CAF Intelligence Branch members made up a significant proportion of the ASIC staff, it also included members from the combat arms, civilian analysts, and personnel from the CSE, the CSIS, the Royal Canadian Mounted Police, and the Canada Border Services Agency.

Deployed in tandem with Task Force AEGIS was Task Force ORION, a BG based on the 1 PPCLI, commanded by Lt.-Col. Ian Hope. His organic intelligence assets included an intelligence officer (S2) with a small staff, a reconnaissance platoon, and an eight-vehicle Coyote LAV reconnaissance/surveillance troop. In theory, the Coyote and UAV troops gave the BG technical collection (SIGINT and imagery) capacity beyond the basics. But they also imposed new and greater data integration and analytical tasks on the S2 staff. Moreover, the Sperwer continued to have reliability issues (e.g., it could not fly during extreme daytime heat). However, even after the CAF deployed specialized FHTs, every BG commander relied on their infantry companies and platoons and the PRT CIMIC teams to act as the BG's eyes and ears. The regular patrols and the CIMIC meetings kept the BG in touch with the population. Patrols did tactical questioning of captured insurgents. Augmented by technical collection, each soldier became a sensor,[44] although they relied heavily on interpreters to gain HUMINT.

During predeployment training Hope had been told that ORION "would have access to incredible intelligence resources that would enable us to execute deliberate plans against pinpoint targets with less risk."[45] And on paper, the ISR assets at the disposal of the coalition looked impressive. The US deployed Predator UAVs, U-2/TR-1 reconnaissance aircraft, and RC-135 RIVET JOINT (SIGINT) and E-8 Joint STARS aircraft. The National Security Agency was generating SIGINT from its ground stations and satellites and from teams inside Afghanistan. US spy satellites also produced imagery. But the Canadians had not been briefed or trained on the American ISR systems. It wasn't until Operation KETARA in April 2006 that a US Army SOF officer was able to familiarize Hope with each capability, its characteristics, and how to best employ it.[46]

However, the operation also demonstrated the limitations of these enablers. Since some had been stripped away to support the war in Iraq,[47] what remained was in high demand among competing coalition members. The BG operations had lower priority than the SOF HVT hunts. Those assigned to the BG were often reassigned during operations, leaving it "relatively deaf and blind."[48] Moreover, even when available, the systems were not always reliable. In addition to interoperability problems, they were plagued by the normal friction associated with combat: "air gaps; low fidelity sensors; receivers that were not rugged enough[;] ... vehicle and equipment breakdown; bad atmospherics and foul weather; restrictions on intelligence sharing ... inherent in coalition operations; and human error."[49] These issues degraded his communications and sensor networks "to the point where they were incapable of producing more than a fleeting glimpse of a portion of the enemy's force." Based on Hope's account, his BG received only fragmentary SIGINT and ASIC reports. So, the reality for the Canadians was that "very limited Intelligence/Surveillance/Reconnaissance ... were available to us, and none of it directly."[50]

Offsetting the limits of these systems, Hope had two non-Canadian assets at his disposal: first, Capt. Zia Massoud of the Afghan National Police. While the Afghan National Police were notoriously corrupt and distrusted by the population, Massoud was seen as a stand-out exception. A close confidant of the governor of Kandahar province and commander of his quick-reaction force, Massoud ran his own network of informants in the Zharey-Panjawayi area. Hope found his information reliable, and Massoud became his "single most important source of intelligence."[51]

Massoud gifted cell phones and gave reward money in exchange for information about Taliban movements. After seeing the effectiveness of this network, Hope appointed him as a liaison officer in his command post, giving Hope direct access to Massoud's HUMINT network. The problem with this arrangement was cultural: Hope taught Massoud to read maps and use grid references, but his informants did not know how to use maps or understand compass directions. They gave "location and direction relative to the compounds of prominent locals and village names—many of which were not on our maps."[52] Their raw information then had to be converted into map grid references, an imperfect and time-consuming process.

Hope's other asset was the provincial Joint Coordination Center (JCC), initially set up by the Americans within the governor's compound. It had its own command post and communications. Initially it had limited resources, but the National Directorate of Security was funneling most of its information into the JCC, which also received intelligence from US sources. So, Hope decided to strengthen it by seconding to it personnel from the BG intelligence staff and adding a signals detachment. Maloney quotes CAF lieutenant-colonel Harjit Sajjan to the effect that "80 percent of TF ORION's intelligence comes from the JCC, not the ASIC back at KAF."[53]

Sajjan was not an intelligence officer; rather, he served as security adviser to Brigadier-General Fraser. Prior to taking command of Task Force AEGIS, Fraser had served on the Bi-National Planning Group in Colorado Springs, where he learned a lot about drugs and gangs from the US Drug Enforcement Administration. That shaped his thinking as he was preparing to deploy his task force. Based on the information then at his disposal, Fraser had decided that the Taliban was "nothing more than a bunch of thugs."[54] In short, the Taliban were a criminal gang. His key takeaway from his Bi-National Planning Group experience was the need to connect with the community that has the problem—develop human links based on respect and trust. "Who knows how to do this?... It's the police. Cops think differently than soldiers. They work a beat. They show up over and over. They get to know people. They help people. In time, people learn to trust them and they tell them things." Community policing yields HUMINT, "an invaluable commodity.... So when I began planning for our rotation in Afghanistan, I knew we needed cops on the team."[55]

Fraser heard that Sajjan, an army reservist and policeman who had worked on gangs in Vancouver, was being posted to Kabul. Fraser had him reassigned to Task Force AEGIS, and told him,

> I need you working with my intelligence guys.... I need your police mentality to help my military intelligence guys understand the Taliban. They're not a formed army; they're thugs, a bunch of pick-up guys running an

operation no different from the gangs you deal with in Vancouver.... You're a policeman.... Go do community policing. There's your community—it's called Kandahar. Get to know the tribal elders and the people they trust. Get me information on what's going on from the Afghan point of view.... [R]eport directly to me when you return.⁵⁶

Fraser later praised Sajjan effusively.⁵⁷ However, Godefroy noted that Sajjan's efforts were problematic in one respect. During the 2006 and subsequent deployments, he "engaged in a personal compartmented analytical effort." Although he was drawing upon "intelligence generated by the ASIC and other parts of the intelligence architecture in theatre, which he used to produce bespoke assessments for the Comd," Sajjan insisted that his product "could only be shared with the Comd directly because of its sensitivity."⁵⁸ While a commander can benefit from receiving different perspectives, Sajjan's approach violated the basic principle that MI be centrally controlled to prevent duplication.⁵⁹ Godefroy says that "successive J2s spent significant amounts of time trying to ensure these activities were integrated, to the extent possible, into the overall intelligence architecture even when their direction and focus was outside of intelligence functional control."⁶⁰

Massoud, the JCC, and Sajjan were not Fraser's only unique sources. Fraser also asked the task force's Muslim padre, Suleiman Demiray, to build relationships with the leaders in the mosques, listen to what they had to say, and report back to him. So, Demiray was another community HUMINT source not under direction of the task force J2.⁶¹

As the Canadian commitment was extended and expanded, so did the intelligence resources at the disposal of CAF commanders. At the apex was the J2, the chief intelligence officer for the task forces and their supporting staff. While Godefroy served as J2 for Roto 5-09 headquarters (February–November 2009), his staff totalled twelve. Some served in the Operations Centre, two served in Planning, one served at the Operational Coordination Centre–Provincial, and four (a major, a captain, and two NCOs) comprised the ISTAR CC.⁶²

There was no permanent, deployable J2 staff in the CAF; it had to be generated from across the CAF intelligence enterprise for each task force headquarters rotation, a process that involved multiple organizations. The Army was the force generator for the headquarters, and its land force area commands were the lead mounting areas. In Godefroy's case, the lead mounting area was the Land Force Western Area, which contained the 1 Canadian Mechanized Brigade Group. Col. Jonathan Vance was the brigade commander and would become the task force commander. To meet requirements set by the NATO-inspired architecture in theatre, where several of the headquarters' joint operational staff branches were headed by lieutenant-colonel division chiefs, the J2 had to be of equivalent rank. But in 2008 there was only one intelligence position in the Canadian Army at that rank: its G2. So, the candidates to fill the J2 position had to be found from CDI resources. They essentially became the force generator for the senior J2 staff position. In May 2008, working from options suggested by the CDI's chief of staff, Vance selected Godefroy, who at the time was serving in the Canadian Forces Joint Imagery Centre and was due for promotion to that rank.[63]

The CDI also led coordination with affected CAF stakeholders to determine what the rest of the intelligence architecture for each rotation should look like: how many people, at what ranks, and in what positions. However, because there was a ceiling on the number of people who could be deployed in theatre, the architecture had to be "massaged"; if more people were needed in one function or unit, that would have to be balanced by reductions in another. Early rotations were usually short-staffed.[64] The result was a compromise: good enough to get the job done.

The J2 was responsible for ensuring that the intelligence architecture was doing what the task force commander needed it to do. This involved directing the process, ensuring that intelligence production was functioning effectively, resolving issues and problems, and doing coordination. The J2 (intelligence) and J3 (operations) worked closely together to execute the commander's intent. The J2 did not run the ASIC—it was a line unit that reported to the task force commander. But the J2 routinely gave direction to the ASIC on the commander's behalf in order to ensure appropriate prioritization of specific intelligence support requirements for operations and planning. The J2 staff effort was dynamic and constant: eighteen-hour days, seven days a week throughout the mission. The J2 was expected to be able to brief on any intelligence topic at any time. This could take the form of oral briefings in person or products disseminated by computer, on paper, or by radio if the commander was out in the field (which Vance often was). The J2 staff also had to brief incoming commanders, all personnel entering theatre, and all visitors so that briefings on the threat and the current intelligence situation were routine and constant. The J2 oversaw the ISTAR CC, which held daily coordination meetings with all Task Force Kandahar elements. More will be said on this below. In addition, the J2 conducted weekly meetings with CAF intelligence staffs to communicate priorities and the commander's intent and to affect any necessary coordination. Battle Group S2s routinely met with the J2 when needed, but the ASIC was the intelligence hub.[65]

Of course, this snapshot from 2009 might not reflect the experience of all J2 headquarters rotations. In fact, Godefroy stressed that "the influence of successive J2's changed with different Rotos, depending upon personal relationships with commanders, and with the commander's understanding of intelligence, their attitudes toward it and expectations of it."[66] One obstacle to that understanding was the fact that it was possible to rise through the Army without being exposed to the intelligence function apart from a notional process during collective training events. Consequently, there was skepticism or naivete about it. Intelligence staffs had to establish their credibility and had to teach their commanders about the capabilities of the various collection activities and about what the architecture supporting the mission could and could not do for them. In Godefroy's case, he found that Vance was a quick study who grasped what intelligence could do. Vance asked good questions, became well informed, and could process important details and effectively integrate them into his operational thinking.

During Godefroy's rotation the ISTAR CC was one of his most valuable assets. It was responsible for collecting, deconflicting, and prioritizing all Task Force Kandahar ISTAR platform requirements and preparing the daily collection plan. It was under his command and control but resided in the Task Force Kandahar headquarters operations centre. The J2 had the lead for identifying the collection priorities, while the J3 was responsible for tasking the platforms that the ISTAR CC coordinated. The two collaborated in providing and deconflicting direction and guidance to the ISTAR CC when necessary.

For example, occasionally a nonintelligence requirement, such as surveillance of a Canadian element in contact with the enemy, might trump an intelligence collection task; in these cases, the J3 and J2 would adjudicate. The Task Force Kandahar collection requirements were fed into RC-South headquarters daily, and the task force made available to its allies any spare Canadian collection capacity while also benefiting from access to lines of tasking for other platforms outside of Canadian control.[67]

From 2009 on, JTF-A had one other major ISR asset under its control: a new UAV troop. Over time, the limitations of the Sperwer had become increasingly apparent. Even before the 2008 Manley Panel report on the Afghan mission recommended it, the CAF had sought an alternative UAV with longer range. The CAF settled on the Heron and leased three of them from MacDonald Dettwiler. Its synthetic aperture radar could deliver "full motion imagery in real time." The detachment deployed to KAF in December 2008, serving as part of the JTF-A air wing, and began flying operational missions in January 2009. While published sources introduce some confusion about who controlled them, during Godefroy's tenure as J2 he was responsible for assigning their collection priorities, while the J3 looked after tasking, with the ISTAR CC coordinating their missions. The Herons flew thousands of hours doing area surveillance and route reconnaissance, observing sites or activities of interest (such as Taliban teams emplacing IEDs), threat identification, and targeting.[68]

Collecting HUMINT was not something unique to the Afghan mission, but it was more fully developed there. By the time CAF operations were under way in Kandahar in 2006, FHT and CSIS operators had established a well-synchronized, albeit personality-dependent, HUMINT team.⁶⁹ Operating under direction of the ASIC commander, the FHT consisted of about a dozen CAF personnel who had been selected and trained in relatively short order. Relying on interpreters and their own language skills, they collected information through contact with the local population and, in some cases, tactical questioning of detainees. Starting in 2009, interrogators were assigned to the team, and the ASIC's headquarters HUMINT staff (J2X) responsibilities expanded to include the coordination of both source handling and interrogation operations. Godefroy says that Vance was actively engaged in providing direction to the use of these resources. In an article that described two operations in which the FHTs delivered timely and accurate information that led to positive outcomes, Vance asserted that "they are an invaluable asset providing critical intelligence in support of operations."⁷⁰

By integrating in-theatre tactical SIGINT with its Canadian-based strategic counterpart, SIGINT made a more significant contribution to operations than it had in previous missions. From 2005 to 2008, as director general of military SIGINT within the CSE, Cmdre. Andrea Siew served as the link between the CSE and the CFIOG, which provided the CAF's tactical SIGINT collection capability. In Afghanistan, they worked for JTF-A J2 staff but were compartmented in a SCIF in the ASIC. The J2 staff would take finished products generated in real time by the CFIOG team, do the analysis, and brief the commander. When Brigadier-General Fraser was appointed to lead Task Force AEGIS, the CSE brought in his command team (all cleared to top secret special access) to brief them on how the national SIGINT organization could support their operations. Siew later went to Afghanistan to meet with Fraser to ensure that SIGINT was meeting his needs. This integrated approach represented, in her view, a major cultural shift within the CSE and "a huge change in the way of doing [SIGINT] business."⁷¹

Determined to bring the CSE and the CAF into closer cooperation, CSE chief John Adams took this initiative a step further. He deployed three CSE officers to Afghanistan: one each to the ASIC, JTF-A headquarters, and the American J2 staff at Bagram airfield. In his view, the benefit of having CSE representatives there was that they could explain to the military what the data they were getting from tactical SIGINT, which the CFIOG did well, would amount to if pushed back to the CSE in Canada. There it would augment what the CSE was collecting from their Canadian sites. Then the CSE would put the package together and send it back to the CAF consumers in theatre. This represented a fusing of national and theatre, strategic, operational, and tactical SIGINT operations. Adams estimated that eventually "about 75–80% of actionable intelligence in Afghanistan was [derived from] SIGINT."⁷²

This kind of two-way flow was not confined to SIGINT. Some of the ASIC's assigned positions were not filled, possibly due to caps on personnel totals in theatre. Fortunately, the more advanced communications available at this time allowed the ASIC at KAF and the Afghan Intelligence Response Team at NDHQ to do simultaneous real-time intelligence analysis seamlessly.[73] That took time to develop because the CDI's intelligence production division first had to be reorganized. It also had to provide analytical support to the ASIC and staff for the new CAF commands while implementing the changes imposed by the *Defence Intelligence Review*.[74]

RC-South had it its disposal a broad spectrum of ISTAR collection systems. In addition to the American platforms already mentioned, the British, Dutch and German contingents deployed a range of reconnaissance aircraft, including jets, helicopters, and UAVs. Between them, they were capable of doing wide-area search, target identification and cueing, IED locating, route reconnaissance, and gathering "pattern of life data."[75] Being a major player in RC-South and having US forces under command gave the CAF access to these ISR assets, although this always depended on tasking priorities and availability due to competing demands from the various coalition partners.

In addition to accessing these collection systems, the CAF benefited from long-standing bilateral and multilateral intelligence-sharing agreements within NATO and the Four/Five Eyes networks. According to Andrew Feltham, once NDHQ had approved sharing arrangements, the JTF-A commander or his delegated subordinates could liaise directly with allied intelligence agencies via formal procedures or informal relationships. This occurred in theatre, where intelligence personnel from the NATO and Australia, Canada, United Kingdom, and United States networks often met separately from other coalition members to share information. It also occurred in Canada through existing channels that fed allied intelligence products to NDHQ. The CSE routinely received SIGINT products from the US National Security Agency and the United Kingdom's Government Communications Headquarters, and the Canadian Forces Joint Imagery Centre received imagery from US aerial and space-based systems. This material could be integrated into analysis produced by the CDI or the CSE or be sent directly to the ASIC.

In addition to these theatre- and strategic-level arrangements, some units took initiatives to optimize their own intelligence collection capabilities. Task Force 1-07, for example, had deployed with a full squadron of Coyote LAVs. The task force commander, Lt.-Col. Rob Walker, grouped them with his battalion's reconnaissance platoon and the sniper section to create a hybrid ISTAR squadron. Fusing those technical and human collection capabilities gave the task force "a powerful information-gathering tool."[76]

SOF were focused primarily on DA missions against HVTs, so they were mostly intelligence consumers. Due to the small size of their DA assault teams, they required precise, accurate intelligence. Moreover, their operations almost always generated detainees, documents, and captured equipment of intelligence value that could be exploited by further SOF or BG operations. They also conducted many of the reconnaissance and surveillance missions that added to the larger intelligence picture. As noted earlier, Canadian SOF operated under the direction of the Coalition Joint Special Operations Task Force–Afghanistan, not under JTF-A. That and the fact that there is limited public data on their activities means that it is difficult to assess their intelligence contribution and value. But as one informed observer put it, "In most instances, there was a collaborative relationship between the SOTF SOIC and the JTF-A ASIC. The ASIC worked on describing the Taliban Network[,] and the SOIC worked on identifying and targeting individuals of importance within the Network. In short, when each organization understood its role . . . it worked very well indeed!"[77] Other intelligence structures accessible to the CAF included the Kandahar Intelligence Fusion Cell, supporting ISAF operations in RC-South, and ISAF's Joint Intelligence Centre in Kabul, which carried out intelligence and surveillance coordination and data fusion for all of the Afghan AOR. It is also possible that some JTF-A requests for information went to the NATO Intelligence Fusion Center, colocated with the US Joint Analysis Center at Molesworth in the United Kingdom. Created in 2006, the NATO Intelligence Fusion Center did 24/7 intelligence analysis and production in support of NATO's military headquarters.[78]

Regardless of originating source—from tactical collectors or from strategic systems and structures—all or most of this data and analysis ultimately reached the ASIC, the Afghan Intelligence Response Team, or both. Just as Darren Knight had remarked with respect to the 1991 Persian Gulf War, Maj. Gordon Ohlke commented that when he first arrived in Afghanistan the flow of intelligence from the various sources, but especially from the United States, "was like drinking from a fire hose, but you adjusted and learned to ask the right questions, narrow your focus."[79] From a purely organizational standpoint it is fair to say that never before had the CAF been "so well supported in the intelligence field in time of war, by both its own collection and analysis assets and those of its allies."[80]

THE IMPACT OF INTELLIGENCE SUPPORT ON OPERATIONS

So, how effective was that intelligence support? Was quantity matched by quality? Did it exert a positive influence on CAF operations? This section draws upon a very limited number of primary and secondary sources. Thus, what follows is a preliminary and tentative assessment. It is also important to remember that counterinsurgency campaigns should not be all about kinetic operations: engaging the insurgents' armed units. It should be about building capacity for self-governance, rebuilding confidence in administrative institutions, economic, and social development including educational and public health programs. It is meant to be people-centric: engaging the local population, improving their quality of life, and giving them a greater stake in their own future.[81]

That was the intent of the Canadian PRT that had arrived in Kandahar in the summer of 2005. But none of that can succeed in an atmosphere of instability and violence. And that was the harsh reality confronting the PRT. The province was insecure; violence was prevalent everywhere, so until some degree of security was restored, it was difficult for the PRT to fulfil its mandate. The killing of Canadian diplomat Glyn Berry in January 2006 and increased Taliban activity stalled PRT activity for several months. Maloney says that Ottawa also removed some of its capabilities, which limited its effectiveness and reduced its security.[82] This put a premium on kinetic operations, which is also reflected in the sources. Unavoidably, this tends to skew the intelligence story toward support to those operations.

The SOF operations in 2005–6 offer a starting point. The JTF2/coalition SOF operation in De Lam Ghar in September 2005 was launched because "intelligence analysts had confirmed [it] was an enemy sanctuary harbouring key Taliban leaders and fanatical insurgents."[83] JTF2's mission was to find, capture, or kill them, in particular Mullah Dadfar. A medium-value target, he was believed to be linked to al-Qaeda jihadists and to report directly to Taliban leader Mullah Mohammad Omar. The analysts assessed that at least thirty to forty-five insurgents were there and specified how they were armed and equipped. But in two separate raids, JTF2 did not capture or kill Dadfar. Although they found some weapons caches, they retrieved nothing of intelligence value. The intelligence that guided the operation may have been correct, but it was not timely. The Taliban had motorcycles and probably had moved out before the SOF arrived.

This may have been the case as well in the JTF2-led operation in Shah Wali Kot mentioned earlier. The intelligence-handling process was slow, so the mounting force lost SA. The SOF encountered heavy fire, which downed one helicopter. The target was meeting nearby but evaded capture. Here the intelligence was close enough, but the delayed exploitation of it and unexpected resistance prevented a successful outcome.[84]

The JTF2 operation into the Bahgran Valley (19 May–8 June 2006) was itself a strategic reconnaissance mission to gather information in advance of a larger coalition operation. The SOF would "focus on ground analysis, ACM [anticoalition militia] communications, HUMINT . . . collection, discussions with local elders/villagers, and questioning [of suspected anticoalition fighters]."[85] Horn says that "reconnaissance information and enemy intelligence they gathered provided an important picture" for the coalition forces deploying into the valley.

The Tarin Kowt SOF operation of July 2006 was intended to kill or capture Taliban leader Osami Bari. Coalition intelligence analysts believed that this would seriously disrupt the Taliban network in the area and that sensitive site exploitation of his compound would reveal material "of great intelligence value" that would lead to follow-on targeting. Unfortunately, the intelligence picture had greatly underestimated the enemy force on the ground, and the raid met unexpectedly quick and fierce resistance. The situation "differed so much from what the intelligence picture painted, particularly from what was supplied by human intelligence . . . , that the task force commander conceded, 'compromise is suspected.'"[86] When the SOF gathered additional information from local sources they learned that most of the fighters who engaged them came from a large *shūrā* being held near the objective. Nevertheless, the mission was considered a success because it inflicted heavy casualties on the Taliban (fifty-seven killed and thirty-five wounded), including Bari and two of his subcommanders. More significant than the body count was the longer-term shaping effects: the raid improved the security posture in Uruzgan for the next several months. This was helpful to the Dutch forces that later deployed there.

This series of operations highlighted two challenges for coalition intelligence: accuracy and timeliness. Given the nature of the enemy and the terrain and the inevitable friction surrounding military operations, even when intelligence was correct it rarely was complete. So, there was always the potential for being surprised. In particular, the Taliban's mobility made timeliness even more important and harder to achieve.

During the Task Force ORION operations in the spring of 2006, Lieutenant-Colonel Hope clearly did not feel that he was always adequately supported by higher-level intelligence, saying that at best "we would be given grid references where there had been a communication [SIGINT] hit on a suspected enemy leader, but seldom details of who or what. . . . This lack of detailed intelligence, combined with the big blunt nature of our LAV-based capability, made it impossible to execute rapid deliberate precision operations from KAF."[87] Therefore, he deployed his task force forward into company and platoon AORs, living among the local population. He explained that "this put us closer to the enemy and if we received 'actionable intelligence,' it shortened our response times and increased our chances of achieving surprise."[88] He went to say,

> It also gave us access to local intelligence. Like beat cops, we became aware of the environment and were able to sense measures of local confidence and the swing of operational momentum. Intuition and trust became central in our efforts to find Taliban forces. Over time we began to decipher which Afghan information sources were reliable (and which were not), and to trust our instinct, regardless of whether or not they were confirmed by higher

intelligence capabilities. I began to trust subordinate commanders to act—
or not—upon this local HUMINT.[89]

Brigadier-General Fraser was impressed by Lieutenant-Colonel Sajjan's HUMINT efforts. Sajjan "started talking with everyone, and he was good at it. He got a whole bunch of information and reported it in substantial detail. The stuff he gathered was primary-source, from the Afghans themselves. We compared that evidence with our other data sources. If all of the sources said the same thing, then the raw data became actionable intelligence.... That's how, over time, we built situational awareness. Based on that awareness, we came up with plans to deliver the effects I was trying to achieve."[90] According to Maloney, Sajjan developed a rapport with all of the intelligence players, including the National Directorate of Security. As a result, he sent "two pages of solid intelligence to Task Force ORION per week. The quality of the information was awesome."[91]

Fraser was also fulsome in his praise for the HUMINT efforts of Padre Demiray, who engaged with the mosque leaders, prayed with them, and listened "over and over, until he learned things we never could have discovered without him there."[92] His report revealed the extent to which the Taliban held sway in Kandahar city's mosques. The government was paying the salaries of only one-quarter of the imams; the rest were beholden to the Taliban, which controlled their messaging. So, they were winning the information war. This led to a change in Afghan government policy: to reform, fund, and retrain the imams in order to break the Taliban's hold over them and change their narrative. Demiray's HUMINT was crucial to improving the SA of Fraser and his staff. They were coming to appreciate the real complexity of the "human geography" of their AOR.[93] Fraser had arrived in Kandahar thinking that he was confronting a mere "pickup gang" of thugs. The SA developed by Sajjan and Demiray proved that notion wrong. Fraser was forced to concede that his troops were fighting a deep-rooted, competent political-military insurgency.[94]

While Sajjan and Demiray tried to get inside the mindset of the population and their influencers and to tease out SA from them, if the CAF was going to protect and win them over, then Hope's BG had to defeat the armed insurgents.[95] He and his successors needed intelligence support to do that. The published accounts show that some aspects worked better than others.

Sean Maloney writes that during Operation KETARA (April 2006) the ISTAR platforms (including EW systems and the Sperwer) were "layered." They fed targeting information to the forward observation officer, Capt. Nichola Goddard, who coordinated the fire plans. Hope, who was at the Tactical Command Post, also received continuous intelligence updates. According to Maj. Bill Fletcher, "The [ISTAR] hits were coming fast and furious."[96] This operation persuaded Hope that while deployed forward in the battle space, the commanding officer should be "the nexus for all critical battlefield intelligence" and should be equipped with the necessary receivers for SIGINT intercepts and imagery. Thereafter, he expanded the Tactical Command Post to include signalers, translators, and the mobile EW team vehicle. The virtue of this for C2 is readily apparent; in Hope's view, "In a close fight, the commander is the best person to synthesize this material and to make decisions regarding movements and fires of his sub-units."[97] However, this perspective and approach could be problematic if it meant that the commander bypassed his professional intelligence staff and usurped their role by doing his own analysis.

The next month, the BG mounted Operation BRAVO GUARDIAN to clear armed Taliban out of the Nalgham townships in the Zharey and Panjawayi districts. The frequent SOF Tier 1 operations in these districts indicated that the Taliban leadership was building up there. During BRAVO GUARDIAN, information from Massoud's network allowed the BG to capture eleven Taliban, having killed or wounded more. During a follow-up operation (JAGRA) in the same area in June, the BG received "periodic radio-fed information bites" from the ASIC and more frequent cell phone messages to Massoud from his informants. He tried to keep the BG informed, but a lack of grid or map references made tracking the Taliban "shear guesswork.... Without any aerial support, maintaining contact with this fleeing enemy was impossible in the close country of Zharie-Panjawayi."[98]

Relying on his own observations and anonymous sources, Sean Maloney offers a critical perspective on the intelligence effort at brigade level during the AEGIS/ORION phase. He suggests that there were problems in intelligence architecture supporting the brigade headquarters and BG. And the perception at the BG level was that the AEGIS J2 staff and the ASIC "did not provide timely intelligence to TF ORION," Hope notes.[99] "The need for fast-reacting operations could not be met ... by the existing architecture ... [that] was based on restrictive Cold War–era compartmentalization of source information and analysis that in turn was based on the fear that the Americans would shut off the pipeline to Canada not only at the tactical level, but also at the strategic level, if the relationship was 'compromised.'"[100]

But as Godefroy points out, information security served a legitimate purpose. It existed not just to ensure that the flow of allied intelligence was not disrupted but also to minimize the possibility that sensitive information would fall into the hands of the insurgents. That could inform them that the coalition knew things about them that they should not know and put the source of that knowledge—whether human or technical—at risk. In any case, it was possible to create intelligence-sharing workarounds that did not compromise source security.[101]

Maloney goes on to assert that "the ASIC generally ignored the JCC, in part because some ASIC people refused to accept that a person [this probably refers to Sajjan] working on finding ways for improving the ANSF [Afghan National Security Force] couldn't be viewed as an intelligence collector."[102] He adds that "elements in the ASIC didn't like this because they viewed it as 'single source' Afghan information and didn't trust it until they could 'wash it' through their processes.... Information had to go through a laborious process: when it arrived, Ian [Hope] and his staff couldn't act on [it] in a timely fashion because the intelligence was so stale."[103] He went on to say that he perceived "a lack of confidence at TF ORION in the ASIC products. On the other hand, some in the ASIC thought that TF ORION was being 'played' by corrupt provincial government officials and wanted to vet all intelligence coming into TF ORION first."[104] In the summer of 2006, the relationships between the various Afghan security agencies were dysfunctional due to the influence of local power brokers in areas such as the Zharey district. Maloney says that the Taliban exploited that disunity before the Canadians figured out what was happening. He adds that "there was a definite requirement for specialists to assess in detail, local power structures: who was who in the zoo and their exact relationships with each other."[105] He felt that the ASIC should have been doing this but did not have the capacity at that time.

This debate yields a number of observations. The tensions between the BG on the one hand and the J2 and ASIC on the other were hardly remarkable. Military history is replete with disputes between line and staff. What also can be seen here is the normal trade-off or balancing act between timeliness and risk. The BG had a legitimate requirement for timely intelligence on which to base its operations, often on short notice. The ASIC, for its part, was correct in insisting that local sources it did not control should be vetted for reliability and their information cross-checked for accuracy. Having a single intelligence channel to the commander also reduced chances for duplication of effort. For this conundrum there was no perfect solution.

Add to this mix the unfamiliar nature of both the AOR and the enemy, the uncertain capabilities and reliability of the Afghan security forces, the need to adapt conventional ISR systems to unconventional targets, and the normal political, operational, and technical challenges of operating within a multinational coalition, and one gains a sense of the complexity of these operations. What is remarkable is that the CAF's intelligence system worked as well as it did under those circumstances.

In July 2006, Hope launched Operation ZAHAR to disrupt Taliban forces that were thought to be gathering in the Pashmul area of the Zharey and Panjawayi districts. The operation involved his full BG plus ANA and Afghan National Police troops and a British Army armoured reconnaissance troop. In this case Hope relied less on his ISTAR systems for hard evidence and more on his personal sense that they were there. Unit leaders did their reconnaissances and gathered HUMINT from locals. Maneuvering task force units generated Taliban radio chatter, but it was only an advance to contact maneuver that revealed where they were.[106]

Operation ZAHAR was the result of what Maloney described as a series of "maneuver to collect" operations whose aims were to provoke the Taliban into moving or generating radio traffic. "That data would be used to validate HUMINT collected by Harj Sajjan and the NDS [National Directorate of Security], and then synthesized into a bigger picture of enemy activity and intentions in the two districts."[107] So, these kinetic operations were not just consumers of intelligence but were also producers of it. Troop presence and maneuvering there prior to ZAHAR also had generated "a significant number of local 'walk-ins' who provided information on the enemy and his movements." This "web of contacts" yielded patterns that showed how the Taliban would react when confronted by coalition forces. The answer was that they would fight hard; they were not to be dismissed. And the most important takeaway from ZAHAR was that the Taliban was embedded deeply in the Zharey and Panjawayi districts. It would take a major operation to remove and replace them with Afghan National Security Force troops.[108]

That operation, code-named MEDUSA, happened in September 2006. It has since been described as "the battle that saved Afghanistan."[109] In fact, its strategic aims were more modest. The ultimate objective was to set the security conditions for establishing the Kandahar Afghan Development Zone. The development zone was meant to bring some economic prosperity and normalcy to the area and to show the population that the Afghan government offered a more promising future than did the Taliban.[110]

Fraser recounts that it had two other strategic goals: to inflict a defeat on the Taliban just as ISAF assumed command of RC-South and to show the United States, NATO countries, and Afghans "that NATO could fight and win battles just as well as the Americans."[111] This translated into two operational objectives: "to maintain freedom of movement along Highway 1 and uphold the security of Kandahar City."[112] MEDUSA was intended to be a four-phase operation whose first (shaping) phase would last until mid to late September. That timetable was abruptly compressed in mid-August when, at a meeting with the governor, local leaders demanded immediate results or they would throw their lot in with the Taliban (some had effectively done so already). So, Fraser came under pressure to act quickly.[113]

To achieve these objectives, he assembled a force of some 2,200 troops. The 1 RCR BG, which had only arrived in theatre at the beginning of August, provided the core of the maneuver units. It was enhanced by a mix of Canadian and multinational forces: artillery, ISTAR assets, engineers, more infantry, SOF, an ANA *kandak*, and a lot of airpower.[114] MEDUSA lasted about two weeks. It is not necessary to recount the battles here. Suffice to say that they were bloody on both sides. The Taliban suffered the heaviest losses but inflicted enough on the ISAF forces to give them pause. In the end, the Canadians and their allies took the ground and achieved their aims. They had won a major but temporary tactical victory. The Taliban eventually returned.

Intelligence played a central role in the operation. This began with intelligence preparation of the battlefield that exploited the combined assets of the brigade, the ASIC, and the BG.[115] The intent, according to Task Force 3-06 intelligence officer Capt. Kris Purdy, was to get "a very clear picture" of what was in the Pashmul/Panjawayi area.[116] "A critical element of our Phase 1 activity was coordinating all our intelligence, surveillance and reconnaissance (ISR) assets to prepare for the battle," Fraser says.[117] "We could watch and listen to them with our sophisticated array of intelligence and surveillance systems. In the air we had Predators ... that fed line of sight video to us in real time. We had Sperwer ... that could send target images back from as far as 150 kilometers away. Other platforms collected data from ultra-high altitudes, while British Nimrod aircraft conducted aerial surveillance. On the ground, other assets gathered intelligence on the Taliban as well."[118]

Their task was target development: tracking HVTs and medium-value targets and identifying key locations such as IED factories, ambush sites, mortar pits, medical stations, and early-warning sites. The brigade intelligence staff relied on "a protocol called F2T2EA ... for the six discrete steps we take to find, fix, track, target and engage the enemy and assess the effect we created."[119] At the same time, the ISR systems would send to the troops the SA they needed to advance effectively onto each objective. The operations staff used that intelligence to develop a template and assign objectives, which evolved as the situation did and as indicated by further reports.[120]

In many respects, the intelligence preparation of the battlefield succeeded. As Fraser recounts, "Using our full combination of intelligence assets, including our network of friendly local nationals, we could track exactly where and when Taliban commanders were setting up their headquarters."[121] Listening in on intercepted communications allowed the Canadians to identify the Taliban's commander for the defense of the area—Mullah Abdul Hanan—and the names and locations of his subcommanders, the forces at their disposal, and how they intended to fight the ISAF force: with a combination of IEDs, mortars, ambushes, and full-on assaults.[122]

Based on that intelligence, the brigade drew assumptions and made plans. But Fraser concedes that often their assumptions were wrong. For example, they had not realized that the Taliban would capture the Mas'um Ghar ridge that overlooked the entire AOR. That change, occurring at the outset of the operation, impressed upon Fraser and his staff that intelligence is "always possibly wrong, possibly incomplete. You can base a plan in part on intel, but you'd better be ready to change it."¹²³ He went on to say that "every day I reminded my officers that we now had 'a clear picture of the enemy with a plus or minus 100 per cent chance of error.'"

Fraser was right to be cautious, because the intelligence picture, while clear in many respects, was less so in others, especially on the exact location of enemy fighting units. After the first day of artillery and aerial bombardment (2 September), locals told the task force that the Taliban were leaving the area. But once C Company had crossed the Arghandab River on 3 September and was advancing toward its objective (the "White Schoolhouse" area), ISR assets began to show that there were plenty of insurgents there. They held fire until the Canadian troops were in an ambush position and then opened up on them from three sides. The chaotic fight that followed ended with the Canadians withdrawing after suffering serious casualties. An intelligence report later that day, probably based on SIGINT, stated that in spite of taking heavy losses themselves, "the enemy believe that they are winning, and their morale is assessed as high."¹²⁴ And to add insult to injury, the following morning C Company was rendered combat-ineffective by a blue-on-blue friendly fire strafing attack by a USAF A-10.¹²⁵

The ambush at the White Schoolhouse prompted the intelligence community to do some soul-searching to figure out what had gone wrong. Was it an intelligence failure on their part? Not surprisingly, they concluded emphatically that it was not. But this requires elaboration. Capt. Kris Purdy claims that the community (which probably included the brigade J2 staff and the ASIC) never assessed that the Taliban were leaving the area. On the contrary, they were saying that the enemy was still there and that they were going to stay and fight, particularly in that area. In fact, they were "wondering why we were going ahead with this feint when we were assessing that they [the enemy] were probably more likely to draw us in [to their kill zones]."¹²⁶

This begs several questions. If the intelligence staff did not claim that the Taliban were withdrawing from that area, who did? How did that report make its way through the system? Was it passed up the chain without comment or validation? Is it possible that it was a Taliban deception, intended to tempt the task force to do exactly what it did? The published sources do not offer unambiguous answers to those questions. One (unidentified) intelligence officer laid the blame firmly on Fraser's shoulders: "The intelligence was clear. . . . The General was clearly informed. And clearly [he] chose to ignore the intelligence. . . . Intelligence can only advise the commander; that was done, he made the decisions."¹²⁷

Lt.-Col. Omer Lavoie, the BG commander, says he felt that brigade headquarters wanted to "rush it through," although he felt that at the time his troops crossed the river "the conditions had not been set and the intelligence picture was not clear."¹²⁸ In his own defence, Fraser felt that he was under pressure from

ISAF headquarters to "get it done."[129] Horn says that according to then Lt.-Col. Shane Schreiber, Fraser's assistant chief of staff for operations, even after the friendly fire incident Fraser was getting calls hourly from ISAF commander Gen. Sir David Richards and his deputy, US major-general Benjamin Freakley, urging him to finish the operation. They were telling him that "this is the most important thing NATO's ever done, the future of NATO rides on this, the future of Afghanistan rides on this."[130] And all that pressure was pushed down to Lavoie.

Even with only personal recollections as a source, this has the ring of truth. After all, the strategic importance of success in Operation MEDUSA had been made clear before it started. Furthermore, this would not be the first military operation in history to be launched in the face of intelligence suggesting that the attackers were facing a more formidable enemy than was expected.

So, was this an intelligence failure? It is difficult to reach a definitive answer. The intelligence preparation of the battlefield was thorough, collecting a lot of crucial information. That the Taliban would stand and fight there was widely known and based on intelligence. What was missing was the exact location and strength of the Taliban force that engaged C Company. This can be attributed to two factors: first, the inability of the ISR systems to penetrate the dense and complex topography to expose the defensive positions at the objective, and second, the foreshortened bombardment of the area before the attack, changed from four days to only one. The first was a technical limitation, and the second was a planning problem brought about by the compressed operational timeline imposed on the brigade by ISAF headquarters. This raises the question of whether the leadership—all the way up the chain—understood the totality of the intelligence picture of the target and the gaps in it yet chose to act anyway. Regardless of its provenance, the incorrect report that the Taliban were leaving the target area added impetus to the pressure on Fraser to act to prevent those enemy forces from escaping. Thus, it seems fair to conclude that the ambush that befell C Company cannot be attributed solely to a failure of intelligence but rather to several intersecting factors. Finally, it is important to acknowledge that in spite of the several setbacks, Operation MEDUSA ultimately achieved its objectives even if only temporarily.

After Operation MEDUSA the Taliban reverted to asymmetric tactics: hit-and-run attacks, IEDs, and suicide bombings. ISAF/coalition forces, including the Canadians, had to adapt to that while they also tried to carry out the development/reconstruction work of the ISAF mission in an AOR that was not yet secure.[131] So, the intelligence mission continued and evolved with the shifting face of battle.

In December 2006 ISAF issued news releases on three precision air strikes in the Zharey and Panjawayi districts. The reports described these operations as "meticulously planned and executed," which suggests that they were launched on the basis of accurate and timely intelligence.[132] Since they were part of Canadian-led Operation BAAZ TSUKA, the strikes probably relied on Canadian-directed intelligence assets. The essential point here is that they indicate that Canadian and other coalition forces increasingly were carrying out ILOs.

In late February, responding to intelligence, a joint CAF/ANA infantry/armour combat team from Task Force 1-07 conducted a cordon and search operation in Howz-e-Medad in the Zharey district west of Kandahar City. The information was accurate, and the search yielded a cache of mortar bombs and rockets. A series of small ambushes followed the search but were suppressed in a matter of minutes.[133] Intelligence may not have predicted them but probably did not need to; based on CAF experiences in 2006, the 2 RCR troops were very likely alert to the possibility.

In March a detachment of the ISTAR squadron (based on the Royal Canadian Dragoons) established a base on the Ghundey Ghar mountain, deploying its Coyote LAVs and other surveillance equipment in overwatch. With this and regular patrolling the BG "cast a wide security cordon" around the Zharey and Panjawayi districts. Together, surveillance and patrolling allowed the BG to observe and listen, thereby adding to the intelligence picture. The BG learned about the local farmers' dependence on the opium crop, which all but indentured them to the Taliban. This knowledge supported the PRT's strategy, which was to take a gradual approach to poppy eradication by focusing on crop substitution while the BG went after the traffickers and insurgents. This paid dividends in the form of an increasing flow of information from the locals about the Taliban and the location of IEDs. The hints included that "ISAF might want to check out that piece of road" and that "foreigners had been seen in that hamlet the other week, milling around a certain house."[134] Not only did these enhance SA and increase operational effectiveness, they were a genuine measure of increased local confidence in the willingness and ability of the Canadians to secure the population in the Zharey and Panjawayi districts.

That said, such sentiment was not universal. The Taliban retained a foothold in the area, especially in Nalgham-Sangsar, and continued to pose a threat to the locals and to the BG. Patrols, searches, and reconnaissance squadron surveillance day and night, combined with information from the locals, yielded useful operational results. In early April the combined information from patrol and human source reports created better SA of the complexity of life in that area but also pointed to a growing threat from Taliban and foreign fighters. With that intelligence in hand, the BG decided to not wait for the Taliban to act first and preempted them. Throughout the month of May the BG launched patrols and probing attacks into the area, keeping the insurgents off balance and never allowing them to seize the initiative. These efforts could not eliminate the Taliban presence in the Zharey and Panjawayi districts, but the BG declined to conduct a larger operation that would risk a high-casualty IED strike (such as one that hit the BG in April) or ambush and a Taliban information operations victory. Instead, the BG continued to deploy quietly at night and to engage insurgent units by day.[135]

Operation SEASONS, launched on the night of 20 June, was typical of these. Intelligence had identified a Taliban unit operating out of Howz-e-Medad in Zharey that was running an IED cell and attacking checkpoints on Highway 1. Sean Maloney says, correctly, that an ILO such as this ideally required multiple sources of information that could be quickly cross-checked against substantial SA about the local community. But in this case, the BG and company commanders would have to rely on incomplete information and their own experience. During a chaotic all-arms battle that began at dawn, a UAV and the sniper teams provided information to update the intelligence picture. As portions of the battle area were cleared of enemy fighters, CAF engineers did sensitive site exploitation and uncovered a significant cache of weapons and explosives. Later, a second sensitive site exploitation revealed more weapons and artillery rounds and other components for making IEDs. As a result of Operation SEASONS, regular commercial and military traffic continued on the highway, an IED cell had been dismantled, and the Taliban was unable to use Zharey as a base for launching conventional operations against ISAF. Nevertheless, the area remained disputed territory.[136]

But accurate intelligence did not always lead to success; at Zalakhan in July 2007 it led to tragedy. Multisource reporting indicated that a new and more experienced IED cell was working in the area. The C Company 3 PPCLI dispatched a joint CAF/ANA combat team to root them out. Unfortunately, a massive IED killed six Canadian soldiers and their Afghan interpreter. The only consolation was that evidence from the explosion, combined with other intelligence, led the task force to two IED factories/storage facilities in Panjawayi. Intelligence eventually tracked the cell responsible for the fatal blast to Nakhonay. Operation PORTER, a joint CAF/ANA/Afghan National Police action on 26 July, led to the arrest of seven men, the seizure of IED-related supplies, and the disbanding of that cell.[137]

Task Force 1-07 had institutionalized the practice of ILOs; they became the norm from 2007. This was apparent in Operation INTIZAAR SMAREY (30 October–1 November 2007) in Arghandab district. The death of a prominent local pro-ISAF leader on 12 October prompted the ASIC to go on heightened alert status. Task Force 3-07 (based on the 3ème Battalion, Royal 22e Regiment BG), deployed its Coyote LAVs into Arghandab, while the ASIC monitored its indicators for signs of insurgent activity. The key source was the Kandahar PRT, which reported a mass exodus of civilians from a district village because the

Taliban had moved in. This was substantiated by large numbers of "panicky" cell phone calls to people in Kandahar City, warning them to get out—the Taliban were coming. Likewise, local nongovernmental organizations reported to their head offices in Kabul that "the enemy was at the gates."[138] These indications and warning reports could not be ignored even if their exact meaning was uncertain. Elements of the task force, along with ANA troops and enablers, moved into two villages, where they encountered a substantial Taliban force. During the subsequent battle, Sperwer and Predator UAVs identified groups of enemy fighters, which became targets for air strikes, and then reported on their withdrawal from the area. A human source also warned the task force about emplaced IEDS, which were located and removed.[139]

In this operation, intelligence contributed to another tactical victory. It started with early warning and was sustained with continuous surveillance of and targeting information for the battle space. It also illustrated the ability of the Canadian theatre intelligence structure to integrate information from both human and technical sources and to disseminate it in a timely fashion to effectively support task force operations.

This pattern continued in 2008. During the defence of Strongpoint Mushan in Panjawayi District in June 2008 and during Operation TIMUS PREEM in Zharey District in August 2008, ISTAR assets, including Sperwer and Predator UAVs, maintained almost uninterrupted surveillance of the battle space. They observed and reported on enemy locations and movements, allowing artillery and air strikes to eliminate those forces and fighting positions.[140]

From January 2008 through December 2010, CAF units conducted 150 ILOs. ISAF news releases stated explicitly that 127 were guided by intelligence; 23 more were described as "targeted" operations, indicating that intelligence directed them to a specific location or person. One hundred thirty-eight operations (92%) led to the capture of known or suspected insurgents, and in 89 cases (59%) at least one of those captured was an HVT. For example, between late May and the end of June 2010, ILOs led to the capture or killing of Taliban district chiefs for the Dand, Maywand, Panjawayi, and Zharey districts. Twenty-five percent of these operations led to the seizure of IED materials or weapons; some were major arms caches. Some 54 ILOs (36%) were guided by intelligence that indicated or confirmed (in a few cases) insurgent activity at a specific location. Sixty-three operations (42%) were launched with data about a specific person, usually an HVT. Overall results seemed to improve over time due to better collection and analysis, a cumulative snowballing effect as successes built on each other, or both. They degraded Taliban activities, though only temporarily in some areas.[141]

The intelligence sources were identified in several cases. First, in June 2010 a tip from a Kandahar resident led to the capture of two foreign fighters from Pakistan. Second, a report in September 2010 stated that a Taliban informer provided information leading to a raid that netted the deputy shadow governor of Zharey. Thirty other ILOs (July–December 2010) were guided by HUMINT, including tips from unidentified sources. Two dozen operations during that period were HUMINT-assisted. In those cases, information from local residents after the operation confirmed the identity of captured suspects. Only two reports stated specifically that operations relied on "all-source" intelligence. Most simply referred to "intelligence reports" or were described as "targeted" DA operations.[142] The latter, including those directed at HVTs, were probably conducted by Canadian SOF, with intelligence support from their SOIC. According to Tony Balacevicus and Bernd Horn, in 2007–8, using all-source intelligence, the Canadian SOF task force removed "an entire generation of Taliban leadership" from their AOR.[143]

This data, even if incomplete, suggests growing effectiveness of CAF intelligence over time and the increasing value of HUMINT. That in turn flowed from local population's confidence that the ISAF and Afghan forces could protect them from Taliban retaliation.[144] Kandahar's police chief confirmed this in December 2008 when he said that "more and more, citizens are calling to warn the police of suspicious activities and behavior."[145] They could report suspicious activity anonymously using a telephone tip hotline.

Solving the IED threat received high priority, and intelligence was central to that. This required a knowledge-based, all-source, and even whole of government approach entailing both defensive and offensive measures.[146] On the defensive side, to defeat the device, the CAF exploited its technological advantages. It synchronized ISTAR assets with operations, such as using SIGINT and surveillance by the Heron UAV to guide task force teams to locate IEDs.[147] But HUMINT also played a significant role. Lt.-Col. Dana Woodworth, commander of the Kandahar PRT, said in December 2008 that 70–90 percent of the IEDs being found in Kandahar were being turned in to the coalition forces by the locals. Echoing the Kandahar police chief's comments, he added that "Kandaharis are showing their confidence in their police and coalition forces by reporting possible IEDs."[148]

Likewise, the CAF's ATN campaign was an all-source effort. HUMINT and SIGINT collection, fusion, and analysis "guided the task force's anti-network operations that focused on finding and neutralizing the bombmakers, the IED team leaders, and their financiers."[149] Many intelligence-led ATN operations removed key Taliban figures and dramatically reduced the number of successful IED attacks between 2008 and 2010. By the end of 2008, more than 60 percent of IEDs in Kandahar province were being found and disarmed before detonation. In 2008–9 only 22 percent of IEDs caused casualties. By 2010 that figure had been reduced to 16 percent.[150] Since the IED was the Taliban's main kinetic weapon, this represented a significant operational success.

But the Taliban responded by increasing the number of IEDs it planted: 1,300–1,500 per month from August 2010 to January 2011.[151] The Canadians and

ISAF struggled to stay ahead of them. The Taliban had "a deep bench" of talent and could replace losses almost as fast as the CAF and ISAF inflicted them.[152]

Dr. Lee Windsor's study of Canadian infantry in Afghanistan noted that "the battle against Taliban IED cells and the effort to protect Canada's Task Force Kandahar consumed ever increasing resources and effort as the campaign went on."[153] While many of those he interviewed felt that the technical and tactical C-IED solutions had been shown to be effective by 2008–9, a few of them, along with a key adviser to the commander of ISAF during the American surge into Kandahar, believed that "the counter-IED struggle constituted a successful Taliban diversion that drew Canadian units and resources away from their core mission of protecting the people of Kandahar."[154] That said, Windsor concluded that freedom of movement on Kandahar's major roads was considered essential for all ISAF units in RC-South, so the Canadians could not simply ignore the problem.[155] In any case, the Taliban's IED offensive created more than a diversion. It was a strategic attrition weapon that raised the human costs of the CAF campaign and had some negative impact on public opinion in the Canadian home front.[156] In effect, each deadly IED was an information operation too.

What ISAF did in response was to exploit its tactical intelligence advantage to support its own information operations. It regularly announced through its news releases that it was acting on intelligence to capture or kill insurgents. For example, news releases from May and June 2010 stated that two Taliban leaders whom ISAF had killed had been tracked for days or weeks.[157] ISAF was in effect telling the Taliban and the Afghan population just how good its intelligence was, that it was able to monitor and follow the insurgents with impunity. This information operation clearly was meant to intimidate the Taliban and to sow doubt and mistrust. Without saying so explicitly, the operation implied that the population was informing on the Taliban, that their communications were compromised, and that their ranks had been penetrated by double agents. Protecting sensitive sources and methods is gospel in intelligence, since releasing that information puts them at risk. We do not know how that decision to go public was reached in these instances. The ISAF J2 and information operations staffs must have concluded that the information operations benefits outweighed the risks. The fact that the 2010 news releases have since been deleted suggests that the issue remained controversial. More important, the available sources do not tell us if those messages had the desired effect on the Taliban.

ASSESSING THE CANADIAN INTELLIGENCE EFFORT IN AFGHANISTAN

The foregoing leaves us with two questions. First, how did the Canadian intelligence effort in Afghanistan adapt to the changing operational environment and missions? Second, did it provide the intelligence support that the CAF needed to achieve its goals?

First, intelligence support to CAF operations changed significantly over the course of Canada's decade in Afghanistan. Out of necessity CAF intelligence expanded in size to meet the demands on it. By mid-decade it was shifting its mental operational focus from conventional war and peacekeeping to counterinsurgency. CAF intelligence was working with OGDs and agencies and with allies in ways and on a scale that had not been done before and created new structures: the ASIC to manage all-source intelligence fusion and analysis and the ISTAR CC to direct and access collection systems, Canadian and allied, tactical in-theatre, and strategic. CAF intelligence also deployed and exploited new and improved collection systems: the Sperwer and then the Heron and other UAVs.

These were remarkable changes, achieved in a relatively short time span. As such, they were not without challenges. Godefroy reminds us that the J2 forward had to manage "a web of intelligence capacity" that included assets within his control (his own staff), those under command of the commander of Task Force Kandahar but subject to the J2's direction (the ASIC), and those under the command of others, accountable to the task force commander, part of the higher chain of command, or serving under the authority of organizations "totally outside" of the commander's influence, such as the CDI, the CSE, and the CSIS.[158] The in-theatre J2 "could coordinate, and conduct limited reallocation of resources, but no more—they generally had to do the best they could to satisfy all competing priorities with the resources at hand, while under constant pressure to respond to critiques or challenges to their role by outsiders who either sought to blame intelligence support deficiencies for their own failings, or ... [to] take credit for the work of the intelligence enterprise."[159] As if this were not enough, the J2 forward also wore two accountability hats: to the task force commander, "for the outputs of the theatre intelligence architecture (assessment and single-source/all-source intelligence production, analytical focus, and force management of allocated resources);" and to the CDI, for meeting intelligence policy-related obligations, for governance, and for managing partnerships with OGDs and coalition partners.[160]

Intelligence challenges were not confined to the J2 level. Windsor's postdeployment interviews with infantry officers and NCOs revealed that there was "room for improvement when it came to enabling infantry units to reap the full benefits of unmanned aerial vehicles (UAVs) and other newly acquired surveillance gear. Their frustration was reflected in ALLC [Army Lessons Learned Centre] reports, which identified the need for more knowledge of ... ISTAR technological capabilities and limits—know what to ask for and how to make the most efficient use of the information that comes from it."[161]

The second change was in the culture within the CAF itself, manifested in the increasing trend toward ILOs. Major Ohlke emphasised the huge difference in army attitudes toward intelligence from the time of the Oka Crisis. Commanders became better at defining what they needed to know and getting those requests back to the intelligence producers.[162] Lt.-Gen. Gauthier was equally convinced that there had been a sea change. "The operational culture and the institutional culture vis-à-vis intelligence in 2009 was night and day ... from what it had been in 2002, let alone in the '90s."[163]

As more commanders bought into the concept of ILOs, intelligence became a more central part of the operational planning and decision cycles. One indicator of this was that despite constant "evolution and improvement" in the ability of higher organizations to produce intelligence, company-level Canadian troops who were either hunting Taliban or interacting with local civilians "always wanted more."[164] By 2009–20 there were enough US and CAF intelligence and ISTAR assets to push them down to companies and platoons "in the form of Intelligence Support Teams." Officers and NCOs from the last Canadian rotations in Kandahar "reported a higher level of satisfaction with the intelligence gathering."[165]

It is important to grasp how significant this change of mindset was. Most commanders at this time still had "a limited, and guardedly sceptical [sic], understanding of what intelligence capabilities could do for them. Many of the capabilities that were accessible to them in theatre had never been seen before; they often had not trained with the use of them, and sometimes even their intelligence staffs were seeing them for the first time. The necessary experience that was required before these capabilities were used to best effect created a learning curve for commanders and intelligence staffs."[166]

But this still begs the question as to whether these changes made intelligence support more effective. The evidence suggests that they did, especially for kinetic operations. It never was perfect, but it improved over time. One constant was the challenge of accuracy and timeliness. Even when the intelligence was correct, it rarely was complete. In fact, Godefroy says, sometimes it raised more questions than it answered, introducing ambiguity and uncertainty that made many commanders uncomfortable.[167] And the Taliban's mobility made timeliness even more important and much harder to achieve. So, there was always the risk of being surprised.

Operation MEDUSA showed that even having good multisystem collection platforms could not ensure that commanders would have all the information they needed, in that case the exact location of enemy forces. Terrain and cover can offset technical advantages, and changes in operational planning can play havoc with intelligence assessments. That in turn can cause tactical setbacks. Nevertheless, CAF and coalition intelligence did contribute to MEDUSA's overall operational success. From that point on, multisource intelligence guided operations. No BG, SOF, CIMIC, or PRT operation ever went into an AOR completely blind or uninformed. In fact, quite the opposite. Infantry leaders from every rotation commented "on the problem of sheer information overload."[168]

In the years that followed, the link between human security and HUMINT was proven beyond all doubt; the one almost always led to the other. Constant troop presence created protection, generating trust that yielded information. Windsor's interviewees reflected usefully about the infantry role in gathering information "and acting as sensors for the Task Force. . . . [T]he Kandahar campaign saw the Infantry sense function elevated to a new level of complexity." They developed new tactics and procedures to "assist with identifying suspects, establishing patterns of routine, and observing hostile network behaviors." Over time, "a more systematic process was developed for maintaining . . . SA about the ground, the enemy, friendly units from dozens of nations, Afghan partners and especially the local Kandaharis they were assigned to protect." Experience showed that "tracking the comings and goings of people requires patient observation skills," which did not emerge naturally and had to be "encouraged and monitored" among the younger soldiers.[169]

But Task Force Kandahar was too small, spread too thin, and too frequently on the move to provide the constant presence that the task required, so the flow of information from observation of and contact with the local population was intermittent. Between 2006 and 2009, some infantry companies created their own ad hoc intelligence cells to keep track of the people in their AOR. These yielded mixed results. The "small infantry sub-units felt they were not well enough connected or equipped to be sensitive to complex cultural and tribal dynamics in Kandahar."[170]

In any case, to ensure reliability, HUMINT had to be cross-checked against other sources. Indeed, the best results were achieved when all collection systems exploited their sources in tandem and their products were integrated and fused into a comprehensive picture of the AOR and the target. This was apparent in the large number of successful ILOs in the 2008–10 period, particularly against Taliban HVTs. ISAF J2 Canadian brigadier-general Jim Ferron praised these DA actions, claiming in 2007 that NATO was "on top of our game right now . . . taking the conflict to the insurgents."[171] It was equally apparent in the C-IED fight. Exploiting all-source fusion that was serving the campaign as a whole dramatically reduced the number of IED strikes and their success/casualty-infliction rate. Even allowing for the limited sources available, the evidence presented here strongly suggests that intelligence provided effective support to tactical kinetic operations.

But the same cannot be said for strategic assessment and cultural intelligence: white SA. In 2009, ISAF J2 US Army major general Michael Flynn wrote a blistering critique of American intelligence in Afghanistan. Given its dependence on the US intelligence community, ISAF intelligence was likewise implicated. He faulted US intelligence for its failure to provide adequate white SA. "Eight years into the war in Afghanistan the U.S. intelligence community is only marginally relevant to the overall strategy."[172] In fact, he felt it was so focused on the insurgent group (i.e., the kinetic dimension) that it could not answer "fundamental questions about the environment in which the U.S. and allied forces operate and the people they seek to persuade." He went further, saying that American intelligence was, "ignorant of local economics and landowners, hazy about who the powerbrokers are and how they might be influenced, incurious about the correlations between various development projects and the levels of cooperation among villagers, and disengaged from people in the best position to find answers—whether aid workers or Afghan soldiers."[173]

In his informed opinion, US intelligence had failed to do what Gavriel argued was absolutely essential: gain an understanding of the cultural geography of the Afghan people. Flynn conceded that focusing on insurgent activities was worthwhile but argued that giving it priority "baits the intelligence shops into reacting to enemy tactics at the expense of finding ways to strike at the very heart of the insurgency." This left the initiative in the hands of the insurgents and diverted attention from the important essential work of asking and answering the questions that would foster cooperation from local populations, who are better placed to identify the insurgents. Flynn likened the war to a violent election campaign, in which "all counter-insurgency is local." Therefore, he argued, "tactical Intel Equals Strategic Intel."[174] After all, the insurgency was for both sides a struggle for legitimacy, which is a state of mind.

The same evidence that shows effective intelligence support for the CAF's tactical kinetic operations also suggests that such support exhibited some of the flaws that Flynn had identified. As part of its overall counterinsurgency campaign the CAF devoted some resources, time, and intelligence capital to the C-IED fight and to finding, capturing, or killing HVTs, that is, reactively focusing on the insurgents rather than proactively dismantling the political-social insurgency itself. It is understandable why they did so. There could be no stability without security, no building without clearing and holding. So, tactical attrition of the insurgents was both necessary and unavoidable. Moreover, political imperatives in Canada put a premium on minimizing casualties, making force protection a priority, hence a visible focus on the C-IED effort.

One former CAF intelligence officer conceded that while the Canadian intelligence structure in Afghanistan was very effective in unpacking the insurgents' networks, the weak link was in understanding the white SA: local demographics, the key players, the influential people, the infrastructure, the nuances of language, and customs.[175] Gavriel might say "I told you so," but he also would say even that information was insufficient, since it lacked the depth of understanding that he feels is needed to counter an insurgency effectively in such a foreign culture. The CAF's white SA intelligence on Kandahar had come a long way since Dr. Calder's 2003 claim that "we don't know anything about this country." But that weak link was never fully overcome. In fact, Canada did not produce a district situational assessment for Kandahar until 2009. And CAF intelligence did not produce it. Instead, an independent research team under contract to the Department of Foreign Affairs and International Trade prepared it.[176] Up to that time, CAF units had to develop their own white SA when they deployed into their AORs by patrolling and holding *shūrās* with local leaders. But until troops moved into villages on a permanent basis, the shortage of troops and their inability to provide continuity in place hampered the local learning process.[177]

But that is not to say the CAF overlooked the white SA issue. Godefroy notes that in 2009 his staff included a two-person white SA analytical cell, staffed by Canadian government civilian analysts. In addition to producing "significant levels of analytical output," they "routinely participated in Key Leader Engagements with senior Afghan military and civilian officials, gathering additional information from the latter meetings." He goes on to say that "like all aspects of the JTF-A intelligence architecture, their work was not always well-used or visible to commanders and operators." This reinforced the impression that "we did not know enough about this aspect to the intelligence problem, and the perception . . . that this was due to intelligence community disdain/neglect/disinterest in this issue." The ASIC also "actively pursued" white SA analysis, and the J2 analysts worked closely and extensively with their geographically focused all-source analyst counterparts in the ASIC.[178] So, even if Flynn's overall assessment of US and ISAF efforts was correct, it cannot be said that the Canadians were ignoring the problem entirely.

Moreover, the high success rate of direct-action ILOs from 2008 on, based on an increased flow of HUMINT, combined with good technical intelligence would not have been possible without some good white SA. This suggests that it was improving in the latter stages of the CAF campaign. While this was not the only factor shaping this complex campaign, the long lead time required to develop cultural intelligence about the Canadian AOR may explain in part the CAF's inability to contain or fully degrade the Taliban insurgency in Kandahar.

To summarize, CAF intelligence effectively managed the changes in intelligence practices required by the war. It relied on a mixture of adapting and innovating structures, technologies, and practices. It grew in size, shifted its focus, and increased collaboration, deepening established relationships with OGDs and allies and developing new ones. It also both encouraged and benefited from a sea change in attitudes of commanders in the field toward the utility and necessity of exploiting intelligence to support their operations.

This in turn allowed CAF intelligence, assisted by its own and allied enablers and intelligence sharing, to produce often timely and mostly accurate—if not always complete—intelligence that could be exploited effectively in the tactical battle for control in Kandahar province. It was particularly effective against Taliban leadership cadres and their networks. This greatly reduced the number of IED attacks and limited the number of CAF casualties. But the focus on insurgent attrition, the prolonged, intermittent development of cultural intelligence, and (until 2009) the insufficient CAF and coalition resources to provide continuous protection of the population, along with the Taliban's untouchable sanctuary in Pakistan and the weaknesses of the Afghan government, meant that the CAF and its allies could not translate victories in the tactical battle for control into a victory in the strategic battle for legitimacy in Kandahar.

NOTES

1. David P. Auerswald and Stephen M. Saideman, *NATO in Afghanistan: Fighting Together, Fighting Alone* (Princeton, NJ: Princeton University Press, 2014), 32–33.
2. John Robert Ferris and James F. Keeley, "The Afghanistan Debate Warms Up," in *Canada in Kandahar*, Calgary Papers in Military and Strategic Studies 1 (Calgary, Alberta: Centre for Military and Strategic Studies, University of Calgary, 2007), i–ii; Lee Windsor, David A. Charters, and J. Brent Wilson, *Kandahar Tour: The Turning Point in Canada's Afghan Mission* (Mississauga, Ontario: Wiley, 2008), 34–36; and Janice Gross Stein and J. Eugene Lang, *The Unexpected War: Canada in Kandahar* (Toronto: Viking, 2007), 178–82.
3. On this conception of insurgency, see David A. Charters, *The British Army and Jewish Insurgency in Palestine, 1945–47* (Houndmills, Basingstoke, UK: Macmillan, in association with King's College, London, 1989), 2–3.
4. Thomas J. Barfield, "Weapons of the Not So Weak in Afghanistan: Pashtun Agrarian Structure and Tribal Organization," in *Culture, Conflict, and Counterinsurgency*, ed. Thomas H. Johnson and Barry Scott Zellen (Stanford, CA: Stanford University Press, 2014), 96–99, 108–9, 114–18; and Thomas H. Johnson, "Religious Figures, Insurgency, and Jihad in Southern Afghanistan," in *Culture, Conflict, and Counterinsurgency*, 120–24, 126, 128–30, 139–41.
5. Nancy Teeple, *Canada in Afghanistan: 2001–2010; A Military Chronology*, contract report (Ottawa: Defence Research and Development Canada, Centre for Operational Research and Analysis, December 2010), 26–27; and Windsor, Charters, and Wilson, *Kandahar Tour*, ix.
6. Teeple, *Canada in Afghanistan*, 26, 28.
7. Teeple, 62; Stephen M. Saideman, *Adapting in the Dust: Lessons Learned from Canada's War in Afghanistan* (Toronto: University of Toronto Press, 2016), 22, table 2.2, 47, 90; and National Defence, "Joint Task Force Afghanistan," Government of Canada, 20 February 2013, https://www.canada.ca/en/department-national-defence/services/operations/military-operations/recently-completed/operation-athena/joint-task-force-afghanistan.html.

8. Windsor, Charters, and Wilson, *Kandahar Tour*, ix, xviii–xix, 20, 38–39, 41–42, 45–46; and Peter Pigott, *Canada in Afghanistan: The War So Far* (Toronto: Dundurn Group, 2007), 135–57.
9. On the National Solidarity Program, see Stein and Lang, *Unexpected War*, 268–69. For critiques of the ISAF PRT efforts, see Sean M. Maloney, *Fighting for Afghanistan: A Rogue Historian at War* (Annapolis, MD: Naval Institute Press, 2011), 89, 132–41; Saideman, *Adapting in the Dust*, 18; and Windsor, Charters, and Wilson, *Kandahar Tour*, 22–23, 41.
10. United States, Department of the Army and US Marine Corps, *The U.S. Army/Marine Corps Counterinsurgency Field Manual: U.S. Army Field Manual No. 3-24; Marine Corps Warfighting Publication No. 3-33.5* (Chicago: University of Chicago Press, 2007), chap. 5, para. 51–80; Joseph J. Collins, *Understanding War in Afghanistan* (Washington, DC: National Defense University Press, 2011), 77; Lawrence E. Cline, "COINdinistas versus Whack-a-Mole: The Debate on Counterinsurgency Approaches," in *The Future of Counterinsurgency: Contemporary Debates in Internal Security Strategy*, ed. Lawrence E. Cline and Paul Shemella (Santa Barbara, CA: Praeger, 2015), 146; Auerswald and Saideman, *NATO in Afghanistan*, 91–92, 102–3; and Lee Windsor, *The Royal Canadian Infantry Corps in Afghanistan*, Dispatches 17.1 (Kingston, Ontario: DND, Army Lessons Learned Centre, 2013), 5–9.
11. Quoted in Windsor, Charters, and Wilson, *Kandahar Tour*, 18.
12. Windsor, Charters, and Wilson, 41–42, 73–74, 99–101, 157–58, 189.
13. Windsor, *Royal Canadian Infantry Corps*, 2.
14. Paul Clarke, "Strategic Communication and COIN Ops in the Emerging Security Environment," in *Future of Counterinsurgency*, 71–73, 77–78; Johnson, "Religious Figures," 140–41; Michael R. Fenzel, "The Maneuver Company in Afghanistan: Establishing Counterinsurgency Priorities at the District Level," in *Culture, Conflict, and Counterinsurgency*, 191–94; Windsor, Charters, and Wilson, *Kandahar Tour*, 72–73, 108; Pigott, *Canada in Afghanistan*, 160–61; and Maloney, *Fighting for Afghanistan*, 24, 40–44, 93–94, 131, 150–53.
15. Alexei J. D. Gavriel, "Incorporating Cultural Intelligence into Joint Intelligence: Cultural Intelligence and Ethnographic Intelligence Theory," in *Culture, Conflict, and Counterinsurgency*, 3–4.
16. Gavriel, 19, 21–22, 40, 41.
17. Quoted in Tony Balasevicius and Bernd Horn, "Intelligence and Its Application to Irregular Warfare," in *The Difficult War: Perspectives on Insurgency and Special Operations Forces*, ed. Emily Spencer (Kingston, Ontario: Canadian Defence Academy Press; Toronto: Dundurn, 2009), 67.
18. Gavriel, "Incorporating Cultural Intelligence," 22.
19. Gavriel, 22–23.
20. Gavriel, 23.
21. Gavriel, 21.
22. Gavriel, 25–29.
23. *U.S. Army Field Manual 3-24*, chap. 3, para. 13, 20–54, 130–36.
24. Gavriel, "Incorporating Cultural Intelligence," 23.
25. Sir Julian Paget, *Counter-Insurgency Campaigning* (London: Faber, 1967), 166.
26. James Godefroy, comments on draft chapter, 23 April 2021.
27. Maj.-Gen. David Fraser and Brian Hanington, *Operation Medusa: The Furious Battle That Saved Afghanistan from the Taliban* (Toronto: McClelland & Stewart,

2018); Maloney, *Fighting for Afghanistan*; and Sean M. Maloney, *War in Afghanistan: Eight Battles in the South* (Ottawa: Magic Light, 2012).
28. Murray Brewster, "Canada's Special Forces Kept Too Many Secrets about Afghan Missions, Says Report," CBC News, 6 September 2018, https://www.cbc.ca/news/politics/special-forces-afghanistan-report-1.4812154.
29. Especially ISAF news releases dated 12 October 2008, 22 December 2008, 22 June 2010, 31 May 2010, 4 June 2010, and 29 June 2010. Since my initial research on this topic the ISAF news releases that were posted at https://www.nato.int/isaf/article/isaf-releases/ are no longer available, as that site has been deactivated.
30. Bernd Horn, *No Ordinary Men: Special Operations Forces Missions in Afghanistan* (Toronto: Dundurn, 2016), Kindle.
31. Maj. Gordon Ohlke, interview with author, June 13, 2019.
32. Matthew Fisher, "IEDs Claimed the Most Canadian Casualties," *Fredericton (NB) Daily Gleaner*, 8 July 2011; and quote from Lt.-Col. R. H. Matheson, *Lesson Synopsis Report (LSR) 09-011 Defensive C-IED TTP Review* (Kingston, Ontario: Army Lessons Learned Centre; Land Force Doctrine and Training System, 17 August 2009), 3.
33. Lt.-Col. R. H. Matheson, *Lesson Synopsis Report (LSR) 09-012 Offensive C-IED TTP Review* (Kingston, Ontario: Army Lessons Learned Centre, Land Force Doctrine and Training System, 14 October 2009), 1–2.
34. Godefroy, comments.
35. Godefroy.
36. Godefroy.
37. Godefroy.
38. Godefroy.
39. Godefroy.
40. Horn, *No Ordinary Men*, chap. 2.
41. Horn, chap. 3.
42. Horn, chap. 5.
43. *Canadian Forces Joint Doctrine Note (2011/01) The All-Source Intelligence Centre*, 6–8, annex B. The staffing figure was provided by a CAF officer. The forensic lab was added in 2009 as the result of a CDI-led project. Godefroy, comments.
44. Maloney, *Fighting for Afghanistan*, 13–15, 93, 109; Lt.-Col. Ian Hope, "Trust: A Critical Element of Task Force Orion," in *Leveraging Trust: A Force Multiplier for Today*, ed. Lt.-Col. Jeffrey M. Stouffer and Craig Leslie Mantle (Kingston, Ontario: Canadian Defence Academy Press, 2008), 32–33; and Ian Hope, *Dancing with the Dushman: Command Imperatives for the Counter-Insurgency Fight in Afghanistan* (Kingston, Ontario: Canadian Defence Academy Press, 2008), 55–56.
45. Hope, *Dancing with the Dushman*, 55.
46. Hope, 82.
47. According to Collins, *Understanding War in Afghanistan*, 77–78, some ISR and SOF units were reassigned, but others remained in Afghanistan. From 2005 on, however, the deteriorating situation in Iraq prevented US reinforcement of the Afghanistan War.
48. Hope, *Dancing with the Dushman*, 82; and Maloney, *Fighting for Afghanistan*, 87.
49. Hope, *Dancing with the Dushman*, 83.
50. Hope, 55.

51. Hope, 43.
52. Hope, 85–86.
53. Maloney, *Fighting for Afghanistan*, 104–6.
54. Fraser and Hanington, *Operation Medusa*, 39.
55. Fraser and Hanington, 38–39.
56. Fraser and Hanington, 40.
57. See Brig.-Gen. David Fraser to Chief Constable (Vancouver Police) J. H. Graham, 16 September 2006, published in Sandy Garossino, "Here's What Harjit Sajjan Really Did with OPERATION MEDUSA," Canada's National Observer, 29 April 2017, https://www.nationalobserver.com/2017/04/29/analysis/heres-what-harjit-sajjan-really-did-operation-medusa.
58. All three quotes from Godefroy, comments.
59. See NATO Standardization Office, *AINTP-1(A) Intelligence Doctrine* (NATO, January 1995), chap. 2, Lt.-Col. Greg Jensen, private papers.
60. Godefroy, comments.
61. Fraser and Hanington, *Operation Medusa*, 41–42.
62. Godefroy, telephone interview with author, 20 April 2021, plus follow-up notes, 23 April 2021.
63. Godefroy.
64. Godefroy; and Godefroy, comments.
65. Godefroy, revised comments on draft chapter, 23 April 2021.
66. Godefroy.
67. Godefroy.
68. Capt. Kyle Welsh, "Task Force Erebus: Providing Essential Support to Canada's Mission in Afghanistan," *Canadian Air Force Journal* 3, no. 2 (Spring 2010): 19–20, 22, 23; Maj. L. H. Rémillard, "The 'All-Source' Way of Doing Business: The Evolution of Intelligence in Modern Military Operations," *Canadian Military Journal* 8, no. 3 (Autumn 2007): 23; and Sgt. Marcus Sterzer, Cpl. Patrick McDuff, and Cpl. Jacek Flasz, "Note to File—The Challenge of Centralized Control Faced by the Intelligence Function in Afghanistan," *Canadian Army Journal* 11, no. 2 (Summer 2008): 97, 100.
69. Comment from a retired intelligence officer.
70. Godefroy, comments on draft chapter; and "CF HUMINT Experts Praised by Allied Forces," *Maple Leaf* 14, no. 3 (19 January 2011): 6.
71. Godefroy, comments; and Capt. (N) Andrea Siew, interview with author, 7 November 2019. Fraser and Hanington make no mention of this.
72. Former CSE chief John Adams, interview with author, 6 November 2019.
73. Siew, interview.
74. Interview with a former DND official who requested anonymity, 4 November 2019. See also chapter 3.
75. *Defence Talk*, 30 August 2010, www.defencetalk.com; *Defence Update*, 13 July 2010, www.defence-update.net; "Return of Tornado Squadron to Germany from Service in Afghanistan," press release, German Federal Ministry of Defence, 30 November 2010, www.bmvg.de; Tech. Sgt. Oshawn Jefferson, "'Crows' Keep Watch over Afghan Skies," US Air Forces Central, 5 March 2010, https://www.afcent.af.mil/Test-Page/Article/223912/crows-keep-watch-over-afghan-skies/; and Craig Hoyle, "RAF Heralds Emergence of 'Combat ISTAR' over Afghanistan," FlightGlobal,

22 March 2010, https://www.flightglobal.com/raf-heralds-emergence-of-combat-istar-over-afghanistan/92529.article.
76. Windsor, Charters, and Wilson, *Kandahar Tour*, 69. See also "2 RCR Battle Group Org Chart," *Pro Patria: Regimental Journal of the Royal Canadian Regiment*, no. 89 (2008): 25.
77. Comments on draft chapter.
78. Col. USAF (ret.) Robert G. Stiegel, "The Origin and Evolution of the Joint Analysis Center at RAF Molesworth," *Studies in Intelligence*, Extracts, 62, no. 1 (March 2018): 29, 35–36.
79. Ohlke, interview with author. He served as J2 Plans at RC-South headquarters and then as officer commanding the ASIC Forward, operating in support of the PRT.
80. David A. Charters, "Canadian Military Intelligence in Afghanistan," *International Journal of Intelligence and CounterIntelligence* 25, no. 3 (2012): 483.
81. *U.S. Army Field Manual 3-24*, 1–25.
82. Hope, *Dancing with the Dushman*, 53; and Maloney, *Fighting for Afghanistan*, 32–33, 35, 133–34.
83. Horn, *No Ordinary Men*, chap. 2.
84. Horn, chaps. 2–3.
85. Horn, chap. 4.
86. Horn, chap. 5.
87. Hope, *Dancing with the Dushman*, 55.
88. Hope, 55–56.
89. Hope, 56.
90. Fraser and Hanington, *Operation Medusa*, 40–41.
91. Maloney, *Fighting for Afghanistan*, 108.
92. Fraser and Hanington, *Operation Medusa*, 42.
93. Fraser and Hanington, 42, 44, 46.
94. Bernd Horn, *No Lack of Courage: Operation Medusa, Afghanistan* (Toronto: Dundurn, 2010), chap. 2.
95. Hope, *Dancing with the Dushman*, 116.
96. Maloney, *Fighting for Afghanistan*, 87; and Hope, *Dancing with the Dushman*, 80.
97. Hope, *Dancing with the Dushman*, 80–81.
98. Hope, 86, 93–105; and Maloney, *Fighting for Afghanistan*, 94.
99. Hope, *Dancing with the Dushman*, 107.
100. Hope, 107–8.
101. Godefroy, comments.
102. Maloney, *Fighting for Afghanistan*, 108.
103. Maloney, 108.
104. Maloney, 109.
105. Maloney, 147.
106. Hope, *Dancing with the Dushman*, 109–11.
107. Both quotes from Maloney, *Fighting for Afghanistan*, 148.
108. Maloney, 148; Hope, *Dancing with the Dushman*, 117; and Fraser and Hanington, *Operation Medusa*, 68.
109. This is the subtitle of the Fraser and Hanington book. See also Windsor, Charters, and Wilson, *Kandahar Tour*, 55; Stein and Lang, *Unexpected War*, 220; and Horn, *No Lack of Courage*, chap. 8.

110. Horn, *No Lack of Courage*, chap. 4; Fraser and Hanington, *Operation Medusa*, 114.
111. Fraser and Hanington, *Operation Medusa*, 68.
112. Fraser and Hanington, 114.
113. Fraser and Hanington, 112–13, 125, 128; and Horn, *No Lack of Courage*, chap. 6.
114. Fraser and Hanington, *Operation Medusa*, 134–35, 137–38, 140–41, 143.
115. Horn, *No Lack of Courage*, chap. 6.
116. Horn, chap. 3.
117. Fraser and Hanington, *Operation Medusa*, 115.
118. Fraser and Hanington, 117. Unfortunately, the Nimrod crashed on the first day of the operation.
119. Fraser and Hanington, 115.
120. Fraser and Hanington, 115.
121. Fraser and Hanington, 116.
122. Fraser and Hanington, 116–17.
123. Fraser and Hanington, 117.
124. Horn, *No Lack of Courage*, chap. 5; and Murray Brewster, *The Savage War: The Untold Battles of Afghanistan* (Mississauga, Ontario: Wiley, 2011), 105.
125. Brewster, *Savage War*, 106–8.
126. Horn, *No Lack of Courage*, chap. 6.
127. Horn, chap. 6.
128. Horn, chap. 6.
129. Horn, chap. 6.
130. Horn, chap. 6.
131. Horn, chap. 9. See also Stephen M. Saideman, "Canadian Forces in Afghanistan: Minority Government and Generational Change While under Fire," in *Military Adaptation in Afghanistan*, ed. Theo Farrell, Frans P. B. Osinga, and James A. Russell (Stanford, CA: Stanford University Press, 2013), 222, 223–24, 227–28, 230, 233–34.
132. "Nowhere to Hide for Taliban Commanders," ISAF, news release no. 2006-360, 13 December 2006; "Precision Air Strike against Insurgent Command Post," ISAF, news release no. 2006-374, 19 December 2006; and "Lethal Air Power Kills Insurgent Leadership," ISAF, news release no. 2006-375, 19 December 2006.
133. Windsor, Charters, and Wilson, *Kandahar Tour*, 96–98.
134. Windsor, Charters, and Wilson, 105, 107–8.
135. Windsor, Charters, and Wilson, 110, 119–21, 129, 159–74, 180–86.
136. Windsor, Charters, and Wilson, 186; and Maloney, *War in Afghanistan*, 128, 130–38.
137. Windsor, Charters, and Wilson, *Kandahar Tour*, 207–13.
138. Maloney, *War in Afghanistan*, 144–46.
139. Maloney, 147–56.
140. Maloney, 224–31, 248–58.
141. The author accessed the ISAF news releases on 3 March and 18–20 May 2011.
142. Charters, "Canadian Military Intelligence," 484–85.
143. Balasevicius and Horn, "Intelligence and Its Application," 64. They do not provide a source for this claim.
144. Windsor, Charters, and Wilson, *Kandahar Tour*, 107–8.
145. "IEDs, Other Munitions Destroyed in Kandahar," ISAF, news release no. 2008-732, 22 December 2008.

146. Matheson, "LSR 09-012," 1, 2; and Maj. C. R. Henderson, "The Need for a 'Whole of Government' Approach to Counter-IED Operations" (unpublished course paper, Master of Defence Studies, JCSP 36, North York, Ontario, Canadian Forces College, n.d.).
147. Colin Freeze, "Canada's Little-Known Spy Agency Comes Out into the Open," *Globe and Mail*, 22 December 2010, https://www.theglobeandmail.com/news/national/canadas-little-known-spy-agency-comes-out-into-the-open/article4260580/; "Counter-IED Starts at 10,000 Feet: HERON Unmanned Aerial Vehicle Contributes to Battle against Improvised Explosive Devices," video, 13 December 2010 (no longer available online).
148. ISAF, "IEDs, Other Munitions Destroyed."
149. Matheson, "LSR 09-012," 1–2; "Interview: Counter-IED Task Force Commander, Part 1, Transcript," *Canadian Army News*, Episode 359 (no longer available online). On the ATN concept, see United States, Department of Defense, "Joint Improvised Explosive Device Defeat Organization (JIEDDO)," https://cbrnecentral.com/profiles/name/joint-improvised-explosive-device-defeat-organization-jieddo/; and Lt. (N) Kevin McNamara, "Battlefield Forensics Helps Counter IEDs," *Maple Leaf* 14, no. 4 (26 January 2011).
150. ISAF, "IEDs, Other Munitions Destroyed"; US, DoD, *Joint IED Defeat Organization Annual Report Fiscal Year 2009*, https://apps.dtic.mil/sti/pdfs/ADA535373.pdf; and Cheryl Pellerin, "Effective Bomb Attacks Decline in Afghanistan," DVIDS (formerly Armed Forces Press Service), 2 March 2011, https://www.dvidshub.net/news/66351/effective-bomb-attacks-decline-afghanistan.
151. Pellerin, "Effective Bomb Attacks Decline."
152. Collins, *Understanding War in Afghanistan*, 77.
153. Windsor, *Royal Canadian Infantry Corps*, 17.
154. Windsor, 17.
155. Windsor, 17.
156. For contrasting perspectives on the Canadian public impact, see John Manley, "Canada's New Role in Afghanistan: Leading Rather Than Following Public Opinion," Policy Options, 1 December 2010, https://policyoptions.irpp.org/fr/magazines/the-year-in-review-2/canadas-new-role-in-afghanistan-leading-rather-than-following-public-opinion/; and Jean-Christophe Boucher, "Evaluating the 'Trenton Effect': Canadian Public Opinion and Military Casualties in Afghanistan (2006–2010)," *American Review of Canadian Studies* 40, no. 2 (2010): 237–58, https://doi.org/10.1080/02722011003734753.
157. ISAF news releases, 31 May, 4 June 2010.
158. Godefroy, comments on draft chapter.
159. Godefroy.
160. Godefroy.
161. Windsor, *Royal Canadian Infantry Corps*, 15.
162. Ohlke, interview with author.
163. Lt.-Gen. (ret.) Michel Gauthier, interview with author, 5 November 2019.
164. Gauthier; Windsor, *Royal Canadian Infantry Corps*, 15–16.
165. Windsor, *Royal Canadian Infantry Corps*, 16.
166. Godefroy, comments on draft chapter
167. Godefroy.

168. Windsor, *Royal Canadian Infantry Corps*, 15–16.
169. All quotes in paragraph from Windsor, 10–11.
170. Windsor, 15–16.
171. Matthew Fisher, "NATO 'on Top of Our Game' in Afghanistan, Intelligence Chief Says," CanWest News, *Ottawa Citizen*, 18 September 2007, https://www.proquest.com/docview/461047675/.
172. Michael T. Flynn, Matt Pottinger, and Paul Batchelor, *Fixing Intel: A Blueprint for Making Intelligence Relevant in Afghanistan*, Working Paper (Washington, DC: Center for a New American Security, 2010), 7.
173. Flynn, Pottinger, and Batchelor, 7.
174. Flynn, Pottinger, and Batchelor, 8, 11–12.
175. Private communication from a retired senior Canadian Forces MI officer, 11 March 2011.
176. Flynn, Pottinger, and Batchelor, *Fixing Intel*, 25n10.
177. Maj. C. Bolduc and Capt. J. Vachon, "Making Strides at the Heart of the Insurgency," *Canadian Army Journal* 13, no. 2 (Summer 2010): 45, 49–51, 53–55.
178. Godefroy, comments.

CONCLUSION

Historians often find it useful to examine events, institutions, and practices of the past through the contrasting lenses of continuity and change. The evolution and operations of Canadian MI and DI from 1970 to 2010 offers considerable scope for this kind of analytical framework.

From a continuity perspective, certain features were relatively constant throughout the period. First, changing terminology notwithstanding, the key elements of the intelligence task remained largely unchanged. Intelligence staffs at all levels had to manage requirements, collection, production, and dissemination. Second, domestic factors, especially budget cuts, meant that until very recently they had to do this without sufficient people, up-to-date equipment, and other resources. Doing more with less was the norm both in the field and at headquarters. Intelligence leaders had to fight not just to gain essential capabilities and resources but also to preserve the ones they already had. They did not always succeed. This meant that intelligence support to strategic decision making and to operations usually fell short of optimal.

Third, they supported both institutions and people who did not understand the utility of intelligence and were ignorant of or indifferent to it until operational necessity forced them to grasp it. Fourth, out of necessity, Canadian MI and DI staffs were skilled at improvising structures, techniques, and systems to offset limited assets. Fifth, their consistent strength lay in tactical intelligence, which generally served them well on operations.

Finally, it is impossible to overstate the value to the CAF and the DND intelligence of being part of the Five Eyes alliance and the NATO intelligence community. This gave them access to systems and products they would not have had otherwise. It enhanced Canada's limited collection and analysis capabilities. Without such access, it would have been difficult for deployed Canadian forces to contribute to coalition operations in the Persian Gulf War, Bosnia, Kosovo, and Afghanistan. Partnership in the alliance gave the CAF a privileged seat at the top table for consultation with allies about intelligence and operational planning. This helped the CAF and the DND develop in-house expertise in certain niche fields such as imagery analysis, which not only supported CAF operations in conflicts such as that in Bosnia but also contributed to coalition intelligence in the Persian Gulf War. As a result, CAF/DND intelligence was able to "punch above their weight" in selected fields alongside allied and coalition partners.

Continuity, therefore, was a significant feature of Canadian MI and DI in this period. This yielded mixed blessings, although some of its positive features outweighed the negatives.

Yet, Canadian MI also experienced considerable change over time, and dealing with change poses a range of challenges. Management theorist Peter Drucker has argued that change is normal and constant for modern organizations; they change because they must, or they will fail.[1] Theo Farrell and Terry Terriff point out that militaries change who and how they will fight. Such change takes the form of different goals, strategies, or structures. Because war is a dynamic phenomenon and the consequences of failure are potentially severe, militaries have to adapt to changes in war or will face defeat. But for the same reasons, they prefer to rely on proven ideas, practices, and technologies. Farrell and Terriff identify three paths to change: innovation, creating or adopting something entirely new; adaptation, adjusting existing means or methods; and emulation, imitating what others do.[2]

Stephen Peter Rosen asserts that military innovation requires an "ideological struggle" over "what the next war will look like and how officers must fight it if it is to be won."[3] Glenn Leonard argues that change occurs most effectively in what he (and others) describe as "learning organizations." Smaller organizations adapt more easily to change than bigger ones. The key features of learning organizations are people ("knowledge individuals") and structure (less vertical and hierarchical), and having a "culture of change."[4] These criteria help us understand how Canadian MI adapted to change from 1970 to 2010.

First, after 1990, the CAF shifted from being primarily a conventional warfighting force to one oriented to low-intensity warfare. The CAF and national DI components had to make that conceptual, cultural, and functional shift as well. Their intelligence target changed dramatically. The Cold War enemy had comprised clearly defined formations that could be identified and quantified and that operated in familiar ways. The new opponents consisted of small groups or individuals who operated in secrecy using unpredictable irregular tactics and information operations. Their center of gravity was political, not military. The evidence suggests that Canada's small MI cadre generally adapted to this change from the bottom up, driven by necessity in the field first, then forcing changes at higher levels.

Second, drawing upon concepts originally conceived for conventional war—the ICAC being a case in point—the intelligence community developed new structures to support operations in the field: the CANIC, the ISTAR CC, the ASIC, and the DGI intelligence response teams. Third, to the extent that these facilitated the coordination and fusion of intelligence from tactical, theatre, national, and allied sources, they also represented the compression of the strategic, operational, and tactical levels of intelligence into a more seamless unified effort, a de facto single intelligence environment. A significant manifestation of this was the closer collaboration between deployed CAF intelligence and the CSE to enhance military SIGINT efforts. These structural changes did not work perfectly but functioned well enough to allow intelligence to more effectively guide tactical operations.

Fourth, the CAF and its intelligence components adopted new ISR collection platforms and the information management systems needed to extract, produce, and disseminate the intelligence that ISR yielded. Four stand out: computers, the Coyote LAV, the UAVs, and the tactical SIGINT support provided by mobile electronic warfare teams. These gave intelligence staffs and the force commanders they served a much greater capacity to understand their battle space and make more informed tactical decisions. Developing in tandem with these was an increasing focus on human source collection, reflecting the different nature of the enemy. These innovations and the trend toward intelligence fusion/integration contributed to the fifth change: the adoption of intelligence-led and -driven operations. This in turn required and reflected a sixth change: a shift in institutional culture within the CAF toward accepting the utility of intelligence. Intelligence moved from the margins of military activity to become a central operational enabler.

Finally, there was a concerted effort to professionalize MI and DI and to raise their profile and authority. The former was reflected in changes in intelligence training and the appointment of professionally trained personnel to lead intelligence staffs and units and to plan and execute intelligence collection activities. The latter was manifested in the appointment of a CDI with greater authority over the defence intelligence community and in the other changes arising from the *DIR*.

In these changes—in operational focus, structure, collaboration, technology, operations, culture, and professional status—we can see innovation, adaptation, and emulation (of Canada's intelligence allies). Although CAF/DND intelligence was part of a hierarchical organization, it seems to have become a learning organization with a culture of change forced by necessity. In this respect, being small probably was a virtue. That may have allowed knowledge individuals to exert influence, although it is hard to prove that point with the evidence at hand.

Taken together, the changes in intelligence support to CAF operations and in CAF personnel attitudes toward the use of that support were truly transformative. This does not suggest that James Cox's study of Canadian DI was wrong in 2004. But the Canadian experiment with intelligence transformation did move on from where it was then, and the Afghanistan War and the *DIR* largely drove that process. Former CSE chief John Adams said, "Afghanistan was a watershed for intelligence. . . . The impetus that Afghanistan brought was quite significant."[5] Capt. (N) Andrea Siew concurred, saying that the Afghanistan War drove the big change in the way the CAF did intelligence.[6] Lieutenant-General Gauthier attributes the changes to the interaction of the war and the *DIR*. "There was a DI transformation which was a result of the DIR, but it was more than just that. If the capacity of DI is ten times today what it was back then, that is due to the DIR and to the effect that intelligence had on operations, at home and in Afghanistan. . . . It was at JTF [joint task force] level that the groundbreaking work was done in concert with other government department representatives [CSIS, CSE]. Fusion, above all."[7]

Gauthier stressed that it was pushed by operational demands and by a willingness on the part of the CAF/DND to take some risks. Gen. Rick Hillier, Gen. Andrew Leslie, and Gauthier himself, all deploying on operations, brought back an intelligence-driven and -led operations mindset with them. That was all part of the *DIR* implicitly. It could not be separated from those improvements in operational intelligence support.[8] It was completed before the war expanded in 2005, but it had initiated changes within DI that made the later innovations possible. One thing it did not—and could not—change was the fact that the pool of CAF intelligence resources, especially specialist personnel such as imagery analysts and interrogators, was too small to meet the demands the war placed on them. Gauthier and the others can be forgiven for expressing professional pride in the changes in which they played significant roles. So, their perspectives are not disinterested. Yet, given the evidence at hand, it is hard to dispute those observations.

So, how did all of this continuity and change impact CAF operations? The record presented here shows that the ability of CAF/DND intelligence structures to support and influence CAF operations waxed and waned over time. There was not a straight line of steady progress from one operation to the next or from the DGI to the CFINTCOM. The extent to which intelligence operated effectively was shaped by a wide range of operational, political, and technological factors, many of which lay outside its control. The CAF/DND intelligence community never had enough people, money, and resources to fulfil its tasks and missions perfectly even during the Afghanistan War, when the CAF benefited from the most comprehensive intelligence support it had ever received. What the intelligence staffs lacked in numbers they made up for in quality and in adapting their skills and tools sufficiently to do the job well enough. They were also fortunate that in overseas operations, they were part of coalitions in which they could draw upon capabilities that the CAF itself lacked. But as shown by operations in Bosnia under the UN, in the Kosovo air campaign, and in Afghanistan, even the very best intelligence collection and production could not compensate for flawed strategic planning or ineffective operations. Intelligence does not work miracles. So, this has not been a story of unvarnished success but rather one of useful accomplishments achieved in the face of adversity.

The October Crisis and the Afghanistan War bookend this study. But, of course, that is not the end of the CAF/DND intelligence story. In 2013 the CDI division within NDHQ was reorganized into CFINTCOM. With some one thousand personnel, headed by a flag-rank commander who was also designated the CDI, CFINTCOM's mandate is to collect intelligence and to "enable intelligence assessment" in order to provide "credible, timely and integrated defence intelligence capabilities, products and services" in support of Canada's national security objectives.[9] To fulfil this mission CFINTCOM has at its disposal a number of specialized, task-tailored components. On the collection side, this includes the Joint Imagery Centre, the National Counter-Intelligence Unit, the Joint Meteorological Centre, the Mapping and Charting Establishment, and Joint Task Force X, which collects human source intelligence. On the assessment side, CFINTCOM deploys five directorates: Intelligence Policy and Partnerships, Intelligence Production Management, Meteorology and Oceanography, Scientific and Technical Intelligence, and Transnational and Regional Intelligence.[10] Not falling under CFINTCOM's jurisdiction but linked for operational purposes are the CSE, the CFIOG, and the deployable collection capabilities organic to formations and units. This adds some two thousand military and civilian personnel to the total performing intelligence tasks.[11]

The creation of CFINTCOM could be said to complete the process of Canadian MI transformation that had been under way for several decades. It had moved from the margins to the center, attaining status equal to that of the four other national-level commands and the Strategic Joint Staff.[12] But as the previous chapters show, this was not a preordained result. Nor should we assume that CFINTCOM is the final iteration of the Canadian MI/DI function. Many factors influenced its path, and alternative outcomes were always—and remain—possible. Indeed, if the past is any guide, CFINTCOM is likely to be buffeted by further policy shifts, fiscal constraints, challenging operational demands, reorganizations, and reviews, the *Defence Intelligence Enterprise Review* (2019) being a case in point. But we should be able to say with a degree of confidence that any future CAF force is unlikely to deploy on operations without some form of all-source intelligence collection and integrated analysis capacity, back-stopped via connectivity to/from national and allied intelligence systems.

Beyond this, what can we say about the future of Canadian DI/MI? The historian who attempts to predict the future must do so with great caution, since the past is an unreliable guide. Armed forces are frequently criticized for "fighting the last war" as they prepare for the next. There is a measure of truth in that, but there is also merit in the saying "Never say never again." The international environment remains as unpredictable and volatile as it has been since the end of the Cold War. Major conventional wars, such as the very recent one in Ukraine, and even nuclear exchanges are still conceivable. And if the recent conflicts in Iraq and Syria are at all typical, we also should expect combatant forces to use chemical weapons, both bespoke and improvised. Neither can we rule out biological weapons. But the most likely operating environments in the foreseeable future probably will be low-intensity and unconventional, not greatly dissimilar from those discussed in this book. Recent CAF operations in Libya, Iraq, and Mali are cases in point. The CAF would forget at its peril what it has learned from these and from its experiences in the Balkans and Afghanistan, for example, the attritional, morale, and political impacts of the IED. That applies as much to the intelligence staffs as it does to commanders, planners, and those at the sharp end.

So, what will be new and different? First, in the kinetic dimension, the merging of nanotechnology and artificial intelligence presents the most significant near-term challenge. It is already manifesting itself in conventional or unconventional conflicts: autonomous or near-autonomous weapons systems, such as small armed drones, that can evade air defence systems and then swarm and overwhelm their opponents' forces.[13] Likewise, maneuverable hypersonic weapons pose an emerging threat in the conventional and nuclear warfare domains.[14] Both new systems have been used in the 2022 Russian invasion of Ukraine with devastating effect.

Second, in the nonkinetic dimension, cyber warfare is likely to be a prominent feature of any future conflict. It entails several capabilities, which may be used simultaneously: destroying or disrupting an opponent's C4ISR systems and the critical infrastructures that sustain the forces on the home front and conducting cyber-based information operations against enemy forces, their governments, their allies, and their domestic political and social structures.[15] Both of these, deployed in tandem with kinetic and special operations, would be intended to prevent an opponent from conducting effective offensive or defensive military actions. While powers such as the United States, Russia, and China can deploy massive cyber warfare resources, they do not have a monopoly on them. Lesser powers such as North Korea and even nonstate actors—insurgents and terrorist groups—have access to cyber warfare skills and tools. They are cheap and easy to use.

This has several implications for Canadian MI and DI. First, they need to retain existing skills and capabilities, including integrated joint operations and fused all-source intelligence. They remain relevant to the operations that the CAF is most likely to undertake.

Second, they need to consider the extent to which computers and related information management systems will play an increasing role in intelligence collection and analysis. Will artificial intelligence, as some suggest, displace human operators, who cannot manage the vast amounts of so-called big data gathered at the speeds needed to process and make sense of it? The CAF and DND intelligence enterprises are just on the cusp of understanding what artificial intelligence and machine learning can provide. It will impact everything from intelligence collection and processing to C2 in a pan-domain (land/air/sea/space/cyber) environment. It raises ethical questions, such as where do humans fit in the automated collection process for space-based collection? The CAF established in 2020 the Joint Operations Fusion Laboratory in order to trial, experiment, and assess these impacts of artificial intelligence and machine learning.[16] But this is just a start.

Integrating artificial intelligence and machine learning into the intelligence function would require yet more reorganization and a substantial investment in advanced information management systems.[17] The CAF and the DND probably will find themselves hard-pressed to afford to do so. But if they do not, they will be marginalized by their allies and outfought by their opponents. Moreover, given the stakes, artificial intelligence and machine learning are only part of the answer in handling big data. The intelligence communities will experience additional cultural shifts regarding innovation, procurement, training, education, and digitalisation. This is not just an MI problem. If indeed the future of defence is digital, it will require a whole of nation response, not one limited to the intelligence cadres of the CAF and the DND.

At the time of this writing, the challenges of providing timely, relevant, and credible intelligence support intended to understand increasingly complex operational environments are not just on the horizon. The pan-domain era of operations has arrived. Experience during recent deployments in Eastern Europe, Iraq, and Mali indicate that the struggle for information dominance—countering narratives and influence—is already joined. Determining how the CAF and DND intelligence enterprises will meet these challenges is an ongoing process whose foundation has been laid by the journeys explored in this book. It has provided an explanation of how the CAF/DND intelligence function developed to its current form. But because of its largely operational focus and limited access to sources, this is only a first step toward understanding, not the last word on the subject. For now, the *1st Canadian Army Intelligence After-Action Review* in 1945 offers an observation that seems likely to remain relevant into the foreseeable future: "Intelligence Organizations of the Army must be flexible."[18]

That is also sound advice for the historian of intelligence. If the author's experience in researching and writing this book is at all typical, then flexibility is a necessary virtue. Since security restrictions will ensure that many original sources are unavailable, then the historian must be willing to pursue other avenues toward knowledge. Decades ago, my mentor Professor Toby Graham gave me a sound piece of advice that has resonated throughout my career: "Collect people." Just as in intelligence work, human sources are essential to the intelligence historian. They are valuable not just for what they know themselves but also for who they know. This book would not have been possible without them. But this means the intelligence historian must be a good listener. It is not enough to ask good questions; one must pay attention to the answers. Professor Graham also said that a good historian must be a good poacher who recognizes the value of perspectives offered by other disciplines and is willing to apply them to history. As suggested in the introduction, that approach is highly relevant to intelligence studies, which by its very nature is multidisciplinary. Two more points will complete this reflection. First, like an intelligence staff, the historian of intelligence must be well organized. Haphazard collection and analysis will not yield useful conclusions. Avoid stovepiping your sources and data; they are bound to cross analytic boundaries. So, your procedures—and your mind—must be trained to fuse that diverse material and to connect the dots. Second, and finally, be patient with your sources and with yourself. Your research may not yield all the answers nor all at once; eureka moments are rare. Be willing to accept that your story is necessarily incomplete. It will be up to others to finish it. But if you have done your job well, you will have shown them the way.

NOTES

1. Peter F. Drucker, *Management Challenges for the 21st Century* (New York: HarperBusiness, 1999), 73.
2. Theo Farrell and Terry Terriff, *The Sources of Military Change: Culture, Politics, Technology* (Boulder, CO: Lynne Rienner, 2002), 4–6; and Lt.-Col. (USAFR) Kathleen A. Mahoney-Norris, "Huntington Revisited: Is Conservative Realism Still Essential for the Military Ethic?" (course paper, National Defense University, National War College, Fort Belvoir, VA: Defense Technical Information Center, 20 April 2001), https://doi.org/10.21236/ADA441680.
3. Stephen Peter Rosen, *Winning the Next War: Innovation and the Modern Military* (Ithaca, NY: Cornell University Press, 1991), 7, 20.
4. Robert Glenn Leonard, "No Lessons Required: The Balkan Wars and Organizational Learning in the British Army before the First World War" (PhD diss., Fredericton, University of New Brunswick, 2011), 45, 49–51, 54.
5. John Adams, interview with author, 6 November 2019.

6. Capt. (N) Andrea Siew, interview with author, 7 November 2019.
7. Lt.-Gen. (ret.) Michel Gauthier, interview with author, 5 November 2019.
8. Gauthier.
9. Thomas Juneau, "The Department of National Defence and the Canadian Armed Forces (DND/CAF)," in *Top Secret Canada: Understanding the Canadian Intelligence and National Security Community*, ed. Stephanie Carvin, Thomas Juneau, and Craig Forcese (Toronto: University of Toronto Press, 2020), 207; and "Canadian Forces Intelligence Command," Government of Canada, 23 June 2014, https://www.canada.ca/en/department-national-defence/corporate/organizational-structure/canadian-forces-intelligence-command.html.
10. "Canadian Forces Intelligence Command."
11. Juneau, "Department of National Defence," 207.
12. Juneau, 202–3.
13. Zachary Kallenborn, "Meet the Future Weapon of Mass Destruction, the Drone Swarm," *Bulletin of the Atomic Scientists* (blog), 5 April 2021, https://thebulletin.org/2021/04/meet-the-future-weapon-of-mass-destruction-the-drone-swarm/.
14. Kelley M. Sayler, "Hypersonic Weapons: Background and Issues for Congress," R45811/v18, CRS Report, Congressional Research Service (Washington, DC: United States Congress, April 26, 2021), 1, 2, 11–13, 14–15, 17, https://crsreports.congress.gov/product/pdf/R/R45811.
15. Bill Robinson, "The Communications Security Establishment (CSE)," in *Top Secret Canada*, 78.
16. I am grateful for Col. Greg Jensen's insights on this.
17. Anthony Vinci, "The Coming Revolution in Intelligence Affairs," *Foreign Affairs* (blog), 31 August 2020, https://www.foreignaffairs.com/articles/north-america/2020-08-31/coming-revolution-intelligence-affairs.
18. *1st Canadian Army Intelligence After-Action Review* (July 1945), in Canada, First Canadian Army, *42-1-0/Int: First Canadian Army Final Intelligence Report* (July 1945).

SELECT BIBLIOGRAPHY

OFFICIAL SOURCES

Canada. Canadian Armed Forces and NDHQ. *CFP 301 (3) Peacekeeping Doctrine*. First draft. Ottawa: NDHQ, June 1992.
Canada. DND. *Adjusting Course: A Naval Strategy for Canada*. Ottawa: Canada Communications Group, 1997.
———. B-GG-005-004/AF-010 *Canadian Forces Information Operations*. Ottawa: DND, 15 April 1998. Lt.-Col. Greg Jensen, private papers.
———. *Canadian Forces Joint Doctrine Note 2011/01: The All Source Intelligence Centre*. 2011.
———. *Canadian Forces Joint Publication 2-1: Intelligence Operations*. 2nd ed. [promulgation draft]. Ottawa: DND, 2021.
———. *The Canadian Navy's Operational Intelligence Surveillance and Reconnaissance (ISR) Blueprint to 2010*. Halifax: Maritime Command, n.d. [ca. 1997].
———. *Challenge and Commitment: A Defence Policy for Canada*. Ottawa: DND, June 1987.
———. *DCDS Planning Guidance—Intelligence, Surveillance and Reconnaissance (ISR) for the CF*. Draft. Ottawa: DND, 7 November 2000.
———. *Defence in the '70s: White Paper on Defence*. Ottawa: DND/Information Canada, 1971.
———. *Intelligence Collection and Analysis Centre Field Trial, Post Exercise Report*. Mobile Command Headquarters, 13 February 1986. Lt.-Col. Greg Jensen, private papers.
———. *MARCOM Capability Planning Guidance 2000*. Halifax: Maritime Command, September 1999.
———. *Shaping the Future of Canadian Defence: A Strategy for 2020*. Ottawa: DND, June 1999.
———. *1994 White Paper on Defence*. Ottawa: DND, 1994.
———. *[1964] White Paper on Defence*. Ottawa: Queen's Printer and Controller of Stationery, 1964.
Canada. DND. Chief—Review Services. *Joint Command Control Intelligence System (JC2IS)*. Ottawa: DND, April 2001.
Canada. DND. Chief of the Defence Staff. *The Aerospace Capability Framework*. Ottawa: DG Air Force Development, 2003.
Canada. DND. Directorate of Maritime Strategy. *Leadmark: The Navy's Strategy for 2020*. Ottawa: DND, June 2001. https://www.files.ethz.ch/isn/15017/ENG_LEADMARK_FULL_72DPI.pdf.

Canada. DND. J2/Director General Intelligence. *Director General Intelligence Report Defence Intelligence Review—Report to the DCDS*. Ottawa: DND, 20 May 2004. CFIHP.

Canada. DND. Vice Chief of the Defence Staff. *Defence Planning Guidance, 2000*. Ottawa: DND, August 1999.

Dowell, Lieutenant-Colonel J.A.E.K. *Intelligence for the Canadian Army in the 21st Century: "Enabling Land Operations."* JADEX Papers 5. Kingston, Ontario: Directorate of Land Concepts and Design, 2011.

English, Allan D. *Command & Control of Canadian Aerospace Forces: Conceptual Foundations*. Ottawa: DND, 2008.

Isbister, C. M. *Intelligence Operations in the Canadian Government*. Ottawa: Privy Council Office, 9 November 1970. CFIHP.

Matheson, Lieutenant-Colonel R. H. *Lesson Synopsis Report (LSR) 09-011 Defensive C-IED TTP Review*. Kingston: ALLC, Land Force Doctrine and Training System, 17 August 2009.

———. *Lesson Synopsis Report (LSR) 09-012 Offensive C-IED TTP Review*. Kingston, Ontario: ALLC; Land Force Doctrine and Training System, October 14, 2009.

NATO Standardization Office. *AINTP-1(A) Intelligence Doctrine*. NATO, January 1995. Lt.-Col. Greg Jensen, private papers.

O'Neill, N. K., and K. J. Hughes. *History of the Communications Branch of the National Research Council*. 7 vols. Ottawa: Communications Security Establishment, 1987. CFIHP.

Teeple, Nancy. *Canada in Afghanistan: 2001–2010; A Military Chronology*. Contract report. Ottawa: Defence Research and Development Canada. Centre for Operational Research and Analysis, December 2010. https://apps.dtic.mil/sti/citations/ADA539606.

United States. Department of the Army and US Marine Corps. *The U.S. Army/Marine Corps Counterinsurgency Field Manual: U.S. Army Field Manual No. 3-24/Marine Corps Warfighting Publication No. 3-33.5*. Chicago: University of Chicago Press, 2007.

United States. Department of Defense. *Conduct of the Persian Gulf War: Final Report to Congress, Pursuant to Title V of the Persian Gulf Conflict Supplemental Authorization and Personnel Benefits Act of 1991 (Public Law 102-25)*. Washington, DC: Department of Defense, 1992.

Wark, Wesley K. *A History of the Creation of Canada's Post–World War II Intelligence Community, 1945–1970*. Ottawa: [Privy Council Office], 2000–2002. CFIHP.

Windsor, Lee. *The Royal Canadian Infantry Corps in Afghanistan*. Dispatches 17, no. 1. Kingston, Ontario: DND; Army Lessons Learned Centre, 2013.

SECONDARY SOURCES

Aid, Matthew M. *The Secret Sentry: The Untold History of the National Security Agency*. New York: Bloomsbury, 2010.

Allin, Dana H. *NATO's Balkan Interventions*. Abingdon, Oxon, UK: Routledge, 2002. https://doi.org/10.4324/9781315000664.

Arkin, William M. "Operation Allied Force: 'The Most Precise Application of Air Power in History.'" In *War over Kosovo: Politics and Strategy in a Global Age*, ed. A. J. Bacevich and Eliot A. Cohen, 1–37. New York: Columbia University Press, 2001.

SELECT BIBLIOGRAPHY

Auerswald, David P., and Stephen M. Saideman. *NATO in Afghanistan: Fighting Together, Fighting Alone*. Princeton, NJ: Princeton University Press, 2014.

Avis, Captain (N) Peter. "Surveillance and Canadian Domestic Maritime Security." *Canadian Military Journal* 4, no. 1 (Spring 2003): 9–14.

Balasevicius, Tony, and Bernd Horn. "Intelligence and Its Application to Irregular Warfare." In *The Difficult War: Perspectives on Insurgency and Special Operations Forces*, ed. Emily Spencer, 53–77. Kingston, Ontario: Canadian Defence Academy Press, 2009.

Bamford, James. *Body of Secrets: Anatomy of the Ultra-Secret National Security Agency; From the Cold War through the Dawn of a New Century*. New York: Doubleday, 2001.

Bashow, Lieutenant-Colonel David, et al. "Mission Ready: Canada's Role in the Kosovo Air Campaign." *Canadian Military Journal* 1, no. 1 (Spring 2000): 55–61.

Berdal, Mats R. *Whither UN Peacekeeping? An Analysis of the Changing Military Requirements of UN Peacekeeping with Proposals for Its Enhancement*. London: Brassey's, for the International Institute for Strategic Studies, 1993.

Bland, Douglas. *The Administration of Defence Policy in Canada, 1947 to 1985*. Kingston, Ontario: Ronald P. Frye, 1987.

———. *Chiefs of Defence: Government and the Unified Command of the Canadian Armed Forces*. Toronto: Canadian Institute of Strategic Studies, 1995.

———. *Transforming National Defence Administration*. Kingston: Ontario: School of Policy Studies, Queen's University, 2005.

Byers, R. B. *Canadian Security and Defence: The Legacy and the Challenges*. London: International Institute for Strategic Studies, 1986.

Carryer, Andrew. *A History of Unmanned Aviation in Canada*. Brampton, Ontario: MacDonald Dettwiler, 2008.

Carvin, Stephanie, Thomas Juneau, and Craig Forcese, eds. *Top Secret Canada: Understanding the Canadian Intelligence and National Security Community*. Toronto: University of Toronto Press, 2020.

Charters, David A. "Canadian Military Intelligence in Afghanistan." *International Journal of Intelligence and CounterIntelligence* 25, no. 3. (Fall 2012): 470–507.

———. "From October to Oka: Peacekeeping in Canada, 1970–1990." In *Canadian Military History: Selected Readings*, ed. Marc Milner, 368–93. Toronto: Copp Clark Pitman, 1993.

———. "The Future of Military Intelligence within the Canadian Forces." *Canadian Military Journal* 2, no. 4 (2002): 47–52.

———. "Out of the Closet: Intelligence Support for Post-Modernist Peacekeeping." In *Intelligence in Peacekeeping*, 33–68. Clementsport, Nova Scotia: Canadian Peacekeeping Press, 1999.

Cline, Lawrence E., and Paul Shemella, eds. *The Future of Counterinsurgency: Contemporary Debates in Internal Security Strategy*. Santa Barbara, CA: Praeger, 2015.

Collins, Joseph J. *Understanding War in Afghanistan*. Washington, DC: National Defense University Press, 2011.

Cordesman, Anthony H., and Abraham R. Wagner. "The Gulf War." [Prepublished manuscript, 1994; revised 2013, 2016; first published as *The Lessons of Modern War*, Vol. 4, *The Gulf War* (Boulder, CO: Westview, 1996)]. Center for Strategic and International Studies, 2016. https://www.csis.org/programs/burke-chair-strategy/lessons-war/gulf-war.

Cox, Brigadier-General (ret.) James S. "The Transformation of Canadian Defence Intelligence since the End of the Cold War." Master's thesis, Royal Military College of Canada, 2004.

Crelinsten, Ronald D. "The Internal Dynamics of the FLQ during the October Crisis of 1970." In *Inside Terrorist Organizations*, ed. David C. Rapoport, 59–89. London: Frank Cass, 2001.

Daalder, Ivo H., and Michael E. O'Hanlon. *Winning Ugly: NATO's War to Save Kosovo*. Washington, DC: Brookings Institution Press, 2000.

Dangerfield, Major-General J. K. "The 1st Canadian Division: Enigma, Contradiction or Requirement?" *Canadian Defence Quarterly* 19, no. 5 (April 1990): 7–14.

Davies, Philip H. J. "ISR versus ISTAR: A Conceptual Crisis in British Military Intelligence." *International Journal of Intelligence and CounterIntelligence* (2021): 1–28. https://doi.org/10.1080/08850607.2020.1866334.

Deere, Captain David N. *Desert Cats: The Canadian Fighter Squadron in the Gulf War*. Stoney Creek, Ontario: Fortress Publications, 1991.

de Graaff, Bob, and Cees Wiebes. "Fallen off the Priority List: Was Srebrenica an Intelligence Failure?" In *The Role of Intelligence in Ending the War in Bosnia in 1995*, ed. Timothy R. Walton, 149–65. Lanham, MD: Lexington Books, 2014.

Dorn, A. Walter. "The Cloak and the Blue Beret: Limitations on Intelligence in UN Peacekeeping." In *Intelligence in Peacekeeping*. Clementsport, Nova Scotia: Canadian Peacekeeping Press, 1999.

Elliot, Major S. R. *Scarlet to Green: A History of Intelligence in the Canadian Army, 1903–1963*. 2nd ed. Ottawa: Canadian Military Intelligence Association, 2018.

Farrell, Theo, Frans P. B. Osinga, and James A. Russell, eds. *Military Adaptation in Afghanistan*. Stanford, CA: Stanford University Press, 2013.

Ferris, John Robert. *Behind the Enigma: The Authorized History of GCHQ, Britain's Secret Cyber-Intelligence Agency*. London: Bloomsbury Publishing, 2020.

Flynn, Michael T., Matt Pottinger, and Paul Batchelor. *Fixing Intel: A Blueprint for Making Intelligence Relevant in Afghanistan*. Washington, DC: Center for a New American Security, 2010.

Fraser, Major-General David, and Brian Hanington. *Operation Medusa: The Furious Battle That Saved Afghanistan from the Taliban*. Toronto: McClelland and Stewart, 2018.

Freedman, Lawrence. *The Transformation of Strategic Affairs*. London: Routledge, for the International Institute for Strategic Studies, 2006.

Garrett-Rempel, Danny. "Will JUSTAS Prevail? Procuring a UAS Capability for Canada." *Royal Canadian Air Force Journal* 4, no. 1 (Winter 2015): 19–31.

Gauvreau, Michael. "Winning Back the Intellectuals: Inside Canada's 'First War on Terror,' 1968–1970." *Journal of the Canadian Historical Association/Revue de La Société Historique Du Canada* 20, no. 1 (2009): 161–90. https://doi.org/10.7202/039786ar.

Gimblett, Richard Howard. *Operation Apollo: The Golden Age of the Canadian Navy in the War Against Terrorism*. Ottawa: Magic Light, for DND, 2004.

Gramer, Lieutenant-Colonel George K. Jr. "Operation JOINT ENDEAVOUR: Combined-Joint Intelligence in Peace Enforcement Operations." *Military Intelligence Professional Bulletin* 22, no. 4 (1996): 11–14.

Hennessy, Michael A., and Todd Fitzgerald. "An Expedient Reorganization: The NDHQ J-Staff System in the Gulf War." *Canadian Military Journal* 4, no. 1 (2003): 23–28.

Hillen, John. *Blue Helmets: The Strategy of UN Military Operations*. Washington, DC: Brassey's, 1998.

Hillier, General Rick. *A Soldier First: Bullets, Bureaucrats, and the Politics of War*. Toronto: HarperCollins, 2009.
Hope, Ian. *Dancing with the Dushman: Command Imperatives for the Counter-Insurgency Fight in Afghanistan*. Kingston, Ontario: Canadian Defence Academy Press, 2008.
Horn, Colonel Bernd. *No Ordinary Men: Special Operations Forces Missions in Afghanistan*. Toronto: Dundurn Press, 2016. Kindle.
———, ed. *In Harm's Way: On the Front Lines of Leadership: Sub-Unit Command on Operations*. Kingston, Ontario: Canadian Defence Academy Press, 2006.
Jenish, D'Arcy. *The Making of the October Crisis: Canada's Long Nightmare of Terrorism at the Hands of the FLQ*. Toronto: Doubleday, 2018.
Jockel, Joseph T. *The Canadian Forces: Hard Choices, Soft Power*. Toronto: Canadian Institute of Strategic Studies, 1999.
Johnson, Thomas H., and Barry Scott Zellen, eds. *Culture, Conflict, and Counterinsurgency*. Stanford, CA: Stanford University Press, 2014.
Lambeth, Benjamin S. *NATO's Air War for Kosovo: A Strategic and Operational Assessment*. Santa Monica, CA: RAND, 2001.
Lebel, Lieutenant-Commander J. A. "The Royal Canadian Navy's Intelligence Function: In Line, Off Focus." JCSP 41: Exercise *Solo Flight*, Canadian Forces College, Toronto, 2015. https://www.cfc.forces.gc.ca/259/290/317/305/lebel.pdf.
MacKenzie, Major-General Lewis. *Peacekeeper: The Road to Sarajevo*. Vancouver: Douglas and McIntyre, 1993.
Maloney, Sean M. *Confronting the Chaos: A Rogue Military Historian Returns to Afghanistan*. Annapolis, MD: Naval Institute Press, 2009.
———. *Enduring the Freedom: A Rogue Historian in Afghanistan*. Lincoln, NE: Potomac Books, 2007.
———. *Fighting for Afghanistan: A Rogue Historian at War*. Annapolis, MD: Naval Institute Press, 2011.
———. *The Hindrance of Military Operations Ashore: Canadian Participation in Operation Sharp Guard, 1993–1996*. Halifax: Centre for Foreign Policy Studies, Dalhousie University, 2000.
———. "'A Mere Rustle of Leaves': Canadian Strategy and the 1970 FLQ Crisis." *Canadian Military Journal* 1, no. 2 (Summer 2000): 71–84.
———. *Operation Kinetic: Stabilizing Kosovo*. Lincoln, NE: Potomac Books, 2018.
Maloney, Sean M., and John Llambias. *Chances for Peace: Canadian Soldiers in the Balkans, 1992–1995; An Oral History*. St. Catharines, Ontario: Vanwell, 2002.
Martin [Martyn], Captain Robert. "Trends in Tactical Intelligence: Global Conflict and the Canadian Forces." *Army Doctrine and Training Bulletin* 1, no. 2 (Fall 1998): n.p. [67–82]. http://publications.gc.ca/collections/Collection/D12-9-1-2E.pdf.
Middlemiss, D. W., and J. J. Sokolsky. *Canadian Defence: Decisions and Determinants*. Toronto: Harcourt Brace Jovanovich, 1989.
Miller, Commodore Duncan E., and Sharon Hobson. *The Persian Excursion: The Canadian Navy in the Gulf War*. Toronto: Canadian Peacekeeping Press and Canadian Institute of Strategic Studies, 1995.
Milner, Marc. *Canada's Navy: The First Century*. Toronto: University of Toronto Press, 1999.
Morin, Major Jean H., and Lieutenant-Commander Richard H. Gimblett. *Operation Friction, 1990–1991: The Canadian Forces in the Persian Gulf*. Toronto: Dundurn, 1997.

Nardulli, Bruce R., Walter L. Perry, Bruce Pirnie, John Gordon, and John G. McGinn. *Disjointed War: Military Operations in Kosovo, 1999*. Santa Monica, CA: RAND, 2002.

Nordick, Colonel Glenn W. *Battalion Command: UNPROFOR (Sector West) Croatia, September 1992 to April 1993*. Personal Experience Monograph. Carlisle Barracks, PA: US Army War College, 1999.

Off, Carol. *The Ghosts of the Medak Pocket: The Story of Canada's Secret War*. Toronto: Random House, 2004.

Pigott, Peter. *Canada in Afghanistan: The War So Far*. Toronto: Dundurn, 2007.

Ramsbotham, Lieutenant-General Sir David. "Analysis and Assessment for Peacekeeping Operations." In *Intelligence Analysis and Assessment*, ed. David A. Charters, Stuart Farson, and Glenn P. Hastedt, 162–74. London: Frank Cass, 1996.

Rémillard, Major L. H. "The 'All-Source' Way of Doing Business: The Evolution of Intelligence in Modern Military Operations." *Canadian Military Journal* 8, no. 3 (Autumn 2007): 19–26. http://www.journal.forces.gc.ca/vo8/no3/doc/remillar-eng.pdf.

Richter, Andrew. *The Revolution in Military Affairs and Its Impact on Canada: The Challenge and the Consequences*. Working paper no. 28. Vancouver: Institute for International Relations, University of British Columbia Press, 1999.

Rostek, Lieutenant-Colonel Michael. "A Framework for Fundamental Change? The Management Command and Control Re-Engineering Initiative." *Canadian Military Journal* 5, no. 4 (Winter 2004–5): 65–72. http://www.journal.forces.gc.ca/vo5/no4/doc/5-4-10-eng.pdf.

Saideman, Stephen M. *Adapting in the Dust: Lessons Learned from Canada's War in Afghanistan*. Toronto: University of Toronto Press, 2016.

Sens, Allen Gregory, and Commission of Inquiry into the Deployment of Canadian Forces to Somalia. *Somalia and the Changing Nature of Peacekeeping: The Implications for Canada*. Ottawa: Minister of Public Works and Government Services, 1997.

Skaarup, Harold A. *Out of Darkness—Light: A History of Canadian Military Intelligence*. 3 [4] vols. New York: iUniverse Inc., 2005. [Unpublished manuscript of volume 4, ca. 2018].

Sloan, Elinor. "Canada and the Revolution in Military Affairs: Current Response and Future Opportunities." *Canadian Military Journal* 1, no. 3 (Autumn 2000): 7–14.

Smith, Hugh. "Intelligence and UN Peacekeeping." *Survival* 36, no. 3 (1994): 174–92. https://doi.org/10.1080/00396339408442755.

Sokolsky, Joel J. *Canada, Getting It Right This Time: The 1994 Defence White Paper*. Carlisle Barracks, PA: Strategic Studies Institute, US Army War College, 1995.

Spencer, Emily, ed. *Special Operations Forces: A National Capability*. Kingston, Ontario: Canadian Defence Academy Press, 2011.

Stein, Janice Gross, and J. Eugene Lang. *The Unexpected War: Canada in Kandahar*. Toronto: Viking, 2007.

Sterzer, Sergeant Marcus, Master Corporal Patrick McDuff, and Corporal Jacek Flasz. "Note to File—The Challenge of Centralized Control Faced by the Intelligence Function in Afghanistan." *Canadian Army Journal* 11, no. 2 (Summer 2008): 96–100.

Stiegel, Colonel USAF (ret.) Robert G. "The Origin and Evolution of the Joint Analysis Center at RAF Molesworth." *Studies in Intelligence*, Extracts, 62, no. 1 (March 2018): 10.

Taylor, Scott, and Brian Nolan. *Tested Mettle: Canada's Peacekeepers at War*. Ottawa: Esprit de Corps Books, 1998.

Tetley, William. *The October Crisis, 1970: An Insider's View*. Montreal: McGill-Queen's University Press, 2006.

Villeneuve, Lieutenant-Colonel Daniel. "A Study of the Changing Face of Canada's Army Intelligence." *Canadian Army Journal* 9, no. 2 (Summer 2006): 18–36.

Ward, Colonel Michael, with Lieutenant-Colonel Ed Gallagher, Major Doug Delaney, and Major Hugh Ferguson. "Task Force Kosovo: Adapting Operations to a Changing Security Environment." *Canadian Military Journal* 1, no. 2 (Spring 2000): 67–74.

Wark, Wesley K. "Favourable Geography: Canada's Arctic Signals Intelligence Mission." *Intelligence and National Security* 35, no. 3 (2020): 319–30.

———. "The Road to CANUSA: How Canadian Signals Intelligence Won Its Independence and Helped Create the Five Eyes." *Intelligence and National Security* 35, no. 1 (2020): 20–34.

Welsh, Captain Kyle. "Task Force Erebus: Providing Essential Support to Canada's Mission in Afghanistan." *Canadian Air Force Journal* 3, no. 2 (Spring 2010): 18–26.

Whitaker, Reginald, Gregory S. Kealey, and Andrew Parnaby. *Secret Service: Political Policing in Canada; From the Fenians to Fortress America*. Toronto: University of Toronto Press, 2012.

Windsor, Lee, David A. Charters, and J. Brent Wilson. *Kandahar Tour: The Turning Point in Canada's Afghan Mission*. Toronto: Wiley, 2008.

Winegard, Timothy C. *Oka: A Convergence of Cultures and the Canadian Forces*. Kingston, Ontario: Canadian Defence Academy Press, 2008.

INDEX

Adams, Maj.-Gen. (ret.) John, 59, 273, 306. *See also* Communications Security Establishment
Adjusting Course: A Naval Strategy for Canada, 22, 76, 77
Afghan Intelligence Response Team, 267, 274, 275
Afghanistan, as Canadian intelligence target, 244, 246–48
Afghan National Army, 260, 261, 262, 264, 280, 281, 288
Afghan National Police, 268, 286, 294. *See also* Massoud, Capt. Zia
Aid to the Civil Power (ACP), 16, 20, 107–9, 111–12, 125, 126. *See also* operations: ESSAY, GINGER, SALON
Airborne Battle Command and Control Center (ABCCC), 157, 165, 226, 227, 242n60
Air Command intelligence (A2), 82–87, 98n76, 220
air intelligence, 32, 33, 82–84, 89, 93, 155–57, 159, 160, 164–65, 190, 219–20, 222
Akwesasne Reserve, 124, 131, 132, 138, 139. *See also* Oka Crisis
Allied Forces Southern Europe (AFSOUTH), 190, 216
Allied Naval Forces, Southern Europe, 177, 190, 191
all-source intelligence, 46, 58, 59, 70, 71, 72, 73, 79, 80, 92, 93, 142, 187, 188, 191–92, 225, 250, 267, 288, 290, 292, 294, 307, 309
All-Source Intelligence Centre (ASIC): structure, 250–51, 267, 297n43; support to operations, 73, 92, 252–54, 256, 260, 265, 268, 269, 270–75, 279–80, 282, 283, 286, 290, 294, 299n79, 305
al-Qaeda, 244, 245, 246, 247, 248, 276
antiaircraft artillery (AAA), 155, 187, 219
antisubmarine warfare (ASW), 14, 16, 17–18, 19, 30, 75, 78, 81, 82, 90. *See also* submarines
Army Lessons Learned Centre, 184, 290
assistant chief of staff for intelligence (SHAPE), 190, 221
assistant chief of the Defence Staff, 17, 34
attaché program, 35, 42, 43, 44
automated data processing (ADP). *See* computers

Balkans Intelligence Response Team, 203, 205, 220, 234, 237
Bassarab, Maj. Rusty, 130, 131, 136, 140
Bastien, Chief Warrant Officer Susan, 202
Bean, Air Vice-Marshal Wilfred, 34, 35
Beauvais, Col. Michel, 90–92
Beharriell, Lt.-Col. Susan, 82, 85
Binda, Maj. Ken F., 44
Bland, Douglas, 15, 16, 24, 61, 109
Bosnia-Herzegovina, war in, 171–93

Bosniak armed forces, 173, 176, 186, 189, 207, 209
Bosnian Croats, 207–9
Bosnian Serb Army, 176, 184, 186, 187, 188, 189
Bowen, Mike, 47
Bruyea, Capt. Sean, 160

Cabinet Committee on Security and Intelligence (CCSI), 69, 107, 111
Calder, Dr. Kenneth, 246, 294
Canadian Airborne Regiment, 70, 109, 114
Canadian air force, 81–82, 85–87, 148. *See also* operations: ECHO, FRICTION
Canadian Air Task Group Middle East, 151–52, 153, 157, 160, 165, 170n75
Canadian Contingent United Nations Protection Force, 184, 186, 187, 188, 200, 202
Canadian defence policy, 13–27, 32, 46
Canadian Forces Base Borden, Ontario, 88, 90
Canadian Forces Base Greenwood, Nova Scotia, 86, 90
Canadian Forces Base Kingston, Ontario, 72, 88, 114, 116
Canadian Forces Base St. Hubert, Quebec, 105, 109
Canadian Forces Base Valcartier, Quebec, 71, 109, 116, 125
Canadian Forces Communication System, 50
Canadian Forces Information Operations Group (CFIOG), 56, 59, 69, 95n9, 202, 205–6, 212n18, 249, 266, 267, 273, 307
Canadian Forces Intelligence Branch, 1, 3, 32, 52, 80, 89, 90, 92, 202*fig.*, 267
Canadian Forces Intelligence Command, 62, 306, 307
Canadian Forces Intelligence Liaison Officers, 248, 257n21

Canadian Forces Joint Imagery Centre, 43, 60, 89, 91, 92, 266, 271, 274, 307
Canadian Forces Middle East (CANFORME), 148, 150, 151, 153, 155, 157–60
Canadian Forces Special Investigations Unit (SIU), 128–30, 131, 133–35, 137, 142, 143n25, 144n39
Canadian Forces Supplementary Radio System, 34, 36, 40n37, 42, 62n5, 69
Canadian Joint Intelligence Committee (CJIC), 30, 35
Canadian National Intelligence Centre (CANIC), 73, 200, 202–4, 205–6, 210, 232, 237, 251, 267, 305
Canadian Security Intelligence Service, 128, 129, 137, 247, 248, 251, 266, 267, 272, 290, 306
Canadian Special Operations Forces, 94, 245, 249, 260, 261, 264–67, 275, 276, 288, 292
Canadian Submarine Analysis Group, 78–79
Canavan, Lt. Dave, 159
CF-5 jet fighter, 81, 82, 114, 128, 130
CF-18 jet fighter, 18, 20, 81, 82, 84, 148, 150–51, 152–53, 155, 157, 160, 166, 168n27, 215, 216, 218, 241n19
CH-124 Sea King helicopter, 19, 78, 82
CH-146 Griffon helicopter, 82, 233, 236
Challenge and Commitment (1987 Defence White Paper), 18
Chambers, Maj. Alex, 96, 99n102
Chassé, Lt.-Col. Henri, 115
Chief of Defence Intelligence (CDI), 53, 55–60, 93, 271, 274, 290, 297n43, 305, 307
Chief of Defence Staff: command role, 15, 16, 17, 21, 23, 25, 26, 35, 43, 46, 49, 54, 55; role in operations, 108, 114, 125, 127, 129, 142, 150, 153, 184, 207, 230, 260
Chief of Intelligence and Security, 34, 42

INDEX   323

Chief Review Services, 50, 53, 54, 59
Chouinard, Brig.-Gen. Jacques, 109
5e Brigade (Groupement) de Combat Mechanisé, 109, 110, 125, 126, 128, 131
civil-military cooperation (CIMIC), 204, 229, 236, 239, 260, 262, 263, 264, 268, 292
Clairoux, Capt. J. V. Gilles, 201
Clark, General Wesley, US Army, 216, 217, 221, 225
combat air patrol missions, 151, 153, 218
Combat/Combined Logistics Force (CLF), 148, 152, 154, 160
combat intelligence, 67, 70–71, 72, 83, 89, 91, 233. *See also* tactical intelligence
Combined Anti-Terrorist Squad, 110, 111
Combined Task Force 440, 177
command and control (C2), 21, 22, 24, 49, 50, 75, 79, 81, 109, 133, 149, 150, 160, 162, 198, 200, 217, 220, 279, 309
command, control, communications, computers, intelligence, surveillance, and reconnaissance (C4ISR), 56, 58–59, 77, 79, 80, 86, 93, 308
Communications Branch of the National Research Council (CBNRC), 31, 34, 36, 68, 69
Communications Security Establishment (CSE), 59, 68, 69, 95n9, 129, 160, 166, 206, 212n18, 267, 273, 274, 290, 305, 306, 307
computers, 22, 36, 45–49, 50, 56, 61, 67, 69, 72, 74, 78, 79, 159, 165, 207, 209, 238, 305, 309
concept of operations, 84, 149, 229, 232, 235
conventional warfare, 71, 238, 290, 304, 305
counter-IED operations, 265–66, 289, 292, 293

counterinsurgency, 92, 256, 259–64, 275–76, 290, 293
counterintelligence, 32, 34, 52, 60, 72, 92, 112, 160, 203, 207, 221, 230, 236, 239, 251, 252, 266, 267
Cox, Brig.-Gen. (ret.), James S., 51, 61, 87, 158, 220–21, 223, 225, 248, 249
CP-121 Tracker aircraft, 114, 121n73
CP-140 Aurora aircraft, 18, 78, 82, 128, 130, 177, 190, 191*fig.*, 245
Crandell, Col. Patrick, 43–44
Crisis Action Team, 150
Croatia, 171–75, 179–81, 183, 189, 207–8; armed forces of, 172, 183, 185, 189; intelligence service of, 207
Cross, UK Trade Commissioner James, 104, 107, 112, 117, 120n53. *See also* October Crisis; operations: ESSAY
cryptologic support detachment, 80
cultural intelligence, 262–63, 292, 294, 295
current intelligence, 36, 41, 43, 50, 51, 79, 83, 158, 203, 221, 271
cyber warfare, 308

Dare, Lt.-Gen. Michael, 106, 108, 109
Davies, Dr. Philip, 73
Dayton Accords, 171, 174, 198, 200, 205, 207, 228
de Chastelain, Gen. John, 47, 150
defence intelligence (DI): organization, 13, 30–40, 41–66, 69, 73, 77, 93, 305–7; support to operations, 115, 158, 166, 170n70, 179, 184–89, 203, 206, 210, 220, 234, 247–48, 251, 267, 303, 305–9
Defence Intelligence Priorities, 37, 52, 247
Defence Intelligence Review (2002–2004), 53–62, 85, 93, 305, 306
Defence in the '70s (1971 Defence white paper), 15–16
Defence Management Committee, 22, 54
Defence Planning Guidance 2000, 23

defence re-engineering program, 21–22, 50, 52
Defence Structure Review, 17–18, 41, 78
Defence White Paper (1964), 15
Defense Meteorological Support Program, 222, 224
Delaney, Maj. Douglas, 236
demining, 177, 199, 200, 211n12
Demiray, Padre Suleiman, 270, 278
Denne, Col. Donald, 250, 254
Department of External Affairs (DEA), 158, 162, 163
Department of Foreign Affairs and International Trade (DFAIT), 178, 179, 185, 248, 294
Deputy Chief of Defence Staff (DCDS): functions, 17, 24, 42, 49–51, 52, 54, 55, 69; support to operations, 114, 150, 153, 188, 220, 230, 237, 247, 248
deputy chief of intelligence and security, 34, 69, 115
Devlin, Brig.-Gen. Peter, 250, 251
Dextraze, Gen. J. A., 17
direct action (DA) operations, 246, 251–56, 261, 264, 265, 267, 274, 288, 292
Directorate of Defence Intelligence (DDI), 41–44, 50, 51
Directorate of Imagery Exploitation (DIE): organization, 42, 43, 48, 50, 51; support to operations, 131, 139, 160, 166, 187, 188, 237, 248
Directorate of Intelligence Plans and Doctrine, 44
Directorate of Intelligence Production (DINTP), 41
Directorate of Scientific and Technical Intelligence (DSTI), 36, 37, 41, 42, 45, 51, 52, 58, 307
Director/Directorate of Intelligence–Air, 32
Director/Directorate of Military Intelligence, 32, 34
Director/Directorate of Naval Intelligence, 32

Director General Intelligence (division) (DGI): organization, 34–37, 42–45, 47–53, 54–55, 58–59, 78, 85, 92; support to operations, 114, 158, 166, 179, 184–89, 203, 206, 210, 220, 234, 247–48, 251, 267, 305
Director General Intelligence Production, 57
Director General Military SIGINT, 59, 273
Director of Communications Security, 68, 69
Director of Current Intelligence, 43
Director of Defence Intelligence and Security Automation, 45, 48
Dorn, Dr. Walter, 178, 181
12e Régiment Blindé du Canada, 116, 121n67, 176, 177
Dowell, Lt.-Col. J.A.E.K., 33, 70, 72
Drenica valley, Kosovo, 231, 234, 235
Drvar, Bosnia-Herzegovina, 206–7, 213n34
Duchaine Report, 109. *See also* October Crisis; Royal Canadian Mounted Police

E-3 AWACS aircraft, 157
E-8 Joint STARS aircraft, 157, 165, 205, 213n30, 222, 224, 226, 228, 268
Earl, Sgt. Kevin, 238
8th Canadian Hussars, 113, 121nn66–67
electronic intelligence (ELINT), 69, 155, 156, 157, 186, 224
electronic warfare (EW), 70, 71, 72, 74, 87; on operations, 114, 116, 128, 130, 133, 137–39, 143n25, 175, 186, 190, 222, 235, 237, 249, 251, 252, 253, 267, 278, 279
Electronic Warfare Coordination Centre, 72, 116
Elliott, Capt. Lisa, 204, 255
Ellis, Adm. James USN, 216, 225
engineer intelligence, 71, 72, 129, 181
engineer operations, 175, 177, 200, 231, 233, 250

Eon, L. G., 35, 36
Ethell, Col. Donald, 178
explosive ordnance disposal, 175, 250

Fenton, Col. Ivan, 237
Fergusson, Maj. Hugh, 232
Ferron, Brig.-Gen. Jim, 292
Fetterly, Dr. Ross, 13
field human intelligence team (FHT), 251, 252, 253, 266, 272, 273
field intelligence support team, 201
Fife, Lt. John, 140
Fitzgerald, Todd, 48, 150
Five Eyes intelligence alliance, 5, 31, 34, 42, 68, 69, 89; support to operations, 117, 160, 166, 181, 184–85, 189, 190, 192, 206, 222, 226, 234, 248, 274, 303
Fleet Ocean Surveillance Information Facility, 191
Fletcher, Maj. Bill, 278
Flynn, Maj.-Gen. Michael, US Army, 292–94
Fogarty, Rear-Adm. William, 151
Forces Mobile Command (FMC), 71, 81, 109, 110, 112, 114, 116, 125–30, 131, 134, 138, 140, 141, 150
forward air controller, 165, 175, 205, 224, 226, 251
forward-looking infrared (FLIR) systems, 233, 235, 236, 239
forward observation officer, 205, 251, 278
Foster, Lt.-Gen. Kent, 125, 129
Foucreault, Col. Michel, 93, 160
Foulkes, Gen. Charles, 31
4 Wing, 82
408 Tactical Helicopter Squadron, 230, 233
419 Squadron, 130
430 Tactical Helicopter Squadron, 233
Franks, Gen. Tommy US Army, 248
Fraser, Brig.-Gen. David, 267, 269–70, 273, 278, 281–83, 284, 298n71
Freakley, Maj.-Gen. Benjamin US Army, 284

French armed forces, 173, 175, 231, 250, 251
Front de Libération du Québec (FLQ), 93, 103–4, 105–6, 107, 108, 110–11, 113–17, 119n32, 120n41. *See also* October Crisis; operations: ESSAY, GINGER
functional review of national defence (1990–1991), 48, 49, 158

Gauthier, Lt.-Gen. (ret.) Michel, 53–55, 57, 59, 61, 62, 74, 177, 248, 291, 306
Gavriel, Alexei, 262–63, 293
General Framework Agreement for Peace. *See* Dayton Accords
geomatics and imagery support team (GIST), 60, 205, 249, 250–51, 266, 281
geomatics intelligence, 51, 128, 188, 205, 213n32, 220, 221, 248
German armed forces, 86, 231, 250, 251, 253, 274
Gervais, Maj.-Gen. Jim, 150
Gimblett, Comdr. Richard, 154
Girouard, Comdre. Roger, 249
Glenfield, Lt. William, 160
Goddard, Capt. Nichola, 278
Godefroy, Col. James, 265, 270, 271, 273, 279, 290, 291, 294
Goldthorp, Dr. Linda, 57
Government Communications Headquarters (UK), 69, 203, 221, 274
Graham, Col. Gordon S., 48

Hague, Brig.-Gen. Ken, 50, 51
Haisell, Maj. Don, 208–9, 214n37
Hanan, Mullah Abdul, 282
Hand, Lt.-Col. Christopher, 261
Heath, Comdre. Ted, 51
Hellyer, Paul, 14–15, 35
Hennault, Gen. Raymond, 54, 230
Hennessy, Dr. Michael, 48, 150
Heron UAV, 87, 89, 272, 288, 290
Hewson, Maj.-Gen. William, 45, 46

Higgitt, Royal Canadian Mounted Police Commissioner Leonard, 106, 111
high-value targets (HVTs), 246, 251, 261, 264, 265, 268, 274, 282, 287, 288, 292, 293
Hillen, Dr. John, 174
Hillier, Gen. Rick, 25, 26, 200, 203, 208, 209, 250, 260, 306
Hisey, Capt. Todd, 233
HMCS *Acadian*, 128
HMCS *Algonquin*, 190
HMCS *Athabaskan*, 152, 164
HMCS *Iroquois*, 190
HMCS *Protecteur*, 152, 154
HMCS *Terra Nova*, 152
Hope, Lt.-Col. Ian, 267–69, 277–80
Horn, Col. Bernd, 264, 266, 276, 284, 288
Huddleston, Lt.-Gen. David, 153
humanitarian operations, 173, 231, 275
human source intelligence (HUMINT), 52, 56, 60, 62, 67, 72, 89, 92; in operations, 110, 113–14, 128, 129–30, 132, 139, 142, 161, 186–87, 208, 209, 210, 235, 251, 253–55, 258n49, 263, 267, 268, 269, 270, 272–73, 276, 278, 281, 288, 292, 294
Hunt, Lt. Christopher, 232, 239, 242n85
Hunter UAV, 222, 223, 235
Hussein, Saddam, 161, 163

ICAC. *See* Intelligence Collection and Analysis Centre
IED. *See* improvised explosive devices
imagery intelligence, 34, 36–37, 42, 43, 45, 48, 50, 51, 60, 67, 72, 89, 90, 92, 304; support to operations, 87, 112, 114, 129, 130, 136, 139, 155–57, 159, 160, 164–65, 166, 180, 187, 188, 197n98, 203, 204, 205, 208, 213n32, 220, 221, 222–23, 224, 228, 236, 237, 248, 253, 266–68, 272, 274, 279, 282
Implementation Force (IFOR), 198, 199, 200, 201, 202, 211n12
improvised explosive devices (IEDs), 261, 264–66, 272, 274, 282, 284–89, 292, 293, 295, 308. *See also* counter-IED operations
indications and warning intelligence, 42, 70, 72, 86, 90, 154, 155, 164, 180, 181, 203, 230, 232, 287
information management, 56, 59, 74, 79, 80, 267, 305, 309
information operations, 73, 74, 107, 115, 141, 205, 209, 221, 230, 231, 240, 255, 259, 262, 263, 286, 289, 304, 308
information technology (IT), 22–23, 50, 60, 67, 88, 157. *See also* computers
information warfare. *See* information operations
infrared line-scan surveillance, 114
insurgency, 106, 198, 215, 259–60, 278, 293, 294
Intelligence Advisory Committee, 42, 43, 69, 163
intelligence analysis, 58, 78, 89, 150, 251, 274, 275. *See also* intelligence assessment; intelligence production
intelligence analysts, 36, 48, 57, 74, 87, 89, 92, 93, 157, 158, 276, 277, 294, 306
Intelligence and Security Complex (ISX), 45–50
intelligence architecture, 46, 54, 56, 58, 77, 80, 86, 87, 93, 204, 221, 266, 270–72, 279, 290, 294
intelligence assessment, 32, 57, 71, 76, 80, 107, 116, 153, 159, 160, 161–63, 164–66, 181, 183, 185–86, 188–89, 221, 222–23, 225–26, 228, 290, 292, 294, 307
intelligence collation, 46, 76, 79, 112, 114, 206, 224–25, 267
intelligence collection: concepts and structures, 5, 31, 32, 35, 37, 42–44, 53, 54, 55, 56–59, 60, 62, 67–68, 69, 70–72, 73, 75, 80, 88, 93; support to operations, 107, 112–14, 128–31, 134, 139, 142, 155–57, 158, 165, 166, 178, 182, 183, 187, 189, 192, 195n39, 201, 202, 203, 204–6, 208, 209, 215, 220–24, 226–27, 228, 233–37, 247–48,

249, 252, 254, 255, 267–68, 272, 273, 274–75, 276–78, 287, 288, 290, 291, 292, 303, 305, 307, 309, 310
Intelligence Collection and Analysis Centre (ICAC), 70–73, 77, 95nn22–23, 128, 130, 131, 135, 138, 142, 252, 305
intelligence coordination, 43, 44, 48, 51, 56, 58, 59, 62, 79, 85, 111, 117, 137, 157–58, 164, 267, 269, 270, 271, 273, 275, 305
intelligence deficiencies: operational, 111, 116–17, 137–38, 139–42, 159, 162–63, 164–65, 178, 179–81, 182–84, 205, 207, 224–26, 228, 235–36, 246–47, 249, 265, 266–67, 268, 276, 277, 279–80, 283–84, 292–94; structural, 43–44, 45–46, 47–50, 53, 57, 70, 82, 86, 92–93
intelligence dissemination, 42, 43, 44, 51, 56, 58, 80, 112, 138, 142, 150, 157, 164, 206, 224–26, 253–54, 269, 273, 277, 279, 282, 287, 303
intelligence doctrine, 44, 51, 70, 72, 73–74, 85, 88, 90, 92
intelligence estimates, 33, 41, 43, 71, 90, 131–33, 141, 178, 188
intelligence exploitation, 75, 135–37, 206–9, 226–27, 238–40, 253–54, 276–77, 278–79, 281–83, 285–89
intelligence fusion, 33, 57, 58, 67–68, 70, 72, 73, 75, 79–80, 93, 128–29, 130, 142, 157, 225, 227, 251, 252, 266, 267, 275, 288, 290, 305, 306, 309
intelligence impact on operations, 74, 112, 115, 192, 210, 227–28, 238–40, 263, 275–89, 291–92, 306. *See also* intelligence exploitation
intelligence interoperability, 46, 49, 53, 58, 67, 76, 77, 164, 226, 228, 268
intelligence-led operations (ILOs), 117, 136, 209, 266, 285–88, 291–92, 294, 305
intelligence liaison, 31, 32, 35, 37, 41, 42, 44, 51, 52, 79, 85, 86, 109, 113, 115, 126, 129, 133, 136, 141, 143n25, 141, 151, 159, 173, 179, 190, 202, 204, 205, 221, 237, 248, 252, 253, 267, 269
Intelligence Policy Committee, 31, 38n12, 68
intelligence preparation of the battlefield, 91, 149, 208, 240, 263, 282, 284
intelligence production, 35, 36, 37, 41–46, 48, 51, 55–58, 62, 79, 84, 95n9, 158, 206, 215, 220, 224–26, 228, 237–38, 265, 271, 274, 275, 290, 307. *See also* intelligence analysis
intelligence "reach-back," 160, 203, 234, 251, 266
intelligence reporting, 33, 42, 57, 68, 69, 112–13, 140, 182, 183–85, 187, 189, 197n99, 201–2, 220, 221–22, 223, 224, 230, 248, 252, 286, 288
intelligence requirements, 17, 24; national, 33, 42, 43–44, 50, 51, 54, 55, 56, 58–59, 67, 72, 80, 83, 85; operational, 112, 154–55, 159, 160, 200–201, 206, 219–20, 231–32, 252, 261, 262–64, 267, 270–72
intelligence sharing, 31, 33, 46, 79, 111, 112, 137, 166, 181, 184–85, 190, 192, 203–4, 226, 228, 234–35, 247, 248, 255, 268, 274, 279, 295. *See also* Five Eyes intelligence alliance
intelligence, surveillance, and reconnaissance (ISR), 59, 67, 73, 76, 77, 79, 80, 86, 93, 157, 222, 226, 238, 240, 268, 272, 274, 280, 282–84, 297n47, 305
Intelligence Surveillance Target Acquisition Reconnaissance (ISTAR), 73–74, 250–53, 256, 270, 271–72, 274, 278, 280, 281, 285, 287, 288, 290, 291, 305
intelligence training, 31, 32, 33, 42, 44, 52–53, 56, 57, 71, 82, 83, 84, 85, 88–93, 128, 132, 139, 142, 210, 233, 263, 305, 309
Interdepartmental Committee on Security and Intelligence, 42, 69
International Police Task Force (IPTF), 199, 204, 207, 208, 229

328 INDEX

International Security Assistance Force (ISAF), 86, 87, 250, 252–55, 259–60, 261, 262, 265, 275, 282, 284, 285, 287, 288, 289, 292–94
internet, 74, 79, 236, 238, 262
interrogation/interrogators, 72, 89, 268, 273, 306
Iraqi armed forces, 148, 151–53, 154–58, 161–63, 165
Isbister, Claude, *Report on Canadian Government Intelligence Operations* (1970), 3, 6, 68, 69

Jackson, Gen. Sir Mike, 229–31
Jensen, Lt.-Col. Greg, 71, 88, 93
Johnston, Capt. Paul, 82
Joint Analysis Center, 190, 196n96, 203, 221, 223, 225, 234, 275
Joint Command and Control Information System (JC2IS), 49, 50
Joint Commission Observer teams, 205
Joint Coordination Centre (JCC), 269, 270, 279
Joint Deployable Intelligence Support System, 183
Joint Forces Air Coordination Center, 164
Joint Imagery Processing Center, 157
joint intelligence centre (JIC), 112, 114, 115, 128, 129, 135, 137, 139, 156, 157, 159, 275
joint operations centre, 112, 114, 221
Joint Photo Interpretation Centre, 34, 36, 42
Joint Reconnaissance Center, 157–58
Joint Special Operations Task Force, 205, 264, 275
Joint Task Force–Afghanistan (JTF-A), 87, 89, 260–61, 264, 267, 272–75, 294
Joint Task Force South West Asia (JTFSWA), 245, 248–49
Joint Task Force 2, 245, 246, 249, 264, 266, 276
Joint Task Force X, 60, 307

Jones, Lt.-Col. Michel, 178–79
J2 (intelligence), 50–52, 53–54, 55, 60, 150, 157–60, 184, 203, 206, 213n32, 220, 232, 234, 236, 237–38, 247, 248, 265, 267, 270–73, 279, 280, 283, 289, 290, 292, 294, 299n79

Kabul, Afghanistan, 86, 91, 244, 250, 252–54, 259, 260, 275
Kabul Multi-National Brigade, 250–53, 255
Kahnawake Reserve, 123, 125–26, 128, 129, 130–36, 140, 141, 145n52. *See also* Oka Crisis; operations: SALON; Warrior Society
Kandahar Airfield (KAF), Afghanistan, 245, 249, 260, 264, 267, 269, 272, 274, 277
Kandahar city, Afghanistan, 267, 281, 285, 287
Kandahar Intelligence Fusion Cell, 275
Kandahar province, Afghanistan, 256, 259, 261, 288, 295
Kanesatake, Quebec, 123–25, 129, 131–32, 139. *See also* Oka Crisis; operations: SALON; Warrior Society
Kenyon, Brig.-Gen. Lloyd, 34–37, 41, 60
key leader engagements, 262, 264, 294
KFOR. *See* Kosovo Force
KLA. *See* Kosovo Liberation Army
Knie, Capt. Linda, 159
Knight, Capt. (N) Darren, 79, 159–60, 275
Koch, Maj. Pat, 237
Kolisnek, Dr. George, 78
Kosovo air campaign. *See* operations: ALLIED FORCE, ECHO
Kosovo Force (KFOR), 215, 228–32, 234–37, 239, 240
Kosovo Liberation Army (KLA), 221, 223, 227, 229, 231–32, 234–36, 238, 239
Kosovo Rotary Wing Air Unit, 233, 235–36, 239

Kuwait theater of operations (KTO), 152, 153, 156. *See also* Persian Gulf War; operations: FRICTION

Lambert, Maj. David, 132, 137
Lambeth, Dr. Benjamin, 222, 224, 225
Laporte, Pierre, 104–8, 110, 117
Lavoie, Lt.-Col. Omer, 235, 283, 284
Leadmark: The Navy's Strategy for 2020, 76
Linked Operation-Intelligence Centers Europe, 204
Lord Strathcona's Horse (armoured regiment), 230, 234*fig.*, 249
low-intensity conflict, 13, 21, 80, 304, 308

MacKenzie, Maj.-Gen. Lewis, 172, 178–81
MacLean, Lt.-Col. Bill, 87
Magee, Maj. Colin, 130, 132, 136
Maloney, Dr. Sean, 107, 109, 113, 114, 120n41, 229, 237, 249, 252, 269, 276, 278, 279, 280, 281, 286
Management Command and Control Re-Engineering Team, 21–22
Management Review Group (MRG), 16, 17
"maneuver to collect" operations, 281
Mapping and Charting Establishment, 51, 60, 129, 131, 248, 307
MARCOM Capability Planning Guidance 2000, 77
Marine Security Operations Centre (MSOC), 80
Maritime Air Group, 81, 86, 91
Maritime Command (MARCOM), 16, 18, 75–77, 78, 79, 80, 81, 114, 158, 159, 164
Maritime Command Vision, 76
Maritime Interdiction Force (MIF), 151–52, 164
Massoud, Capt. Zia, 268–69, 270, 279
Mayer, Maj. Jerry, 89, 90, 92, 99n102, 159
McCann, Warrant Officer Matt, 160
McKillop, Capt. David, 182
McNaughton, Lt.-Gen. (ret.) D. M., review by, 49
Medak Pocket battle (Croatia), 175, 182–83, 185, 186
media, 53, 108, 110, 127, 133, 135, 141, 142, 155, 161, 162, 187, 192, 221, 222, 262
meteorological intelligence, 72, 222, 224, 307
military intelligence battalion (US Army), 203, 234
militia/reserve intelligence (training) companies, 52, 70
Milner, Maj.-Gen. Dean, 204–5
mines, 133, 154, 177, 181, 199, 201, 205, 235, 239, 254. *See also* improvised explosive devices
Minister of National Defence (MND), 14–15, 16, 18, 19, 32, 35, 42, 69, 153, 245
missiles, 19, 37, 42, 75, 117, 153, 154, 156, 158, 164, 186, 218, 225, 233, 254
Mitrovica, Kosovo, 237, 240
Mohawk Tribe, 123–24, 126, 128, 129, 131, 132, 134, 136, 139–42. *See also* Oka Crisis; Warrior Society
Montreal, Quebec, 104, 107, 108, 109, 111, 114, 116, 120n53, 123, 126, 127, 130; police force of, 104, 110, 111, 112
Moore, Lt.-Col. David, 176
Morneau, Lt.-Col. Jacques, 141
Multi-National Division South-West (MND-SW), 200, 203, 206, 208
Multinational Support Unit, 208, 209

Nalgham-Sangsar, Afghanistan, 279, 285
Nardulli, Bruce, 226
national command element, 230, 233, 237, 242n76
National Defence Act, 105, 108, 125
National Defence Command Centre, 57
National Defence Headquarters (NDHQ): operational intelligence and, 114, 129,

National Defence Headquarters (*continued*) 131, 138–39, 141, 158, 159, 163, 166, 179, 192, 201, 202–3, 206, 207, 237, 238, 274; organization, intelligence, and, 16, 17, 22, 25, 34, 35, 47–50, 52, 80, 81, 83–85, 89, 93, 148, 150, 307

National Defence Intelligence Centre (NDIC), 41–43, 45, 51, 52, 114, 184, 185–89, 190, 192

National Defence Operations Centre, 43, 114, 129

National Directorate of Security (Afghanistan), 254, 255, 269, 278, 281

national intelligence support team, 234

National Special Centre, 36, 42, 51

naval intelligence, 32, 75, 77–80, 154, 189–92, 249

Naval Task Force/Group, 21, 33, 75, 150, 151–52, 154, 158, 164, 166, 244, 245, 249. *See also* operations: FRICTION; Persian Gulf War

Nightingale, Captain Wayne, 160

Nimrod aircraft, 157, 282, 300n118

1994 Defence White Paper, 19–20, 22, 75

Nordick, Brig.-Gen. (ret.) Glenn, 59, 66n87, 70, 172

North American Aerospace/Air Defence Command (NORAD), 14, 16, 18, 20, 43, 81, 83, 84, 85, 86, 156, 164

North Atlantic Treaty Organization (NATO): Canada in, 13, 14, 16, 17–18, 20, 21, 37, 43, 50, 70, 73, 75, 81, 83, 84, 215, 216, 218, 244, 250, 259, 303; operational intelligence and, 149, 162, 174, 177, 181, 184–89, 190–92, 198–99, 200, 203–5, 215, 216–17, 219, 220–28, 230, 234, 255, 265, 270, 274, 275

O'Blenis, Lt.-Gen. David, 156
O'Brien, Lt.-Col. D. G., 141–42
observation, 67, 68, 82, 140, 178, 181–82, 204–5, 206, 222, 232, 234*fig.*, 236, 246, 251, 278, 292

October Crisis, 16, 103–22, 123, 127. *See also* Front de Libération du Québec; operations: ESSAY, GINGER

Offensive Psywar Guidelines, 115

Ohlke, Maj. Gordon, 128, 129, 133, 136, 138, 140, 265, 275, 291

Oka Crisis, 48, 73, 123–47, 159, 239, 252, 291. *See also* Mohawk Tribe; operations: SALON; Warrior Society

O'Leary, Lt.-Col. Paul, 71

1 Canadian Air Division/Group, 81, 82, 84–87

1 Canadian Division Intelligence Company, 70–73, 128, 129, 130, 134, 135–36, 137, 138, 140, 141, 142, 143n25, 201, 252

1 Canadian Signals Regiment, 114, 121n62, 128

open-source intelligence, 155, 184, 222

operational intelligence, 30, 49, 70, 77, 158, 210, 263, 306

Operational Intelligence, Surveillance and Reconnaissance Blueprint to 2010, 77, 79–80

operations: ALLIANCE, 199–200; ALLIED FORCE, 215–28; APOLLO, 245–49; ATHENA, 250–302; BAAZ TSUKA, 285; BRAVO GUARDIAN, 279; CAVALIER, 175; DESERT STORM, 148, 149, 152–53, 156, 165–66; EAGLE EYE, 223; ECHO, 215–28; ESSAY, 105, 108–10, 112; FRICTION, 148–70; GINGER, 105, 108, 109, 112–14; HARMONY, 174–75, 178–83; HARPOON, 246; INTIZAAR SMAREY, 286–87; JAGRA, 279; KETARA, 268, 278; KINETIC, 215, 228–40; MEDUSA, 264, 281–84; PALLADIUM, 200–210; PORTER, 286; QUARTERBACK, 239; SALON, 123–47; SEASONS, 286; SHARP GUARD, 177, 189–92; TIMUS PREEM, 287; WESTAR, 207–8;

WHIRLWIND, 254; WOLVERINE, 239; ZAHAR, 280–81
Osborne, Lt.-Cmdr. Shawn, 91
Ottawa (capital of Canada), 105, 107, 108, 113, 121n67, 130, 138, 158, 160, 166, 179, 192, 202, 237, 267, 276
OV-1 aircraft, 114

P-3 Orion aircraft, 78, 157, 205
Panjawayi District, Afghanistan, 267, 268, 279–81, 284, 285–87
Pashmul village, Afghanistan, 280, 282
Pashtun identity, 259
patrolling, 33, 68, 113–14, 121n67, 127, 135, 152, 153, 164, 175, 178, 179, 187, 190, 195n39, 202, 204, 206, 208, 210, 218, 230, 234*fig.*, 235, 237, 238, 250, 252–54, 255, 285, 294
Pattee, Maj.-Gen. R. Percival, 46–47
peace-enforcement, 23, 166, 172, 198–99, 200, 215, 216–19, 229
peacekeeping, 14, 16, 17, 20, 21, 23, 39n22, 76, 110, 127, 135, 142, 145n78, 166, 171–74, 175, 178, 183, 200, 207, 210, 231, 261–62, 290
Persian Gulf War, 22, 23, 48, 49, 81, 82, 84, 148–70, 224, 303–4. *See also* operations: FRICTION
Predator UAV, 222, 224, 227, 228, 235, 268, 287
prime minister's office, 107, 111, 115
Princess Patricia's Canadian Light Infantry (PPCLI), 172, 175, 182–83, 230, 233, 245, 267, 286
Pristina airfield, Kosovo, 231, 235, 239
Privy Council Office, 42, 247
Probert, Lt.-Col. Rhe Ap, 90, 183, 184
Provincial Reconstruction Team (PRT), 260–61, 262, 268, 276, 286, 288, 292
psychological operations (psyops). *See* information operations
Purcell, Maj. Mike, 252, 255
Purdy, Capt. Kris, 282, 283

radar, 33, 87, 114, 140, 153, 155–57, 165, 186, 190, 197n98, 219, 222–24, 235, 241n32, 251, 272
radio, 113, 114, 130, 133, 138–39, 145n67, 180, 223, 249, 262, 271, 279, 281
raids, 111, 113, 114, 116, 126, 127, 132, 136, 207–9, 239, 254, 276, 277, 288
RC-135 RIVET JOINT aircraft, 157, 222, 235, 242n53, 268
reconnaissance, 70, 72, 82, 113–14, 126, 131, 157–58, 175, 176, 179, 182, 187, 200, 201, 205, 208, 216, 221–22, 228, 230–31, 233, 234*fig.*, 235–36, 237, 240, 246, 249, 250–52, 257n33, 264, 267, 268, 272, 274, 275–76, 280, 285
"Red Crown" ship, 191
Regional Command-South (RC-South), 259, 264, 265, 272, 274, 275, 281, 289
Reid, Maj.-Gen. Roland, 69
Revolutionary Strategy and the Role of the Avant-Garde, 106, 115. *See also* Front de Libération du Québec; October Crisis
revolution in military affairs (RMA), 22–23, 60, 67, 73, 157, 166
Richards, Gen. Sir David, British Army, 284
Richter, Dr. Andrew, 22–23
Ritchie, A. E., 107
Roy, Brig.-Gen. Armand, 136
Royal Canadian Dragoons, 208–9, 213n27, 231, 233, 237, 250, 285
Royal Canadian Mounted Police (RCMP), 104–6, 108, 110–13, 114, 115, 116, 118n22, 126, 128–29, 130, 131, 141, 251, 267
Royal Canadian Navy (RCN), 14, 22, 23, 30, 33–34, 75, 78, 96n37, 152. *See also* Maritime Command; operations: APOLLO, FRICTION, SHARP GUARD
Royal Canadian Regiment (RCR), 112–13, 126, 128, 129, 130, 131–32,

Royal Canadian Regiment (*continued*)
    136–37, 176, 200, 206, 207–8, 213n34,
    231, 233, 237, 250, 261, 264, 281, 285
Royal 22e Regiment, 128, 130, 144n51,
    175, 176, 178, 250, 286
rules of engagement (ROE), 110, 126,
    139, 150, 152, 173–74, 175, 176, 192,
    218
Russian/Soviet armed forces, 16, 18, 19,
    33, 37, 71, 75, 78–79, 90, 162, 231, 235

Saideman, Dr. Stephen, 244
Saint-Pierre, Maurice, 109, 110
Sajjan, Lt.-Col. Harjit, 269–70, 278, 280,
    281
Samson, Brig.-Gen. Patricia, 247
satellites, 57, 155–57, 187, 221, 222, 224,
    228, 237, 268, 274, 309
Schreiber, Lt.-Col. Shane, 284
scientific and technical intelligence. *See*
    Directorate of Scientific and Technical
    Intelligence
searches, 87, 105, 109, 110, 113, 126, 127,
    135–37, 175, 224, 228, 236, 240, 264,
    274, 285
secure compartmented intelligence
    facility (SCIF), 36, 42, 248, 249, 251,
    273
"sense" function, 73, 74
sensitive site exploitation, 245, 252, 254,
    255, 277, 286
sensors, 33, 57, 75, 76, 86, 87, 155,
    156–57, 190, 191, 220, 222, 224, 226,
    233, 235, 242n53, 251, 268
Serbia, 189, 198, 215, 217, 223, 235;
    armed forces of, 216–18, 223, 226,
    229
Shah Wali Kot, Afghanistan, 266, 276
*Shaping the Future of the Canadian
    Forces: A Strategy for 2020*, 23
Short, Lt.-Gen. Michael USAF, 216–17
Siew, Capt. (N) Andrea, 49–50, 59–60,
    77, 90, 158–59, 273, 306

SIGINT/EW operations center, 249, 251,
    252
signals intelligence (SIGINT), 30, 31,
    34, 36, 38n15, 42, 58, 59–60, 62, 67,
    68–69, 70, 79, 90, 91, 95n9, 114, 117,
    130, 134, 138, 142, 155, 156, 157,
    160, 166, 181, 187, 202, 203, 205–6,
    212n18, 213n32, 221–24, 235, 248–49,
    251, 253, 266, 267, 268, 273, 274, 277,
    279, 283, 288, 305
situational awareness (SA), 22, 72, 76, 94,
    114, 132, 155, 158–59, 190, 192, 204,
    207, 210, 230, 232, 237, 276, 278, 282,
    285, 286, 292–94
Skaarup, Maj. (ret.) Harold, 3, 71, 210
Slade, Rear Adm. John, 46, 48, 49, 158
Sloan, Dr. Elinor, 22, 23
Sokolsky, Dr. Joel, 20, 21
Somalia, Canadian armed Forces in, 2,
    23, 91, 238, 256
sonar, 33, 77–78, 155
Sound Surveillance System, 33, 34
Special Handling and Evaluation
    Detachment, 221
Special Investigations Unit (SIU).
    See Canadian Forces Special
    Investigations Unit
special operations forces (SOF), 24, 25,
    94, 154, 155, 160, 163, 203, 205, 223,
    234, 236, 245, 249–50, 251–52, 253,
    256, 260, 261, 264–66, 267, 274–75,
    276–77, 279, 281, 288, 292, 297n47
Special Operations Intelligence Centre
    (SOIC), 73, 266, 267, 268, 275, 288
Spencer, Dr. Emily, 263
Sperwer UAV, 86, 87, 250, 251, 252,
    253*fig.*, 267, 272, 278, 282, 287, 290
Srebrenica, Bosnia, 174, 176, 185, 186, 188
Stabilization Force (SFOR), 198–200,
    201–4, 205–10, 211n5
Starnes, John, 106, 118n22, 119n32
strategic intelligence, 37, 45–46, 51, 52,
    55, 57, 68, 85, 90, 93, 184, 201, 221, 263

Strategic Operations Centre: prime minister's office, 107, 111; Royal Canadian Mounted Police, 111
submarines, 19, 33, 75, 77, 78–79, 154, 189, 218
Summers, Comdre. Ken, 150–51, 153, 159, 164
suppression of enemy air defences, 217–19
Supreme Allied Commander Europe, 216, 217, 221
Supreme Headquarters Allied Powers Europe (SHAPE), 188, 189, 190, 221, 225. *See also* North Atlantic Treaty Organization
Sûreté du Québec (SQ) (provincial police), 109–14, 120n53, 123, 124–26, 127, 129, 131, 133, 135, 136–37, 141, 145n72
surveillance, 4, 20, 22, 33–34, 56, 59, 73, 76, 77–80, 82; in operations, 111, 114, 128, 133, 142, 157, 177, 178, 182, 188, 191, 204–5, 208, 222, 223–24, 228, 230, 233, 234*fig.*, 235–36, 239, 240, 245, 246*fig.*, 249, 252, 254, 257n33, 267–68, 272, 275, 282, 285, 287, 288, 290

Tactical Integrated Planning Centre, 222
tactical intelligence, 72, 110, 117, 220, 249, 264, 289, 303. *See also* combat intelligence
tactical psychological warfare teams, 262, 263
tactical questioning, 268, 273
Taliban, 245, 246, 250, 259–61, 262, 264, 266, 269, 272, 275, 276–79, 280–83, 284, 285–89, 291, 292, 294, 295
targeting process, 57, 84–85, 155, 160, 164–65, 187, 217, 219, 220–27, 228, 242n55, 251, 253–54, 267, 272, 275, 277, 278, 287
Task Force Aegis, 267, 269, 273, 279

Task Force Aviano, 215, 218, 219, 220, 228, 241n18
Task Force Falcon, 234–35
Task Force Kandahar, 265, 271, 272, 289, 290, 292
Task Force Kosovo, 229, 230–32, 235, 237, 238–40
Task Force 1-07, 261, 274, 285, 286
Task Force Orion, 267, 277, 278
Task Force 3-06, 282
Taylor, Lt.-Col. Ray J., 47–48
technical intelligence, 32, 42, 294. *See also* Directorate of Scientific and Technical Intelligence
technology, impact on intelligence, 22–23, 47, 50, 75, 77, 80, 87, 88, 93, 139, 166, 200, 305
Tenhaaf, Lt.-Col. William, 112
Tetley, William, 108
Thiffault, Comdre. Jean-Pierre, 245, 248
transformation of Canadian military intelligence, 55, 60–62, 67–100, 306–7. See also *Defence Intelligence Review*
Tremblay, Maj. A., 138
TRINITY intelligence facility, 79, 91
Trudeau, Prime Minister Pierre, 16, 36, 106–7
Turcot, Maj.-Gen. Gilles, 109
2 Combat Group, 108, 109, 113
2 Electronic Warfare (EW) Squadron, 114, 128, 130

U-2 aircraft, 157, 187, 197n96, 197n98, 222, 224, 235, 268
unification of the Canadian Armed Forces, 34
United Nations, Mission in Kosovo (UNMIK), 229, 231, 235
United Nations Protected Areas (UNPA), 172, 173, 175, 176, 189
United Nations Protection Force (UNPROFOR) 171–73, 175, 176, 177–84, 185–89, 192–93, 205, 210

unmanned aerial vehicle (UAV), 23, 72, 86–87, 89, 205, 222–24, 226–28, 235, 250–51, 252, 253*fig.*, 256, 260, 267, 268, 272, 274, 286, 287, 288, 290, 305. *See also* Heron UAV; Predator UAV; Sperwer UAV
Uruzgan province, Afghanistan, 259, 267, 277
US Central Command (CENTCOM), 149–50, 156, 157, 158, 159, 160, 245, 248, 249
US Central Command Air Forces (CENTAF), 149, 151, 159, 160, 164
US Central Intelligence Agency, 36, 156
US Defense Intelligence Agency, 36, 45, 52, 156, 160, 186, 187, 221
US European Command, 190, 225
US National Reconnaissance Office, 156, 222, 224, 241n30. *See also* satellites
US National Security Agency, 156, 187, 221, 235, 268, 274
US Naval Forces Central Command (NAVCENT), 149, 151, 248
US Navy (USN), 33, 75, 77, 79, 96n37, 150, 151, 158, 160, 191, 245, 246, 248, 249
USS Blue Ridge, 151, 160
USS John C. Stennis, 248
USS Lasalle, 160

Vance, Col. Jonathan, 270–71, 272–73
Vance, Lt.-Gen. Jack, 45–47

vehicle checkpoint, 135, 175, 176, 181, 182, 235, 236, 286
Vice-Chief of Defence Staff (VCDS), 16–17, 34, 42, 45–47, 49, 54, 106, 107, 108, 109, 114, 120n41
Villeneuve, Maj. Daniel, 232

Walker, Lt.-Col. Rob, 274
Walsh, Maj. Jerry, 235
Ward, Col. Mike, 230, 232, 240
War Measures Act (WMA), 103, 105, 107, 112, 115, 116
Warrior Society, 126, 127, 130, 131–34, 135–36, 142n5
Warsaw Pact, 37, 70, 71, 162
Weekly Intelligence Review, 43–44
Weeks, Brig.-Gen. Reginald, 41
"White Schoolhouse" battle, Afghanistan, 283
Windsor, Dr. Lee, 289, 290, 292
Winegard, Dr. Timothy, 136, 140, 141
Woodworth, Lt.-Col. Dana, 288

Yugoslav Crisis Cell (YCC), 50, 51, 184, 188, 189. *See also* Balkans Intelligence Response Team
Yugoslav People's Army (JNA), 172, 173, 180, 187, 222

Zdunich, Maj. Andrew, 252, 258n49
Zharey District, Afghanistan, 268, 279, 280–81, 284–86, 287–88

ABOUT THE AUTHOR

DAVID A. CHARTERS is a senior fellow at the Brigadier Milton F. Gregg Centre for the Study of War and Society at the University of New Brunswick and a retired professor of military history. He is the author of *Whose Mission, Whose Orders? British Civil-Military Command and Control in Northern Ireland, 1968–1974* (McGill-Queen's University Press, 2017) and a coauthor of *Kandahar Tour: The Turning Point in Canada's Afghan Mission* (Wiley, 2008).

www.ingramcontent.com/pod-product-compliance
Lightning Source LLC
Chambersburg PA
CBHW032013300426
44117CB00008B/1015